C++ and C Debugging, Testing, and Reliability

Grace Lrai

To Anita, with all my love

C++ and C Debugging, Testing, and Reliability

The Prevention, Detection, and Correction of Program Errors

David A. Spuler

Computer Science Department
James Cook University

Prentice Hall

Sydney New York London Toronto Tokyo
Singapore Mexico City Amsterdam

© 1994 by David A. Spuler

All rights reserved. No part of this publication may be reproduced, stored in a retrieval system, or transmitted in any form or by any means, electronic, mechanical, photocopying, recording, or otherwise, without written permission of the publisher.

All warranties, representations, promises, conditions and statements in relation to this book [and/or software] are to the full extent permitted by law excluded. The liability of the author and Prentice Hall to any persons whatsoever in relation to this book is limited to the cost of replacing the book or the cost of obtaining equivalent goods, whichever is the lowest amount.

Acquisitions Editor: Andrew Binnie
Production Editor: Fiona Marcar
Cover design: The Modern Art Production Group, Prahran, Victoria

Printed in Australia by McPherson's Printing Group

 3 4 5 98 97 96 95 94

ISBN 013 308172 9

National Library of Australia
Cataloguing-in-Publication Data

Spuler, David
  C++ and C debugging, testing and reliability.
  Bibliography.
  Includes index.
  ISBN 0 13 308172 9.
  1. C (Computer program language). 2. C plus plus (Computer program language). 3. Debugging in computer science. I. Title.

005.133

Library of Congress
Cataloging-in-Publication Data

Spuler, David
  C++ and C debugging, testing and reliability / by David Spuler.
  p.   cm.
  Includes bibliographical references and index.
  ISBN 0 13 308172 9.
  1. C++ (Computer program language). 2. C (Computer program language). 3. Debugging in computer science. I. Title.

QA76.73.C153S698   1994   94–14211
005.1'4—dc20   CIP

Prentice Hall, Inc., *Englewood Cliffs, New Jersey*
Prentice Hall Canada, Inc., *Toronto*
Prentice Hall Hispanoamericana, SA, *Mexico*
Prentice Hall of India Private Ltd, *New Delhi*
Prentice Hall International, Inc., *London*
Prentice Hall of Japan, Inc., *Tokyo*
Prentice Hall of Southeast Asia Pty Ltd, *Singapore*
Editora Prentice Hall do Brasil Ltda, *Rio de Janeiro*

PRENTICE HALL

A division of Simon & Schuster

Contents

Part II: Catalog of common errors

Chapter 12   General forms of error   177

Chapter 13   Lexical errors   185

Chapter 14   Expression errors   192

Preface

This book is intended for intermediate or advanced C/C++ programmers, and aims to improve their programming by reducing the frequency of programming errors. Readers are assumed to be reasonably fluent in C or C++. No introductory discussion of either C or C++ is provided in this book; for such an introduction readers are referred to a good general textbook such as my own book, *Comprehensive C*. There are a small number of cases where aspects of the languages are discussed because even the experienced programmer may not be aware of the details.

The accompanying diskette

All being well, this book should be distributed with a source code diskette containing programs and documents, including:

- source code of large programs that do not appear in the book
- source code of (smaller) example programs from the book
- program libraries coded by various authors
- documentation provided by vendors of commercial products

Please note that the material on the disk is not all free software. All material written by the author remains copyright © David Spuler, 1993. A legitimate purchase of this book grants you limited but quite flexible usage rights; see the file "copying" on the source code disk for details. Any material not written by the author is subject to the particular copyright arrangements by the author(s) of the document or program.

Books by the same author

If you like this book, you might also like my other two books, both published by Prentice Hall. More detailed descriptions are provided on this book's accompanying software diskette, but I will briefly describe the two books here. The bibliographic details are:

SPULER, David A., *Comprehensive C*, Prentice Hall, 1992.

SPULER, David A., *C++ and C Efficiency: How to Improve Program Speed and Memory Usage*, Prentice Hall, 1992.

The first book is *Comprehensive C*, which is a general textbook on the ANSI C language, divided into two parts. Part I examines the C language in detail and is therefore appropriate for courses teaching the C language (indeed, *Comprehensive C* has been adopted for a number of university courses). Part II presents advanced chapters on topics such as efficiency, debugging, portability, program style, large programs, advanced pointer usage, and UNIX systems programming. Thus Part II will interest the intermediate and advanced C programmer.

My second book is *C++ and C Efficiency: How to Improve Program Speed and Memory Usage*. As the title suggests, this book is entirely devoted to the topic of writing programs that are fast and small. Some of the specific topics covered include run-time efficiency, space efficiency, algorithms, code transformations, measurement, estimation, and compiler optimization techniques.

Policy on commercial product reviews

This book contains reviews of a number of commercial products related to testing and debugging in C or C++. All reviews present the opinions of the author. The author makes no warranty regarding the accuracy of any information in the reviews, or the integrity of the companies involved. These reviews are provided as a service to readers who may wish to supplement their current set of tools with good commercial tools.

Unfortunately, the coverage of existing tools is by no means complete, because of the limited amount of time and resources available to me. Products for review were chosen in an informal manner from information about products in magazine advertisements and articles, and Internet postings. No doubt there are good companies with relevant products that have not been reviewed, but this was unavoidable. Furthermore, the amount of time available for reviewing products was very limited, thus making it impossible to test all features, and hence I have relied heavily on product documentation to ascertain the important features of many products. Where time permitted, I have asked firms to check the relevant copy for factual correctness.

Having made all these negative comments about the reviews, I hope nevertheless that they are useful to readers. I received no fee for any of the reviews and have no commercial interest in any of the companies. If I have provided a reasonably unbiased and accurate picture of the products, then I have succeeded in my aim.

Bug reports

A book is a very large document and it would be foolish to expect it to be wholly correct, despite the massive amount of effort that I (and others) have expended to ensure its correctness. The author will be interested to hear of all forms of errors, including typos, typesetting glitches, bugs in example programs, portability problems in programs, erroneous information, and so forth. As they are discovered, the problems can hopefully be corrected for later printings and/or diskette updates. The author can be contacted by postal mail at the following address:

David Spuler
c/o Spuler & Associates
P.O. Box 1262
AITKENVALE QLD 4814
AUSTRALIA

Acknowledgments

Naturally, the ideas in this book didn't all come out of my own head, and there are many, many people to whom I owe thanks. First and foremost, a very special thank you to Anita Markovic without whom this book would not have been. A number of friends and colleagues have reviewed sections of this book and/or provided some of the numerous suggestions: Cameron Gregory, David Bonnell, Stuart Kemp, Ahmed Sajeev, Jayesh Thakrar, Geoff Tollefson, Geoff Sutcliffe, Robert Goodwill, John Farrell, and Jian-nong Cao.

The Internet news groups `comp.lang.c`, `comp.std.c`, `comp.lang.c++`, `comp.std.c++`, `comp.software-eng`, `comp.software.testing`, and `comp.compilers` have provided a useful source of information and I have corresponded with a number of colleagues in these forums. My thanks go to (in no particular order) Jos Horsmeier, Stuart Hood, Harald Winroth, Conor Cahill, Brian Marick, Richard O'Keefe, Mats Henricson, Steve Clamage, Graham Dumpleton, Dwight Wilson, Richard Mazzaferri, Thomas Breuel, Brian Minard, John Panzer, Doug Gallinat, Shaun Davey, Castor Fu, Norman Ramsey, Terry Woodings, and the many others whom I have lost track of.

The FAQ list for `comp.lang.c` written by Steve Summit and also the FAQ list for `comp.lang.c++` written by Marshall Cline were both very valuable sources of ideas.

As always, the staff at Prentice Hall were very conscientious. My thanks go to Andrew Binnie, Fiona Marcar, Chris Richardson, and Liz Guthrie for coordinating the process of bringing out the completed book. In addition, the referees supplied by Prentice Hall (Andrew Blucher and John Boutland; others anonymous) were very encouraging and provided dozens of useful suggestions for improvement.

David Spuler

Trademarks

Part I

Techniques
and
tools

Chapter 1

Introduction

In the early days of programming there was little importance placed on error-free programs. There were no such things as "errors," only "undocumented features." However, the modern programmer is repeatedly reminded of the importance of writing correct programs. Although there is no way to avoid all mistakes, there are techniques that can prevent mistakes and make it easier to track down the cause of an error. With the ever-increasing reliance on computer software it is becoming very important to develop programs without errors.

1.1 Why a book on debugging?

Reliability is the modern programmer's goal. In the past it was program efficiency that was the most important aspect of programming, with computer time being the most expensive resource, but the decrease in hardware cost has changed the focus of cost-effectiveness toward reducing the programmer's time. Currently the problems of testing and debugging consume the major portion of development time. I hope this book will contribute to reducing the time spent by programmers on these tasks, to free them for more productive work. Hence, this book is intended to aid the professional programmer at a number of levels, including:

(a) finding errors in a program (testing)
(b) finding the causes of errors in a program (debugging)
(c) writing more robust code (reliability and exception handling)

Originally, the idea for this book was coverage of C/C++ debugging and testing, a topic for which there appeared to be no books available. However, the book's charter soon grew to include extra topics such as exception handling and software quality assurance.

The coverage of C and C++ in one work is uncommon, but debugging is a topic where most comments apply to both languages. C++ is a superset of C and almost all of the techniques applicable to C can be applied to C++. Special C++ techniques that are available because of the C++ extensions are also discussed in many sections throughout the book.

1.2 Notable features of the book

The book has the broad aim of covering all aspects of testing, debugging, and reliability. Some of the specific areas to which attention has been paid are now highlighted:

Practical techniques. Part I covers a variety of techniques and tools for testing, debugging, exception handling, and defensive coding.

Theoretical issues. In addition to practical issues, a number of more theoretical issues are discussed in various chapters. General procedures for high-level reliability are discussed in Chapter 6, and this complements the more practical advice on reliable coding practices in Chapters 9 and 10. The relatively new idea of Software Quality Assurance (SQA) is examined in Chapter 5.

Commercial and public domain tools. Chapter 11 examines a large number of C and C++ software tools that are important for debugging and testing. Many of these tools are freely available, and yet are not widely known.

Catalog of errors. All chapters in Part II form a long listing of numerous common pitfalls for programmers in the C or C++ languages. Thus it is not a collection of techniques, but a catalog of errors, which the programmer should browse through so as to be wise to the dangers.

Symptoms catalog. A catalog of common error symptoms is provided in Appendix A, which is intended to be used when solving a particular debugging problem. The programmer can look up the particular symptoms and see suggestions as to what errors may be causing them. Thus this catalog is a form of reverse index into the error catalog in Part II.

1.3 Origin of the term "debugging"

An error in a program is commonly called a "bug," and the process of removing "bugs" from a program is correspondingly called "debugging." The origin of these terms is an amusing historical anecdote.

The developers of one of the earliest computers, the Mark II, used the state-of-the-art hardware of the time, namely, valves and relays. Their computer was huge by modern standards and the circuitry took up an entire room. One day the computer stopped working for some unknown reason and it took them some hours to locate the cause. A large moth had been caught in one of the relays and battered to death by the contacts. Naturally, the scientists wrote a lengthy logbook entry about the incident, and they even taped the offending insect into their logbook. However, that was certainly not the end of the story. Such occurrences of insects bringing the computer down soon became all too frequent. The length of the logbook entries for such events quickly dwindled, until the scientists simply wrote "debugging" to explain how their time had been spent.

This anecdote is presented in Robert Binder's book *Application Debugging*, which even presents a photograph of the moth taped into the logbook. Admittedly, other sources regard this story as "specious," but it does make for an interesting little tale.

1.4 Further reading

Although there are a great many general books on debugging, testing, reliability, and related techniques, there seem to be only a few books that relate specifically to C or C++. In fact, this gap in the literature relating to C, and even more so for C++, was the motivation for writing this book.

One important book discussing debugging in C is Andrew Koenig's gem *C Traps and Pitfalls*, which discusses a great many of the common pitfalls for C programmers over the years. Methods of avoiding these pitfalls are discussed, and various aspects of writing portable code are also examined.

Another excellent book is *Effective C++* by Scott Meyers, which has the appropriate subtitle "50 specific ways to improve your programs and designs." All 50 sections are relevant to the process of improving the reliability of C++ programs. According to my calculations, at least 20 of the 50 relate to specific C++ coding pitfalls, another 10 relate to C++ design pitfalls, and the remaining sections cover a variety of issues, such as avoiding common inefficiencies and general ideas for improving C++ coding practices.

Stephen Davis has written a C++ book, *C++ Programmer's Companion*, with a focus on testing and debugging that is over 600 pages, divided into 3 main parts. Part 1 discusses the economics of debugging, designing, and coding in C++, and also has two chapters on specific C++ pitfalls (one is specifically about C++ pointer pitfalls). Part 2 covers testing and maintenance methods, debugging tools, and offers a sample debugging session. Part 3 is a reference manual explaining all error messages from the Borland and Microsoft C++ compilers.

Kernighan and Plauger's book, *The Elements of Programming Style*, discusses numerous stylistic issues of programming and mentions a number of common errors.

Of the growing number of general C textbooks, a few contain discussions of debugging or testing, usually as part of a general coverage of the language. My own book, *Comprehensive C*, contains a chapter on debugging from which this book has grown. The book *Advanced C Tips and Techniques* written by Paul Anderson and Gail Anderson contains a good chapter on debugging techniques, including debugging output, use of the preprocessor, assertions, and catching memory allocation errors. Another book with a large chapter on debugging is *Topics in C Programming* by Stephen Kochan and Patrick Wood; it discusses `lint`, debugging output, the `ctrace` utility, and the `sdb` symbolic debugger. Numerous other C books contain smaller sections on debugging or testing: David Masters' book contains a chapter entitled "Program Efficiency and Testing"; Herbert Schildt's book has a chapter called "Efficiency, Porting and Debugging"; and Ken Pugh's book contains numerous sections on various aspects of debugging, including a short discussion of common errors.

Of the many C++ general textbooks available, there are a few that contain discussions of various aspects of debugging, testing, or reliability. Bjarne Stroustrup's classic text *The C++ Programming Language* (which covers all of C++) mentions various pitfalls in passing, and contains an excellent chapter on the use of the ANSI C++ exception handling syntax for improved reliability. James Coplien's book on advanced C++ programming mentions some common errors in various sections and discusses how to avoid them, notably examining the four-function C++ class idiom in detail.

The amusing etymology of the term "debugging" appears in Robert Binder's book *Application Debugging* (which discusses debugging of COBOL programs), including a photograph of the moth taped into the logbook.

ANDERSON, Paul, and ANDERSON, Gail, *Advanced C: Tips and Techniques*, Hayden Books, 1988.

BINDER, Robert, *Application Debugging*, Prentice Hall, 1985.

COPLIEN, James O., *Advanced C++ Programming Styles and Idioms*, Addison-Wesley, 1992.

DAVIS, Stephen R., *C++ Programmer's Companion: Designing, Testing and Debugging*, Addison-Wesley, 1993.

ELLIS, Margaret A., and STROUSTRUP, Bjarne, *The Annotated C++ Reference Manual*, Addison-Wesley, 1990.

KERNIGHAN Brian W., and PLAUGER, P. J., *The Elements of Programming Style*, McGraw-Hill, 1974.

KOCHAN, Stephen G., and WOOD, Patrick H., *Topics in C Programming* (rev. edn), John Wiley and Sons, 1991.

KOENIG, Andrew, *C Traps and Pitfalls*, Addison-Wesley, 1989.

MASTERS, David, *Introduction to C with Advanced Applications*, Prentice Hall, 1991.

MEYERS, Scott, *Effective C++: 50 Specific Ways to Improve Your Programs and Designs*, Addison-Wesley, 1992.

PUGH, Ken, *All on C*, Scott, Foresman/Little, Brown Higher Education, 1990.

SCHILDT, Herbert, *C: The Complete Reference*, Osborne-McGraw-Hill, 1987.

SPULER, David A., *Comprehensive C*, Prentice Hall, 1992.

STROUSTRUP, Bjarne, *The C++ Programming Language* (2nd edn), Addison-Wesley, 1991.

Chapter 2

Debugging techniques

The detection and correction of errors in programs is usually called *debugging*. For the most part there is no standard method of debugging programs and much responsibility rests on the programmer's creativity and ingenuity in finding the cause of a program's malfunction. However, there are a number of useful techniques that programmers can use to aid in the debugging of programs.

Another important aspect of debugging is being aware of the common errors that a program can contain. There are a number of errors that occur frequently in C programs, and these are examined in Part II.

2.1 Overview of debugging techniques

There are a large number of techniques that programmers use for debugging programs. Some of the debugging techniques we will be discussing include:

- desk checking
- postmortem debugging
- symbolic debuggers
- debugging output
- assertions and self-testing code
- keyboard interrupts
- debugging libraries and tools

Desk checking refers to the simple technique of a programmer sitting down with a printout of the source code and looking through it for obvious errors. Unfortunately, desk checking is not often a very effective method of debugging. The obvious problem is that the programmer is examining his or her own code, and is likely to see what should be there rather than seeing what actually is there. It is somewhat more effective if the programmer examines the source code some time after it has been written, thereby reducing familiarity with the material. However, the method should not be relied upon too heavily when trying to ensure reliability.

Postmortem debugging involves examining a program "dump" that has been produced due to some abnormal failure. Typically, a symbolic debugger is used to ease the process, rather than trying to directly decipher the hardware addresses. Postmortem debugging offers an almost immediate solution to detecting the cause of a particular problem. Unfortunately, not all operating systems offer this dump facility, and the faults that cause a dump will also differ between operating systems.

The symbolic debugger can also be used to debug the program in a more general sense. The programmer runs the program from within the debugger and sets breakpoints to control execution. The values of variables can be examined at run-time, and function calls can be monitored carefully. When used properly these tools are a highly effective method of finding an error. However, a programmer should not fall into the trap of using a symbolic debugger to *test* a program because this form of testing is not easily reproducible; symbolic debuggers should be used only when a particular failure has been identified. A number of symbolic debuggers are examined in Chapter 11.

A common alternative to using a symbolic debugger is adding output statements to a program to print out important information at various points in the program. Judicious use of output statements can be highly effective in localizing the cause of an error, but this method can also lead to huge volumes of not particularly useful information. One useful feature of this method is that the output statements can be selectively enabled at either compile-time or run-time.

The programmer should ease the debugging task by making the program "easy" to debug. One useful method of catching program failures is making the program apply checks to itself. The `assert` macro is one convenient method of performing simple tests, and larger code fragments can be used for more complicated tests. Self-testing code has the major advantage that it will catch such errors early, rather than letting the program continue, and cause a failure much later.

An interesting but rarely used debugging procedure is to trap keyboard interrupts such as those from the `<ctrl-c>` key sequence. These interrupts cause the execution of a signal handler, which can output debugging information, such as a report on the current heap state.

The final debugging method in our list is other tools and libraries. Programmers should make the most of the existing tools and code libraries to help the debugging process. However, this chapter will not examine them in full; instead numerous debugging libraries are developed in Chapter 3 and a detailed discussion of a number of debugging tools is provided in Chapter 11.

2.2 A debugging methodology

When presented with the problem of a program with a specific failure, programmers use their own debugging method. However, there are a number of not-so-common steps that programmers should consider before "leaping in" and using their favorite method:

> Enable compiler warnings.
> Enable compiler run-time traps.
> Use a static checker.

The program should be made to compile cleanly (i.e., without warnings). Any warning can be a cause of an error and should be examined carefully. Using a compiler and/or static checker to test for common errors can be a great time-saver even if the simple errors found this way only occur rarely. These tests can be performed quickly and will save much time in the long run.

Only when the compiler and static checker (e.g., `lint`) have failed to identify the problem should the next phase of debugging begin. This is the phase where the programmer's creative ability is put to the full test. Different debugging methods are best for different forms of program failure. For example, a "segmentation fault" on a UNIX machine is easily found by using a symbolic debugger such as `dbx`. Methods such as using a symbolic debugger, printing debugging output, and self-testing assertions can all be used to complement each other.

2.3 Making the correction

An important part of the debugging phase that is often neglected is actually making the correction. You've found the cause of the failure, but how do you fix it? It is imperative that you actually understand what caused the error before fixing it; don't be satisfied when a correction works and you don't know why. Another common pitfall is to make the correction and then not test whether it actually fixed the problem. Furthermore, making a correction will often introduce a new bug; hence it's a good idea to use extensive regression tests (see Section 4.6) after making an apparently successful correction.

2.4 Don't blame the compiler

The biggest temptation when faced with an error you do not understand is to blame the compiler. However, though compiler bugs are not as uncommon as one would hope, there is probably a 99% or more chance that it is *your* mistake, especially if you are just learning the language.

There is an even larger temptation to place the blame on the compiler if the code suddenly fails when optimization is invoked. Because of the complexity of optimization technology, there have been many well-known errors in optimizers. However, there are a large number of errors that may not cause failures when compiled in one way, but may cause failures with other compiler or optimizer settings; see Section A.4 for a listing of some of these common errors. A compiler or optimizer bug is a very convenient excuse, but also an unlikely excuse.

I remember well the first time that I demonstrated this form of human frailty while learning the C language. A program wasn't working, and after some debugging effort, the problem was traced to a `for` loop that was executing only once instead of many times. An experienced programmer can probably diagnose the error from the single statement in the previous sentence, but the program's behavior seemed very strange to me. Although I don't remember the exact code, the loop was similar to:

```
for (i = 0; i < n; i++);
    {
    /* do something */
    }
```

Instead of repeating n times, the loop body was executed only once. The error is, of course, the semicolon after the for loop, which does not cause a syntax error, but makes the for loop empty and causes the loop body to be executed only once, after i has been incremented from 0 to n.

Finding this error took me a great deal of time and effort. I spent a lot of time trying to determine the problem with debugging output statements, but with no success. Then, beginning to suspect a compiler bug, I created assembly output using cc -S. Sure enough, the assembly code showed the compiler generating instructions where control prematurely returned to the top of the loop. The compiler was "erroneously" placing the branch instruction before the first statement of the loop body. Finally I demonstrated my "compiler bug" to a friend, who immediately pointed out the extra semicolon. A little knowledge is a dangerous thing.

2.5 Postmortem debugging

Postmortem debugging is a particular method of using a symbolic debugger to examine a "dump" of the program's state, which was produced by the operating system upon detection of some abnormal condition. This is a well-known technique under UNIX, where a "core" file is produced for errors such as a segmentation fault or bus error. However, the technique is not limited to UNIX, and applies to any operating system capable of providing some form of stack dump. Let us now discuss postmortem debugging in both the UNIX and Windows contexts.

2.5.1 UNIX postmortem debugging

Postmortem debugging under UNIX requires the examination of the "core" file after the program has terminated abnormally with a message to the effect of "core dumped"; the most common causes of the core dump are segmentation violations and bus errors. The effect of a core dump is that the entire program memory contents (including stack, heap, and global variables) are dumped to a file. Although the method of examining the core file depends on the symbolic debugger used (e.g., sdb, dbx, etc.), the basic idea remains the same. The debugger is used to examine the core file to determine the state of the program when it failed. A stack trace of all functions called is usually available, and the values of variables can be examined. Note that for useful debugging it is often necessary to compile the program using the "-g" option to the compiler, so that symbolic information is left in the executable for use by the symbolic debugger. If this symbolic information is not available, the debugger will not be able to translate the machine addresses in the core file into symbolic names, and will only be able to present hardware address values.

The most common use of postmortem debugging is in the detection of the cause of some abnormal termination such as a "segmentation fault" or "bus error." However, the method can be invoked upon the detection of a number of other errors, either by the user or within the program itself. If the programmer, while testing the program, encounters an error and wishes to perform postmortem debugging, it is a simple matter of pressing the two-key sequence <ctrl-\> to send the SIGQUIT signal to the program and thereby provoke a core dump (assuming this signal is not trapped by the program).

If the program itself detects an error of some sort (e.g., control reaches a point where it should not), the program can terminate abnormally and produce a "core" file. The simplest method in ANSI C or C++ is to call the abort standard library function, which will usually provoke a core dump under UNIX:

```
abort();        /* suicide with core dump */
```

Another method in ANSI C or C++ under UNIX is to use the raise library function, which sends signals to the program itself:

```
raise(SIGQUIT);     /* suicide with core dump */
```

If this function is not available, as is the case in some pre-ANSI implementations, it is also possible to use the UNIX library functions kill and getpid, as follows:

```
kill(getpid(), SIGQUIT);    /* suicide with core dump */
```

2.5.2 Windows postmortem debugging

Unfortunately, as with most of the "smaller" personal computer platforms, programs running in unprotected MS-DOS do not have the capability of producing a dump, and therefore postmortem debugging is not possible. Typically, the program will simply crash rather than detect and report memory violations.

However, because Windows can run in protected mode, it offers a feature whereby such failures (e.g., UAEs and GP faults) are detected and do produce a dump of the program state. The details of the technique depend on the postmortem debugger you are using; consult your debugger's documentation regarding support for postmortem debugging. Further discussion of postmortem debugging under Windows can also be found in Matt Pietrek's article in *Dr Dobbs Journal*.

PIETREK, Matt, "Postmortem Debugging," *Dr Dobbs Journal*, September 1992, pp. 18–31.

2.6 Symbolic debuggers

The symbolic debugger is a highly versatile debugging tool which works at both ends of the compilation process — it coordinates debugging effort between the final machine code and the original source code by translating machine addresses into symbolic names. Although some programmers (myself included) prefer using a symbolic debugger only for postmortem debugging, it can be used as a very general debugging tool by executing the program from within the debugger itself.

Symbolic debuggers are also called "source code debuggers" if they are fancy enough to operate directly from the source code files. Thus, we could separate debuggers into "symbolic debuggers," which work only with the executable (and a postmortem dump), and "source code debuggers," which also work directly with the source code files. However, we won't consider this classification any further, and will refer to all forms as symbolic debuggers or even as just debuggers.

This section introduces the use of debuggers as a debugging tool, with a brief overview of what this class of tool usually provides. There is an immense variety of existing symbolic debugger tools, some commercial and some public domain, and naturally there is great variation between products. A number of symbolic debuggers are discussed in more detail in Chapter 11.

The basic features provided by symbolic debuggers are very similar. Some of the most useful features typically offered by a symbolic debugger include:

- stack traces
- breakpoints
- conditional breakpoints
- "watching" data locations
- single-step execution

These features can be used to start, stop, and restart execution, while examining program data values and the call stack. Facilities to "watch" a location are particularly useful, because the programmer is notified of any changes to that location. A good debugger will automatically stop execution when a location changes; others will require the user to step through the code and manually examine the window for any changes. This technique has a few specific debugging applications:

- watching address 0 to catch NULL assignments in MS-DOS
  — for Turbo Debugger watch the expressions: `*(char*)0,4m` and `(char*)4`
- watching `errno` to catch library errors

The single-step execution procedure may not handle C++ `inline` functions particularly well, typically stepping over them rather than stepping through their internal statements. For better checking of `inline` functions there are a few alternatives: (a) some compilers have an option to make all `inline` functions out-of-line instead; (b) use a macro to change the meaning of the `inline` keyword:

```
#define inline /*nothing*/
```

This avoids using `inline` functions but will not be effective for class-local functions declared inside the `class` declaration, because they neither use nor need the `inline` keyword.

2.6.1 Coding functions for debuggers to call

An important technique in the usage of symbolic debuggers is writing functions specifically to be called from within the debugger. These can usually be functions with and without parameter lists, as debuggers provide methods of passing arguments to called functions.

For example, such functions might perform self-tests or produce reports on the status of some large data structure. Section 2.11.1 shows how to use the symbolic debugger to configure debugging code at run-time. Note that any variables that are modified by these functions should be qualified as `volatile` to make the compiler aware that these variables may be modified in unpredictable ways.

Functions for debugger usage need not be from the particular application. A useful example of calling functions from a debugger would be the `print_block_list` function from the `mymalloc` library in Section 3.1. Furthermore, many commercial tools also provide functions for this purpose; for example, Purify offers many API functions that can be called from a debugger, such as to print the current heap status.

2.7 The preprocessor and debugging code

The preprocessor offers a number of important techniques for the introduction of debugging code into a program. The most useful techniques arise from the use of conditional compilation (i.e., `#if`, `#ifdef`, etc.) and macro expansion (i.e., `#define`). Let us first examine the use of conditional compilation for the introduction of debugging code into a program.

A typical example of debugging code is the use of debugging output statements such as C style `printf` or C++ style `cerr` statements. The main problem with using debugging output is the need to remove these output statements when the program is complete. The preprocessor can be used to aid in the removal of these statements. Instead of actually being removed from the source code, they are simply ignored during compilation using the preprocessor's conditional compilation directives. For example, a `printf` debugging output statement is placed inside a preprocessor `#ifdef-#endif` pair:

```
#ifdef DEBUG
    printf("Entered function print_list\n");
#endif
```

When the program is compiled, the debugging `printf` is compiled only if DEBUG is defined. The DEBUG symbol can be defined by `#define` in a header file (which must be included in all files), or preferably defined using an option to the C/C++ compiler (e.g., `cc –DDEBUG` under UNIX). Therefore, the method offers a simple method of ensuring that all debugging code has been removed from a final production run — simply undefine the preprocessor macro symbol.

2.7.1 #ifdef versus #if

The choice between `#ifdef` and `#if` must be made when using any form of conditional compilation, regardless of whether it occurs within source files (e.g., to hide debug statements) or inside header files (e.g., to set a parameter, or define a macro). Naturally, this decision applies only to binary on-off macro tests; any macro with multiple values will usually be tested by `#if`.

The use of `#ifdef` is a little cumbersome if the macros are in a header file, since removing the debugging code will require that the macro never be defined. This can be achieved by deleting or "commenting out" the `#define` or by an explicit `#undef` directive.

Both `#if` and `#ifdef` support removal of debugging code from single files by placing a `#undef` line somewhere *after* the `#include` line that includes the header file defining the macro. If compiler options are used to set the macro, the `#undef` can appear anywhere at the top of the file (i.e., compiler options are like having a macro definition as the first line of the file). The #if method can also use a redefinition of the macro to 0 to remove the debugging code from one file.

The #if method is slightly more convenient when using header files. The slight difference is that the symbol DEBUG can be #define'd to 0 in the header file, rather using #undef. Debugging code can be removed by changing the number in the #define DEBUG line in a header file from 1 to 0. The method has the advantage of improving readability because debugging code depends on a line that is always present, rather than on a #undef line that may be absent.

The different behavior of #if and #ifdef with the various possible macro definitions is summarized in Table 2.1 Note that the -D option to UNIX's cc compiler defines a macro to "1" by default rather than as being without any replacement text; see (f) in Table 2.1. This may not be the same for all compilers, so consult your local compiler's documentation to determine the effect of the -D option without an explicit statement of the replacement text and also to determine whether -D is indeed the option that defines macros for your compiler!

Table 2.1   Effects of macro definitions

Macro definition	#ifdef test	#if test
(a) Undefined; no definition	False	False
(b) #define DEBUG 1	True	True
(c) #define DEBUG 0	True	False
(d) #define DEBUG /* nothing */	True	Error
(e) #undef DEBUG	False	False
(f) cc -DDEBUG (UNIX)	True	True
(g) cc -DDEBUG=1 (UNIX)	True	True
(h) cc -DDEBUG=0 (UNIX)	False	False

The safest method is to always either define a macro as "1" or leave it undefined, because both #if and #ifdef have the same behavior for these two definitions, thus avoiding any problems should programmers have inadvertently used the wrong conditional "if" test. Preferably the header file method would use (b) and (e); the compiler option method would use (g) and (h), or their local equivalent. The definition of a macro as "1" or nothing is easily achieved via compiler options, but is a little more difficult to achieve with header files because editing header files can be a pain. On the other hand, header files have some advantages over compiler options, as we will now discuss.

2.7.2 Header files versus compiler options

When using conditional compilation based on a preprocessor macro name, another choice is whether to define the macro name in a header file or via compiler command-line options (typically the -D option).

Header files are neat in combination with #if macro in that the configurable options are all together and defined as either 1 or 0; an even more user-friendly header file would allow other macro names such as "yes," "no," "on," and "off" instead of 1 and 0.

One danger of using compiler options is that changing them will not necessarily cause all files to be considered "old" and be recompiled automatically. The danger arises of inconsistencies between the different source files. However, if a header file is changed, a correctly designed `makefile` or some other form of automated rebuild facility will know to recompile all source files using the header file.

On the other hand, similar errors can arise owing to header file usage if a `makefile` is incorrectly designed, or if one of the source files does not `#include` the correct header file. The latter problem can be avoided to some extent by ensuring that a linker error arises for files that do not include the header. For example, by ensuring that `DPRINTF` is not both a macro and a function name (i.e., it isn't a recursive macro, but instead a macro expanding to a differently named function call) any files that use `DPRINTF` but do not include the header file will report an undefined `DPRINTF` function at link-time. In summary, header files and compiler options have their own specific pitfalls, and the choice is a matter of preference.

2.7.3 A debugging statement macro

An alternative method of using debugging statements without the annoying requirement of paired `#ifdef`-`#endif` directives is to use a special macro. For example, debugging output statements can be written as:

```
DBG(    printf("Entered function print_list\n");    )
DBG(    cout << "Entered function print_list\n";    )
```

where the DBG macro is declared in a header file as:

```
#ifdef DEBUG
#  define DBG(token_list)    token_list
#else
#  define DBG(token_list)    /* nothing */
#endif
```

Whenever debugging is enabled, the statements inside the DBG argument are activated, but when debugging is disabled they disappear completely. Thus this method offers a very simple method of removing debugging code from the production version of a program.

The DBG macro may be considered poor style since it does not mimic any usual syntax. However, it is a neat and general method of introducing debugging statements, and is not limited to output statements.

2.8 Debugging output in C's printf style

A common method of debugging a program is placing output statements at strategic positions in the program. These statements may print out contents of variables, or indicate entry to a function or loop. This output information is examined to determine the source of a bug.

At its best, this method can be a good way of tracing a program's execution in order to find the cause of a failure; at its worst it can lead to reams of useless output that the programmer must wade through to find the cause. This worst case can be avoided by proper use of a consistent library for debugging output, preferably offering run-time configurability so that useless output can be suppressed. Such a library will be discussed later, but first we must discuss the most basic methods of using debugging output.

The main problem with using debugging output is the need to remove these output statements when the program is complete. Naturally, conditional compilation via #if or #ifdef can be used to aid in the removal of these statements as discussed in detail in Section 2.7. Similarly, a general debugging statement macro such as DBG in Section 2.7.3 can be used. However, it becomes annoying to place #ifdef-#endif pairs around every debugging output statement, and the DBG macro doesn't have a neat syntax. A better alternative is to use the preprocessor to automatically delete every occurrence of the debugging printf statement using macro expansion, without the need to use a #ifdef-#endif pair.

This can be partially achieved by using a different function for debugging output, which we will call DPRINTF. The DPRINTF function is then declared as a preprocessor macro with different replacement text, depending on whether debugging statements are enabled at compile-time. Instead of multiple #if/#ifdef lines throughout the code, they are present only in the header file that defines DPRINTF.

2.8.1 A single fixed-argument DPRINTF macro

The simplest form of DPRINTF macro allows only one argument. The following DPRINTF macro outputs a single string:

```
#ifdef DEBUG
#define DPRINTF(x) fprintf(stderr, "%s\n", (x))
#else
#define DPRINTF(x)    /* Nothing: calls expand to empty text */
#endif
```

The manner of usage is simply:

```
DPRINTF("Entered function print_list");
```

When DEBUG is defined, the DPRINTF call will expand into an fprintf call; when DEBUG is not defined, the DPRINTF call will expand into empty text (it is effectively deleted).

Another use of special macros is to print out expressions rather than strings as shown above. For example, macros could be defined cleverly using the # stringize preprocessor operator as:

```
#define PRINT_INT(x)     printf("%s = %d\n", #x, (int)(x))
#define PRINT_FLOAT(x)   printf("%s = %f\n", #x, (float)(x))
```

The methods above have the limitation of only allowing one argument to DPRINTF. There comes a time when the flexibility of printf is desired in such debugging output. Although using more than one argument isn't difficult, all DPRINTF calls must have a fixed number of arguments, so the flexibility is not present. This is not so easily achieved because of the problem that printf accepts a variable number of arguments and there is no way in C or C++ to define a single macro name to accept a variable number of arguments. The alternatives are the use of different macro names or variable-argument functions.

2.8.2 Multiple DPRINTF macros

A simple way of allowing multiple arguments is to define a different macro for each number of arguments:

```
#define  DPRINTF1(s, x1)       fprintf(stderr, s, (x1))
#define  DPRINTF2(s, x1, x2)   fprintf(stderr,s, (x1), (x2))
...
DPRINTF1("%d", x);
DPRINTF2("%d %s", y, str);
```

The method of removing such debugging output in production code is to use macros that expand into nothing.

```
#define  DPRINTF1(s, x1)       /* nothing */
#define  DPRINTF2(s, x1, x2)   /* nothing */
```

This use of multiple numbered macros is one good choice of debugging output method. It is certainly the simplest method whereby the two important factors are easily achieved:

1. There is no need to use #ifdef-#endif pairs.
2. The debug output can be easily removed.

2.8.3 Removal methods for a single DPRINTF macro

There are also a number of tricky ways of using the preprocessor to allow removal of debugging statements without resorting to multiple macros. The two methods we consider are the "(void)" type-cast method and the "if(1){}else" method. One preprocessor trick that may be considered is:

```
#ifdef DEBUG
#define DPRINTF fprintf
#else
#define DPRINTF  (void)
#endif
```

The DPRINTF statement looks exactly like an ordinary fprintf statement, allowing multiple arguments to the one DPRINTF macro:

```
DPRINTF(stderr, "Entered main:   %d %d \n", x, y);
```

This way works normally when DEBUG is turned on, but when debugging is turned off there is no function call. Each DPRINTF call expands to be a "do-nothing" expression consisting of brackets around an expression where the comma is now the comma operator. The above DPRINTF statement becomes:

```
(void) (stderr, "Entered main:   %d %d \n", x, y);
```

which should have no effect unless there are side effects in the arguments (e.g., function calls). The "(void)" type cast before the expression is intended to prevent compilation warnings about discarding a value. This method of eliminating the DPRINTF statement is not very efficient because the expression may still be evaluated at run-time. A good optimizer should remove the above statement, but if any of the arguments contain function calls, the optimizer is unlikely to remove them. Unfortunately, this method may also cause a deluge of warnings from good compilers about "null effect" statements if the type cast does not prevent such warnings.

There is a much better method of removing DPRINTF statements without using a (void) type cast. The trick is to use an if statement with a constant expression, which the compiler should recognize and optimize away:

```
#ifdef DEBUG
#define DPRINTF fprintf
#else
#define DPRINTF  if (1) {} else fprintf
#endif
  ...
DPRINTF(stderr, "Entered function: main %d %d \n", x, y);
```

When debugging is turned off, the above statement becomes:

```
if(1){} else fprintf(stderr, "Entered main:   %d %d \n", x, y);
```

The fprintf statement is never executed, and the compiler should not generate code for the if condition (i.e., the test with the literal 1). Therefore, the above if statement should not generate any code that is executed at run-time. However, the compiler might not be smart enough to elide the unreachable fprintf statement from the executable code, leading to unnecessary space wastage but no run-time cost; in this case a type cast to void can be used in addition to the "if(1){}else" trick:

```
#define DPRINTF  if (1) {} else (void)
```

Note that it would be incorrect to use "if(0)" instead of "if(1){}else," since it could lead to an error involving mismatched else statements (see Section 20.8 for an example). There must always be an else keyword to match any if keyword inside a macro that is to represent a statement.

2.8.4 Expression-like DPRINTF calls and their removal

The "if(1){}else" removal method has the slight disadvantage that it is a *statement*, not an *expression*, whereas an fprintf call is an expression. Consider the problem if the program uses DPRINTF in an expression context, such as in a for loop initializer:

```
for(i = 0, DPRINTF("entering for loop") ; ... ; ...)
```

This will work well when debugging is enabled, but the removal method creates an if statement, which will cause a syntax error at the DPRINTF call. The solution is to use the ternary conditional operator, ?:, to create an equivalent expression. The DPRINTF removal definition becomes:

```
#define DPRINTF  (1)?0:   /* equivalent to if(1){}else */
```

Thus the expression becomes a fixed ?: test that should also be elided by the compiler's optimization phase. The ?: operator must have the 2nd and 3rd operands of the same type, so the use of 0 as the first condition is neat because 0 can be converted to most basic types, including pointers.

This method has a minor drawback of precedence errors involving other operators to the left of DPRINTF. The error is fundamentally identical to the problem with bracketing the entire replacement text of a macro as in Section 20.5, and cannot be avoided because a bracket cannot be appended to the right of the macro. Thus the DPRINTF expression stays "open at the right side" and the precedence error can arise because of operators on the left. As an example of the error, consider the following use of the return value of DPRINTF:

```
count = count + DPRINTF("i = %d\n", i);
```

Whenever DPRINTF is disabled, the expression becomes:

```
count = count + (1)?0:printf("i = %d\n", i);
```

and this is an error because the ?: test becomes "count+(1)" rather than just "(1)", and the printf could even occur if count is -1, although DPRINTF was supposed to be disabled. Fortunately, such precedence errors will be rare because the most common operators that would be applied to DPRINTF expressions — the assignment operators and the comma operator — do not cause a precedence error. However, as shown above, other operators with higher precedence, such as the arithmetic operators, can cause errors.

Although occasionally useful, such expression-like uses of DPRINTF are probably undesirable and it may be preferable to receive a warning for them. This is a stylistic decision to be made when defining a project's debugging output method.

2.8.5 The double bracket method

Another common method of using debugging output macros is to use a parameterized DPRINTF macro:

```
#ifdef DEBUG
#define DPRINTF(x) fprintf x
#else
#define DPRINTF(x)       /* expand to nothing */
#endif
```

Note that the x macro parameter is *not* bracketed in the replacement text, although that would be the usual style to prevent macro argument precedence errors. In this case, bracketing x would prevent the technique from working.

The DPRINTF calls must use a double pair of brackets around the argument list:

```
DPRINTF((stderr, "Entered main:  %d %d \n", x, y));
```

The trick is the double pair of brackets in the call to DPRINTF. The extra brackets are needed so that "fprintf x" expands out to have brackets around the parameter list. The preprocessor is smart enough not to use commas within nested pairs of brackets as macro argument separators (instead they are treated as a token in the current macro argument), and when debugging is turned off, the DPRINTF statements are totally eliminated by the preprocessor. Thus this is a slight improvement over the "if(1){}else" removal method because it does not even require a semismart optimizer to eliminate the statements.

However, the use of double brackets is not very appealing and it would also be better to leave out the specification of stderr, possibly to allow an easy change from stderr to stdout for debugging output.

2.8.6 The ctrace debugging output method

One ugly method of allowing a change from stdout to stderr is the following macro style used internally by the ctrace utility (see Section 11.6.1). The DPRINTF macro is declared as follows in a header file:

```
#if DEBUG
#if USE_STDOUT
#    define  DPRINTF     printf(
#else
#    define  DPRINTF     fprintf(stderr,
#endif
#else   /* not debugging */
#    define  DPRINTF     if(1){} else printf(
#endif
```

The call to DPRINTF omits the left function call bracket:

```
DPRINTF "%d %d", x, y);
```

This method is not recommended because it is never good to use a preprocessor hack that does not mirror an existing syntax construct.

Unfortunately, there appears to be no pretty way to define a macro such that it can optionally print to stdout and stderr (i.e., without stderr explicitly stated in the debugging statement). This limitation arises because variable-argument macros are not supported in C or C++. However, it is possible to declare a variable-argument function.

2.8.7 A variable-argument DPRINTF function

The cleanest solution is to write your own variable arguments list function that calls either vprintf or vfprintf with its argument list. This method uses a variable-argument function when debugging, and macro tricks to remove the statements when not debugging. The advantages of this method are:

1. no use of #ifdef-#endif pairs
2. statements easily removed by macros
3. no need to put stderr in the format
4. uses printf-like syntax

The only disadvantage is the need to write a function (whereas other methods would just call the printf function). However, the implementation of a variable-argument function is not difficult and one implementation of the DPRINTF function using the macros in <stdarg.h> is shown below:

```
#include <stdio.h>
#include <stdarg.h>

void DPRINTF(char *format, ...)
{
    va_list p;

    va_start(p, format);
    vfprintf(stderr, format, p);
    va_end(p);
}
```

The removal of DPRINTF statements when debugging is no longer required is best achieved using the if(1){}else method. The main header file should include something similar to:

```
#ifndef DEBUG    /* if not debugging */
#define DPRINTF   if(1){}else printf
#endif
```

2.8.8 A pre-ANSI nonprototyped DPRINTF function

When using a non-ANSI C compiler that doesn't support <stdarg.h> it is often possible to use the old non-ANSI header file <varargs.h>. The use of the macros is slightly different, but the principle is the same. The modified function becomes:

```
#include <stdio.h>
#include <varargs.h>

void DPRINTF(va_alist)
va_dcl                  /* no semicolon here */
{
    va_list p;
    char *format;

    va_start(p);
    format = va_arg(p,char*);
    vfprintf(stderr, format, p);
    va_end(p);
}
```

There is also a hack solution that uses a nonprototyped function declaration of DPRINTF. Using a nonprototyping definition of DPRINTF, there is no checking of function arguments and you can send as many or as few as desired. Any missing arguments will be garbage, but this is not a problem because, if correct, the format string will never cause DPRINTF to request their use. This method will usually fail for floats and doubles (%f), but it is often successful for %s if pointers are compatible with int. This method has dubious portability (notably the fact that ANSI C allows a nonprototyped function call supplying too few arguments to fail), but as it is mainly used in the development phase of a program, portability considerations may not be important.

```
void DPRINTF(format, x, y, z, any, number)
char *format;
int x, y, z, any, number;
{
    fprintf(stderr, format, x, y, z, any, number);
}
```

Again, the best method of automatically removing the debugging code is:

```
#define DPRINTF if(1){}else printf
```

2.8.9 DPRINTF macros in C++

The C++ language offers some extra tricks that can be used with DPRINTF. These may be useful to a C++ programmer who happens still to prefer printf-like output statements; they may also be important when writing code that must be used with both C and C++, or when converting existing C code to C++ code.

An alternative removal method is to declare DPRINTF in a header file as an inline function that does nothing, as shown below:

```
#ifndef DEBUG     // if not debugging
inline void DPRINTF(char *format, ...)    // WORKS?
{
    // do nothing
}
#endif
```

The intention is that inlining the empty "do nothing" function will cause it to have no effect at run-time. Unfortunately, this method is not always effective since the compiler is likely to ignore the "inline" request for variable-argument functions (naturally, this is compiler-dependent). There may still be a "real" function call to a non-inlined version of DPRINTF at run-time, resulting in inefficiency. One solution is to use the "if(1){}else" removal method in addition to the empty inline function.

Another issue that may be relevant in C++ is that DPRINTF uses the <stdio.h> output library, and may not mix too well with output from the <iostream.h> or the older <stream.h> libraries. An alternative macro definition of DPRINTF that may be considered is:

```
#define DPRINTF    cerr.form
```

This makes use of the form facility in the C++ output libraries, which is almost identical to printf. This ensures that DPRINTF macros use C++ streams instead of the <stdio.h> library.

2.8.10 Line numbers and filenames

One neat feature of the `assert` standard library macro is that it tells you what line of what file caused the error. This behavior can be produced for debugging output statements so as to trace program execution more easily. Naturally, the technique uses the `__LINE__` and `__FILE__` preprocessor standard macros, which expand into an integer constant representing the line number and a string literal representing the filename, respectively. Note that a neat extension `__FUNCTION__` is supported by newer versions of Gnu's `gcc` compiler, but using this macro is not portable.

For the fixed-argument macro methods such as in Section 2.8.1 there is little difficulty in incorporating the line number and filename. For example, a single-argument string output function becomes:

```
#define DPRINTF(x) \
   fprintf(stderr, "File %s, Line %ld: %s\n",    \
               __FILE__, (long)__LINE__,(x))
```

Note that the use of `%ld` and the conversion to `long` of `__LINE__` appear because `%d` could fail on 16-bit implementations if `__LINE__` exceeded 32767.

However, there is a difficulty in passing them to the `DPRINTF` function, because it accepts a fixed number of arguments, and there are no variable argument macros in C or C++. The simplest solution is to print them before calling `DPRINTF`; the macro appends an `fprintf` call before `DPRINTF` using the comma operator:

```
#define DPRINTF (void) fprintf(stderr, "File '%s', Line %ld:",\
               __FILE__, (long)__LINE__), DPRINTF
```

The initial `(void)` type cast prevents the programmer from testing the return value of `DPRINTF` and receiving the wrong value instead. For example, without the type cast, if the user tried `"ret=DPRINTF(....);"` then `ret` would be set to the return value of `fprintf`.

However, if the `DPRINTF` function is required to perform more useful processing of the line and filename, such as if it is a run-time configurable output function that should not always output the line number and filename, then passing the line number and filename is more difficult. The solution is to use two global variables, which are set by the `DPRINTF` macro and accessed by the `DPRINTF` function. The following global variable definitions are assumed to be present in one source file:

```
long int line_num;
char *file_name;
```

The equivalent `extern` declarations of these global variables should be in the same header file as the `DPRINTF` macro definition, which is an expression involving the comma operator, as follows:

```
#define DPRINTF   (line_num = __LINE__,  \
                  file_name = __FILE__, \
                  DPRINTF)
```

Pre-ANSI preprocessors may fail on the recursive macro, although it is legal in ANSI C. If this is the case, the problem can be removed by using a different name for the function called by the DPRINTF macro, say DPRINTF_HIDDEN. In fact, this may be preferable in any case since it will cause a linker error about an undefined DPRINTF function if the header file containing the DPRINTF macro is ever accidentally not included. If DPRINTF is a recursive macro on top of a same-named function, failure to include the header file will cause a function call without the assignments to the global variables, resulting in the use of the old values of the line number and filename.

2.8.11 Flushing output buffers

An important point to note when producing debugging output is that output to stdout is line buffered. A line of output to stdout is not printed until a \n is sent to stdout. This means that if a program crashes (e.g., segmentation fault), any output in the buffers will not appear on the screen. For this reason, it is a good idea to have a \n at the end of every debugging printf — otherwise you may be misled as to the location of the crash. The simplest method of avoiding this problem is to use stderr, which is always unbuffered, so that error messages appear immediately.

However, there are situations when it is important that output go to stdout or to a log file and there is no automatic output flushing. One method of avoiding the problem of lost output is to use the setbuf library function declared in <stdio.h> to turn off buffering for stdout:

```
#ifdef DEBUG
    setbuf(stdout, NULL);
#endif
```

Alternatively, if you have defined your own debugging printf macro, modify it to flush output buffers each time using the fflush library function:

```
#define DPRINTF(str)    printf("%s\n", (str)), fflush(stdout)
```

This is difficult to do in the DPRINTF macro calls using variable-arguments, but the trivial solution is to place the fflush statement inside the DPRINTF function body instead.

2.9 Debugging output using C++ streams

The previous sections have examined a variety of methods of controlling the output using a C-style DPRINTF function. Let us now examine how the C++ programmer would control debugging output produced by C++ streams.

The simplest method of producing output such that it can be later removed by conditional compilation is the use of #ifdef-#endif directive pairs:

```
#if DEBUG
    cerr << "Value of i is " << i << "\n";
#endif
```

The DBG macro as described in Section 2.7.3 may also be considered:

```
DBG( cerr << "Value of i is " << i << "\n";  )
```

Another alternative is to use multiple macros for differing numbers of outputs:

```
#ifdef DEBUG       // if debugging
#define DEBUGOUT1(x)      cerr << (x) << "\n"
#define DEBUGOUT2(x,y)    cerr << (x) << (y) << "\n"
#else  // not debugging
#define DEBUGOUT1(x)      // nothing
#define DEBUGOUT2(x,y)    // nothing
#endif
  ....
DEBUGOUT1(a);
DEBUGOUT2("b = ", b);
```

In fact, most of the macro tricks used for defining the C-like DPRINTF output macro can be used in C++. However, a few extra tricks are possible with the additional C++ features.

In Section 2.8.1 we saw how to define C macros for printing out expressions, with a different macro required for each type. In C++ the superior type-safety features of the <iostream.h> output library can be used so that all types use the same macro:

```
#define PRINT(x)       (cerr << #x << "= " << (x) << "\n")
```

This macro can be defined to "nothing" using #define for removal from production code.

Yet another neat trick that uses C++ features is to use the fact that << builds a subexpression. This method uses only one macro, but later arguments must be added with << operators rather than commas:

```
#ifdef DEBUG       // if debugging
#define DEBUGOUT(x)      cerr << x
#else
#define DEBUGOUT(x)      // nothing
#endif
  ....
DEBUGOUT(a);
DEBUGOUT("b = " <<  b);
```

Note that the parameter x is *not* bracketed in the replacement text (which is contrary to the usual good macro style).

Unfortunately, all these macro tricks look like function calls rather than the usual stream output style. A clever use of preprocessor macros makes it possible to use the usual << output stream style. A simple solution is to name a new stream, say DEBUGOUT, and use the following macros in a header file:

```
#if DEBUG       // if debugging
#define DEBUGOUT   cerr
#else
#define DEBUGOUT   if(1){} else cerr
#endif
  ...
DEBUGOUT << x << y;
```

The use of the "if(1){}else" trick for removal of the statements from production code is discussed in detail in Section 2.8.3. Again it may be preferable to use the ?: operator instead if DEBUGOUT appears in expression contexts; this is also discussed in Section 2.8.3. Note that the "(void)" removal method cannot be used for this C++ stream style; one possibility is:

```
#define DEBUGOUT  (void)0       // DOES NOT WORK
```

The problem is that the resulting << expression will likely receive compilation diagnostics about type errors because the legal operand types of the built-in << operator are limited.

The inclusion of line number and filename in the debugging output is much simpler than it was for the C-like DPRINTF call, with no need for hidden global variables. One possibility is:

```
#define DEBUGOUT  cerr << "Line " << __LINE__  \
                       << ", File: '" << __FILE__  \
                       << "' "
```

2.10 Multiple levels/areas of debugging output

For any nontrivial project, the use of only one form of debugging output level soon becomes too inflexible. Using a binary on/off compile-time flag is too limited because all of the output appears when debugging is enabled. It is more useful to allow selective choice of output, so that only the output of interest to the current debugging problem can be examined. Firstly, we will examine how to make this type of selection at compile-time, and then in Section 2.11 we will deal with run-time configuration.

Although this classification of output statements can be done in many ways, I have found the two most common to be the use of either:

1. multiple independent debugging output "areas"; or
2. a single debugging output "level".

The term "areas" is my own, intended to convey the idea that each debugging area has its own identification and can be selected independently of other areas. The simplest method of achieving this method at compile-time is the use of multiple macro names throughout the code:

```
#if DEBUG_INSERT
    ... /* output statements for insert function */
#endif

#if DEBUG_SEARCH
    ... /* output statements for search function */
#endif
```

Thus all the debugging statements dependent on each different macro name are independent of each other, and the programmer can select which are important at compile-time. Naturally, it is far more flexible to make this change at run-time and this is discussed in Section 2.11.

The use of a single level means that a value is set to indicate the current level of debugging interest, and all debugging statements must indicate how important they are. This idiom is like having a "verbosity level" on the amount of debugging output produced. At compile-time the debugging level can be supported using a single macro name in a global debugging header file:

```
#define DEBUG_LEVEL  5
```

and the #if-#endif pairs around output statements become:

```
#if DEBUG_LEVEL >= 3
    ... /* output statements for level 3 */
#endif
```

The use of #if-#endif pairs is irritating when overused, and a better way of supporting both the "level" and "area" idioms is to specify an extra argument to the debugging output statements. This can be achieved in both the C and C++ style of output:

```
DPRINTF(3, "Level 3 output: x = %d\n", x);
DEBUGOUT(3) << "Level 3 output: x = " << x << endl;
```

Although this appears straightforward, there are a few issues to consider with the addition of the extra argument.

2.10.1 Debugging printf statement for multiple levels/areas

The use of different output levels means that the DPRINTF function must be modified to accept another argument, and this affects the choice of macro style. All of the various styles of DPRINTF macro have been implemented fully in the disk files "debugout.c" and "debugout.h" in the chap2 directory (note also the C++ versions in "tracer.cc" and "tracer.h") and the important points are summarized herein.

There is little difference when implementing the variable-argument DPRINTF function of Section 2.8.7; the only issue is an extra int argument for the level, and the requirement to test that level for validity. The line and filename must still be passed as hidden global variables.

The most noticeable difference appears in the double bracket style of Section 2.8.5, because the two pairs of brackets must be separated to allow the debugging level as an extra macro argument. The DPRINTF call becomes quite strange in appearance:

```
DPRINTF(1, (stderr, "x = %d\n", x));
```

where the simplest macro definition is of the following form:

```
#define DPRINTF(level, args)  \
        if(DEBUG_FLAGS[level] == 0) \
          { /* disabled -> do nothing */ } else   \
              fprintf args
```

2.10.2 Debugging C++ stream for multiple levels/areas

The alteration of the C++ stream-like debugging output macros for the extra level argument is quite straightforward. The various macros for C++ have been implemented fully in disk files "tracer.cc" and "tracer.h" in the chap2 directory (compare the C version in "debugout.c" and "debugout.h"). The method of building a subexpression using << is changed very little, requiring only the appropriate processing of the level; the new syntax looks like:

```
DEBUGOUT(1, "x = " << x << ", y = " << y);
```

The more stream-like style of debugging output macro is also changed very little; only extra processing of the level argument is required. Even the output of line and filename is the same — they are output before beginning the user-supplied << sequence. The new style of debugging stream looks like:

```
DEBUGOUT(1) << "x = " << x << ", y = " << y << endl;
```

One possible macro definition of DEBUGOUT is:

```
#define DEBUGOUT(level)   \
    if(debug == 0 || DEBUG_FLAGS[level] == 0) \
        { /* nothing */ } else \
            DEBUGOUT(level) << "File " << __FILE__ \
                    << ", Line " << __LINE__ << ": "
```

As always, the only removal method is the "if(1){}else" method.

2.11 Run-time configuration of debug output

It is possible to alter the debugging output macros (using any of the C or C++ output styles we have examined) to allow selective enabling and disabling of different classes of debugging output. There are a number of methods of changing debugging output without recompilation:

1. manual alteration within a symbolic debugger
2. in-code program support
3. command line arguments
4. environment variables
5. debugging file

The use of a symbolic debugger allows changes during execution (i.e., when the debugger is executing the program), whereas the other methods are more useful for altering the levels at the start of each execution.

Compile-time configuration can be easily combined with run-time configuration. For example, it may be desirable to use a single DEBUG macro name to disable all forms of debugging output, thus allowing simple removal for the production version while still permitting run-time configuration during development.

2.11.1 Changing debug level in a symbolic debugger

When using a symbolic debugger to test a program it can be useful to turn the extra debugging output on and off *during program execution.* There are two ways this can be supported:

1. `volatile` global variables
2. callable API functions

Any decent symbolic debugger will permit the alteration of program variables, and hence debugging output can be changed at a specified breakpoint in the program. This is facilitated by using a global variable instead of the preprocessor symbol, DEBUG. The symbolic debugger can then be used to physically access the location of this variable, and turn debugging on and off. Note that a global variable used this way must be declared as `volatile` so that tests are not elided by the optimizer. In the simplest form of debugging output, the compile-time `#ifdef`-`#endif` pair is replaced by a run-time variable test:

```
if (debug) {
    ...            /* Debugging output code */
}
```

The use of callable functions to turn debugging on and off is also possible. For example, as a simple interface, the program could include the `debug_on` and `debug_off` functions:

```
extern volatile int debug;
void debug_on(void)  {  debug = TRUE;  }
void debug_off(void) {  debug = FALSE;  }
```

Note that the debugging output code must still test the global `debug` variable as shown above, and that the `debug` variable must still be declared as `volatile`.

The use of `volatile` variables and callable API functions can be generalized to allow setting of debug levels or areas. For example, the debug level could be a single `volatile` integer, and the set of area flags could be a `volatile` array of integers. This idea is implemented in source disk file "`debugout.c`" in the chap2 directory, using the `debug` integer variable and the DEBUG_FLAGS array. An extension would be to provide a callable function to set the level or enable/disable debugging areas, since most symbolic debuggers will allow functions to be called with arguments specified from within the symbolic debugger.

The use of a symbolic debugger can be combined with the other methods of command-line arguments, environment variables, or text files. In fact, it is recommended to also use some other method, because symbolic debugger alterations are not easily reproducible and are of little benefit to regression testing.

2.11.2 In-code program support of debug-level changes

A fairly general way of making a program easy to debug is to provide debugging options within the program itself. For example, if it is a menu-based program, one or more extra menu entries related to enabling/disabling of debugging output are usually not difficult to add. Unfortunately, this form of in-code support is a little too intrusive in that it may be difficult to remove for the production version of the program.

One form of less intrusive in-code support for debugging is to use keyboard interrupts to generate signals, and then use a special handler for those signals. For example, a program could detect <ctrl-c> as the SIGINT signal, and the handler would then start up a small interactive menu enabling the user to examine and change the state of the debugging levels.

The debugging output library implementation that appears in the disk files debugout.c/debugout.h (C version) and also tracer.cc/tracer.h (C++ version) provides this facility; the main function need only call the following function to install a handler for SIGINT that brings up a text-based menu allowing debugging areas to be examined, set, or cleared:

```
debug_install_SIGINT();
```

Note that all variables that can be modified by this signal handler must be declared as volatile.

The signal handler for SIGINT simply returns to restart normal execution after the user has finished with the menu. This is usually possible, but signal handling is inherently a nonportable part of C and C++. This return-and-continue may cause some low-level system functions to return with a failure code; consult your manuals for details about the effects of a signal handler returning.

Removing this form of signal-based debugging support from the production version of a program is a simple matter of not installing the handler, perhaps ignoring the signal instead.

2.11.3 Command-line arguments setting debug levels

When using command-line arguments to set the debugging levels, arguments are passed to the program at execution-time. For example, the notation:

```
a.out  -d1 -d2        # UNIX-style
prog   -d1 -d2        # DOS-style
```

can be used to set the debugging areas 1 and 2 on (i.e., turn debugging output on for these areas).

Using command-line arguments requires that the main function accept two parameters: argc and argv. These parameters are used to examine any command line arguments passed to the program.

An implementation is provided in disk files debugout.c/debugout.h (C version) and also tracer.cc/tracer.h (C++ version), which provides the debug_arguments function, which accepts three arguments: argc, argv, and a character indicating what to name the debugging options. An example of using the debug_arguments function to detect -d command-line arguments would be:

```
main(int argc, char*argv[])
{
#if !PRODUCTION
    debug_arguments(argc, argv, 'd');    /* detect -d options */
#endif
  ... /* body of main() */
}
```

The implementation on the source code disk (i.e., chap2 directory, files debugout.c, debugout.h, tracer.cc, tracer.h) uses the debugging "area" idiom, and allows space and comma-separated integers for each -d option, and does allow multiple options, which are processed left to right. A number of special strings are allowed: the words yes, on, and all in either all lower case or all upper case will enable all debugging areas; similarly the companion words no, off, and none will disable all debugging areas.

The implementation given in the source code disk also provides a useful feature — removing the debugging arguments from the argv array. The modification of argv is supported by ANSI C, and should be highly portable in both C and C++. With this feature, the program can test for debugging arguments first using a separate debugging function, and then pass the new set of arguments to the main command-line option handling code. Therefore, the main option handler need not know about debugging options at all, and support for this feature can be disabled completely for the production version.

Note that the facility of debugging command-line arguments is particularly useful for script-based regression testing suites. It is useful to ensure that regression testing performs the maximum amount of self-testing.

2.11.4 Environment variables setting debug levels

Environment variables, if supported by the operating system, can be used to communicate with the program. The program could examine a single variable to determine what level to turn on (i.e., if the variable is set to 5, turn on up to level 5), or a number of variables could be examined (one per debugging level).

The implementation provided on the source code disk (i.e., chap2 directory, files debugout.c, debugout.h, tracer.cc, tracer.h) examines a single environment variable with the name passed to the function debug_getenv as a string. This version implements the "area" idiom, requiring the environment variable to consist of a number of integers separated by whitespace or commas. The same special words as mentioned for command-line arguments are supported: yes, no, on, off, all, none. The main function simply calls the function debug_getenv with the required name; for example:

```
main()
{
#if !PRODUCTION
    debug_getenv("DEBUG");        /* examine the DEBUG variable */
#endif
  ... /* body of main() */
}
```

The debugging output areas can be changed by altering environment variables using operating system commands; consult your local operating system documentation for details. For example, in C-shell (csh) under UNIX, use the following command to enable debugging areas 1, 2, and 3:

```
setenv DEBUG 1,2,3        # C-shell UNIX style
```

The Bourne shell (sh) style is:

```
DEBUG=1,2,3               # Bourne-shell UNIX style
export DEBUG
```

It is advisable to report a visible message whenever a debugging environment variable is detected. This is simply to prevent the environment variable from being retained during final testing of the product. After all, the final user's environment will probably not contain this variable.

2.11.5 Text file setting debug levels

A text file containing numbers indicating what levels of debugging printout to enable can be examined at the start of program execution. The program determines what flags are specified in this text file and sets those debugging levels on. In this way it is only necessary to change this data file to change the debugging output produced by the program. For example, to enable debugging output areas 1 and 2, the text file might contain only one line:

```
1 2
```

If the single "level" idiom is used, the file would probably only contain a single integer value.

The use of a debugging text file is implemented on the source code disk (i.e., chap2 directory, files debugout.c, debugout.h, tracer.cc, tracer.h) as the debug_file function, which requires the filename string as its argument. A typical use of this function in the main function would be:

```
main()
{
#if !PRODUCTION
    debug_file("debflags.txt");   /* load debug flags */
#endif
 ... /* body of main() */
}
```

This version implements the debugging "areas" idiom, allowing the specification of integer areas. The text file can be formatted in any manner, with integers separated by whitespace or commas. The following special words, as mentioned for command-line arguments, are supported: yes, no, on, off, all, none.

One minor point: it is advisable to report a visible message whenever a debugging file is detected so as to ensure its removal during final testing of the product. The end user will not have such a file, and it is inappropriate to perform the final tests with the file available.

2.11.6 Run-time configuring of C++ streams/files

A full C++ version of a run-time configurable debugging output library is available as disk files `tracer.cc` and `tracer.h` in the `chap2` directory. The functions for configuring based on command-line arguments, environment variables, strings, and text files are mostly unchanged; the only alterations are cosmetic ones to use `cerr` rather than `fprintf` for error reports. The main change is the method of allowing run-time configurable changes between `cerr` and a log file.

In C the problem of switching between `stderr` and a log file is simply a matter of using a `FILE*` variable that either points to `stderr` or to an open file. However, how can this be done at run-time for a stream-like output statement such as the one below?

```
DEBUGOUT(1) << "x = " << x << ", y = " << y << endl;
```

At compile-time it is a simple matter of choosing between `cerr` and an `ofstream` open file. The run-time trick in C++ is to make the `DEBUGOUT` macro call a function that returns a reference to an `ostream` object. The basis of the `DEBUGOUT` function (ignoring processing of the level) is effectively:

```
ostream& DEBUGOUT(int level)
{
    if (! debug_is_logfile)
        return cerr;
    else {
        assert(debug_stream != NULL);
        return *debug_stream;
    }
}
```

The class `ofstream` is declared in `<fstream.h>` and is a derived class of `ostream` declared in `<iostream.h>`, which is the type of `cerr`. Thus the "`ostream&`" return type of `DEBUGOUT` is returning a reference to the base class, and `<<` will output to the correct form of stream.

The only other changes are to modify the `debug_stderr` and `debug_logfile` configuration functions to open and close the `ofstream` object for the log file. The opening and closing of the log file is facilitated by using `new` and `delete`. Allocating an `ofstream` object using `new` calls the constructor to open the file, and the corresponding `delete` will execute the destructor to close the file.

2.12 Redirecting output

Output redirection is a convenient feature of both the UNIX and DOS environments that can be used to aid in debugging programs that use the debugging output method. When programs generate a large amount of output it can be very useful to redirect this output into a file. After program termination, the output text can be examined using any text editor. To redirect output to a file under either DOS or UNIX, use the notation:

```
a.out > file        # UNIX-style
program > file      # DOS-style
```

If a large amount of debugging code is generated, serious consideration must be given to which output stream the debugging output will go. Using `printf`, the output goes to standard output, `stdout`. If program generates nondebugging output itself, the debugging output can be sent to the standard error output, `stderr`. This is done by changing the `printf(...)` to `fprintf(stderr,...)`. The advantage of sending debugging output to `stderr` is that `stdout` and `stderr` can be redirected separately in most environments. The UNIX environment allows redirection of both output streams, and DOS allows `stdout` to be redirected to a file, whereas `stderr` is fixed to the console. For example, the output redirection shown above will redirect `stdout` to a file, and send `stderr` to the console in both UNIX and DOS environments.

Under UNIX there is a method of throwing away unwanted output. This can be useful for throwing away all output to `stdout`, but allow messages from `stderr` to appear on the screen. The special file `/dev/null` is used for this purpose. Any output redirected to this file is thrown away. To throw away output to `stdout` use the command:

```
a.out >/dev/null     # UNIX only
```

Under MS-DOS the `nul` file is used to throw away unwanted output, using the syntax:

```
program  > nul       # MS-DOS only
```

The `stderr` output stream can be redirected under UNIX, but not under DOS. When program output is to `stderr`, the usual redirection will not redirect the error messages. Only `stdout` will be redirected, and `stderr` will be sent to the terminal as usual. To redirect both `stdout` and `stderr` to the same file under UNIX using the C-shell, use:

```
a.out >& file        # UNIX C-shell
```

Under UNIX the two streams, `stdout` and `stderr`, can be separately redirected using one of the following notations:

```
(a.out > file1) >& file2    # UNIX C-shell (csh)
a.out  > file1  2> file2    # UNIX Bourne-shell (sh)
```

With these commands `stdout` is redirected to "file1" and `stderr` to "file2."

2.13 Assertions: <assert.h>

The task of debugging can be made much easier by making the program apply tests on itself during program execution. A good way of testing conditions that should be true is the use of assertions. Assertions are a form of self-testing code. An assertion is made that a condition is true. If it is not true when the assertion is executed, the program prints out an error message indicating which assertion failed and then terminates.

Assertions should be used only to test conditions that should be true, but that might not be if there is a bug in the program. Assertions should not be used to test conditions about input data, because terminating on incorrect data is not very appropriate. Assertions should never replace an exception handler.

There is the standard library macro, `assert`, defined in the standard header file `<assert.h>`, which provides a useful assertion facility. Use of this macro is highly recommended, as it is part of the standard library and its performance is quite adequate — it reports the line and the filename where the error was found (in some implementations, the failed boolean condition is also given in text form). The format of an assertion is just like a function call:

```
assert(condition);
```

The condition can be any arbitrary expression, even containing function calls. This expression is evaluated by the program at run-time.

A nice feature of assertions is that they produce a form of program documentation that is executable. For example, in the code below:

```
#include <assert.h>

if (color == WHITE)
    ...
else {
    assert(color == BLACK);
    ...
}
```

the assertion is similar to a comment stating that `color` must be `BLACK` in the `else` clause. The advantage over using a comment is that if, for some reason, `color` is neither `WHITE` nor `BLACK`, the assertion will detect this error.

Where and how often to use assertions is a matter of style. Generally, assertions should be used for improbable situations only. One common use of assertions is to detect `NULL` pointer dereferences. For example, the code:

```
assert(ptr != NULL);
ptr->next = NULL;
```

prevents `ptr` from being dereferenced if it is `NULL`. Under UNIX this has the advantage over just allowing a segmentation fault that, although the program still crashes, at least the line number causing the crash is known. Under DOS and other operating systems the use of `assert` is very useful to detect the problem, since a run-time failure may not occur immediately from a `NULL` dereference.

Another valuable use of assertions is to test the validity of function arguments during development of the program. These tests can then be removed from the production version of the program using the method we will now discuss.

2.13.1 Removing assertions

In the final version of the program it is often desirable for performance improvement to remove the assertions from the code. This is easily achieved using conditional compilation. The `assert` macro uses the symbol `NDEBUG` (no debug) to inhibit all assertions. The most common method is to use a compiler command-line option such as:

```
cc -DNDEBUG file.c
```

Alternatively, if NDEBUG is defined *before* the line including <assert.h>, assertions become empty statements:

```
#define NDEBUG
#include <assert.h>
```

When assertions are disabled using either of these methods, all calls to the assert macro expand to an empty statement. Note that defining NDEBUG has no effect if it appears *after* the header file <assert.h> has been included. Therefore, special care should be taken about where to define NDEBUG.

2.13.2 Writing your own assert macro

There is nothing special about the assert macro in the standard library, and for some additional flexibility it is possible to define your own assert macro. For example, it would be possible to have the assert macro invoke an exception handling routine rather than terminating. Another reason for using your own assert macro would be to prevent a core dump under UNIX by calling exit rather than abort to terminate the program (the standard library assert macro usually causes a core dump).

One way to define assert is shown below. The stringize preprocessor operator, #, is used to print out the offending condition in text form. If the stringize operator is not supported in a non-ANSI implementation, it is not possible to print out the failing condition and the assert macro can only report that some assertion failed:

```
#define assert(exp) if (exp) {} else   \'
                     printf("Assertion failed: %s\n", #exp), \
                     exit(EXIT_FAILURE)
```

Defined this way, a failed assertion will print the offending condition in text form (using the stringize preprocessor operator), and then terminate (without a core dump).

Note that to use your own assert macro, the file must be called "assert.h" and the #include line must be modified to become:

```
#include "assert.h"   /* not <assert.h> */
```

Alternatively, it is often possible to leave the <assert.h> notation in the program and use a compiler option to cause the compiler to search another directory for header files before searching the system directory. The required compiler option is –I under UNIX and in many other implementations.

Another alternative is to use a different name for the macro (e.g., my_assert) and use a different header filename (e.g., "my_assert.h"). This is probably better, since using a different name makes it obvious that the standard library macro is not being used.

An improved version of assert would output the message to stderr, and output the line number and filename of the failed assertion (as done by the standard library assert macro). The line number and filename can be found using the special preprocessor macro names: __LINE__ and __FILE__.

```
#define assert(exp) \
        if (exp) {} else    \
           fprintf(stderr,   \
               "Line %ld, File '%s', Assertion failed: %s\n", \
               (long)__LINE__, __FILE__, #exp), \
           exit(EXIT_FAILURE)
```

If assertions are to be removed after program development, the preprocessor can be used to help. Using the method below, assertions will be ignored if NDEBUG is defined:

```
#ifndef NDEBUG
#define assert(exp)
           /* etc.  as given above */
#else
#define assert(exp)  ((void)0)    /* do nothing */
#endif
```

Note that using the following macro declaration when NDEBUG is declared is slightly dangerous:

```
#define assert(exp)  /* nothing */
```

Obscure errors can arise if a semicolon is missing from a call to the assert macro if declared this way. Refer to Section 20.7 and Section 20.8 for more discussion of this obscure macro error. However, if assertions are removed only after they have first been used, the compiler would have caught any missing semicolons as compilation errors. The "nothing" macro may be preferable for those compilers that warn about a "null effect" statement from the "((void)0)" method.

2.13.3 Leaving assertions in production code

It is common practice to remove assertions from production code, and yet this may be an unwise decision. This has been compared to using lifevests on the mainland but discarding them when going out to sea. There is certainly a case to be made for leaving assertions in production code. Although this may slow down program execution slightly, a program failing gracefully because of a failed assertion is far better than an ungraceful crash resulting in lost data.

Therefore, one useful effect of leaving assertions in the code is to cause graceful termination when an assertion fails. For some programs it may be satisfactory to terminate using the default method provided by the compiler's version of the assert macro. However, other programs will require extra work to be performed, such as the closing of files. One method of declaring assert to allow a useful shutdown is:

```
#define assert(exp) \
        if (exp) {} else    \
           graceful_assert(__LINE__, __FILE__, #exp)
```

where the graceful_assert function is defined something like:

```
void graceful_assert(long line, char *file, char *mesg)
{
    /* .. shutdown actions here ... */
    fprintf(stderr, "FATAL INTERNAL ERROR: ");
    fprintf(stderr, "Line %ld, File '%s', Assert failed: %s\n",
            line, file, mesg);
    exit(EXIT_FAILURE);
}
```

An alternative to termination that may be worth considering is to "keep going" even if an assertion fails. Removing the `exit` call in the above function would allow the program to continue even after an assertion has failed. Under some conditions this might be desirable, such as when the correctness of an assertion is not of paramount importance to program execution.

A design method worth considering is to use more than one form of assertion, depending on how crucial a given condition is to program success. For example, a `harmless_assert` macro could be used to indicate a condition that should be true, but is not highly important. A corresponding `crucial_assert` macro would indicate a condition that must be true for the program to continue operating. The declarations of these macros might be:

```
#define crucial_assert(exp) \
        if (exp) {} else    \
          graceful_assert(__LINE__, __FILE__, #exp),  \
          exit(EXIT_FAILURE)

#ifdef DEBUG
#  define harmless_assert(exp)  crucial_assert(exp)
#else
#  define harmless_assert(exp)       \
        if (exp) {} else    \
          graceful_assert(__LINE__, __FILE__, #exp)
```

The above declarations assume that `graceful_assert` does not terminate. The failure of a "harmless" assertion during the debugging phase will cause termination, but will continue execution in production code. Another variation would be to make `harmless_assert` calls disappear in production code by defining it to expand into nothing; this would be the best alternative if producing warning messages in the midst of program execution is not desirable.

2.13.4 Assertions are not exception handlers

Assertions should never attempt to replace an exception handler. The `assert` macro should never be used to check for bad input, or for library function error return values. For example, the use of `assert` to check that the return value of `malloc` is not NULL is bad style:

```
p = malloc(sizeof(*p));
assert(p != NULL);     /* Bad style */
```

Is it really appropriate for the program to terminate with an obscure assertion failure message? The awful trick with string literals:

```
assert(p != NULL && "Malloc failed");
```

can make a slightly more self-explanatory error diagnostic with the phrase "Malloc failed" somewhere in the text (since most modern implementations of assert will stringize the expression). However, a far better solution is an exception handler that either produces a more graceful diagnostic or attempts to keep the program running.

2.13.5 Non-ANSI assert syntax

A common mistake in the use of the assert macro is to omit the semicolon after the macro call. Because of the way in which old pre-ANSI C compilers defined assert, some programmers use the following style of assertions:

```
assert(x != 0)   recip = 1.0 / x;
```

The idea is that the code after the assert macro is executed only if the assertion succeeds. Hence the above code avoids division by zero. However, this code should not compile on an ANSI C compiler because it relies on the implementation of an assert macro as an if statement with an empty else clause such as:

```
#define assert(y)   if(!(y)) { __assert(....); }  else
```

This type of definition of assert would expand into code giving the required characteristics:

```
if (! (x != 0)) { __assert(....); } else  recip = 1.0 / x;
```

The absence of the semicolon after the right brace is not a syntax error and the code will compile and run correctly. The assignment statement after the assert macro occurs only if the assertion succeeds. However, the ANSI C standard and the draft ANSI C++ standard require that assert be an *expression*, not a *statement*. Therefore, a standard-conforming implementation of assert must look like an expression, such as:

```
#define assert(x)   ( (x) ? (void)0 : __assert(...))
```

In this case the missing semicolon in the pre-ANSI style of assertions will cause a compilation error. Hence this style of assertions relies on the idiosyncrasies of pre-ANSI C compilers and should be avoided. The correct method of using assert has exactly the same run-time behavior, with the assignment occurring only if the assertion succeeds; the only difference is the extra semicolon:

```
assert(x != 0);
recip = 1.0 / x;
```

2.14 Self-testing code

During the development of a program, it can be very useful to have the program check itself for errors. It checks for any incorrect conditions, and if they occur, some action is taken. During program development, an appropriate action could be to print out an error message and terminate.

When program development is complete, these checks can be removed. Alternatively, the checks can remain, and a more useful exception handling routine can be installed using the `setjmp` library function (see Section 8.1). Instead of exiting the program when a problem is encountered, this exception handler is called using the `longjmp` library function. Almost anything is better than a crash.

Complex data structures are good candidates for self-checking code. The program could perform consistency checks on the data structures, after each insertion and deletion. Often some extra data is useful to compare against. For example, an incremental count of names in a symbol table can be maintained by incrementing on insertion and decrementing on deletion. This count variable can then be compared against a function that counts the number of names actually stored in the symbol table data structure. This idea is illustrated below:

```
      insert(table, node);              /* Insert node into table */
#if SELF_TEST
      count++;                                    /* update count */
      if (count != count_elements(table)) {   /* correct? */
          internal_error("Element count wrong");   /* error */
      }
#endif
```

When the self-checking code indicates an error, the first place to look is in the self-checking code itself. It is at least as likely to be wrong as the data structure functions, and nothing is worse than checking an entire B-tree insertion function only to discover that the sense of the condition in the checking `if` statement was wrong!

2.14.1 Specialized self-testing macros

There are a number of common errors that can be detected by placing self-testing macros or functions throughout the code. A good example of this form is checking array bounds. Instead of assertions such as:

```
assert(0 <= i  && i < MAX);
```

it may be better to use specialized bounds checking macros. Repeatedly using the above code is error-prone since the programmer can easily mistype the `<=` and `<` tests. The following macro is more elegant and also more reliable:

```
#define bounds_check(i, size)  \
        assert(0 <= (i) && (i) < (size))
  ...
bounds_check(i, MAX);  /* Better */
```

Manually checking every instance with an explicit test is prone to errors of omission. However, until compiler implementors realize the need for run-time error checks of this type, it is probably the best that we can do.

2.14.2 Removing self-testing code

It may be desirable to remove self-testing code when building the production version of a program. However, the comments relating to the dangers of assertion removal made in Section 2.13.3 also apply to self-testing code. It may be better to leave self-testing code in the production code, so as to exhibit graceful termination when an error occurs. If self-testing code is left in the program, the `internal_error` function should be written so as to exhibit good behavior. It might also be desirable to make `internal_error` into a macro defined so as to pass `__LINE__` and `__FILE__` on to another function that performs the real work (similar to the method of declaring your own `assert` macro in Section 2.13.2).

Nevertheless, many programmers wish to remove self-testing code for the production version so as to improve efficiency. For specialized macros such as the `bounds_check` macro of the previous section, this can be achieved by declaring it as an empty macro:

```
#define bounds_check(i, size)   /* nothing */
```

For large blocks of self-testing code, the simplest method is to surround each block with an `#ifdef`-`#endif` pair, as used in the example above. Self-testing code is then removed by appropriately setting the values of the controlling macro names.

Another method is to use a macro such as the DBG macro declared in Section 2.7.3. The self-testing code would then appear as:

```
DBG(  count++;      )
DBG(  if (count != count_elements(table)) {   )
DBG(      internal_error("Element count wrong");  )
DBG(  }  )
```

An alternative use of DBG with multiple statements is valid, provided that the enclosed statements do not include any comma tokens (unless they are nested inside matching brackets). The presence of a comma would separate the tokens into two or more macro arguments and the DBG macro requires only one:

```
DBG(
    count++;                                  /* update count */
    if (count != count_elements(table)) {   /* correct? */
        internal_error("Element count wrong");   /* error */
    }
)
```

An alternative formulation of a macro for installing self-testing code using a block-style is as follows:

```
#if !PRODUCTION    /* if using self-test code */
#define SELFTEST  /* nothing */
#else
#define SELFTEST  if(1) {} else
#endif
    ....
SELFTEST {
    /* block of debugging or self-testing statements */
}
```

This binary on/off decision about self-testing code is not the most desirable condition. The natural extension is to implement the "areas" idiom as discussed for debugging output, to allow configuration of what self-testing code is executed for a particular run. A macro definition of SELFTEST(level) has been hooked into the run-time configuration library for debugging output in the source disk implementation (i.e., debugout.c and debugout.h in the chap2 directory). The macro is:

```
#define SELFTEST(level) \
        if(debug == 0 || DEBUG_FLAGS[level] == 0) \
          { /* do nothing */  } else
```

This uses the same "debug flags" array as the debugging output commands. Naturally, a better implementation would allow separation of the areas for debugging output and self-testing code, but this is left as an extension for the reader.

2.15 Using keyboard signals for debugging

Keyboard interrupt signals are an advanced feature that can be used for debugging purposes. They are mainly useful under UNIX, where they are always supported. The DOS environment supports the SIGINT signal for the keyboard interrupt <ctrl-c>, but does not support keyboard interrupts for <ctrl-\> or <ctrl-z>.

The idea is to set up a signal handler for SIGINT, the interrupt signal generated by <ctrl-c>, so that this handler prints out debugging information whenever the user presses <ctrl-c>. This method has occasional utility, but has major disadvantages, such as the fact that any data used by the handler must be available globally.

The code below illustrates how to set up a handler for the <ctrl-c> interrupt (i.e., the SIGINT signal). The debugging function prints out the data currently in the array (which must be a global variable to allow the handler to access it).

```
#include <stdio.h>
#include <stdlib.h>
#include <signal.h>

int arr[10];              /* Array is Global variable */

void handler(int sig)
{
    int i;
                            /* Print out debugging info */
    for (i = 0; i < 10; i++)
        printf("%d  ", arr[i]);
    printf("\n");
    signal(SIGINT, handler);  /* reinstall for some systems */
}

main()
{
    int i;

    signal(SIGINT, handler);
    printf("Running ....\n");
    for (i = 0; ; i = (i + 1) % 10)
        arr[i] = rand() % 100;
}
```

Other possibilities for useful debugging functions include API functions from existing libraries or tools. For example, the `print_block_list` function of the `malloc` debugging library discussed in Section 3.1 could be called, thus allowing the user to examine the status of the memory heap at any point in the program.

Trapping `SIGINT` means that <ctrl-c> no longer stops the program. It can be stopped under UNIX using <ctrl-\>, but this causes a core dump. Under DOS the program can usually be stopped using another key sequence, such as <ctrl-break>. An alternative under UNIX that would allow <ctrl-c> to still work is to trap the `SIGQUIT` signal generated by <ctrl-\> or `SIGTSTP` generated by <ctrl-z>.

Unfortunately, there is one problem with this approach of using signals to produce debugging output. Although signals act mostly like interrupts, there are a few situations where the last instruction is not restarted. Some UNIX system calls, including `read` and `write`, will fail and return −1 and set `errno` to `EINTR` if they are interrupted by a signal. This means that when using this signal-trapping approach for debugging it is important to examine the return value of some functions for which the return value is usually ignored, such as input and output functions.

Another problem is to ensure that the global data being examined is not currently corrupted. For example, if the `print_block_list` function is called, the user must ensure that <ctrl-c> is pressed only when no heap allocation is occurring; otherwise there is the danger that the internal data structure examined by `print_block_list` will be corrupt. One possibility here is to modify the definition of the wrapper functions in the library to block `SIGINT` during their operations, so as to ensure that `print_block_list` can never examine corrupt data.

2.16 Further reading

Although debugging programs is a huge area, there appears to be relatively little written about debugging C or C++ programs. The book by Anderson and Anderson contains a good chapter on debugging techniques under C that covers topics such as preprocessor macros, debugging input, assertions, and signals. Similarly, the book by Kochan and Wood contains a chapter on debugging in C that covers `lint`, the preprocessor, `ctrace`, `sdb`, and run-time configurable debugging output. Koenig's book is also an interesting discussion of programming errors in C, although it is more comparable with Part II of this book.

ANDERSON, Paul, and ANDERSON, Gail, *Advanced C: Tips and Techniques*, Hayden Books, 1988.

BATES, Rodney M., "Debugging with Assertions," *The C Users Journal*, Vol. 10, No. 10, October 1992.

KOCHAN, Stephen G., and WOOD, Patrick H., *Topics in C Programming* (rev. edn), John Wiley and Sons, 1991.

KOENIG, Andrew, *C Traps and Pitfalls*, Addison-Wesley, 1989.

2.17 Extensions

1. Design a C++ library of `DPRINTF` debugging output functions that are overloaded based on parameter types. The library should allow optional specification by the user of an integer debugging level and a `FILE*` stream, allowing at least the following usage methods:

    ```
    DPRINTF(1, "x = %d\n", x);
    DPRINTF(1, stderr, "x = %d\n", x);
    DPRINTF(stderr, "x = %d\n", x);
    ```

2. Modify the run-time configurable debugging output library presented in this chapter to support the single "level" idiom rather than the "area" idiom (which has been implemented). This will allow only one integer configuration parameter in the environment variable, text file, or command-line arguments.

3. Modify the `DBG` macro of Section 2.7.3 to accept a debugging level as the first argument, and make it compatible with the run-time configuration library.

4. Write your own `assert` macro that dumps the run-time stack using the UNIX `StackDump` function in the file "chap2/stkdump.c" on the disk.

5. Implement an extended assertion macro that allows "levels" or "areas" of assertions to be enabled. Thus it is a special case of a configurable `SELFTEST` macro. The form of the call would be:

    ```
    ASSERT(level, condition);
    ```

6. Implement an extended run-time configuration library that separately specifies "area" flags for:

    - debugging output;   `DPRINTF(1,....);`
    - self-testing code;   `SELFTEST(1) {...}`
    - assertions;   `ASSERT(1,...);`

    For example, use `-d` options for debug output flags, `-s` options for self-tests and `-a` for assertions in the generalization of the `debug_arguments` function.

7. Implement a run-time configurable debugging output package using the debugging "area" idiom, but with the extra feature of string names rather than integers. *Hint:* use an internal search table to store the currently enabled names.

8. Modify the run-time configurable debugging output library to allow some form of comments in the debugging text files. For example, ignore all characters after #.

9. Design a run-time configuration library that allows mid-execution changes to debugging levels via files or environment variables. For example, it could check the modification timestamp of a text file before each debugging output statement, and reload the options if the file has changed.

10. Modify one of the `malloc` debugging libraries in Chapter 3 to allow calls to `print_block_list` from within signal handlers for `SIGINT` or `SIGQUIT`. The signal must be blocked during updates to the library's internal data structure.

Chapter 3

Debugging libraries

This chapter examines a number of libraries for the detection of various forms of programming errors. Typically these libraries involve one of two methods of intercepting calls to standard library functions or other primitives:

1. interception at compile-time using preprocessor macros
2. interception at link-time using function definitions

A number of successful commercial tools are based on these principles, and understanding how these tools can be implemented also yields insight into the benefits that may be obtained from them. To some extent, the libraries discussed in this chapter might be considered as substitutes for the commercial tools. However, the chances are that the commercial versions will be implemented more efficiently, and offer many more useful features. The features of the libraries I present are somewhat limited, although useful, and their efficiency has not been of paramount importance (e.g., a friend of mine complained that the `mymalloc` library, which uses a singly linked list as its base data structure, was a little bit too slow for his application that allocated 60,000 blocks).

There are many extra features with which you might wish to augment the libraries presented herein. Ideally, the libraries should be fully customizable, at both compile-time via conditional compilation and at run-time via API functions. Some of the things that should be customizable are different actions on the detection of various errors, the formats of error messages, and the various reports presented. For example, when debugging C++ programs, one might wish to exit on a fatal error such as a double-`delete`, but continue for a `delete` of `NULL`, which although rather strange, is not actually an error in C++ — it is fully defined as being a safe null effect operation. Some potential changes are suggested as extensions at the end of the chapter.

3.1 Catching memory allocation errors in C

The use of the dynamic memory allocation functions, `malloc`, `calloc`, `realloc`, and `free`, is fraught with danger because these functions perform no error checking. Problems that can occur are blocks being freed twice, blocks being freed that were never allocated by one of these functions (e.g., mistakenly freeing an array variable), and accessing a block that has already been freed (i.e., a dangling reference). These errors cause immediate problems, but there is one problem with less immediate consequences. If a program allocates many blocks of memory but never frees them, it may eventually run out of available memory, and fail. This problem of the accumulation of unused memory (often called *garbage*) is called a *memory leak*.

One reasonably simple method of detecting problems with memory allocation is to add your own error-checking front end onto the existing functions, and such a front end is presented below. The front end maintains a list of allocated blocks, and when a call to `free` or `realloc` passes an address, these functions check that the address is of a block that is currently allocated. If the block's address is not on the list, this is an instance of one of the two problems above related to freeing a nonallocated block. Using this method of intercepting library calls using macros, the following problems can be detected:

- `free` of a nonallocated block
- `free` of an already freed block (double `free`)
- `free(NULL)` — legal in ANSI C/C++ but unusual enough to deserve warnings
- allocation failure — legal but unusual enough to deserve warnings
- memory leakage and garbage accumulation

The implementation of the new memory allocation functions is quite straightforward. The new `malloc` and `calloc` functions store information about the allocated block on a linked list of blocks, as well as actually duplicating the functionality of the real functions (i.e., calling the real `malloc` or `calloc` to get the address of a new allocated block). Both `free` and `realloc` check that the address is actually an allocated block and terminate the program with an error message if it is not valid. If the address is valid, the block is removed from the list, and freed using the real `free` function. The `realloc` function also allocates a new block in a manner identical to that for the new `malloc` function.

A function called `print_block_list` is provided that prints out the current status of the heap, indicating how many blocks are available. To detect a memory leak, this function can be called from the program being tested at the end of execution (e.g., as an `atexit` function). If any blocks are currently allocated, their source can be traced because the line numbers of the statements creating the blocks are recorded. Thus, to detect a memory leak, the last few lines of the `main` function might well be:

```
#if DEBUG_MEMORY
    print_block_list();
#endif
```

The `print_block_list` function can be called at any point in the program where information about the current state of memory allocation is useful. In fact, the `#if`-`#endif` pair is not necessary here because the header file "`mymalloc.h`" will convert `print_block_list()` to whitespace if `DEBUG_MEMORY` is not defined. However, the use of `#if`-`#endif` makes it clearer that the function is called only when memory allocation debugging is enabled.

Unfortunately, one common problem with memory allocation cannot be detected automatically using the method here. The use of wayward pointers from dangling references or array references out of bounds cannot be as easily detected as the freeing of unallocated blocks. To provide a partial solution, two functions are provided to check that pointers are valid. The `check_pointer` function checks if the pointer points to the start of some block, and can be used to trap dangling references. The `check_address` function checks if the pointer is inside some block, and can be used to detect bad array references. However, it is the responsibility of the programmer to explicitly check every pointer dereference, which requires code such as:

```
#if DEBUG_MEMORY
    check_pointer(p);      /* Check p points to a valid block */
#endif
    *p = s;                /* Dereference p */
```

Once again, the `#if`-`#endif` pair is unnecessary because "`mymalloc.h`" will expand `check_pointer` into whitespace if debugging is disabled. The use of `#if`-`#endif` makes this fact clearer, but it may be preferable not to waste the lines of source code.

The addition of an error-checking front end causes errors to be detected but slows down the program, and the error checking should be removed for the final version. Thus the front end should be easy to add to the program and easy to remove. A simple method of achieving this is to use the preprocessor to change all calls to `malloc`, `calloc`, `free`, and `realloc`. The inclusion of the header file "`mymalloc.h`" causes all calls to these functions to translate to the new functions `mymalloc`, `mycalloc`, `myfree`, and `myrealloc`. Extra arguments are also added to pass the line number and filename to the new functions. The macro definitions become akin to the following macro wrapper for `malloc`:

```
#define malloc(size)        mymalloc(size,__FILE__,__LINE__)
```

The header file also defines the functions `print_block_list`, `check_pointer`, and `check_address` for the programmer to use in the program.

Header file inclusion sets the error checking on only if the preprocessor symbol `DEBUG_MEMORY` is defined before the inclusion of "`mymalloc.h`," and the error checking can be used in the manner:

```
#define DEBUG_MEMORY  1    /* 1 if want allocation debugging */
#include "mymalloc.h"
```

The error checking can be removed as simply as setting `DEBUG_MEMORY` to 0. Alternatively, the `DEBUG_MEMORY` macro can be set by a compiler command-line option (e.g., `cc -DDEBUG_MEMORY=1` under UNIX).

When the debugging is required, the source file containing the function definitions must be compiled and linked with the rest of the program. The source code for the function definitions is given in disk file "mymalloc.c" in the chap3 directory. Note that this file can be used for both C and C++ debugging.

3.1.1 Limitations of the memory allocation library

This tricky method of using preprocessor macros to catch common errors has a number of limitations. One has already been mentioned: the inability to detect uses of wayward pointers or array references out of bounds.

Another problem is that the method relies on source code access and any memory allocation in linked object-code libraries will not be detected by the wrapper functions. For example, if the startup code calls malloc, this will not be detected. Fortunately, this is not a major limitation since in many cases we are not interested in the allocation performed by the standard libraries, and also because any standard library use of free to deallocate this memory is also hidden — the debugging library does not notice any anomalies.

A more dangerous problem occurs when a library allocates memory for the programmer, but expects deallocation to be performed in the programmer's code. In this situation the memory debugging library may detect a call to free with no matching allocation. The solution to this problem appears to be writing wrappers for those functions using this sort of allocation. The method of writing extra wrappers is examined below (although for a slightly different purpose). The only difference between the discussion below and writing wrappers for a third-party library function is that the "real" version of the function (i.e., the one in the third-party library) does not need to be changed since it is already calling the real malloc at object-code level; this is indeed fortunate since there is no way to change the function in the third-party library.

3.2 Catching new/delete errors in C++

Because the C++ new and delete allocation primitives are operators rather than function calls, it is not possible to intercept these allocation requests with preprocessor macros, as was possible for the malloc family. However, C++ has a feature enabling link-time interception of new and delete by defining global versions of them. Fortunately, this is a feature supported by the ANSI C++ standard, and not just an idiosyncrasy of particular implementations.

This feature allows the definition of a linkable debugging library for examining C++ allocation requests. In this case there is no need to modify the source code to include a header file (although Section 3.3 shows a version that does use this method); this library is used simply by linking its object file with the other object files from the project. The linker then uses the new definitions of the global new and delete rather than the standard versions. The full versions are given in disk file "link_new.cc" in the chap3 directory. The basis of the method is the definition of overloaded new and delete using the following forms:

```
//----------------------------------------------------------------
//  Replacement for GLOBAL NEW operator
//----------------------------------------------------------------

void* operator new (size_t size)
{
    // ... allocate block of size requested
}
//----------------------------------------------------------------
//  Replacement for GLOBAL DELETE operator
//----------------------------------------------------------------

void operator delete (void *ptr)
{
    // ... deallocate block at address 'ptr'
}
```

3.2.1 Limitations of the linkable new/delete library

Problems will arise if the project already defines global new and delete operators, in which case they should be modified to include error-checking facilities.

A limitation of this method is that not all allocation requests are available to the global versions of new and delete. If any class defines class-specific versions of new and delete, then these local versions will be called instead of the global versions (although the global versions are still called for array allocation requests). Therefore, this library cannot detect errors if a class implements its own fancy memory allocation policy, such as a memory pool. However, it will may detect some errors if the local operators call the global versions to allocate memory.

Another limitation of the method of overloading global new and delete is that there is no portable method of detecting mismatches related to new, new arr[], delete, and delete[], because the same new and delete operator functions are called for array and nonarray allocation requests.

3.3 Augmenting the malloc debug library for C++

The linkable versions of the overloaded new and delete operators can be combined with the malloc debugging library from Section 3.1 to present an improved version with enhanced debugging features. The library can then detect errors in both C-style and C++-style memory allocation, including inconsistent mixing of both allocation schemes such as:

* block deallocated by free was allocated by new; and
* block deallocated by delete was allocated by malloc.

However, the disadvantage in relation to the linkable new/delete debugging library is the need to modify the source code to include a header file (as is required for the mymalloc C-based allocation library). If this header file is not included, the C-style memory allocation functions are not intercepted, and only C++ memory allocation error checking occurs. This library is implemented in disk files "mymalloc.c" and "mymalloc.h," which are the same as for the C version; these files support both C and C++ and detect C++ compilation via the __cplusplus macro.

3.3.1 Limitations of overloading new and delete

An annoying limitation of the C++ error detection library shown here (with overloaded global new and delete) is that the error messages do not report line number or filename. Macros are not used for new or delete, and hence there is no use of __LINE__ or __FILE__.

This feature is not difficult to add to the library and is left as an exercise to the reader. The macro definition of the delete macro simply sets two global variables using a comma expression:

```
#define delete (ext_line=__LINE__,ext_file=__FILE__), delete
```

The macro for delete is very simple because delete is a void expression, and its returned value is never used. Choosing a good macro for new is more difficult because its return value is used. One neat solution I discovered was the use of the ?: ternary conditional operator to set global variables as follows:

```
#define new ((ext_line=__LINE__,ext_file=__FILE__),0)? 0 : new
```

This works correctly with an = token before new in both assignment statements and initialized declarations. However, there is a precedence problem with type casts applied to new, such as:

```
char *p = (char*)new int[100];   // RECEIVES ERROR
```

The type cast operator has higher precedence than ?: and hence is bound to the test condition of the ?: operator. The type cast is not applied to the returned new expression, and a compilation error occurs. One simple solution is the use of brackets:

```
char *p = (char*)(new int[100]);   // OK
```

Thus the situation with type casts is not serious: all problems will receive compilation error, and can be corrected manually. In any case, it is bad style to use this form of pointer type casting. Other obscure macro-related precedence errors can arise if other operators are applied to new, but the only obvious legitimate reason is the use of overloaded operators, which would occur rarely. Most such problems would receive compilation errors, but a pathological example is shown below that will always print 0 rather than the value of the returned pointer, which is thrown away:

```
#include <iostream.h>
  ....
cout << new char;
```

Note that there are no problems with passing a new operation directly as a function argument, which is probably the third most common operation on new, after = and type casting.

Note that the macros for new and delete will not affect the use of any user-supplied (nondebugging) class-local new or delete member functions, except that they will have reduced efficiency because of the preceding assignment to ext_line and ext_file.

A number of other possible macros were examined for new and found to fail. The most obvious was the use of a comma expression as in the delete macro:

```
#define new ext_line = __LINE__, ext_file = __FILE__, new
```

However, although this method works for new operators used in expressions, it fails for new operators in declarations such as:

```
char *p = new char[100];
```

which expands into:

```
char *p = ext_line=__LINE__, ext_file=__FILE__, new char[100];
```

This results in a compilation error because the comma is not an operator in this context; instead commas separate multiple declarations, and thus ext_file is declared as a local char variable and the last part is treated as "char new char[100]," which is an erroneous declaration. Various alternative macros using commas are no better:

```
#define new (ext_line=__LINE__,ext_file=__FILE__),new   // FAILS
#define new (ext_line=__LINE__,ext_file=__FILE__,new)   // FAILS
```

The only other possible solution is to use the new operator's placement syntax, which is an obscure C++ feature that very few programs ever use. However, it suits our purposes here quite well. The macro definition becomes:

```
#define new  new (__LINE__, __FILE__)
```

This can be caught by a global new operator defined as shown below:

```
void* operator new (size_t size, long ext_line, char *ext_file)
{
    // etc
}
```

However, the use of placement syntax can cause compilation errors for any existing user-specified (nondebugging) class-local new operators, and also requires the definition of extra debugging global and class-local new operators. Hence the use of ?: as shown above seems superior as a macro replacement for new.

3.4 Class-specific memory allocation debugging

The C++ facility to provide class-specific overloaded versions of new and delete can be used to enhance the C++ version of the memory allocation debugging. By modifying the class declaration to use a macro name, in this case, CLASS_MEMORY_DEBUG, all class-specific calls to new and delete will be intercepted. Thus this method requires a little more source code modification than just including a header file; it requires adding a macro call to class declarations needing testing, and also the inclusion of the "classnew.h" header file. The full versions of this library are available on the source disk as "classnew.cc" and "classnew.h" in the chap3 directory. The main additions to the header file "classnew.h" compared with "mymalloc.h" are:

```
//-----------------------------------------------------------------
// DebugMem class for memory debugging;  mostly hidden to user
//-----------------------------------------------------------------

class DebugMem {       // Class used to reduce name space pollution
    public:
        static void *new_alloc(size_t size, char*file, long int line);
        static void deallocate(void *ptr, char*file, long int line);
};

//-----------------------------------------------------------------
// inline versions of class-local NEW/DELETE for class header
// Made into a macro for easy usage
//-----------------------------------------------------------------

#define CLASS_MEMORY_DEBUG        \
  public:                         \
    void* operator new (size_t size) \
    { return DebugMem::new_alloc(size, __FILE__, (long)__LINE__); }    \
    void operator delete (void *ptr) \
        { DebugMem::deallocate(ptr, __FILE__, (long)__LINE__); }
```

The usage method for this library is the same as for other libraries in this chapter. All source files should include "classnew.h", and the macro name DEBUG_MEMORY should be set to 1 before inclusion of this header file, or by using a compiler option. The only addition is the need to add the macro CLASS_MEMORY_DEBUG to all class declarations requiring testing. There is no need to surround it with #if/#endif pairs since it will become whitespace when DEBUG_MEMORY is not set. An example usage is:

```
class Obj {
    // .. body of the class
    CLASS_MEMORY_DEBUG
};
```

This macro provides the class with inline definitions of class-specific new/delete operators, and thus will not work for classes that already have these features.

The main advantage of this method is catching class-related mismatches between array and nonarray allocation and deallocations. Errors such as delete[] used on a nonarray block, and using plain delete on an array block, should be identified for the classes that use the macro. The following code should provoke an error from the library at run-time:

```
Obj * p = new Obj;
delete [] Obj;       // ERROR!
```

Testing this file showed up an error in my compiler (g++/gcc) where the class-local new operator was called for new[] operations, instead of the global new operator that is correct for array allocations. This compiler bug resulted in errors about legitimate usage of delete[]. Thus it is wise to test the library with a small test file and determine if the error messages are correct.

An extension to this library would be to enhance the macro to accept the class name as an argument. This would allow better error reporting, such as reporting the class for which class-local new and delete were called, or what type of object a block of memory was. However, the actual number of extra errors caught this way would be minimal since it is unlikely that one class-local delete will deallocate memory from a different class-local new.

3.5 Linkable memory allocation debugging for C

The macro interception method of detecting problems with malloc and free has the disadvantage that all source files must be modified to include "mymalloc.h" and then recompiled. A more convenient method is to use a linkable memory allocation debugging library. This is merely linked with the other object files to rebuild the executable, and does not require source code modification. It also has the advantages of catching all allocation requests, whereas the macro interception method may miss some (e.g., third-party libraries in object form).

However, there are a few problems in portably building a linkable library. Firstly, it must be possible to write your own functions named malloc and free, and link them. The ANSI C standard says that redefining any library function causes "undefined behavior." Fortunately, many C/C++ implementations permit the replacement of library functions with new definitions, but this is not guaranteed.

Secondly, there must be some way to implement malloc and free in terms of other memory allocation primitives. There is no portable method to achieve this, simply because malloc and free are themselves the only portable method. There are a few possible methods:

- Use some other memory allocation functions
  (e.g., sbrk under UNIX, or farmalloc for Turbo C/C++).
- Use the C++ new and delete operators.
- Use realloc (if it's never used in the program).
- Write your own low-level memory allocation functions.

Using either of the first two methods, other C functions or the C++ operators, will work only if these functions do not themselves call malloc or free internally; if they do, an infinite loop will occur.

The use of realloc is an interesting possibility, since it can be used to mimic both free and malloc/calloc, and so linkable versions of free, malloc, and calloc could be provided that simply call realloc. However, this can be dangerous if realloc is actually used by the program being tested (or in third-party libraries). In this case, any blocks allocated/freed by realloc will not be intercepted by the debugging library, and the error checking can be corrupted. Nevertheless, it's a possibility if you're someone who never uses realloc.

The following C source file illustrates how the linkable memory allocation debugging package can be developed using compiler-specific non-ANSI memory allocation primitives. The version below uses Turbo C/C++'s non-ANSI heap memory allocation functions: farmalloc, farcalloc, farfree, and farrealloc. Naturally, this method is not portable because it uses non-ANSI functions. It works only by "accident" in that farmalloc does not appear to be implemented in terms of malloc (at least, this is the case in my version of the compiler), and therefore does not cause an infinite recursion. The source code for this "toy" version is the file "linkmall.c" in the chap3 directory of the source code disk.

The header file "linkmall.h" is listed below and also appears in the chap3 directory of the source disk. It need not be included by any of the other source files, unless the programmer desires to use the three API functions defined in the library: print_block_list, check_reference, or check_pointer. If so, the DEBUG_MEMORY macro must be defined as 1, using either #define or a compiler command-line option; if it is not defined, any calls to these three functions will be macro expanded into "nothing" statements.

```
/*-----------------------------------------------------------*/
/* LINKMALL.H: linkable malloc debugging functions           */
/*-----------------------------------------------------------*/

#if DEBUG_MEMORY        /* Only include if DEBUG_MEMORY is set */

#undef check_reference
#undef check_pointer
#undef print_block_list

                /* check that p is pointing inside some block */
#define check_reference(p)   check_address(p)

                /* check that p is pointing to a block */
#define check_pointer(p)     check_valid(p,4)

void print_block_list(void);
int check_valid(void *address,int type);
int check_address(void *address);

#else  /* not debugging; change some functions to nothing */

#define check_reference(p)   /* nothing */
#define check_pointer(p)     /* nothing */
#define print_block_list()   /* nothing */

#endif
```

3.6 debuglib: a C/C++ debugging library

The above method of detecting memory allocation errors by writing wrapper functions for the malloc, calloc, and free functions can be generalized to catch a greater variety of errors. I have developed a source code library of wrapper functions for many of the standard library functions; it is called the "debuglib" library. This library consists of a header file "debuglib.h" and a single source file "debuglib.c" containing the function definitions; the source code for both files is given on the source disk as files debuglib.c and debuglib.h in the chap3 directory.

The manner of usage of the debuglib library is similar to that of the memory allocation debugging package. All files must include "debuglib.h" at the top of the file. The macro name DEBUGLIB must be defined *before* the inclusion of this header file (e.g., by declaring it as a compiler -DDEBUGLIB option). All source files are then compiled and linked together (with the debuglib object file) and the program is executed.

3.6.1 Errors detected by debuglib

The debuglib library detects a large number of errors related to the use of standard library functions. In summary, debuglib finds three major sources of errors:

1. memory allocation errors
2. file usage errors
3. bad arguments to library functions

The debuglib library builds on the `malloc` debugging library presented earlier in this chapter, and thus finds all of those forms of memory-related errors. However, debuglib also uses wrappers for other library functions unrelated to memory allocation, and has a larger range of error checks. The simplest of these checks is for bad function arguments (e.g., `NULL` pointers passed to `strcmp`), but there are also more fancy checks such as testing whether arguments to various `<string.h>` functions represent bad heap addresses (e.g., testing whether a `strcpy` operation overwrites a heap block). This extends the level of memory-related error checking to detect errors occurring in other library functions; these errors would not be found by the `malloc` debugging libraries in this chapter.

A major improvement of `debuglib` in relation to memory allocation debugging libraries is the error checking of all file operations using `<stdio.h>` functions. Some of the many file errors detected are:

- file handle "leaks" (i.e., files opened but never closed)
- bad filename or mode to `fopen`
- inconsistent operations on files (e.g., writing to a read-only file)
- bad `FILE*` handles used (e.g., writing to an already-closed file)

The implementation of this form of file checking is analogous to the implementation of memory allocation debugging since both file handles and memory blocks are *resources*. Thus the debuglib library maintains an internal table representing information about known `FILE*` handles.

3.6.2 Changing debuglib error output

Although the debuglib library does not contain many configuration options, there are a few choices, and a small number of API functions that can be called. This allows rudimentary control over the error checking and error message output of the library.

The default method of reporting errors is to print them to `stderr`. The `debuglib` library supports a number of methods of changing this so that error messages go to a log file. The simplest method is changing the default execution manner at compile-time (i.e., when compiling `"debuglib.c"`). This is quite acceptable since `debuglib` is probably not a system library and the source code should be available to you. Changing the macro declaration of `DEFAULT_MODE` within the `"debuglib.c"` source file will change the default error reporting method. The default filename for the error log file is `"debuglib.log"` in the current directory.

An alternative method is to change the error reporting method at run-time by calling either of the two functions `debuglib_file` or `debuglib_stderr`:

```
debuglib_stderr();              /* errors go to stderr */
debuglib_file("errs.log")       /* errors go to "errs.log" */
```

If the argument to `debuglib_file` is NULL, the default filename of the log file, "debuglib.log," is used.

Naturally, if the choice between `stderr` or a log file is not flexible enough, there is always the possibility of changing the source code of the `error` function in the source code file "debuglib.c."

The error-reporting process can be suppressed during execution using the two companion functions `debuglib_on` and `debuglib_off`. They apply to both screen and file error reporting. Their usage can be prefixed with `#ifdef-#endif` pairs using the macro name DEBUGLIB:

```
#ifdef DEBUGLIB
    debuglib_on();
#endif
```

There is no need for the `#ifdef-#endif` pair if "debuglib.h" is always included; if DEBUGLIB is not defined, these two functions expand to empty expressions. However, the use of the `#ifdef` method is recommended since the `#include` lines might later be removed from production code.

An alternative to using `debuglib_on` and `debuglib_off` is to use the global `int` variable `debuglib`, which is nonzero when error reporting is enabled. The `debuglib` variable is also useful for run-time testing whether error reporting is currently enabled, such as:

```
#ifdef DEBUGLIB
    if (debuglib) debuglib_file(NULL);
#endif
```

3.6.3 Limitations of the debuglib library

The `debuglib` library uses wrapper functions hidden behind tricky macro definitions. Therefore, it depends on compilation to change the standard library calls into calls to the wrapper functions. Consequently, the `debuglib` library cannot be used on precompiled object code libraries (e.g., as built by `ar` under UNIX, or with `tlink` from Turbo C++).

The range of errors that can be caught by `debuglib` is not as wide as one would wish. The library can only intercept standard library function calls, and cannot error check other statements for errors. For example, although `debuglib` can often catch errors when `strcpy` overwrites too far, it won't catch errors such as:

```
str[i] = 'a';
```

which may be erroneous if `i` is too large or negative. Because many errors cannot be caught by `debuglib`, it should not be viewed as a panacea for library function errors. Just because `debuglib` reports no errors doesn't mean that there aren't any!

3.6.4 debuglib for C++

All of the intercepted standard C library functions are also C++ library functions, and the debuglib can be used with C++ programs as well as C programs. The debuglib library has been coded such that it is valid as both ANSI C and C++ code. It also includes new/delete checking when compiled with a C++ compiler (tested via the __cplusplus macro). The resulting "debuglib++" library tracks the usual C-style standard library functions as well as uses of the global new and delete operators. This library is presented as disk files debuglib.c and debuglib.h in the chap3 directory, which are both combined C/C++ source files.

3.7 Further reading

The idea of using macro wrappers to trace memory allocation errors is not new. Indeed, a number of high-quality free and commercial tools based on this principle are now available. Macro wrappers were also used by William Smith, who examined macro tricks to detect incorrect return values, and also recursive macros to detect common range errors with mathematical functions.

A good solution to Extension 3(c), which requires the detection of array overruns in the allocation debugging libraries, is provided by Stephen Davis in his book. His method neatly supports overrun detection at both ends of the block using the "magic value" idea. A struct is used for memory block allocation that has a "prologue" field with a magic value immediately before the main data. The allocated data block is introduced using the well-known method of a char[1] structure field as the last member; note that this is the char[0] method converted to ANSI C/C++ that disallows zero-sized arrays. A neat trick is used to force the main data onto an aligned address — an "int:0" bit-field structure member is used to align to a word boundary. Thus the struct is of the form:

```
struct {
    // ... other stuff
    char prologue;    // magic value preceding data
    int :0;           // force alignment
    char data[1];     // start of main data
};
```

Overruns at the end of the block are detected by the fairly obvious tactic of allocating a larger block than necessary, and storing a magic value at the upper end of the block.

Scott Robert Ladd has also presented a linkable allocation debugging library for C++ allocation using global new and delete operator definitions.

DAVIS, Stephen R., *C++ Programmer's Companion: Designing, Testing and Debugging*, Addison-Wesley, 1993, pp. 343–351.

LADD, Scott Robert, "Debugging Dynamic Memory in C++," *PC Techniques*, Vol. 3, No. 5, December/January 1993, pp. 38–43.

SMITH, William M., "Debugging with Macro Wrappers," *The C Users Journal*, Vol. 10, No. 10, October 1992.

3.8 Extensions

1. Modify the user interface of the memory allocation debugging libraries, either C or C++ versions, to allow the following extra features:

    (a) extra conditional compilation choices
    (b) extra run-time choices (e.g., suppress errors at run-time)
    (c) number or name the errors for selective enabling/disabling
    (d) class errors as harmless or fatal, and allow selections based on these classes.

2. Modify the reporting of garbage blocks from the `print_block_list` function from the C or C++ memory allocation debugging libraries so as to show:

    (a) group counts of the number of blocks of each size
    (b) group counts of blocks allocated by `malloc`, `calloc`, `new`, etc
    (c) total memory requested by the program in all allocation requests
    (d) maximum heap memory ever used by program (i.e., the "high-water mark")
    (e) total memory used by all garbage blocks
    (f) total memory wasted internally by the linked list

3. Modify the basic algorithms behind the memory allocation debugging libraries, either C or C++ versions, to allow the following extra features:

    (a) faster data structure than a singly linked list (i.e., speed up deallocation)
    (b) once-only `atexit` registration of garbage summary reporting
    (c) detect array overruns by storing "magic values" at the ends of blocks; see Davis [1993, pp. 343–351]
    (d) detect deallocations of stack addresses as a special case (possible portably?)
    (e) allow "aging" of blocks in terms of number of allocations (improve on the choice between freeing or marking as permanently inactive)

4. Improve the error reporting of the memory allocation debugging libraries by producing a dump of the run-time stack using the UNIX `StackDump` function in the `"chap2/stkdump.c"` disk file.

5. Implement the method of passing `__LINE__` and `__FILE__` to the overloaded global `new` and `delete` operators, as shown in Section 3.3.1.

6. Modify a C++ memory allocation debugging library to use a single class name, such as `DebugMem`, with `static` member functions, rather than polluting the global name space with names such as `print_block_list`; the equivalent call would become:

    ```
    DebugMem::print_block_list();
    ```

    What problems does this present for removing these calls when the library's debugging facilities are not used? Is the `"if(1)else{}"` removal method adequate?

7. Modify the class-specific memory allocation debugging library to accept the class name as an argument to the CLASS_MEMORY_DEBUG macro, allowing slightly better error messages and error checking.

8. Alter the focus of the memory allocation debugging libraries from an error-reporting one to one of enforcing fault-tolerance. Instead of reporting an erroneous operation, the library will simply prevent it, thus improving reliability of the program using it.

9. Improve the memory allocation debugging libraries to handle non-ANSI allocation functions, such as Borland C/C++'s farmalloc family of functions.

10. Improve the overall usefulness of the debuglib library:

    (a) improve the user interface configurability — enable/disable errors
    (b) improve the format of error reports (e.g., make it customizable)

11. Modify the algorithms used by debuglib to increase error detection facilities:

    (a) detect stack addresses (impossible portably)
        (e.g., warn about setbuf with a stack variable)
    (b) detect string constant addresses (impossible portably)

12. Increase the number of wrapper functions used in debuglib to find all errors related to functions from:

    (a) the ANSI C standard library
    (b) standard UNIX library functions (e.g., open, close)
    (c) standard DOS non-ANSI functions (e.g., farmalloc)
    (d) the X Windows library

Chapter 4

Testing techniques

Testing is the process whereby flaws in a program's operation are discovered by executing the program with sample inputs. It is distinguished from debugging in that testing is the process of finding flaws, whereas debugging is the process of determining the causes of the flaws and also correcting them. Naturally, there is some overlap in testing and debugging methods in that errors and their causes are often discovered simultaneously. However, it is important to view testing as a separate process that determines whether a program correctly meets its specifications.

The traditional method of testing a program was for the programmer to interactively supply test inputs to the program. However, experience has shown that this is not the most effective method of removing errors from programs. The testing process must be applied more rigorously.

There are a number of other test methods that can be applied in addition to the ordinary interactive testing. Desk checking refers to manually examining the source code in hardcopy form (i.e., poring over printouts), looking for obvious coding errors. Code inspections and walkthroughs are two common methods of team testing whereby a group of programmers examines the source code in hardcopy form.

Some of the test techniques that actually use the computer are embedded test drivers, top-down testing with function stubs, and regression testing. Self-testing code called test drivers can be embedded in source files to test individual modules. Top-down testing refers to building a prototype of the system when some important facilities are imitated by short function "stubs"; this allows the general form of the program to be tested early in the development phase. Regression testing is an important general testing method whereby all test cases are stored and later reused to ensure that a change to the program has not introduced a new error causing it to fail tests performed earlier.

Note that a number of software tools for C/C++ testing are discussed in Chapter 11. Perhaps surprisingly, there are a couple of good tools that are freely available.

4.1 Management guidelines for testing

There are some important guidelines to follow about testing from the point of view of *management* of large projects. The single most important guideline is:

Programmers are poor at testing their own code.

There is a natural human tendency to test the program only on cases that the programmer has thought to handle, and also an understandable reluctance to break what you've just built; see Weinberg [1971] for an interesting study of psychological aspects of programming. Using an independent tester will often uncover a great many more errors. Therefore, it is good policy for a large organization to establish a group specializing in testing (or at least to ensure that code is tested by programmers other than author of the code).

An organization should recognize that a substantial part of software development will consist of testing and debugging. Code inspections and walkthroughs are important options in setting up an organization's testing policy (although they are by no means the only choices). The use of static checkers such as lint can also be a useful technique for ensuring some basic level of reliability. The output from lint, or even the warnings from the compiler, can be examined independently and could also be used as input for code inspection meetings.

The testing process should never be part of the programmer review process. If a programmer is criticized for writing code where too many errors are revealed, this may cause the programmer to think twice about reporting errors that they have themselves discovered. This guideline is particularly important in team testing (i.e., code inspections or walkthroughs) because the programmer who wrote the code is often the person to discover the majority of errors found in such meetings.

4.2 Test what you ship: retain debugging code

The testing guideline of "test what you ship" may seem quite an obvious one, but might be difficult to achieve in some circumstances, such as where different versions of a program exist for multiple platforms. The idea is to test the program that the end user will be running, not an in-house development version of the program. Obviously, the final testing phase of a product should be of the production version.

In addition, there are some methods of making earlier testing phases closer to the production version than usual. For example, it is reasonably common for a program to be using assertions, self-testing code, and debugging output statements, which are removed when the final version is constructed. Although preprocessing tricks should make the removal of these debugging statements transparent, there is always the potential for a problem (e.g., what if one of the debugging statements inadvertently contained an important side effect?). The alternative policy I recommend is to leave these assertions and debugging statements in the final version. As discussed in Section 2.13.3, the assert macro calls can be made into a more user-friendly bug report, and this idea can be generalized to any other self-testing functions in the program. The debugging statements can be left in the code by enabling them only when a particular run-time option is chosen (and perhaps when an environment variable is also set, so as to lessen the possibility of the user stumbling into the debugging mode); this run-time debugging option is used by testers and developers, but not usually by the end user. Some of the advantages of this policy are:

- Early testing phases are more relevant to the final product.
- Assertion failure can be graceful rather than a crash (e.g., no lost data).
- Debug mode allows easier debugging at a remote site.
- Debug mode allows a detailed bug report from the end user.

The main disadvantage is, of course, the inefficiency of leaving these statements in the program. The code size may be much larger than without them, and the run-time efficiency will suffer, although this loss in speed needn't be particularly great. Most assertions are a simple inexpensive conditional test, but those that are more costly can be implemented using a different macro, say, `expensive_assert`, which is enabled only in debug mode. For example, the run-time option to enable debugging mode will set a particular global variable, say, `debug`. All of the expensive assertions, self-testing functions, and debugging output functions will test this global variable before calling the appropriate function, so that the only loss in efficiency for the end user is a single conditional test (rather than the cost of a function call). For example, assuming `debug` is the "boolean" global variable (a fancier implementation might allow it to be a debugging level), the expensive assertions, self-testing functions and debug output statements would be implemented similarly to:

```
#define expensive_assert(cond) ( debug? assert(cond) : (void)0)
#define self_test_fn(x)     ( debug? real_test_fn(x) : (void)0)
#define DPRINTF        (!debug)? (void)0 : debug_printf
```

In this way, the global variable `debug` is tested before the function call, and this test is the only cost for the end user. The only difficult part of the above method is the definition of the debugging output statement `DPRINTF`; the above macro declaration assumes that `DPRINTF` accepts a variable number of arguments. Section 2.8 covers the many issues of debugging output statements in much more detail.

Note that larger blocks of self-testing code that are not implemented as functions could be placed inside an `if` statement:

```
if (debug) {
    /* .. self-testing code */
}
```

The use of `debug` could also be hidden behind a macro so as to make changes to it easier. Note that the use of `!debug` prevents dangling `else` macro errors as discussed in Section 20.8:

```
#define SELF_TEST  if(!debug){} else

SELF_TEST {
    /* .. self-testing code */
}
```

4.3 Code inspections and walkthroughs

Code inspections and walkthroughs are both structured management techniques for testing programs by examination of the source code by a team of people including the author. The difference between code inspections and walkthroughs is not great; both are meetings that examine source code with the intention of identifying errors. Code inspections examine source code line by line for any errors; walkthroughs use a number of test cases to "walk through" the flow of the program on particular inputs.

The code inspection process is a method of team testing that is based on the source code. As discussed by Myers [1979], the inspection team typically includes a small number of people: the program author, a code inspection "moderator," and one or more "test specialists." The moderator and test specialists could come from a special department responsible for code testing in an organization. The moderator is responsible for scheduling the code inspection and distributing source code to all participants in advance of the meeting, and also "leads" the code inspection. The moderator ensures that the meeting does not get sidetracked into unimportant discussions (e.g., how to *fix* bugs).

During the meeting the programmer demonstrates the source code of the program, statement by statement, and explains the purpose of the code. The code is examined with a checklist of common errors in mind, some of which are simple errors such as confusing = and ==, while others are of a more complex nature such as whether a conditional test is correctly phrased for the given problem. The choice of an appropriate checklist is discussed in the next section.

The meeting typically lasts one or two hours, and does not rush through masses of code, but rather takes time to understand all code. Therefore, large programs may require a number of such meetings, and it is the moderator's responsibility to organize them.

A walkthrough differs slightly from a code inspection. Rather than examine each line of code, the aim of a walkthrough is to follow program execution from a number of test cases. There is no actual use of the program in execution; instead execution is performed "manually" by the team members. Any important values of variables should be recorded on paper or on a whiteboard. (Although all of the literature on this technique examined by the author uses the "manual" method, there seems no reason why the step-by-step mode of a symbolic debugger could not be used to guide such testing sessions. Perhaps some innovative organization will try out this method of testing.)

During the code inspection or walkthrough, all errors found by the process are recorded by the moderator. This list of errors is later supplied to the programmer for correction, and the moderator keeps a list so as to ensure at a later meeting that such errors have been corrected. It may be necessary to reinspect a piece of code to ensure that errors have been fixed correctly.

A few common mistakes are made in implementing this process of team testing via code inspections and walkthroughs. The first is the natural tendency of members to attempt to fix errors when they are found. Discussions aimed at fixing the errors should be discouraged by the moderator (unless there seems to be some inconsistency that may indicate a major design error); a code inspection should focus on error identification and leave the solution process to the programmer.

Another means whereby the effectiveness of code inspections and walkthroughs can be subverted is using them as programmer evaluations. If the number of errors is used to judge a programmer, this suppresses the desire to find as many errors as possible. These meetings should be seen as a way to improve the programmer's program, not as a means of judging the programmer.

In summary, these methods of team testing offer a practical management method of ensuring reliability on a large scale. They are not a panacea, but are more effective in detecting errors than simply having programmers test their own code. In a sense, these methods are often just a structured method of forcing the programmer to test properly — experience has shown that the programmer is the team member who identifies the majority of errors because the close scrutiny of the code makes errors more obvious.

4.3.1 Designing a checklist for code inspections

Every organization using code inspections should maintain a checklist. The checklist should not be viewed as a finalized list; instead it should be continually modified and updated by the testing department of an organization. A number of example checklists for C/C++ are available in the written and electronic literature and these provide a good starting point. The software engineering textbook by Frakes, Fox, and Nejmeh [1991] presents a checklist for C, and Brian Marick has one available via FTP. A C++ checklist has also been prepared by John Baldwin and is freely available.

BALDWIN, John T., "An Abbreviated C++ Code Inspection Checklist," Testing Foundations, 1992 (available via FTP to cs.uiuc.edu in directory pub/testing as filename baldwin-inspect.ps).

FRAKES, William B., FOX, Christopher J., and NEJMEH, Brian A., *Software Engineering in the UNIX/C Environment*, Prentice Hall, 1991, Appendix E, pp. 244–248.

MARICK, Brian, "A Question Catalog for Code Inspections," Testing Foundations, 1992 (available via FTP to cs.uiuc.edu in directory pub/testing as filenames inspect.n and inspect.ps).

4.3.2 Static checkers and code inspections

An important point to consider is the extent to which items on the checklist can be verified automatically by a source code checker such as lint or even just the compiler with all warnings enabled. It has already been mentioned that the output from such checkers can be considered part of the code inspection process. If a checker is used in this way, there is little point in listing very common errors on the checklist. Hence, if some form of checker is used, a number of common errors can be removed from the checklist; some likely candidates for removal are:

assignment in conditional expression
type mismatches in printf/scanf arguments
function has return; and return exp;
function does not have return on all paths

In this way, the use of the output from a static checker can reduce the complexity of the code inspection process — a portion of the inspection has been automated! A number of checkers capable of this task are examined in Chapter 11.

4.4 Embedded test drivers

Bottom-up testing refers to a testing procedure that applies at the low levels of a program — that is, it applies at the function level. A very effective testing method is to test each function or group of functions as it is developed. The simplest method of doing so is to embed test drivers into each source file. A test driver consists of a `main` function that is conditionally compiled on the basis of some macro name, say TEST. A simple example is shown below:

```
/*----------------------------------------------------*/
/* Sum the numbers from 1 to n, inclusive             */
/*----------------------------------------------------*/

int sum(int n)
{
    int i, total = 0;

    for (i = 1; i <= n; i++)
        total += i;
    return total;
}

/*----------------------------------------------------*/
/* Embedded test driver code here                     */
/*----------------------------------------------------*/
#ifdef TEST

#include <assert.h>

main()
{
    assert(sum(1)  == 1);
    assert(sum(2)  == 3);
    assert(sum(10) == 55);
    assert(sum(-1) == 0);    /* test bad cases */
    assert(sum(0)  == 0);
}
#endif
```

This example shows an effective method of using `assert` macro calls to test the function. Whenever the function is to be tested, the single file is compiled separately from the rest of the project and then executed. The macro symbol TEST must be defined at compilation such as:

```
cc -DTEST sum.c
```

The use of `assert` macros or other self-testing code is particularly good in combination with test drivers because it allows *reproducible* testing. There is no need for the programmer to supply input to the program, and therefore no part of the testing process is stored in the programmer's head.

Depending upon your preference, it may be desirable to make a test driver print a message such as "No errors found" when it has completed all its tests with no detected errors. Such an output will also be useful when automating the process of bottom-up testing, simply because redirecting the output of the test to a file won't result in an (uninformative) empty file.

The example of an embedded test driver given above had an important property — the self-testing functions in the source file were self-sufficient. There was no need to call other functions from other files, and this allowed the single file to be compiled in isolation from the rest of the project. In practice, this may be true of low-level C modules or C++ classes, but it is more difficult to apply bottom-up testing to higher-level modules or classes that call other functions or classes. One possible solution is to write function "stubs" for the functions from other files so as to mimic their action without requiring their full inner details (note that the definitions of these stubs must be surrounded by `#ifdef TEST` directives). The alternative is a more general testing regime that compiles more than one file at a time for a self-test, but becomes more difficult to organize.

4.5 Top-down testing: function stubs

The idea of top-down testing is to start by testing the overall performance of the system and then gradually modify it so that it performs its more intricate low-level tasks. In practice, this means that the top-level modules are coded in full to get the correct flow of control, but lower-level modules are not fully functional — they are simulated by "function stubs." A function stub is intended to mimic the action required of the function without actually doing all the work (i.e., it is a small amount of code that will later be replaced by the fully coded function). When writing function stubs the aim is to simulate the task without actually coding it all up. Unfortunately, it is far easier to explain what a stub should do than to write one in practice. The problem lies in how closely it must mimic the required tasks. For example, a stub could return a dummy value indicating success without really doing anything else. This will work satisfactorily for some functions, but in other cases it might mean that an error in using this function is not identified because it always reports success.

Top-down testing has the major advantage that a working prototype of the system is developed early, rather than just writing individual modules in isolation. Seeing the project already off the ground is a great morale booster for the software team. There is also the advantage that any major errors in the overall design are identified early in the development. However, there are disadvantages to this method in that the writing of stubs for functions is time-consuming and far from trivial. There is also the difficulty in reproducing top-down tests; this contrasts with bottom-up testing, where the low-level tests can often be easily reproduced (e.g., using embedded test drivers).

In practice, it is probably best to employ a mixture of top-down and bottom-up testing procedures. Top-down testing with function stubs produces a working program early in development, and as the stubs are "fleshed out" they can be tested individually using bottom-up techniques.

4.6 Regression testing

The traditional approach to testing has been for the programmer to run his or her program interactively, supplying any required input. This has been and still is an effective technique on a small scale, but it has some major drawbacks when used on larger projects. That isn't to say that this simple form of testing should be avoided, but that it should be complemented by other, more robust testing techniques.

The main drawback to interactive testing is that it is not *reproducible*. The programmer has to remember what input was supplied to the program to provide that test case. Over the development period the programmer is likely to use a large number of test cases, which are later forgotten. It is far better to record test cases so that they can be later applied by the programmer and also by people other than the programmer — that is, so that the tests are reproducible. There are a number of methods of using reproducible testing. For example, input and output can be redirected from/to files (i.e., store the test cases in files), and embedded test drivers are a reproducible testing method (where the test cases are stored in the code).

Any form of reproducible test method can be used to perform *regression testing*. Regression testing is a test method that is commonly used as part of program maintenance, where tests are performed again to ensure that changing the program has not introduced a new bug (i.e., to check that all the old tests still succeed). Regression testing need not only be performed during maintenance, but should be performed throughout program development. However, test cases and their output produced by the programmer responsible for the software should be viewed with some suspicion, because of the natural tendency to miss "obvious" errors. Therefore, the output results produced by test cases should be scrutinized to ensure that the correct output is produced (i.e., don't simply store these output files for a later regression test without viewing them first).

The simplest method of regression testing is to document all test cases, stating the input sequence and the expected results. This idea is the formal "test plan" document. Testing specialists can manually reconstruct the test cases and inspect the result for correctness. However, any manual process is likely to be error-prone and it is far more effective to make use of the computer to automate the regression testing process.

There are two basic methods of automated testing — use a commercial product or build your own testing tools. The remainder of this chapter examines methods you might use to build your own tools for regression testing, and a few automated testing tools are discussed in Chapter 11.

4.7 Regression testing via I/O redirection

The simplest method of storing a test case for later reuse is to use input redirection from a file. Instead of being typed at the command-line, the commands are stored in a file and the program is executed with its input redirected from that file, and its output redirected to another file. Under both UNIX and DOS the execution manner would look similar to the following command:

```
program < test_file > output_file
```

When performing regression testing there should be an earlier version of the output file from a previous testing procedure. The new output file should be compared with the old version to detect any differences. Under UNIX the diff utility can be used to great effect; the command has the form:

```
diff output_file old_output_file
```

The diff command will produce no output if the files are the same, but if they differ it will produce output in a special form indicating where the differences arise. The following script file for Bourne shell runs a program with a number of test cases:

```
#!/bin/sh
#
#   Shell script for regression testing
#      using I/O redirection
#

FILES="test1 test2 test3"       # Test cases
TESTDIR="testdir"        # Directory containing test cases
PROG="a.out"             # Program name
OPT=""                   # Program options
for f in $FILES
do
                    # Execute the program with I/O redirection
        $PROG $OPT   < $TESTDIR/$f   >temp.out
        if test -r "$TESTDIR/$f.out"
        then
                                # Does exist; test if same
                diff temp.out $TESTDIR/$f.out
                if test "$?" = 0
                then
                        echo $f regression test successful
                else
                        echo "*****" $f FAILED REGRESSION TESTING "*****"
                fi
        else                                    # Doesn't exist
                cp temp.out $TESTDIR/$f.out    # Copy it there
        fi
done
rm temp.out        # remove temporary file
```

MS-DOS supports the comp utility that is useful in writing batch files for regression testing. In other environments it may be necessary to write one's own file comparison tool.

The use of I/O redirection is limited to programs that use only standard I/O methods. Any program that uses other forms of input is not suitable for this method of testing using input redirection. Such input methods include mouse movement or button presses, joystick input, file input, or even nonblocking terminal input (i.e., if the program "knows" about its terminal, such as by using ioctl under UNIX or polling the keyboard using kbhit in Turbo C++). Furthermore, I/O redirection can only save screen output using the standard I/O library; any form of graphical output, file output, communications, or hardcopy output cannot be saved with output redirection. Therefore, the method of I/O redirection is limited to a small set of programs that use input from stdin and output to stdout or stderr (either via C's <stdio.h> or C++'s <iostream.h>). This method is particularly useful under UNIX, where most programs satisfy these criteria, but is almost useless on personal computers where most programs will use graphical displays and nonblocking input.

4.8 Regression testing of file-based programs

It is fairly simple to extend the idea of I/O redirection to a program that uses file input or output. For example, a client management system will have one or more data files containing important information. Therefore, when performing a regression test it is important to have copies of the data files in addition to the input commands (which can be supplied using input redirection). Consequently, each different test case for regression testing on such a program would be a different directory containing a number of files:

- redirected screen input
- redirected screen output
- data files before execution
- data files after execution

The script file to test the program would perform a number of steps for each regression test instance:

- Copy the old data files to the directory containing the executable.
- Execute the program with input and output redirected.
- Compare the new output file with that in the test directory.
- Compare the new data files with those in the test directory.

4.9 Regression testing of interactive programs

As mentioned earlier, the method of regression testing using I/O redirection is not effective when programs use mouse input or nonblocking keyboard input, or use graphical output. So how can you test an interactive menu-based program? Probably the best method is to use a commercial testing tool, as many now have the facility to "capture" and "playback" keyboard or mouse input and graphical output. In fact, an X windows testing tool typically relies on the capture of *events*. A few automated testing tools are briefly examined in Chapter 11.

4.10 Regression testing with embedded test drivers

A good method of regression testing is to make use of test drivers embedded in each file (see Section 4.4). Each source file in turn is compiled and executed with the macro name, say TEST, defined with a compiler option (e.g., -D under UNIX). If the test drivers simply use assert or some other self-testing method to detect failures, it is merely a matter of compiling and executing the program and watching for abnormal termination. If care is taken to ensure that the program always returns a meaningful termination code via exit, the termination status of the program can be examined in a shell script or batch file. The following shell script for Bourne shell (i.e., sh) tests a number of files using embedded test drivers:

```
#!/bin/sh
#
#   Shell script for regression testing
#     of embedded test drivers.
#

FILES="file1.c file2.c file3.c"      # Source files which
                                     # contain drivers
CC="cc"                   # Compiler name
CCOPT="-DTEST"            # Compiler options; set macro name
for f in $FILES
do
        $CC $CCOPT  $f          # Compile the file alone
        if test "$?" = 0
        then
                echo $f compiled successfully
        else
                echo "*****" $f FAILED TO COMPILE "*****"
                continue
        fi

        a.out  2>1 >/dev/null         # Execute the test driver
        if test "$?" = 0
        then
                echo $f executed test successfully
        else
                echo "*****" $f FAILED REGRESSION TESTING "*****"
        fi
done
```

The above method is applicable only to self-testing driver code. If the test drivers create output or require input it is necessary to use a technique similar to that for I/O redirection (see Section 4.7), whereby the results from each test driver are stored, and compared with earlier executions.

4.11 Further reading

Glenford Myers has written a high-quality general text on the issue of software testing, which applies to all programming languages. There are not many books discussing testing with C or C++ in great detail. One book that does so is *Software Engineering in the UNIX/C Environment* by Frakes et al. The use of code inspections and walkthroughs is examined, and a checklist for C is given in an appendix. The implementation of regression testing under UNIX is also examined, including how to use shell scripts for this purpose. A number of other books briefly mention different aspects of testing in C. For example, the use of the preprocessor for embedded test drivers is discussed in the book by Anderson and Anderson.

ANDERSON, Paul, and ANDERSON, Gail, *Advanced C: Tips and Techniques*, Hayden Books, 1988.

FRAKES, William B., FOX, Christopher J., and NEJMEH, Brian A., *Software Engineering in the UNIX/C Environment*, Prentice Hall, 1991.

MYERS, Glenford J., *The Art of Software Testing*, John Wiley and Sons, 1979.

Chapter 5

Software quality assurance

Any discussion of program reliability will inevitably border on a discussion of "quality" in its more general sense — the overall quality of products and services rendered by an organization. There is a massive amount of business literature about quality, and similar issues have begun to appear in discussions of software quality. The most predominant modern methodology seems to be Quality Assurance (QA) and this chapter examines some of the QA ideas in application to software.

Before we begin, however, a little caveat: I am by no means an expert on QA and have relied heavily on advice from others and available written material. If you are intending to follow the ISO accreditation path for your organization, please seek the advice of a qualified consultant.

5.1 What is quality assurance?

Quality Assurance is a general term for any policy aimed at improving quality. However, a particular QA methodology now has the official backing of standards of the International Organization for Standardization (ISO), which we will now discuss.

ISO-standardized QA offers a generic methodology for improving overall product and service quality within any organization. The most fundamental idea of ISO's QA is the requirement to standardize and explicitly document all procedures used by employees in the organization. Typically, all these documented procedures are placed in a Quality Manual and/or Procedures Manuals, which are very important documents in the QA methodology. Employees are required to follow the documented procedures when performing a given task. The fundamental idea can be summed up as "document what you do, and do as you've documented." Since it's fairly obvious that accurately documenting procedures and following them correctly should improve quality, this part of QA can be described as "formalized common sense."

The highest level of QA implementation in an organization is official "accreditation" or "certification" with ISO-9000. This indicates that an external assessor has visited the firm and certified that all the appropriate requirements of the ISO-9000 standard have been met. Note that it is the firm that is certified, not a particular product.

An important part of QA is that the QA process is itself well-documented. There are a large number of official QA standards available, as shown in Table 5.1. Among other things, these standards specify which general procedures should be documented.

Table 5.1 Official ISO standards for QA

Standard	Purpose
ISO-9000	Guidelines and selection of standards
ISO-9001	QA in design, development, production, installation & maintenance
ISO-9002	Subset — QA in production and installation
ISO-9003	Final inspection and test
ISO-9004	Quality management and quality system elements
ISO-9000-3	Guidelines for application of ISO-9001 to the software industry

The ISO-9001, ISO-9002, and ISO-9003 standards are all general QA standards, not specifically aimed at the software industry. ISO-9000-3 is the SQA standard that relates QA to software development. Note that these standards are typically available under different naming schemes in different countries, as shown in Table 5.2.

Table 5.2 Naming of national standards

ISO standard	Australia	UK
ISO-9000	AS3900	BS5750
ISO-9001	AS3901	BS5750 Part 1
ISO-9002	AS3902	BS5750 Part 2
ISO-9003	AS3903	BS5750 Part 3
ISO-9004	AS3904	BS5750 Part 4
ISO-9000-3	AS3900.3	BS5750 Part 13

In the United Kingdom there is an interesting initiative called the the TickIT project, which aims to apply the ISO-9001 standard to the software industry. TickIT has the following contact details: The DISC TickIT Office, 2 Park Street, London W1A 2BS, UK; telephone: +44-71-602-8536; fax: +44-71-602-8912.

5.2 Criticisms of QA

Not everyone agrees on whether QA is a good idea, and this even applies to ISO-standardized QA. The most common objections to QA can be summarized as:

1. QA is not a panacea for quality software.
2. QA is not the only path to quality software, and QA is not the easiest.
3. QA is too general to be of any practical use.

1. Certainly, QA is no panacea, and ISO QA accreditation should not be taken as a guarantee that a firm offers a high-quality product. However, what QA does guarantee is that the quality issue is being given attention and overall quality should be high.

2. Naturally, QA is not the only path to quality. Formalized QA is a relatively recent managerial idea, and there are quality products from firms without a QA policy. However, it is likely that these firms used ideas similar to QA, although they may not have explicitly documented the fact. QA is a rigorous and formalized method of improving product quality.

3. QA is indeed quite a general idea. The fundamental idea of QA is to provide a framework for quality standardization, which the particular organization modifies to suit its needs. Thus QA is not even specific to software companies, and we must look to the SQA philosophy for industry-specific material. Unfortunately, even the existing SQA material is quite general (because it must cover a variety of machines, programming languages, etc.), and a lack of specific information may be a valid criticism of SQA at present. Indeed, this is the only major criticism of SQA that I tend to agree with and hence later sections of this chapter attempt to rectify the problem by providing my own particular opinions on what low-level procedures should be standardized in the quality manuals when developing products using C or C++.

5.3 Putting the S into SQA

QA is a set of general techniques for improving quality within an organization, and is applicable to all kinds of industries. The software industry is one area of application of QA ideas, and it is certainly an area that needs it — the software industry has one of the biggest quality problems. This application of QA to the software industry has become known as SQA, and although the SQA area is in its infancy, there is already some specific material on SQA (see the further reading section).

There is now even an official QA standard specific to the software industry called ISO-9000-3. In fact, there are many more software quality assurance standards available but they do not come from the ISO body (i.e., they are probably good standards but are not relevant to ISO QA accreditation). A variety of software standards from IEEE, DoD, NATO, and many others are discussed by Gordon Schulmeyer, who traces the history of SQA standardization:

> SCHULMEYER, G. Gordon, "Standardization of Software Quality Assurance," in Handbook of Software Quality Assurance (2nd edn), Schulmeyer & McManus, eds, 1992, pp. 92–117.

Unfortunately, there are no official ISO QA standards for the specific use of the C and C++ programming languages. The standards tend to address general areas such as "testing" but not low-level aspects of how programs should be structured. Because of this lack of C/C++ material, many of the later sections of this chapter represent my own opinions as to what procedures should be standardized at the lower levels of C/C++ software development. However, note that these sections are not necessarily requirements of ISO QA, although hopefully they are complementary. These sections represent issues I would investigate if I were managing a large software organization (which I don't), and I encourage organizations to combine their high-level quality programs (be it using official ISO standards or otherwise) with this sort of analysis of low-level issues.

5.4 Software Engineering Process Group (SEPG)

The idea of a SEPG comes from the literature on software quality assurance, but it is not a requirement of ISO QA. It should be complementary to ISO QA, as it has the same fundamental aim, but may not interest those who are merely seeking official ISO accreditation.

The aim of having a SEPG is to make a particular group responsible for overseeing the quality issues in the software production process in a large organization. The overall responsibility of the SEPG is to determine whether existing methodologies are effective, to research the alternatives if they are not, and to coordinate the use of these methodologies in other departments within the organization. Thus some of the specific responsibilities of the SEPG become:

- Evaluate programming aids — software tools, code libraries.
- Evaluate coding style standards.
- Evaluate procedure documents — testing, debugging, maintenance, reuse, etc.
- Document the various tools, procedures and methodologies.
- Train employees to use the various tools, procedures, and methodologies.

Thus the SEPG is similar to the idea of a "code librarian" that has been advocated by some writers. The idea of a single individual as a code librarian may be more appropriate than a SEPG for smaller organizations. The code librarian should maintain a library of existing code and make it easily available for use by programmers. This includes issues such as providing adequate documentation and training programmers to use the new coding tools/libraries.

Some of the first code to be collected by the SEPG or the code librarian should be libraries related to debugging, testing, and reliability. The following types of libraries could be specially designed for the project or organization, or alternatively, commercial products could be purchased:

- `new`/`delete` debugging libraries
- `malloc` debugging libraries
- exception handling macro libraries
- error reporting libraries
- `assert` macro libraries
- debugging output libraries
- self-testing code macro libraries

For further discussion of the SEPG idea, refer to the following article on software quality by Baker and Fisher:

BAKER, Emanuel R., and FISHER, Matthew, J., "Software Quality Program Organization," in *Handbook of Software Quality Assurance* (2nd edn), Schulmeyer & McManus, eds, 1992, pp. 49–74, esp. pp. 63, 67, 69–72.

5.5 Project-wide procedures for reliability

The manner of use of debugging and testing features of the programming language and environment should be standardized within a project and probably even within an organization. It is important to establish procedures aimed at enhancing reliability on a large scale. The programming-level procedures that should be examined include:

- coding procedures
  - — use of debugging/testing features within code
  - — coding style
- debugging procedures
- testing procedures
- Maintenance procedures

Naturally, for such standards to be of practical use they must be:

- documented explicitly
- available easily
- encouraged/enforced — training, monitoring, etc.

These three requirements are explicitly met by the ISO SQA methodology: procedures are documented in the Quality Manual, which is available to everyone, and the various training and accreditation requirements of QA satisfy the last requirement. However, note that the following suggestions of low-level areas to standardize are not explicit requirements of ISO accreditation.

5.6 Project-wide coding procedures

Programmers should be educated about what the C/C++ languages offer as debugging and testing aids, and also about the particular usage style recommended within the project. The idea of coding procedures usually evokes images of coding details such as brace indentation and naming conventions. Although important, these are not the only coding issues worthy of standardization. Hence the low-level issues of coding style are deferred to Section 5.7, which covers coding style standards, and this section examines the coding issues related to debugging and testing that tend not to be covered in existing coding style standards.

5.6.1 Exception handling method

An obvious starting point for ensuring program reliability is defining the method of handling unexpected and exceptional conditions, arising either from unexpected or incorrect human input, or from internal program failures. The alternatives are listed below, ranging from the use of the new ANSI C++ exception facilities to the lazy termination approach:

- exception handling method
    — ANSI C++ exception handling syntax using `try`/`catch`/`throw`
    — macro libraries using C features
    — macro libraries using pre-ANSI C++ features
    — explicit ad hoc use of `longjmp` (not recommended)
    — termination via `abort` or `exit`

The choice of method will depend on various issues such as (a) what language is being used (i.e., C, pre-ANSI C++, or ANSI C++) and (b) whether existing code is already using a particular method (in which case you may be stuck with it). Regardless of the method chosen, the actual actions to be undertaken during handling of exceptions must be designed and coded appropriately, but this is a separate issue. As discussed in Section 6.3, a hierarchical design of the exception handling mechanisms is preferred for all nontrivial methods.

In addition to the overall design of the exception handling scheme, there are a variety of particular cases that should be examined in detail. Some of the most common failures include memory allocation failure, library failures (especially file errors), and signals, and the following is a brief list of issues requiring consideration:

- memory allocation failure handling in C
    — test all `malloc` call return values?
    — or redefine `malloc` to a different function?
    — use a `malloc` debugging library instead? (similar to redefining `malloc`)

- memory allocation failure handling in C++
    — test all `new` operator return values?
    — redefine the default handler using `set_new_handler`?
    — use a single new handler for all allocation failures?
    — or use a hierarchical nested method of installing multiple new handlers?

- standard library error handling
    — which library function error returns to check?
    — file error handling treated differently?
    — `errno` handling and `<errno.h>`

- signal handling
    — ignore which signals?
    — install graceful-termination handlers for fatal signals such as `SIGSEGV`?
    — install log file output handlers for nonfatal signals such as `SIGINT`?

5.6.2 Error reporting of detected internal failures

Error reporting is a special case of exception handling design, although there is naturally some overlap in the decisions to be made. If the chosen method of handling various internal failures is to report the failure to the user, then one of various reporting methods must be chosen.

- error reporting of detected internal failures
    — ERRPRINTF C-style or ERROUT C++ stream style?
    — screen output and/or use a log file?
    — what method in development phase?
    — what method in production code?
    — use more than one form of error (e.g., recoverable versus fatal)?
    — report recoverable failures to the user?
    — use calls to a tool's API functions? (e.g., garbage memory report)
    — compile-time configurable? #if/#ifdef? header file or compiler option?
    — run-time configurable?

There are a variety of specific decisions to make, such as whether to use C or C++ style, and whether to use different methods in development versus production versions of the product. For example, during development it may be desirable to invoke a run-time debugger or the API function of a debugging tool, whereas this facility may be removed from the production version (although there is a case to be made for leaving it in!).

An important issue is whether all failures have the same status, or whether they are classified in groups. The simplest classification is a binary grouping into recoverable and nonrecoverable, which would be treated differently (e.g., reporting only nonrecoverable errors to the user in the production version). More complicated groupings are possible, such as the "levels and areas" idea of debugging output (see Section 2.10), in which case it becomes important to consider whether the behavior for the various classes of failures can be configured at compile-time, run-time, or both.

5.6.3 Debugging output statements

A large number of methods of defining debugging output macros and libraries were presented in Chapter 2. The use of output statements should be standardized rather than allowing each programmer to define his or her own method.

- debugging output statements
    — use debugging output statements at all?
    — printf-like C style?
    — or C++ ERROUT stream style?
    — what is the name of the macro(s)?
    — single level, or multiple "levels" or "areas" of debug output?
    — log file or stderr? both? configurable?
    — compile-time configurable? #if/#ifdef? header file or compiler option?

— run-time configurable?
    (a) text file of flags
    (b) command-line arguments
    (c) environment variables
— report use of text file or environment variable (reminder for later removal)
— leave statements in production code? (run-time configurable only)
— symbolic debugger configuration support (e.g., API functions)

The first decision is naturally whether to use debugging output statements at all, since their use can involve considerable effort. If the answer is affirmative, the next choice is whether to use a C or C++ style of output (i.e., `printf`-like versus `cout`-like); it may be possible to use both styles (e.g., if both forms merely go to `stderr` anyway), although there are difficulties involved in mixing `<stdio.h>` and `<iostream.h>` libraries in areas such as log files.

The next decision is what facilities to use in the output library. The simplest is a single form of statement, with a binary on/off flag, but this is not very useful for nontrivial projects. A more useful scenario is the use of multiple "levels" or "areas" of debugging output, which can be configured either at compile-time or run-time. Compile-time configuration involves using either different macro names for `#if` or `#ifdef`, or a single "debug level" macro. Run-time configuration requires the use of command-line arguments, environment variables, or text files, or some combination of the three. Compile-time and run-time configuration can be combined, such as to allow run-time configuration during development, but total removal from the production version. This may be desirable because run-time configuration is less time-efficient than compile-time configuration because each macro must test whether it is enabled (and less space-efficient because each debugging output statement takes up code space), whereas compile-time configuration allows complete removal of the statements. For further details on compile-time versus run-time configurability refer to Section 2.11.

There are a few other practical issues related to run-time configurability. Consideration must be given to whether to leave debugging output in the production version of the program. With compile-time configurability this isn't an option because the output would then always appear, but with run-time configurability the output statements could be left in the program to allow better on-site debugging and/or user bug reports. For example, requiring an environment variable to be set to enable them should prevent the user accidentally tripping over these features. If an environment variable or file of flags is used for run-time configuration, it is advisable to visibly report this to the user, simply to remind testers to remove the features (they won't be in the user's environment).

Finally, when using run-time configuration, the use of a symbolic debugger can be supported in two ways: (1) by declaring all variables involved in setting debugging levels as `volatile`, so as to indicate that they may be changed externally to the program; or (2) by defining special API functions, such as `debug_on()` and `debug_off()` to turn debugging output on and off, which can be explicitly called within the symbolic debugger.

5.6.4 Self-testing code usage

The insertion of code to test important conditions can be an important technique for making a program easy to debug. Hence, a standard method of introducing such code should be agreed within a project.

- self-testing code usage
    - use self-testing code at all?
    - method of handling failure?
    - use only a few macros such as a `bounds_check` macro?
    - or use facilities for entire code blocks? (e.g., `SELFTEST{ ... }` style)
    - what is the name of the macro(s)?
    - single level, or multiple "levels" or "areas" of self-testing code?
    - leave in production code?
    - run-time configurable?
        (a) text file of flags
        (b) command-line arguments
        (c) environment variables
    - report text file or environment variable (reminder for later removal)
    - symbolic debugger configuration support (e.g., API functions)

Perhaps the most important issue is what should happen when self-testing code identifies an internal failure. Naturally, this will depend on the severity of the failure, and should be tied in with the choices made with regard to exception handling and error reporting, as discussed above.

An important issue is the classification and configurability of the self-testing code statements. The simplest idea is one `SELFTEST` macro that is either on or off using a single `#if` macro name. However, more advanced ideas of "levels" or "areas" of `SELFTEST` macros are also worth considering. Different levels of self-testing statements allow flexible choice as to what tests are enabled, which may be important if some self-tests are too slow to use regularly. The issues are exactly the same as those for a debugging output library and the reader is referred to Chapter 2 for discussion of various configuration methods (especially Section 2.11 for run-time configurability).

The issue of whether to leave self-testing code in production code differs slightly from debugging output, because self-testing code can be left in even if only compile-time configuration is present. However, leaving run-time configurable self-testing code in a production version can be useful, so as to allow better on-site debugging and/or bug reports, by turning on the more expensive tests. Naturally, run-time configuration will lose some efficiency in the production version because each self-testing macro will involve an integral test to determine whether it is enabled; with compile-time configurability the self-testing macros can have no time or space cost in the production version.

5.6.5 assert macro usage

The `assert` macro is a special form of self-testing code that is supported by the C and C++ languages in the header file `<assert.h>`. Thus although the issues are similar to those for self-testing code, there are a few specialized issues to address.

- `assert` macro usage
    - use the `assert` macro at all?
    - leave in production code?
    - or compile out using the NDEBUG macro?
    - if left in, use default failure, or redefine for graceful failure?
    - if redefined, use more than one type of assertion?
    - run-time configurable?
        - (a) text file of flags
        - (b) command-line arguments
        - (c) environment variables
    - report use of text file or environment variable (reminder to remove them later!)
    - symbolic debugger configuration (e.g., `volatile` variables or API functions)

The general issues are the same as for self-testing code, such as whether to use assertions at all, and whether to leave assertions in production code. However, because of `<assert.h>` there are a few "lazy" options regarding the method of assertion removal and the choice of failure outcome. If the system `<assert.h>` header is used, the macro name NDEBUG can be defined to remove assertions (usually as a compiler option such as "`cc -DNDEBUG`" under UNIX), and there is also the default failure method of calling `abort`. Thus the decision must be made whether to use the existing facilities in `<assert.h>` or to redefine `assert` to have improved semantics, in which case the issues are exactly those of designing any self-testing macro.

5.6.6 Debugging tools/libraries in-code support

Many tools, particularly run-time debugging tools, require some form of support within the C/C++ source code. A typical example is calls to API functions supported by a tool. All tools will have their own issues to resolve, and we will only briefly discuss `lint` and symbolic debuggers:

- `lint` in-code support
    - `#ifdef lint` to hide intentionally weird constructs
    - e.g., defining a ZERO macro for the "`do...while(ZERO)`" trick
    - `/*NOTREACHED*/` and other `lint` comment directives
- symbolic debugger in-code support
    - variables modifiable within debugger should be `volatile`
    - callable API functions (e.g., memory library garbage report function)
    - e.g., configurability of debug output using variables and/or API functions

5.7 Coding style standards for C and C++

Quite a lot has been written about coding style for both C and C++. In fact, more has been written about coding style than about standardizing the other programming activities such as testing and debugging methods. Most of the literature focuses on relatively low-level reliability, including issues such as code layout and naming. While these are important things to standardize, coding style isn't the only programming activity that should be standardized. Nevertheless, it is an important area worthy of consideration when improving program development quality.

My favorite discussion of C coding style is the excellent book by David Straker. In addition to discussing the various coding style issues in great detail, his book discusses the pragmatic aspects of implementing a standard within an organization. I recommend it to anyone involved in the development of an organization's coding standard.

There are many references to be examined when creating a coding style standard for your organization and a short list is as follows:

HENRICSON, Mats, and NYQUIST, Erik, "Programming in C++: Rules and Recommendations," Technical Report, Ellemtel Telecommunication Systems Laboratories, Sweden, 1990–1992 (see Bibliography for acquisition details).

STRAKER, David, *C Style: Standards and Guidelines*, Prentice Hall, 1992.

5.8 Project-wide debugging procedures

Debugging is an activity performed by the programmer that can be addressed by a project-wide standard. In this section, the term "debugging" is considered to be the process of attempting to find the *cause* of a program failure that has been discovered by "testing." During debugging, programmers are usually left to their own devices, and tend to rely on their favorite method (e.g., the symbolic debugger) when a more methodical solution would often have found the error more quickly. As discussed in Section 2.2, some of the steps worth considering for inclusion in the standard debugging procedure are as follows:

- Enable compiler run-time traps (e.g., stack overflow).
- Enable compiler warnings (Note: warnings should always be enabled anyway).
- Use a static checker such as `lint`.
- Link in a memory allocation debugging library.
- Link in a run-time debugging tool (e.g., Purify, Sentinel, etc.).
- Enable debugging output trace statements (if present in the code).
- Enable assertions or self-testing code (if present in the code).

Some of these steps will require support during the coding phase. For example, it is advisable to use run-time configuration of assertions, self-testing code, and debugging output so that these can be enabled by the programmer without recompilation. These features should also be configurable within a symbolic debugger, either by providing functions callable from within the debugger (e.g., API functions such as `debug_on` and debug_off), or by using `volatile` global variables that can be modified from within the debugger (e.g., a single integer "debug" variable could be set on and off within the debugger).

Some of these debugging steps should probably be used at all times during development, rather than only being brought to bear upon a particular debugging problem. In fact, all of the following are candidates for permanent inclusion in the basic procedure for executing a program: compiler run-time and compile-time warnings, static checkers, run-time debugging library, run-time debugging tools.

Naturally, this debugging methodology should not be too harshly enforced. A good programmer will often have a fair idea of the cause of the error, and may find it quickly using his or her favorite method. Nevertheless, there are many horror stories of bugs taking days to find when a static checker (for example) would have found the problem in 5 minutes. Probably the best approach is to encourage programmers to use better methods, at least in the initial phases of debugging. This will rule out the most common classes of errors and ensure that programmers only use their ingenuity for truly difficult errors. Making programmers aware of the advantages of the various methods, as well as making them easily available (e.g., in project-wide code libraries), will hopefully reduce the average time spent in debugging.

5.9 Project-wide tool usage procedures

The software tools used by the programmer should be examined closely. Issues worth standardizing are what tools are used, how they are used, and when they are used.

- compiler
    — which compiler?
    — what options to use?
        — enable debugging information? (e.g., -g under UNIX)
        — enable compile-time diagnostics?
        — enable run-time diagnostics? (e.g., stack overflow)

- static checker usage
        — which checker? (a) `lint`? (b) `gcc -Wall`? (c) PC-Lint/FlexeLint?
        — what options to use?
        — in-code support (e.g., the "#ifdef lint" construct)

- run-time debugging libraries, tools, etc.
        — which library? more than one? commercial products?
        — leave debugging features in production code?
        — what compile-time/run-time options to use?
        — use default failure, or redefine for graceful failure?
        — in-code support? (e.g., calls to API functions)

- symbolic debugger
        — which debugger?
        — in-code support?

Naturally, there are many more tools than the four categories examined above. All tools should be examined closely, even apparently mundane areas such as which text editor programmers should use.

5.10 Project-wide testing procedures

Testing is perhaps the most obvious candidate for standardization, and most organizations have already formalized guidelines for the test process in the lead-up to a product release. A short list of some of the issues that should be standardized is presented below.

Who does the testing?
   — separate testing teams within the organization?
   — outside testing companies?
code inspections
   — use code inspections at all?
   — what checklist?
   — use of static checker output? `lint`? `gcc -Wall`? Flexe-Lint/PC-Lint?
   — what team members? how many?
   — use hardcopy printouts or code browser for code examination?
   — manual or computer-assisted recording of the process?
coverage analysis
   — which tool?
   — branch coverage?
   — statement coverage?
regression testing method
   — manual or automated?
   — if automated, which tool(s)?
embedded test drivers
   — use embedded test drivers at all?
   — what name to use? (e.g., `#ifdef TEST`)

When formalizing these standards it may be important to have separate testing procedures for different phases of program development. For example, testing for alpha and beta releases may differ from testing for the final release; the update testing procedure after code maintenance may also be worth a separate set of procedures. Naturally, the steps in these various forms of testing will be similar, but the emphasis and extent of testing may be different.

5.11 Extensions

1.   Even if you're not seeking QA accreditation, the idea of documenting procedures
can be beneficial. Develop a complete set of "reliability improvement" documents
for your project or organization, for standardizing the following areas of the
software cycle:

- debugging procedures
- testing procedures
    — code inspection checklist
- coding procedures
    — usage of debug/testing in-code features
    — coding style standard
- tool usage procedures
- maintenance procedures

2.   Are there any other areas in the software cycle that you recognize as in need of
standardization for your organization? How about the following?

- project specification procedures
- efficiency performance improvement procedures
- documentation procedures — development, testing/checking, maintenance
- portability/porting procedures
- reusability procedures — how to reuse software
- first release procedures and upgrade release procedures
- customer support procedures — e.g., user bug report handling procedures

5.12 Further reading

Naturally, there are many good books on quality and QA in particular. More recently,
books and other documents on SQA have appeared. The Internet FAQ list maintained by
Markus Kuhn is an excellent document with useful general information about standards,
such as addresses of standards institutes in all countries. Unfortunately, the FAQ does not
address ISO-9000 in great detail, but the FTP site maintained by Markus Kuhn contains a
large document that does discuss ISO-9000.

ISO 9000 News, "ISO-9000 Quality Standards in 24 Questions," available via FTP to
`ftp.uni-erlangen.de` in the directory `pub/doc/ISO/english` as file
`ISO-9000-summary`.

JURAN, J.M., and GRYNA, Frank M., *Quality Planning and Analysis* (3rd edn),
McGraw-Hill, 1993 (especially Chapter 23).

KUHN, Markus, "Standards FAQ," Frequently Asked Question (FAQ) list for the
Internet news group `comp.std.misc` (acquisition details in Bibliography).

SCHULMEYER, G. Gordon, and McMANUS, James, I. (eds), *Handbook of Software
Quality Assurance* (2nd edn), Van Nostrand Reinhold, 1992.

Chapter 6

High-level reliability

The correct method of solving the software problem appears to be a "religious" issue in the sense that everyone has different opinions on what should be done. Apart from discussing the merits of C and C++ as programming languages, this chapter largely ignores the "higher" issues of designing a super-duper programming environment. Until someone designs the DWIW (do what I want) programming language, we are stuck with what we have, and must make the best of it. Hence most of this chapter deals with specific methods aimed at achieving improved reliability at the top level within the usage constraints of C and C++.

An important aspect of writing reliable programs is to write programs that continue to function even when an error or exception has occurred. A program should be able to recover from errors such as failure to write to a file or running out of dynamic memory. The program should cope "as well as possible" with such unexpected conditions. In some situations it can continue, in others it can try again (e.g., ask for another filename), and in some cases the only alternative is a graceful program termination.

6.1 Levels of reliability

When designing a program it is important to consider how reliable it must be. If it's a small program used only by the programmer, then it probably won't matter too much if it crashes occasionally. However, if it is life-critical software, it must always perform correctly, even under exceptional conditions. The issue of reliability can be thought of as a number of levels of program correctness:

1. compiles with no errors
2. compiles with no warnings
3. runs with no run-time failure
4. runs with correct output on expected input
5. runs as correctly as possible on both expected and unexpected input

All programs certainly must compile without error. The issue of compilation warnings is often ignored, but it should be given consideration. A high-quality program will not provoke any compilation warnings, nor even any warnings from `lint` (or another static checker).

The next level is that it must run without a fatal run-time failure. The program should not "hang" or cause a "core dump," or cause any other form of abnormal termination.

Naturally, the next level of reliability is that the program, as well as never terminating abnormally, should produce the correct results on expected input. This means that it will perform correctly if given correct input within expected ranges.

The highest level is a program that runs "as correctly as possible" on all input, expected and unexpected. It should never terminate abnormally, should always produce the correct results on expected input, and should perform as correctly as it possibly can when the inputs (or the environmental conditions) are exceptional. This type of coding is usually referred to as "exception handling" code.

6.2 Exception handling alternatives

What should a program do when faced with some unexpected condition? The answer obviously depends on the severity of the condition. Some of the many alternatives are:

- Try again.
- Ignore the problem.
- Correct the problem.
- Ask for help with correcting the problem.
- Return an error value.
- Set a global error flag.
- Gracefully terminate the program (e.g., `exit`).
- Ungracefully terminate the program (e.g., `abort`).
- Jump to a safe place using `longjmp`.
- Jump to a safe place using `goto`.
- Throw an exception object (ANSI C++ only).

Which alternatives can be applied depends on the situation. As an example of the "try again" method, when prompting for input, problems due to bad input can be solved by simply prompting for input again.

The "correction" method is an honorable aim but is quite difficult to achieve in practice. If something goes wrong the chances are that the program won't know enough to fix it, or alternatively, coding enough information to fix the problem will become prohibitive in itself. Nevertheless, correction is possible in some problem domains; an example is the correction of parsing errors by a compiler.

A special case of the correction method is to ask the user for help. An example is prompting the user for an alternative filename when a file fails to open.

An example of ignoring the problem is the method of handling underflow of many of the `<math.h>` functions — many functions simply return zero (i.e., the closest possible valid result). The method of returning an error value is used by many library functions: `malloc` returns `NULL`, `fopen` returns `NULL`, etc.

The global `errno` variable, used by many of the standard library functions, particularly those in `<math.h>`, is an example of using a global error flag. `errno` is usually used in conjunction with some other method: returning an error value, or ignoring the problem.

A particularly common method of handling some forms of error is to terminate the program with an appropriate error message. For example, when a software tool cannot find the file it is supposed to operate upon, the usual method of solution is to report an error and allow the user to rerun the program with a corrected filename.

The ANSI C++ language allows a special form of exception handling syntax using the keywords `try`, `catch`, and `throw`. This is a huge improvement over many of the above methods, although it should be noted that an exception handler that "catches" the exception will probably have to resort to one of the techniques in the above list. Exception handling in C++ is discussed in Chapter 7.

Another useful technique is to use a nonlocal jump via the `longjmp` library function. Under some circumstances it may be adequate to use `goto` to jump to exception handling code within the current function, but as `goto` is limited to be within a function, the `longjmp` method is the only way to jump between functions.

6.3 Hierarchical organization of exception handling

The manner in which a program will perform exception handling is an important design consideration in C and C++ programs. In general, a good design of an exception handling system is hierarchical, with subsystems handling those exceptions that they can, and propagating exceptions that they cannot handle to the next level. The global exception handling code should be invoked only when lower-level handlers cannot cope.

There are some alternatives to consider when choosing an implementation of exception handling. Some possibilities for hierarchical exception handling are:

- ANSI C++ exception handling syntax
- `longjmp`-based exception macro libraries
- returning an error status

The recent ANSI C++ exception handling syntax is inherently hierarchical in that when an exception is thrown, all handlers above it in the call stack will be tried.

The C/C++ exception handling macro libraries in Chapter 8 are also a good method of implementing a hierarchical scheme; in fact, they lead to an overall design similar to that from ANSI C++ exceptions, although they are a little less elegant.

Perhaps surprisingly, the method of returning an error status, either as a function return value or as an extra function argument, can be used to build a hierarchical scheme. It involves some extra work in that the status must be checked at all levels before operating on the data, but it can be made to work. The overall idea is to try to handle an exception, but if it cannot be handled, to pass it back to the calling function, which must then deal with it. An example of this idea is the traditional manner of dealing with `malloc` failure: pass back a NULL pointer and make the caller deal with it. Thus a NULL pointer will be passed back until an appropriate block of code handles the problem.

6.4 Heterogeneity of C/C++ exception handling

There are so many aspects of C/C++ reliability that exception handling will consist of many special cases. For example, some of the many exceptional conditions that can arise are:

- software exceptions (e.g., `throw` in ANSI C++, `longjmp` in C)
- `assert` or self-test failure (special forms of software exceptions)
- allocation failure: C's `malloc` or C++'s `new`
- `set_terminate` handler calls (ANSI C++: unhandled exception)
- `set_unexpected` handler calls (ANSI C++: unexpected exception)
- signals (e.g., `SIGSEGV` for `NULL` dereference under UNIX)

The simplest issue is the software exception, which is just the method you are using to raise an exception detected by the program itself. For example, you may be using ANSI C++ exceptions or `longjmp`-based macros

As you can see from the above list, special cases are rife in C and C++. The aim for a homogeneous method of exception handling is then to convert all other forms of exceptions to use the chosen method. Let's assume for simplicity that you are using the recent ANSI C++ exception handling syntax.

Some of the simpler exceptions to handle are the self-testing macros and `assert` calls that you use. These should be changed so as to throw an exception, which is not difficult for your own self-testing macros, and only slightly more difficult for the `assert` macro — replace it with your own by using your own `"assert.h"` header file instead of `<assert.h>`.

Allocation failure is another special case of exception that must be detected and converted to a thrown exception. For example, `malloc` failure can be caught using macro wrappers and `new` failure can be intercepted using `set_new_handler`. The macro wrapper method for `malloc` has some limitations (e.g., the need for source code access in third-party libraries) but can be used to call a wrapper function that throws an exception when the real `malloc` function fails. The handling of `new` failure in C++ by `set_new_handler` is simple enough to do: install a handler function that throws an appropriately named exception. Note that any attempt to reclaim unused memory from inside a handler function complicates the exception handling process so greatly that it may be advisable not to bother!

The `set_terminate` and `set_unexpected` handler functions are solved in a similar fashion to `set_new_handler`: each should have installed a function throwing an exception.

Signals represent by far the biggest problem, despite the fact that the `signal` function has the common form of installing a handler function. It is not possible to portably throw an ANSI C++ exception from a signal handler, nor is it possible even to portably `longjmp` out of a signal handler. Thus the problem must be solved in a platform-specific manner, or else make the handler simply perform some rudimentary cleanup and then terminate the program.

The end product of all this effort is hopefully a homogeneous exception handling system, where each particular form of "trouble" has its own name (or for ANSI C++ exceptions, its own *type*), by which it can be handled in an appropriate manner.

6.5 Program verification — correctness proofs

Another commonly discussed issue in software reliability is *program verification*, by which we mean the theoretical method of automatically "proving" that a program satisfies its specification (rather than the less theoretical use of the term in the buzz-phrase "verification and validation"). Program verification seems to be widely viewed as a panacea for reliability problems. However, this is not necessarily so. Although verification will surely be an important technique in the future, it certainly doesn't guarantee bug-free programs. The verification process compares a program with a set of *specifications*, and the fundamental problem is that these specifications may be wrong. No matter what language or syntax is used to define specifications, they must always be written by people, and people will make mistakes. If the specifications are incorrect, the best that verification can achieve is to prove that the program is incorrect (i.e., it correctly does the wrong task). Despite these misgivings, verification will certainly be a useful method of identifying errors in programs, or at least in identifying inconsistencies between a program and its specifications (i.e., verification can find errors, but can never really ensure their absence). Unfortunately, a practical verification tool for C or C++ seems a long way off.

6.6 C/C++ reliability is a sad joke?

One of the most fundamental reliability issues is whether reliability is achievable in C or C++. My personal feeling is that C/C++ are definitely not the best languages for reliability. Let's face it: C came to prominence because of its low level and its efficiency, not because of its safety. The length of Part II in this book is testimony to the huge number of ways that programmers can err in C/C++, and I didn't even get onto errors in logic! C is not an easy language to learn and has many counterintuitive features to trap the programmer. C++ is hardly better in this respect, because it has even more features that don't always mesh well together. The main quality of good programming language design that C and C++ both lack is "orthogonality," that refers to different features interacting in the same manner with other features. There are far too many special cases to learn and I must admit that I find the common claim that C is a "small" language to be quite amusing (although in response to this, Peter Jones, my reviewer, invites me to "*Try COBOL!*").

However, having said all that, I believe a reasonable level of reliability is achievable using either C or C++. Would anyone use C or C++ if reliability weren't achievable? Well, maybe you'd better not answer that, but I still claim that if C/C++ are used well, they can produce good-quality software. All programming languages suffer from errors in logic and I don't see that C/C++ will cause more such errors. Arguably, C and C++ have more potential nonlogic errors than many programming languages (see Part II if you're not convinced), but the majority will show up as failures during testing in the same way as logic errors should. For the most persistent errors, such as errant pointers, there are now many techniques and tools for preventing and/or detecting these problems.

Overall, the choice of programming language is only a small part of the process of producing high-quality software. There are many other factors, such as the testing procedures, the training of programmers, and the software tools used during production.

6.7 Further reading

Bjarne Stroustrup presents a good discussion of these high-level reliability issues in a C++ context as part of his general C++ textbook, *The C++ Programming Language*. Although often focusing on usage of the ANSI C++ exception facilities, much material can be applied in a general sense to C++ reliability.

One good general reference textbook on reliability is that by Glenford Myers. Despite being almost 20 years old, the material is still mostly relevant to modern-day programming.

MYERS, Glenford J., *Software Reliability: Principles and Practices*, John Wiley and Sons, 1976.

STROUSTRUP, Bjarne, *The C++ Programming Language*, Addison-Wesley, 1991.

Chapter 7

ANSI C++ exception handling

A new facility for exception handling has recently been added to the C++ language by its designer, Bjarne Stroustrup. This exception handling syntax has been accepted by the ANSI C++ committee and will be supported by the ANSI C++ standard when it finally appears. However, at the time of writing (1993) there are still very few C++ compilers that actually implement the new exception handling features, although most vendors are rushing to add this feature to future releases. Therefore, the syntax represents a very useful technique for future C++ code but is not highly portable across platforms at the current time. Nevertheless, an overview of the exception handling features is now presented.

The new exception handling facilities are part of the language proper, rather than merely being a new function or class library. This explains the delay in vendor support, because the addition of exceptions requires changes to the compiler's parsing and code generation phases.

Exceptions do require some run-time support (i.e., run-time instructions) which may reduce efficiency. However, the facilities are designed so that a good implementation of the facilities should not reduce efficiency if no exceptions occur.

7.1 Exception handling syntax: try, catch, and throw

The exception handling features introduce three new keywords to the language: `try`, `catch` and `throw`. The basic syntax of the exception handling is:

```
try {
    // code having its exceptions handled
}
catch(exception1) {
    // handle exception 1
}
catch(exception2) {
    // handle exception 2
}
catch(...) {
    // handle all other exceptions
}
```

The `try` block specifies the main block of code, and the one or more `catch` blocks specify the code to be executed upon exception. That is, the `try` block is the usual code, and `catch` clauses represent *handlers* for exceptions.

The argument to `catch` specifies which exceptions are to be handled by a `catch` block. Note that `exception1` and `exception2` as above are type names, not variable names; this will be further explained below.

The `...` (ellipsis) token can be used to specify that the handler applies to "all other exceptions." This clause is optional and when it is absent an uncaught exception will cause handlers to be sought in outer scopes. Naturally, a `catch(...)` clause must be the last `catch` clause.

An exception is generated by a `throw` statement; `throw` is a new C++ operator. The syntax of a `throw` statement is:

```
throw expression;
```

A handler is never allowed to resume or continue execution, and thus a `throw` expression can never return. Hence `throw` expressions have `void` type.

When an exception is thrown, the call chain is searched for an exception handler specified by a `catch` clause that handles the exception (i.e., a `catch` clause where the type matches the type of the exception thrown). If an exception handler is found, a process called "stack unwinding" occurs, which causes the invocation of destructors of all automatic objects in scopes on the way up the call chain to the handler. Thus destructors have an important relationship with exceptions, which we discuss in Section 7.9.

7.2 An example: file doesn't open

A complete example of the use of exceptions is shown below. The following code attempts to open files for reading, and throws an exception if the file cannot be opened:

```
#include <stdio.h>
#include <stdlib.h>
#include <iostream.h>

class Open_Failure { };    // exception class

FILE* open_file(char *filename)
{
    FILE *fp = fopen(filename, "r");
    if (fp == NULL)
        throw Open_Failure();    // note the brackets
    return fp;
}

main()
{
    char *filename = "not_exist.c";
    try {
            FILE *fp = open_file(filename);
            // ... do something with file
    }
    catch(OpenFailure) {
        cerr << "File " << filename << "failed to open\n";
        exit(1);
    }
    exit(0);
}
```

Note how a "dummy" class is declared for the exception. It is usual for an exception to have a unique type, and declaring a class with no members is a simple method of achieving this.

Note also that the `throw` expression uses brackets; these serve to call the constructor for the exception class. The following would be incorrect:

```
throw Open_Failure;    // WRONG!
```

It is wrong to simply throw a type name; an object or variable must be thrown. In the example above, an `Open_Failure` object is thrown, but the `catch` clause does not actually use the object. Section 7.5 shows how the thrown object can actually be used.

7.3 Rethrowing an exception

It can happen that a handler for a given exception finds that it cannot adequately handle the exception. In this case it is possible to "rethrow" the same exception in the hope that a handler in one of the calling functions can handle it properly. The C++ syntax for the "rethrow" operation is simply:

```
throw;
```

Naturally, a rethrow operation is only valid when an exception has occurred. Therefore, it is possible to rethrow from within a `catch` clause; it is also possible in a function called by the `unexpected` function, which is discussed in Section 7.8. A typical example of the use of rethrow is:

```
try {
  // .. something
}
catch (Some_Exception) {
  // .. partially handle the problem
  throw;      // rethrow to an outer handler
}
```

A minor detail is that the object rethrown is the original exception object, rather than a newly created object. This has implications, for example, when a base class exception object is caught by value (rather than by reference); see Section 7.6 for more details.

7.4 Unhandled exceptions cause termination

When an exception is thrown for which there is no corresponding exception handler, the default action is program termination with some appropriate system-dependent message — the `abort` library function is called.

If a more graceful termination of the program is required, the `main` function can use a `catch(...)` clause to catch all exceptions as shown below:

```
#include <stdlib.h>

main()
{
    try {
        // ... do the real work
    }
    catch(...) {    // catch all exceptions
        // ... shut down gracefully
        exit(EXIT_FAILURE);
    }
}
```

Alternatively, the `set_terminate` function can be used to override the default behavior for an uncaught exception. The default behavior for an uncaught exception is to call the `terminate` function, which calls `abort` to terminate program execution. The `set_terminate` function is used to specify a different function to be called by the `terminate` function. The prototype declaration for `set_terminate` is:

```
typedef void (*ptr_fn)(void);
ptr_fn set_terminate(ptr_fn);
```

Note that `ptr_fn` is introduced here just for convenience of presentation, and is not a type declared by ANSI C++.

The argument to `set_terminate` is a pointer to the new function (typically just the function name). This "pointer to function" argument is stored internally, and will be called whenever the `terminate` function is called (i.e., for an uncaught exception, when stack corruption is detected, or a destructor throws an exception during stack unwinding). The return value of `set_terminate` is the previous function; this value can be saved and used to reinstate the default behavior. The default function called by `terminate` is `abort` (i.e., the return value from the first call to `set_terminate` will be `&abort`).

The function supplied to `set_terminate` must never return. Typically, the function performs whatever cleanup is required and then terminates gracefully by calling the `exit` library function, as in the example below:

```
#include <stdlib.h>
#include <iostream.h>
#include <new.h>        // declare set_terminate

void shut_down()
{
    cerr << "Program received an uncaught exception\n";
    exit(EXIT_FAILURE);
}

main()
{
    set_terminate(&shut_down);
    // .. start the program
}
```

7.5 Catching exception objects

So far, all our `catch` handlers have caught type names only. However, the exception thrown is an object or value, not a type. To catch and use this object, and any data it contains, the `catch` clause can be modified to declare both a type and an object name, similar to a parameter declaration in a function.

This feature makes it easy to supply an exception handler with any amount of extra information by storing it in the object thrown. This information can be stored either as the value of an exception of built-in type, or as data members of an exception class. A simple example of using a built-in type is shown below. The exceptions thrown are strings, which are caught as exceptions of type `char*`, and their value is accessed to produce an error message:

```
try {
    char *p = new char[100];
    if (p != NULL)
        use_memory(p);
    else
        throw "Heap Memory Exhaustion";
}
catch(char* str) {
    cerr << "***EXCEPTION CAUGHT***: " << str << endl;
    exit(EXIT_FAILURE);
}
```

More typically, an exception class is declared with one or more data members that are used to transmit the information. Such an example follows:

```
#include <stdlib.h>
#include <iostream.h>
#include <limits.h>

class Overflow {
    public:
        int x, y;  // values causing overflow
        Overflow(int a, int b) : x(a), y(b) { }
};

void check_add_overflow(int a, int b)
{
    if (a >= 0 && b >= 0 && a > INT_MAX - b) {
        throw  Overflow(a,b);     // Object thrown
    }
    else if (a < 0 && b < 0 && a < INT_MIN - b) {
        throw  Overflow(a,b);     // Object thrown
    }
}

main()
{
    try {
        check_add_overflow(INT_MAX, INT_MAX);
    }
    catch(Overflow o) {      //   o is the overflow object
        cout << "Overflow from " << o.x << " + " << o.y << "\n";
    }
}
```

Naturally, the object thrown can be constructed in any manner. Although the examples of exception classes shown so far have all had constructor calls in `throw` statements, this is by no means necessary.

The `catch` clause above is less efficient than it could be because the `Overflow` object is constructed using a copy constructor at the beginning of the `catch` clause. A `catch` clause is analogous to a function parameter declaration. Efficiency can be improved by using "catch by reference" in the same way as "pass by reference" of function parameters improves efficiency, as I discuss in my recent book *C++ and C Efficiency*, also published by Prentice Hall. In addition to efficiency, catch by reference is important for derived exceptions which we now discuss.

7.6 Exception hierarchies

When using exceptions it is often desirable to handle groups of exceptions with the same block of code. There are a few ways to achieve this in ANSI C++. An inelegant method is to declare the different exceptions as different values with the same type. In this manner the exception handling code catches an object of the exception type and uses a `switch` over the different values to distinguish the exception. This can be implemented using a class with data members, or somewhat preferably as an `enum` declaration:

```
#include <stdlib.h>
#include <stdio.h>
#include <iostream.h>

enum File_Error { Open_Failure, Write_Failure, Read_Failure };

FILE* open_file(char *filename)
{
    FILE *fp = fopen(filename, "r");
    if (fp == NULL)
        throw Open_Failure;   // No brackets; throw value
    return fp;
}

main()
{
    try {
            FILE *fp = open_file("dummy");
            // ... do something with the file
    }
    catch (File_Error f) {
        switch (f) {                        // YUK! Ugly switch!
            case Open_Failure:
                cerr << "File won't open\n";
                break;
            case Write_Failure:
                cerr << "Write failed\n";
                break;
            case Read_Failure:
                cerr << "Read failed\n";
                break;
            default:
                cerr << "File Error\n";
                break;
        }
        exit(EXIT_FAILURE);
    }
    exit(EXIT_SUCCESS);
}
```

This method is not very elegant, and elimination of the `switch` statement has long been one of the aims of OOP in general, and of `virtual` functions in particular. Fortunately, better OOP style permits the `switch` to be eliminated in this area as well.

The C++ exception handling package permits exceptions to be grouped into hierarchies using inheritance. After all, classes declaring exceptions are no different from any other classes and inheritance can be used. The `catch` clause is smart enough to know about the type hierarchies so as to catch a derived exception class with a base class `catch` clause. The above example of file errors can be implemented far more elegantly using inheritance and `virtual` functions:

```
#include <stdio.h>
#include <stdlib.h>
#include <iostream.h>

class File_Error {
  public:
    virtual char* name()              // Virtual function!
      { return "File Error"; }
};

class Open_Failure : public File_Error {  // derived class
    public:  char* name() { return "Open Failure"; }
};
class Write_Failure : public File_Error {  // derived class
    public:  char* name() { return "Write Failure"; }
};
class Read_Failure : public File_Error {  // derived class
    public:  char* name() { return "Read Failure"; }
};

FILE* open_file(char *filename)
{
    FILE *fp = fopen(filename, "r");
    if (fp == NULL)
        throw Open_Failure();  // Need brackets
    return fp;
}

main()
{
    try {
        FILE *fp = open_file("dummy");
        // ... do something with the file
    }
    catch (File_Error &f) {  // Note: catch by reference
        cerr << "File Error caught: " << f.name << "\n";
        exit(EXIT_FAILURE);
    }
    exit(EXIT_SUCCESS);
}
```

Note that the exception object is "caught by reference" in the `catch` clause. If it were not a reference to a `File_Error`, then f would always be a "real" `File_Error` object, constructed using a copy constructor, and that name would be reported. The use of a reference type prevents this conversion to the base class and ensures correct behavior, not to mention being more efficient as well!

The importance of exception hierarchies is not merely to use `virtual` functions as in the example above. Using derived exception classes makes it easy to write code that handles groups of exceptions. For example, using the class hierarchy from above it is very easy to write `catch` clauses that single out particular exceptions, but have a "default" `catch` clause with the base class that handles the rest of that group of exceptions:

```
class File_Error { };  // base class
class Open_Failure  : public File_Error { };  // derived class
class Write_Failure : public File_Error { };  // derived class
class Read_Failure  : public File_Error { };  // derived class

main()
{
    try {
      // .. whatever
    }
    catch(Open_Failure) {
        // handle file opening failure
    }
    catch(File_Error) {
        // handle any other file error
    }
}
```

7.7 Function interface specifications of exceptions

Another feature of ANSI C++ exception handling is the possibility of specifying in the function prototype declaration exactly what exceptions can be thrown by the function. The types of all exceptions possibly thrown by a function are listed after the parameter list; for example, consider the following function prototype declarations:

```
void open_file(char *)  throw(Open_Failure);
void check_add_overflow(int a, int b)  throw(Overflow);
```

These specify that `open_file` can only throw `Open_Failure` exceptions, and `check_add_overflow` can only throw `Overflow` exceptions.

A function without any `throw(..)` interface specification is assumed to throw any exception. No restriction is the default, so that a programmer need not be concerned with interface specifications unless they are required:

```
void any_exception();
```

A function that cannot throw any exceptions is declared using an empty list:

```
void no_exceptions()  throw();
```

These interface specifications are an opportunity to document the behavior of the various functions. It is much easier to examine the function prototype than to search through source code (if it is actually available) for all the `throw` expressions and determine what types are thrown.

Using interface specifications in function definitions also allows the compiler to check the specifications. Unfortunately, the compiler cannot completely determine the correctness of the specifications at compile-time, because any function (without such an interface specification) that is called by the function might return any exception. However, ANSI C++ requires the run-time detection of a function that throws an exception not specified in its interface specification. When this is detected, the program calls the unexpected library function, which we now consider.

7.8 unexpected and set_unexpected

The unexpected function and its companion, the set_unexpected function, are very similar to the terminate and set_terminate library functions discussed in Section 7.4. The default behavior of unexpected is to call the terminate library function. This default behavior can be changed by specifying a different function to be called as the argument to the set_unexpected library function. The prototype declaration of set_unexpected is:

```
typedef void (*ptr_fn)(void);
ptr_fn set_unexpected(ptr_fn);
```

The return value of set_unexpected is the previous handler function (initially the terminate function); this value can be saved and used to reinstate the default behavior.

The set_unexpected function is useful when termination is not desirable. The function supplied to set_unexpected can rethrow the exception in the hope that a handler elsewhere can cope with it. However, it seems likely that if it wasn't in the interface specification then it won't be handled somewhere else; therefore, a better policy may be to throw a new exception to indicate this condition, such as a special exception named Unexpected or similar, and modify the main function to catch that exception as shown below:

```
class Unexpected { };      // exception class

void throw_Unexpected()
{
    throw Unexpected();
}

main()
{
    set_unexpected(&throw_Unexpected);
    try {
        // .. rest of the main function
    }
    catch(Unexpected) {
        cerr << "Unexpected exception was caught\n";
        // .. graceful shutdown or restart
    }
}
```

Note that a function supplied to set_unexpected cannot return normally, the result being undefined by ANSI C++. The best that could be hoped for would be a return, with a garbage return value, from the function whose interface specifications were violated.

7.9 Destructor techniques using exceptions

Destructors have a special relationship with ANSI C++ exception handling because destructors of automatic objects are executed during the stack unwinding process after an exception has been thrown. In a certain sense these techniques are "tricks," but they do not really deserve such a negative tag since they are based upon a well-defined and well-documented relationship between destructors and exceptions. The use of objects with carefully defined destructors also has the advantage of being less error-prone than the explicit use of cleanup code, because these destructors can be coded once only, whereas the programmer must remember cleanup code in all code blocks.

7.9.1 Explicit cleanup code

The simplest method of introducing cleanup code to be executed in the event of an exception is to use the `catch(...)` clause to catch all exceptions and then rethrow. For example, to ensure an allocated block is deallocated, use the following method:

```
void fn()
{
    char *mem;

    try {
        mem = new char[100];    // allocate the memory
        use_the_mem(mem);       // use the memory
        delete [] mem;          // deallocate
    }
    catch(...) {   // catch all exceptions; cleanup code here
        cerr << "Exception caught..cleanup code used\n";
        delete [] mem;          // deallocate
        throw;                  // rethrow
    }
}
```

7.9.2 Cleanup code using destructors

A more general method of ensuring that temporary memory is deallocated is to use a special class with a destructor that deallocates the memory. The simplest example is such a method for allocation of `char` type memory:

```
class SafePtr {          // Memory allocation class
    private:
        char *mem;    // pointer to actual data
        SafePtr();                      // disallow default constructor
        SafePtr(const SafePtr &);       // disallow copy constructor
        void operator=(const SafePtr &);    // disallow = operator
    public:
        SafePtr(int size) {             // Constructor allocates
            mem = new char [size];
        }
        ~SafePtr() { delete [] mem; }  // Destructor deallocates
        operator char*()        // Conversion operator
            { return mem; }
};

void fn()
{
    SafePtr mem(100);    // allocate the memory
    use_the_mem(mem);    // use the memory
}
```

Now the destructor for mem causes deallocation on normal function return and also during stack unwinding from an exception. Therefore, there is no need for any try or catch block to clean up this memory block.

7.10 Summary

- ANSI C++ exceptions are new and may not be supported by all C++ compilers.
- Three new keywords are used: try, catch, and throw. A try block holds mainstream code, a catch block holds exception handlers, and a throw statement raises the exception.
- Throwing an exception causes "stack unwinding," including destruction of automatic objects.
- Uncaught exceptions cause termination unless intercepted using set_terminate.
- Exceptions are distinguished by catch clauses on the basis of their *type*.
- Exceptions throw objects, not types, and therefore can easily transmit data between a throw statement and the catch handler.
- Exception hierarchies and derived exception classes are supported by catch handlers.
- Exception objects that may be derived objects should be *caught by reference*.
- Interface specifications permit compile-time checking of throw statements and run-time detection of unexpected exceptions.

7.11 Further reading

The ANSI C++ exception handling syntax is quite new, and appears mainly in the writings of its designer, Bjarne Stroustrup. His general-purpose C++ textbook, *The C++ Programming Language*, contains an excellent chapter on the new exception handling facilities, not only covering the syntax and semantics, but also examining some of the issues involved in using the facilities to enhance reliability.

A more detailed description of the technical issues involved in the use and implementation of exceptions is given in *The Annotated C++ Reference Manual* by Margaret Ellis and Bjarne Stroustrup. The technical level of the material is high enough that reading this book is probably not of great importance to the average programmer, but it does contain important material.

ELLIS, Margaret A., and STROUSTRUP, Bjarne, *The Annotated C++ Reference Manual*, Addison-Wesley, 1990.

STROUSTRUP, Bjarne, *The C++ Programming Language*, Addison-Wesley, 1991.

7.12 Extensions

1. Design and implement a nontrivial class, paying special attention to the exceptions. Some example classes you might consider are:

    - vector class (exceptions such as bad array index, bad size, etc.)
    - string class (exceptions such as buffer overflow)
    - complex number class (exceptions such as arithmetic overflow, divide by zero)

2. Find an existing class you have written and add exceptions to it. Is this more difficult than designing the class around exceptions in the first place?

3. Generalize the `SafePtr` class in Section 7.9.2 to all types of memory by making it a template. *Hint:* This is mainly a matter of converting all occurrences of `"char"` to a type parameter.

4. Implement a `SafeFILE` class analogous to the `SafePtr` class in Section 7.9.2 that ensures that a C-style `FILE*` file handle is always closed when an exception occurs. Note that the C++ file I/O class library `<fstream.h>` already provides this functionality, and therefore performs better than `<stdio.h>` in conjunction with exception handling.

5. The `try`/`catch`/`throw` facilities can be thought of as "just another form of flow control" rather than as referring only to exceptional conditions. It is effectively a nonlocal `goto` similar to `setjmp` and `longjmp` that allows jumps "up" but not "down" the call stack. Experiment with the facilities provided to gain a greater understanding; for example, try the following:

    - Implement a loop that exits only via throwing an exception.
    - Implement a function that exits only via throwing an exception.
    - Can you enter a loop for the first time using `throw`? Why or why not?
    - Can you enter a loop for the second time using `throw`? Why or why not?

6. In theory, exceptions can be implemented so that they have only marginal impact on run-time efficiency, except when an exception is actually thrown. Time or profile a test program containing a tight loop both with and without exception handling to examine how closely to the ideal your compiler performs.

Chapter 8

Exception handler macro libraries

This chapter presents a number of preprocessor macro libraries that hide the details of using setjmp and longjmp for exception handling in both C and C++. As far as C++ programs are concerned, this chapter may well be obsolete by the time you read these words, as the ANSI C++ exception handling should be available in the near future. However, the libraries presented herein should be useful when dealing with older C++ compilers, and for the implementation of exception handling in ANSI C.

The libraries have been presented with names similar to the ANSI C++ exception handling keywords try, catch, and throw. For a refresher course on this syntax of ANSI C++ refer to Chapter 7.

8.1 setjmp and longjmp in C

The setjmp and longjmp ANSI C standard library functions are the only way to perform nonlocal jumps in C or pre-ANSI C++. The goto statement can jump only within the current function, and therefore setjmp and longjmp functions must be used when an exceptional condition is detected that necessitates a nonlocal jump. However, in ANSI C++ the preferred method is to throw an exception using the throw operator; the ANSI C++ exception facilities are discussed in Chapter 7.

The setjmp and longjmp functions are companion functions. To use these functions it is necessary to include <setjmp.h> and to declare a variable of type jmp_buf (declared in <setjmp.h>) that is accessible to both setjmp and longjmp (usually a global variable). setjmp is called to set up the location where a later longjmp call will jump back to. When called the first time setjmp will return zero, indicating that it has been called normally. When longjmp is called later, the effect will be as if setjmp had just returned with a nonzero value. The longjmp function unwinds the stack and fixes up the system registers (whose previous values were stored in the jmp_buf data object) to mimic the effect of returning from a call to the setjmp function. Therefore, the standard method of calling setjmp is to test its return value:

```
#include <setjmp.h>
jmp_buf env;          /* global variable */

if (setjmp(env) != 0) {
    /* .. setjmp returns nonzero */
    /* .. exception has occurred */
    /* .. program has longjmp'd to get here */
}
else {
    /* .. normal start of program */
}
```

The manner of calling longjmp is to supply it with the env variable used by setjmp and a nonzero integer error code. The simplest method is:

```
longjmp(env, 1);
```

A typical method of using setjmp and longjmp for exception handling is illustrated below for a menu-based program. When an exception occurs, the longjmp function is called to return back to menu.

```
#include <setjmp.h>

jmp_buf env;

main()
{
    if (setjmp(env) != 0) {
        /* Error: longjmp'd to here */
        /* perform any clean up & restart the menu */
    }
    /* Got here via normal start OR via longjmp call */
    menu();      /* present the main menu */
}
```

A number of common errors involving setjmp and longjmp are discussed starting at Section 18.12 and these should be examined before using the functions.

8.2 setjmp and longjmp in C++

The setjmp and longjmp functions operate in exactly the same manner in C++ as they do in C. Because they are part of the ANSI standard C library, they are also part of the C++ standard library. Hence these functions are a useful alternative to proper exception handling in pre-ANSI C++ implementations that do not fully support exceptions.

However, there is one major problem with using longjmp in C++ — destructors are *not* called for local objects. In fact, the problem is worse in that whether destructors are called by longjmp is actually "undefined" and although most compilers don't call destructors, some implementations do so, and we have a portability problem across C++ implementations.

This failure to execute destructors is a major difference between the use of longjmp and the ANSI C++ throw statement, which does correctly destroy local automatic objects. Therefore the use of longjmp is more precarious, being prone to errors such as leaving files open or creating garbage memory.

There are a few solutions to this problem with destructors. An inelegant solution is to hand-code in the `setjmp` handling block any cleanup code that would have been performed by a destructor. Another possibility is to derive the class for objects requiring destruction by `longjmp` from a base class that helps `longjmp` to call the appropriate destructors. This is most easily achieved within a macro library, and Bengtsson's library (see Section 8.8) is one example with its use of a `Resource` base class.

8.3 Horsmeier's exception handling library for C

The power of the C preprocessor can be used to create a suite of exception handling macros. The following method of using macros to hide `setjmp` and `longjmp` calls was communicated to the author by Jos Horsmeier, and the macros and functions below are based upon those written by him in 1988. The following macro library is available on the source code disk in the `chap8/horsmier` directory.

The basis of the method is to use macros that cleverly extend the syntax of C to make it similar to the syntax of C++ exception handling. A block of code that must have its exceptions handled is surrounded by a TRY and ENDTRY pair, and followed by one or more CATCH blocks:

```
TRY {
   /* something */
} ENDTRY
CATCH(Exception1) {
   /* handle exception 1 */
}
```

Different exceptions are represented by `int` codes that are chosen by the user of the exception macros. When a (software) exception is found by the program, it uses the THROW function to raise an exception, which is "caught" by the exception handling code. The exception may be "thrown" in the current function, or in any function called by these functions:

```
THROW(MALLOC_FAILURE);
```

An example of a program using these macros for exception handling is given below:

```
#include <stdio.h>
#include <stdlib.h>

#include "except.h"

enum { MALLOC_FAILURE, BAD_INPUT };    /* exception codes */

void *my_malloc(int n)
{
    void *p;

    p = malloc(n);
    if (p == NULL) THROW(MALLOC_FAILURE);
    return p;
}
```

```
char* get_string(int max)
{
    int i = 0;
    int ch;
    char *s;

    s = my_malloc(max);
    do {
        ch = getchar();
        if (ch == EOF || ch == '\n') {
            s[i] = '\0';
            return;
        }
        else
            s[i++] = ch;
    } while (i < max - 1);
    THROW(BAD_INPUT);
}

main()
{
    char *s;

    TRY {
        s = get_string(20);
    } ENDTRY
    CATCH(MALLOC_FAILURE) {
        printf("Malloc failed\n");
    }
    CATCH(BAD_INPUT) {
        printf("Bad input\n");
    }
}
```

The main advantage of using these macros is shown in the example above. Without the exception macros it would be quite painful to handle cases where malloc fails, or where the program received bad input. However, using the macros allows the separation of the code for such "exceptional" conditions, and makes the code more readable.

8.3.1 Implementing the exception handling macros

The macros work by hiding setjmp and longjmp calls from the user. A TRY block calls setjmp so as to store the location of where the exception returns to, and a later THROW call uses a longjmp call to return to the exception handling code. The most important macro definitions in the header file are:

```
#define TRY          if (setjmp(ExceptIst()) == 0) {
#define ENDTRY       ExceptRls(); }
#define CATCH(x)     else if (ExceptError == (x))
#define THISEXCEPT   ExceptCode()
#define ALLOTHERS    else
```

Note that THROW is a function, not a macro.

Also needed is a C/C++ source file containing declarations of the functions that do most of the hard work. This file is available in the chap8/horsmier directory on the source code disk.

8.3.2 Limitations of the exception handling macros

There are some unfortunate limitations of the macro approach to exception handling. The major problem is that flow of control must always fall through to the bottom of the TRY block, so that the CATCH macro can "clean up" the exception handling correctly. This means that the return statement cannot be used to return from the current function from within a block that has its exceptions handled:

```
TRY {
    ... return;    /* ERROR */
} ENDTRY
CATCH(...)
```

Similar restrictions apply to the use of other jump statements such as break, continue, and goto. If any of these statements cause the flow of control to bypass the closing ENDTRY macro, the exception handling for the rest of the program is corrupted, and will possibly cause a run-time failure.

Another limitation is that it isn't portable to call THROW from within a signal handler, because it isn't portable to call longjmp from a signal handler. Although it will often behave correctly, a signal can occur at any moment, and could have left important data structures corrupted (e.g., the malloc internal free list). As always, the most portable method of handling signals is to print a message and exit. Therefore, although it is enticing to declare signal handlers that catch common signals (e.g., SIGINT) and THROW an exception, it isn't a portable solution.

8.4 Amsterdam's exception library for C

Jonathan Amsterdam in the August 1991 issue of *Byte* magazine presented a method that differs slightly from Jos Horsmeier's method in that it avoids calling malloc to allocate jmp_buf records. Instead, a stack of jmp_buf records is built on the C internal stack by using automatic jmp_buf variables. Each TRY macro declares a local jmp_buf variable after its opening left brace, and the address of this variable is threaded through a linked list of pointers. The advantages of this method are that stack allocation and deallocation should be faster than malloc and free, and also that there is no need to be concerned with malloc failure.

Although the use of addresses of local variables may appear dangerous at first, it is safe because the addresses are removed from the linked list whenever control flow moves back up past the TRY macro. Thus these addresses can be used only by the exception handling library while they are currently active on the program stack. Of course, the safety of the method relies on consistent use of the exception handling library, and any form of failure might arise if the normal exception handling methods are bypassed.

The idea of using automatic stack variables is a general solution to the problem of allocating jmp_buf records that applies to both C and C++ exception libraries. The stack-based solution has also been used by various implementations such as the C++ library of Leary and D'Souza, and Harald Winroth's library for C. In fact, Jos Horsmeier has modified his library to use this technique and it is available on the source code disk in the chap8/horstack directory.

8.5 Hood's exception library for C

Another interesting exception library has been shown to me by Stuart Hood and is available on the source code disk in the `chap8/hood` directory. The overall syntax is dissimilar to the ANSI C++ style, with separate "handle" and "unhandle" statements — the `EXHandle` macro instates some exception handler code, and the `EXUnhandle` macro removes the corresponding handler. A sample usage looks like:

```
EXHandle(free_array, EXCEPT_ALL, { free(array);  } );

/* ... code using the array variable that may raise exception */

free(array);  /* normal free (i.e., no exception) */
EXUnhandle(free_array);
```

The design of the paired macros is very clever, making good use of ANSI stringizing and token pasting (i.e., the # and ## macro operators). The requirement of explicit pairs of macros may seem error-prone, but there is support for run-time mismatch detection. The argument `free_array` above serves as a character string identifier for the handler, and must match in handle/unhandle macro pairs.

8.6 Winroth's exception library for C

Harald Winroth has presented a macro library for exceptions in ANSI C, with a number of neat features, including exception hierarchy support, unwind-protect, and callbacks. Let us examine the details of the method.

Winroth uses macro calls where code blocks are placed as arguments to the macro, leading to large macro calls. The `TRY` macro call has the form:

```
TRY( try_code_block , catch_code_block );
```

and the `CATCH` macro only has a code block as the second argument:

```
CATCH(exception , handler_block );
```

An example of this usage in practice shows that huge sequences of code are placed inside the macro arguments:

```
TRY (
  {
    /* try block:  do something useful */
    ......
  },  /* Note the comma! */
  {
    /* handler block ... one or more CATCH's */
    CATCH(lib_error, { /* code to handle lib_error */  } );
    CATCH(disk_full, { /* code to handle disk_full */  } );
  }
);
```

All exceptions reach the start of the handler block. Therefore, code appropriate for all exceptions (i.e., equivalent to `catch(...)` in ANSI C++) should be placed after all other `CATCH` macros. Code for all exceptions could be placed anywhere in the handler block, such as before all `CATCH` macros or between two, but this usage is more difficult to convert later to ANSI C++. Placing all default code after the CATCH calls simulates the idea that catch(...) must be the last handler. However, note that the default code must end with a continue statement to restart execution after the TRY block; otherwise the library doesn't know that the exception has been handled and will test for CATCH macros in outer run-time scopes.

Some other specific features of the macro library are:

- continue in a main or handler block will skip to after the TRY macro.
- break in a main block is a run-time error.
- break in a CATCH continues within the handler block after that CATCH.
- break in a handler block but not in a CATCH is a run-time error.
- CATCH in the wrong place is a run-time error.
- A successful CATCH will continue execution after the TRY macro.
- TRY blocks can be nested.
- goto into or out of blocks can corrupt the exception handling.
- longjmp usage can corrupt the exception handling.
- "THROW(exception)" causes rethrow (exception is a special variable).
- Rethrowing outside a handler block is a run-time error.

8.6.1 Limitations of large macro calls

In my opinion, the method of declaring exception handling code using Winroth's macros is far more cumbersome than some of the other macro methods, and also suffers because it is unlike the ANSI C++ exception syntax. There are also a few minor problems (other than its unusual syntax) with this use of macros. Some deficient compilers may have preprocessors that fail on such large macros, although good compilers should not have any problems for "reasonable" size code blocks.

Another minor problem is that any commas that are not nested inside brackets will start a new macro argument, and lead to compilation errors (hopefully). Note that braces do not hide commas from the preprocessor's macro argument collection process. Hence, consider the following code:

```
TRY (
    {    int i,j;        // WHOOPS!  Comma starts new argument
         j = fn(i,i+1);  // This comma would have been ok
    },
    { ....  });
```

Despite my complaints about its appearance, this method of large macros is a practical alternative to the C++-like syntax used by Horsmeier's method. It allows the treatment of entire code blocks as macro arguments, and they can be moved around or repeated within the macro replacement text.

8.6.2 Exception hierarchies using structs

The most strikingly useful feature of Winroth's method is a clever method of simulating C++ exception hierarchies using nested C `struct` definitions. Suppose you wish to represent the following hierarchy of exceptions:

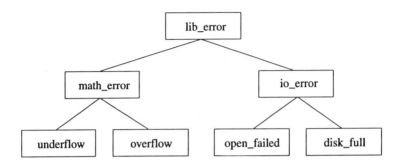

In Winroth's exception library this would be represented as an "exception domain" by a nested `struct` definition, where each `struct` represents an exception domain, and each `int` member is a leaf in the hierarchy:

```
typedef struct {
    struct {
            int underflow;
            int overflow;
    } math_error;
    struct {
            int open_failed
            int disk_full;
    } io_error;
} lib_error_type;
extern lib_error_type lib_error;    // declare exception object
```

This `struct` declaration and extern variable declaration can appear in a header file. `lib_error` must be defined as a global variable in one source file. Note that we cannot use a `static` variable because it is the address that is used by the CATCH macros, and using a `static` variable in the exception header file would lead to multiple addresses for the same exception.

The equivalent ANSI C++ exception hierarchy would be coded as:

```
class lib_error { };
    class math_error : public lib_error { };
            class underflow : public math_error { };
            class overflow : public math_error { };
    class io_error : public lib_error { };
            class open_failed : public io_error { }
            class disk_full : public io_error { };
```

To use these exception domains with Winroth's library, the CATCH macro simply catches the appropriate variable or field. Some alternatives are:

```
CATCH(lib_error, {..})                      // all library errors
CATCH(lib_error.math_error, {..})           // all math errors
CATCH(lib_error.io_error.disk_full, {..}) // disk_full only
```

In the C++ versions, these exceptions could be caught as below. The main difference is that there is no need to explicitly specify the outer domains:

```
catch(lib_error)       // all library errors
catch(math_error)      // all math errors
catch(disk_full)       // disk_full only
```

Note that Winroth's method permits more than one independent exception hierarchy (simply defined as a separate global `struct` variable). It is not a requirement that all exceptions be derived from one base group, as has been the case with other methods (e.g., Vidal's method). However, this is desirable for portability to platforms with nonlinear address spaces (see below). Also, Winroth's method cannot simulate multiple inheritance in the exception hierarchy, but then who needs it?

Although Winroth's exception library applies only to C, this idiom of simulating exception hierarchies using `struct` members can be applied to any of the C++ libraries. This makes it possible to design this exception facility using C++-like exception hierarchies, allowing the code to upgrade to ANSI C++ features *without changing the design*. Although there is significant change to the coding style, the exception hierarchy can remain the same. Therefore, this method is an important building block for an exception macro system.

8.6.3 Implementation details of exception domains

The implementation trick used by the CATCH macro to ensure that it catches the correct domain is that it catches *addresses*. The exception y is handled by a CATCH(x) clause if the addresses satisfy:

```
&x <= &y <= &x + sizeof(x)
```

Therefore, the method requires special care if the memory organization is not linear. The danger is that of getting "false successes" from this test for pointers in different segments, and the wrong CATCH handler will be used. For example, for a segmented DOS architecture it becomes important what types of pointers are compared (i.e., huge pointers are needed). One safety method is that declaring all exception types within one `struct` declaration will ensure that all addresses can be meaningfully declared; alternatively, *defining* all exception objects in one source file will often ensure their addresses are within the same segment.

8.6.4 Implementation details of run-time errors

Another very neat implementation trick is the method of ensuring run-time errors for various failures within the library. Let us examine how the trick is used to detect return statements inside a TRY block. The keyword return is defined as a self-referencing macro (legal in ANSI C and draft ANSI C++) that involves a compile-time test, conceptually similar to:

```
#define return if(sizeof(hidden) > 1) { ERROR(); } else return
```

The trick is a hidden global variable name (i.e., hidden here) that is redefined as a different type in local scopes. The library defines the hidden variable globally with type char, and the TRY macro defines a local variable of the same name as type long. Thus whenever a return occurs inside a TRY block it sees the local long variable that has size at least 4 and complains; but outside of any TRY blocks the compiler sees only the global char variable with size 1 and produces no error.

This clever use of two variables with the same name but different types allows the use of sizeof as a compile-time test. The efficiency of legitimate return statements should not be affected since any good optimizer will elide this test because it has constant value at compile-time.

All run-time errors in Winroth's exception library rely on this trick, which provokes a run-time error based on a compile-time test. In fact, it wouldn't be too hard to modify the method to ensure a *compile-time* diagnostic. One method would be to define the local version of the hidden variable as a struct and perform an impossible operation such as < upon the hidden variable. Unfortunately, the error message produced by such an error would probably be quite obscure, although this could be slightly improved by making the hidden variable name self-explanatory.

8.6.5 Unwind-protect

Another feature of Winroth's library is the UNWIND_PROTECT macro that provides a method of ensuring that a block of code is always executed, under both normal and exceptional control flows. The syntax of this macro is:

```
UNWIND_PROTECT( main_block, cleanup_block );
```

8.6.6 Limitations

One limitation of Winroth's method is that jump statements will corrupt the jmp_buf stack if improperly used. Because only C is used, the C++ popper class idiom of Bengtsson cannot be used. This problem is partially solved by requiring the use of a macro tryreturn inside TRY blocks; using return inside a TRY block should invoke a run-time error. However, the use of goto in and out of blocks is still dangerous.

All variables can be used as exceptions, but since it is actually their address being used, it is dangerous to use automatic local variables, as they may have been destroyed by the time the appropriate CATCH is reached. Exception variables should be global variables, typically declared in a single header file and defined in a single source file.

8.7 Vidal's Lex-based filter for C++

The library presented by Carlos Vidal is different from the other methods discussed in this chapter in that it is not a preprocessor macro library. Rather than use a library of macros, the idea is to use an extra filter tool in the compilation process, to convert the ANSI C++ exception style to C++ code using only pre-ANSI C++ features. Such a filter is presented in the paper as a script for Lex, a lexical analyzer widely available under UNIX. The use of a filter increases flexibility by removing the limitations of the preprocessor. The main novel features of Vidal's method are support for:

- function interface specifications (!)
- `unexpected` and `set_unexpected`
- `terminate` and `set_terminate`
- both `catch(type)` and `catch(type param_name)`

However, even with this extra flexibility, there are still many features of ANSI C++ exceptions that Vidal's method does not support. Some such limitations are:

- Exception classes must inherit from an `Exception` base class.
- Exception classes must define size and type functions.
- Stack unwinding does not call automatic object destructors.
- `return`/`goto`/`break`/`continue` in a `try` block may cause problems.

Regarding the last limitation, although I have no way of testing it, it also seems that any jump statements, such as a `return` statement, inside a `try` block will skip past the "Exh::stk--" stack popping code and cause inconsistency of the stack of `jmp_buf` objects, causing unknown failure of this method.

Overall, Vidal's idea of the use of a filter is a great improvement over using preprocessor macros, although I believe some of the limitations of his implementation could be removed. For example, the execution of destructors and failure due to jump statements could perhaps be handled using Bengtsson's resource and popper class idioms. With these minor problems fixed, the use of a filter has incredible power, as evidenced by the fact that Vidal's method calls `unexpected` upon failure of built-in run-time checking of function interface specifications!

8.8 Bengtsson's exception library for C++

Johan Bengtsson presents an interesting exception handling library. His report first discusses the theory of various methods of handling exceptions, including using ANSI C++ exceptions, and then presents a macro library to simulate ANSI C++ exceptions using pre-ANSI C++ features.

This macro library uses the macro names TRY, CATCH, THROW, and RETHROW. The underlying method, as always, is the use of `setjmp` and `longjmp` by these macros. The syntax used by the method is:

```
TRY {
    // main block
}
CATCH(int throwCode) {
    // handler block
}
```

The syntax is quite limited in that only one CATCH block is allowed, which must handle all exceptions. Furthermore, there is no discrimination of CATCH blocks based on exception types; all exceptions have integer type. All failures cause execution of the closest CATCH, and the only way to handle the exception at a higher level is to RETHROW.

8.8.1 Popper class to avoid return problems

One notable feature of Bengtsson's method is the "popper" class that is used to avoid problems with jump statements (i.e., return, goto, break, and continue) skipping over destructors for objects declared in the TRY block. The TRY macro declares a local automatic popper object, which has a destructor that pops the TRY-stack of jmp_buf variables. The definition of TRY and CATCH are effectively:

```
#define TRY        if(setjmp(....) == 0) { Popper _popper;
#define CATCH(x)   } else
```

Compare the CATCH macro with that of Horsmeier's method, which has an ExceptRls call before the closing right brace that pops the jmp_buf stack. The difference here is that the destructor Popper::~Popper() performs the jmp_buf stack pop operation implicitly. Using the popper class idiom, the destructor execution automatically ensures that the TRY/CATCH level is correct if either:

(a) execution falls through the closing right brace of the TRY block; or
(b) a jump statement skips past this right brace.

Only (a) is guaranteed by an explicit pop operation before the CATCH's right brace, such as in Horsmeier's method. Unfortunately, this popper class idiom uses C++ features (i.e., destructors) and cannot be used by exception macros for C, such as Horsmeier's method.

8.8.2 Resource class for destructor calls in stack unwinding

Another interesting feature of Bengtsson's library is the method of calling destructors during stack unwinding using a Resource class. Although this method doesn't automatically ensure destructor calls, the programmer can ensure that a particular class has its objects deallocated by making it inherit from Resource (i.e., the new class becomes a derived class of Resource). The constructor and virtual destructor of the Resource base class then maintain a stack of objects to be destroyed when THROW is called. Note that a stack ensures destruction in reverse order to construction.

Unfortunately, this method of calling destructors from a common base class has disadvantages such as:

(a) dynamically allocated objects are destroyed (not just automatic objects);

(b) objects inheriting from Resource should not be stored as data members.

Note that the dynamic object problem could be resolved nonportably using an InStack function as shown by Leary and D'Souza's method. The restriction on storing any Resource-inheriting objects as data members of other objects (especially those that do not inherit from Resource) arises because the member object may be destroyed without destroying the outer object.

8.9 Leary/D'Souza's exception library for C++

Sean Leary and Desmond D'Souza have presented another method that uses C++ features to mimic ANSI C++ exceptions. The method uses the macros TRY, CATCH, ADNCATCH, ENDCATCH, and THROW, with the basic syntax:

```
TRY {
    // main code
}
CATCH(type, var_name) {
    // handler code
}
ADNCATCH(type,var_name) {    // Additional catches
    // handler code
}
ENDCATCH
```

The method offers the flexibility to throw entire objects, with the minor restriction that exception class objects must be derived from an Exception class, which is common practice in any case.

Exception handling is based upon the character string representing the name of the exception object's type. All exception classes must define a unique name, and thus exception objects are distinguished using a simple form of run-time type inference. Unfortunately, this allows no possibility of defining exception hierarchies and catching classes of exceptions.

The method used by Leary and D'Souza to destroy automatic objects during stack unwinding is the same as that used by Bengtsson, but has a new twist. All object classes needing to be destroyed in this manner must inherit from the Unwind class; the idea is identical to Bengtsson's use of a Resource base class. The constructor and virtual destructor of Unwind maintain a stack of objects to be destroyed when an exception is thrown (a stack ensures destruction in reverse order of construction). The new twist is that they overcome the problem that dynamically allocated objects will be destroyed by defining an InStack function that determines whether an object is automatic. Unfortunately, the method is inherently nonportable, and the implementation presented works only for Borland C++ small model.

There are various other notable features of this implementation:

- `Throw(Obj)` and `Throw()` are distinguished by C++ function overloading.
- `Throw()` causes a rethrow operation.
- The equivalent to C++'s `catch(...)` is `CATCH(Exception,ptr_name)`.

8.10 Building blocks from the libraries

All of the various exception handling macro libraries offer various features with advantages and disadvantages. However, the different authors have mixed these features in various ways, and it hasn't always been clear which ideas are compatible with each other. That is the purpose of this section — to identify the building blocks, and examine their orthogonality or lack thereof. This should help you to build your own exception handling library if none of the existing ones suffice. I have identified the following important building blocks for exceptions in both C and C++:

- Winroth's exception domains (hierarchies) using `struct`s and addresses
- Winroth's run-time errors for bad use of `return` (macro trick with `sizeof`)
- allocation for `jmp_buf` stack — Horsmeier's `malloc` calls
- allocation for `jmp_buf` stack — Amsterdam's automatic variables
- allocation for `jmp_buf` stack — Hood's global fixed-size array

There are also some building blocks that require C++ features:

- Bengtsson's "popper" class to handle jump statements (i.e., `return/goto`)
- stack unwinding of destructors using Bengtsson's `Resource` class
- run-time type identification implemented in exception objects
- exception objects inheriting from a single `Exception` base class

There are also at least three separate styles of syntax for the exception handling code:

- Winroth style of large macros — i.e., use of code blocks in macro arguments
- ANSI C++ syntax imitation (e.g., Horsmeier's or Leary/D'Souza's methods)
- Hood's separate handle/unhandle macro syntax; dissimilar to C++ syntax

Some of these building blocks are orthogonal, and can be used in combination with others. For example, Winroth's exception domains using `struct`s could be easily combined with a different macro style, such as the ANSI C++ imitation style used by Horsmeier and Leary/D'Souza.

However, other combinations of primitives are less compatible. For example, Winroth's `struct` method appears incompatible with the use of an `Exception` common base class, because the former requires treatment of addresses of objects, and the latter passes objects by reference at the throw-point.

One possibility that none of the authors used was to stringize the type argument to `CATCH`, and explicitly test for the string `"..."` as a special case. However, this is difficult to do; for example, the method of Leary and D'Souza does stringize the type argument in the `CATCH` macro, but also makes use of the same macro argument without stringizing, which would cause a compilation error from the CATCH (. . .) usage.

Another important issue to address is whether the method must use only the C/C++ preprocessor (as with the building blocks above) or whether the use of another tool in the compilation process is acceptable. For example, Vidal's method uses a separate language filter, built using a Lex script, to preprocess the ANSI C++ code (using ANSI exception syntax) into pre-ANSI C++ code. Using an extra filter step provides much more flexibility, but the extra phase during compilation may be a headache.

8.11 Further reading

This chapter has examined the work of a number of people, all presenting various methods of exception handling technique using macros in C or C++ to hide setjmp and longjmp calls. The bibliographic details of the relevant papers are listed below. A few of these papers have not been examined in detail because they were discovered relatively "late" in the writing process. A case in point is the good paper by Lee, which is an early version of a setjmp based exception library. The overall syntax is:

```
BEGIN
   ....
EXCEPTION
   ...
   WHEN(Exception name)
      ....
   WHEN(Exception name)
      ....
END
```

Exceptions have char* type and are declared as variables. One minor caveat: the macro NEW_EXCEPTION relies on macro parameter expansion within strings, and must be converted to use the # stringize operator for ANSI C and C++.

Another exceptions package discovered late is a good package that is freely available via FTP. It was created by Ross N. Williams and publicly released in September 1993. It is available by anonymous FTP to the site "ftp.adelaide.edu.au" in the directory pub/funnelweb/examples. The author of the package can be contacted at: Dr Ross N. Williams, Rocksoft Pty Ltd, 16 Lerwick Avenue, Hazelwood Park 5066, Australia; phone: +61 8 379-9217 (24 hours). Although distributed as an example of literate programming using the *FunnelWeb* literate programming tool, it is also a very useful package for C programmers in its own right. The "readme" file for the package is available on the source code disk in the chap8/williams directory.

AMSTERDAM, Jonathan, "Some Assembly Required: Taking Exception to C," *Byte*, August 1991, pp. 259–264.

BENGTSSON, Johan, "C++, Without Exceptions," Telia Research, Lulea, Sweden (available via FTP to euagate.eua.ericsson.se in directory pub/eua/c++ with filename Exceptions_920511.ps.Z).

ERDELSKY, Philip J., "A Safer setjmp in C++," *C Users Journal*, Vol. 11, No. 1, January 1993, pp. 41–44.

LEARY, Sean, and D'SOUZA, Desmond, "Catch the Error: C++ Exception Handling," *Computer Language*, October 1992, pp. 63–77.

LEE, P.A., "Exception Handling in C Programs," *Software — Practice & Experience*, Vol. 13, 1983, pp. 389–405.

MILLER, W.M., "Error Handling in C++," *Computer Language*, May 1988, pp. 43–52.

MILLER, W.M., "Exception Handling Without Language Support," *USENIX C++ Conference Proceedings*, Denver, Colorado, USENIX Press, 1988.

VIDAL, Carlos, "Exception Handling," *C Users Journal*, Vol. 10, No. 9, September 1992, pp. 19–28.

WINROTH, Harald, "Exception Handling in ANSI C," Computational Vision and Active Perception Laboratory (CVAP), Royal Institute of Technology (KTH), Stockholm, Sweden (available via FTP to `ftp.bion.kth.se` in directory `cvap/2.0` as file `exception-1.2.tar.Z`).

8.12 Extensions

1. Improve on Horsmeier's macro library by:

    (a) using Winroth's method of run-time errors for bad `return` statements; and
    (b) using Amsterdam's stack allocation of `jmp_buf` variables.

2. Improve Vidal's method by using Bengtsson's C++ popper class idiom.

3. Develop a library using Winroth's exception domains with nested `struct` definitions, but using a syntax similar to ANSI C++ rather than the "large" macro method.

4. Investigate methods of destroying automatic objects during stack unwinding, such as Bengtsson's resource class idiom for improvement of Vidal's Lex-script method.

5. Investigate the use of filters such as `sed`, `awk`, or `perl` for use with exception libraries; compare their effectiveness with Vidal's Lex-script method.

6. [Hard] Design an exception handling library that uses a general run-time type information system supporting exception hierarchies.

Chapter 9

Reliable C++ coding

9.1 Handling C++ new operator failure

The C++ memory allocation operator new has similar behavior to malloc when memory is exhausted. The default behavior is for new to return zero (i.e., NULL) whenever it cannot allocate enough dynamic memory. However, the programmer can use the set_new_handler library function declared in <new.h> to specify a function that is called when new can find no free memory.

Typically the set_new_handler function is called in initialization code in main. This will automatically cause every use of the new operator (except when new is overloaded for a particular class) to call this function on allocation failure. The simplest action is to terminate gracefully:

```
#include <iostream.h>
#include <stdlib.h>
#include <new.h>          // declare set_new_handler()

void memory_handler()
{
    cerr << "Internal error: out of dynamic memory\n";
    exit(EXIT_FAILURE);
}

main()
{
    set_new_handler(&memory_handler);
    // .. the rest of the program
}
```

9.1.1 Finding more memory

If the programmer knows where to find it, the handler function can deallocate some memory using delete to make more memory available to new. In this case, the handler function makes the memory available for new by delete'ing it and simply returns (rather than calling exit). If the handler returns, the new operator will keep trying to find memory and will call the handler again and again if it cannot find any more memory. Therefore, carelessly returning from a handler will cause an infinite loop.

119

Unfortunately, such an advanced strategy of finding more memory to use is often not available. In special cases, the program might be using a data structure based on allocated memory that it can deallocate and then use a less memory-intensive approach. For example, a data structure using an allocated cache could deallocate that memory and use a slower, noncached scheme. A toy example of a class with a cache is shown below:

```
//-----------------------------------------------------
// Memory allocation with cache
// When short of memory, caching is abandoned
//   and the memory used for the cache is freed
//-----------------------------------------------------

#include <iostream.h>
#include <stdlib.h>   // declare exit() etc
#include <new.h>      // declare set_new_handler()

//-----------------------------------------------------

class Obj {
 private:
    enum { FALSE = 0, TRUE = 1, CACHE_SIZE = 1000 };
    static Obj *cache;   // cache of objects
    char x[1000];
 public:
    static void init_cache() { cache = new Obj[CACHE_SIZE]; }
    static int free_cache();
};

Obj *Obj::cache = NULL;   // initialize static data member

//-----------------------------------------------------

int Obj::free_cache(void)
{
    if (cache != NULL) {
        delete [] cache;   // free the cache
        cache = NULL;      // clear the cache pointer
        return TRUE;       // freed cache
    }
    else                   // cache == NULL
        return FALSE;      // cache already freed or never set up
}

//-----------------------------------------------------
// Handler to be installed by set_new_handler
//-----------------------------------------------------

void my_new_handler()
{
    cerr << "My new handler executing..\n";
    if (Obj::free_cache())
        cerr << "Warning, low memory, freeing cache!\n";
    else {   // cache has already been freed
        cerr << "Out of memory, cache already free.\n";
        exit(EXIT_FAILURE);
    }
}
```

Another advanced idea for reclaiming memory is to implement a garbage collector that is used to find more memory whenever new fails, but that is beyond the scope of this book.

Even if more memory can be reclaimed there are still difficulties. One major problem is a limitation of the handler mechanism — it is impossible to determine (portably) how many bytes are required to satisfy the failing allocation request. The handler function must reclaim memory with no idea of how much is required.

9.2 Hierarchical use of set_new_handler functions

If we require different handling actions for allocation failure for different parts of the program, the problem of maintaining the `set_new_handler` function becomes more complicated. An inelegant possibility is to still use a single handler function, which determines what actions are required. However, this idea is impracticable because it destroys the independence of different modules. It is therefore better to install different handlers for subparts of the program.

The simplest method of using multiple handlers in a hierarchical manner is to install them on entry, and restore the old handler on exit. This can be achieved by using the "old handler function" return value of `set_new_handler` as follows:

```
void some_function()
{
    typedef void (*ptr_to_fn)();
    ptr_to_fn old = set_new_handler(&local_handler);
    // ... do the work
    (void)set_new_handler(old);    // restore old handler
}
```

Note that in ANSI C++, each local handler would throw an exception (after any appropriate cleanup) that would be caught by the module's top-level `try`/`catch` block.

The above method of paired `set_new_handler` calls around code requiring a particular sequence of code has a few limitations. First, it is cumbersome to use and therefore error-prone. Second, an ANSI C++ exception thrown in the code block will by-pass the second `set_new_handler` call, and not restore the old handler.

To overcome both these limitations, we define a new class called `Handle_New` for installing allocation failure handlers. The class declaration is shown below:

```
#include <new.h>  // declare set_new_handler()

class Handle_New {
  private:
    typedef void (*ptr_to_fn)();
    ptr_to_fn old_fn;
    Handle_New();    // disallow zero-argument constructor
    Handle_New(const Handle_New&); // disable copy constructor
    operator=(const Handle_New&);  // disable = operator
  public:
    Handle_New(ptr_to_fn f) { old_fn = set_new_handler(f); }
    ~Handle_New() { (void)set_new_handler(old_fn); }
};
```

A constructor installs the handler and the destructor restores the old one. The destructor ensures that ANSI C++ exceptions cannot corrupt the process and with that the second objection is overcome. The first objection about the method being cumbersome is also overcome because the new handler installation method is very simple: declare a local automatic variable passing the function as an argument:

```
void some_function()
{
    Handle_New temp(&local_handler);
    // ... do the work
}
```

The name of the local automatic variable does not matter because it is only a "dummy" object that is never used explicitly; only its construction and destruction are important. The variable name could even be the same for all uses of the class in different scopes.

The method is not even limited to function-level scope; different handlers can be installed in inner scopes or even in the same sequence of statements, simply by declaring another local automatic variable. The destruction of local variables in reverse order to their construction ensures the correct order of restoration of the handler. However, care must be taken if the method is used in this manner, because a variable's scope is sometimes counterintuitive; if in doubt, use braces to create a new block around the variable declaration that extends to the point where the old handler must be restored.

9.2.1 Throwing exceptions and set_new_handler

The simplest method of handling new failure in ANSI C++ is to use the inherently hierarchical nature of ANSI C++ exceptions. The handler function for allocation failure will not perform any cleanup but will merely throw an exception, such as:

```
class NEW_FAILURE { } ;   // exception class

void throw_new_failure()
{
    throw NEW_FAILURE();
}
```

This function is installed by set_new_handler at the start of program execution, such as in the main function. Handling allocation failure in a hierarchical manner is then a matter of using catch blocks with the appropriate cleanup statements at the appropriate design levels:

```
try {
  // .. do the work
}
catch (NEW_FAILURE) {
  // .. handle allocation failure
}
```

Note that although the "throw in handler function" ANSI C++ method is usually preferred to the Handle_New class, the latter may still be useful in ANSI C++ if any of the handlers attempt to reclaim memory and retry the allocation. Having one handler attempting to work out what memory can be reclaimed is difficult to implement. It is better to install local handlers in a hierarchical manner via the Handle_New class.

Note that the same considerations apply when using the longjmp-based exception macro libraries of Chapter 8 with pre-ANSI C++. In a manner analogous to ANSI C++ exception handling, the inherent hierarchy of these macro calls is often preferable to the use of the Handle_New class idiom. In this case, the new failure handler function installed by set_new_handler will simply call longjmp (hidden behind a macro), and an earlier setjmp call (also hidden behind a macro) will handle the failure.

9.2.2 Testing new's return value for NULL

In some situations it may be simplest to test whether the return value of the new operator is NULL, rather than have a handler function called. Testing the return value allows lower-level allocation failure handling than the handler function method; it is also analogous to the traditional handling of malloc failure, and the program may already contain an allocation failure handling system based on testing for NULL pointers.

This is simple if the program never installs any handlers using set_new_handler. The default behavior of new for allocation failure is to return NULL. Thus if the program has never installed a handler, there is no difficulty in testing new for NULL return values. The issues are similar to those discussed in Section 10.1 for checking malloc return values.

However, even if the program does use handlers, it may be occasionally desirable to examine the return value of a particular allocation so as to perform specific recovery. To examine the return value of new we must first remove any existing handler. Installing NULL as the handler will cause no handler function to be called for allocation failure and new will return NULL if it fails. As mentioned above, NULL is the default handler at program startup. The simplest method of installing NULL for a single statement (or sequence of statements) is to use the fact that set_new_handler returns the address of the old handler function:

```
typedef void (*ptr_to_fn)();
ptr_to_fn old = set_new_handler(NULL);   // remove old handler
char *p = new char[100];
set_new_handler(old);           // reinstate old handler
if (p == NULL) {
        // .. Out of memory; deal with it here
}
```

The Handle_New class idiom in Section 9.2 can also be used to test the new return value for NULL, simply by installing NULL as the handler. If a single allocation statement is to be NULL-tested rather than using a handler, simply place a block around the allocation statement and declare a block-local Handle_New object with NULL as the constructor argument:

```
{ Handle_New temp(NULL);    // remove existing handler
  x = new char[100];
}   // old handler reinstated here by destructor
  if (x == NULL) {
     // .. handle new failure
  }
```

9.3 Coding your own set_malloc_handler function

The standard C memory allocation library does not support a handler similar to the standard C++ set_new_handler method for the new operator, and always returns NULL for allocation failure. However, we can define our own library of wrapper functions for malloc, calloc, and realloc that do support this idiom; the wrapper functions are called by redefining the names using #define such as:

```
#define malloc(x)    handled_malloc(x)
```

A limited form of such a library supporting only malloc and calloc has been presented in directory chap9 as the files "mallhand.c" and "mallhand.h" on the source disk. The malloc wrapper with support for the handler is shown below:

```
void *handled_malloc(size_t n)
{
    void * ret = malloc(n);    /* call the real malloc */
    if (ret == NULL && malloc_handler != NULL) {
        do {
            (*malloc_handler)();   /* call handler */
            ret = malloc(n);       /* call malloc again */
        } while (ret == NULL);     /* until found some */
    }
    return ret;    /* non-NULL or else no handler */
}
```

This follows the C++ new operator's style of repeatedly calling the handler until memory can be allocated. This style can lead to infinite loops, and since we are coding the library ourselves, we are in a position to change it; a number of choices are discussed in the extensions at the end of the chapter.

The main limitation of this technique is its use of macros to intercept calls to malloc and calloc. This requires source code access to all files (which must #include a header file) and does not permit allocation failure in third-party object code libraries to be handled. However, interception at link-time is difficult to do portably, as discussed in Section 3.5.

This library offers a simple manner of calling a user-specified function for allocation failure with C style memory allocation. The major advantage of this style is consistency with the C++ style of allocation failure handling, allowing most of the discussion about using the C++ set_new_handler standard library function also to apply to our new function set_malloc_handler.

9.3.1 Using the same handler for malloc and new

The previous section has shown how to handle C and C++ allocation failure in a similar manner. The obvious generalization is to use the same handler functions for both new and malloc failure.

The simplest method is merely to convert all malloc/calloc allocation requests to use new. Thus the handler for new failure will be called for malloc failure, simply because new is doing the allocating. Various methods of converting C functions to C++ allocation operators are discussed in the next section.

If we wish to use different handlers for `malloc` and `new` failure, but still have the same set of functions being usable by both, then the issue is more complicated: we must still maintain the `set_malloc_handler` function of the previous section. For the same handler to be effective, it is desirable that both `new` and `malloc` schemes use the same form of allocation. If the same scheme is not used by `malloc` and `free`, there is very little possibility of usefully reclaiming unused memory (i.e., the handler would have to try to reclaim *two* different types of allocated memory). For this reason the implementation in source disk file "chap9/mallhand.cc" converts `malloc/free` requests into C++ new/delete requests. However, note that it removes the existing new handler so that the C++ allocation handlers are not used for C allocation failure. The `handled_malloc` wrapper function becomes:

```
void *handled_malloc(size_t n)
{
    void * ret;
    ptr_to_fn old;

    old = set_new_handler(NULL);   // remove handler
    ret = ::new unsigned char[n];
    (void)set_new_handler(old);   // restore old handler
    if (ret == NULL && malloc_handler != NULL) {
        do {
            (*malloc_handler)();   // call handler
            old = set_new_handler(NULL);   // remove handler
            ret = ::new unsigned char[n];
            (void)set_new_handler(old);   // restore old handler
        } while (ret == NULL);   // until found some
    }
    return ret;   // non-NULL or else no handler
}
```

Unfortunately, this version does not work with my version of g++ under UNIX, because the new operator seems to report an error message when failure occurs and there is no handler; it should simply return NULL. Thus the calls to the `::new` operator with `set_new_handler(NULL)` as the statement before it, do not return NULL for failure. However, the implementation given above should work in a standard-conforming C++ implementation.

9.4 Converting C's malloc/free to C++'s new/delete

Occasionally it may be desirable to convert all the `malloc` family of operations in a C++ program to use `new` and `delete` instead. This choice may be prompted by reasons such as efficiency (the C++ operators may be faster) or reliability (to avoid errors from mixing C and C++ allocated blocks).

The simplest method of converting C allocation to C++ is to write wrapper functions that use `new` and `delete` and `#define` the C allocation function names to call the wrapper functions. However, this suffers from the inefficiency of an extra function call, and requires an object code library linked in.

A more efficient method that overcomes both of these disadvantages is to use preprocessor macros for the C functions. The header file to perform the change is shown below:

```
#include <string.h>  /* declare memset */
#include <stddef.h>  /* declare size_t */

#undef malloc
#undef free
#undef calloc
#undef realloc

    // used to avoid multiple occurrences of macro parameters
static size_t cplus_calloc_size;
    // temporary to hold return value
static void * cplus_calloc_ret;

#define malloc(x)    ((void*)(::new unsigned char[x]))
#define free(ptr)    (::delete[] (ptr))
#define calloc(x,y)  ((void*)(cplus_calloc_size=(x)*(y), \
        cplus_calloc_ret = ::new unsigned char[cplus_calloc_size], \
        (cplus_calloc_ret? \
            memset(cplus_calloc_ret, 0, cplus_calloc_size) : 0), \
        cplus_calloc_ret))
// Impossible to do realloc portably;  can't find old block size
#define realloc(x,y)  (cerr << "ERROR: realloc not supported\n")
```

The only difficulty is that `realloc` cannot be portably mimicked using either macros or wrapper functions, unless care is taken to record allocated blocks and their sizes. The size of the existing block cannot be portably discovered, and it is required in the macro to determine how much of the old block to copy to the new block.

Note that the conversion of C allocation to C++ occurs at the source code level rather than the object code level, and cannot be easily changed for third-party object code libraries.

The reverse change of `new` and `delete` to use C allocation features is easily achieved at link level by overloading the global `new` and `delete` operators, as shown for the C++ allocation debugging libraries.

9.5 Constructor failure

One of the most difficult reliability problems to deal with is a constructor that fails to fully construct an object. For example, allocation might fail for an object requiring dynamic memory, or a file required by an object might not open. The solution in ANSI C++ is straightforward — throw an exception. However, until exceptions arrive, we must use some other alternative; some of the most common methods are:

- `longjmp` out using a macro library (see Chapter 8).
- Set a status bit in the object, and inspect it after construction.
- Do very little in the constructor; provide a member function for initialization.

There isn't much to say about the `longjmp` method that isn't covered in Chapter 8; handling constructor failure just becomes part of the overall exception handling scheme. However, the other methods are more involved.

9.5.1 Using a status field for constructor failure

The use of a status bit in an object is a very common technique, which is general in application, but quite cumbersome to use. The basic idea is to use a status data member in each object that indicates its current "state." The constructor sets the status bit to "good" only when the object is fully constructed; thus the class declaration and constructor look similar to:

```
class Obj {
    private:
        enum { GOOD = 1, BAD = 0 };
        int status;     // status nonstatic data member
    // .... rest of the class
};

Obj::Obj()
{
    status = BAD;
    // ... rest of the constructor
    status = GOOD;
}
```

Note that if construction fails in some way, it is usually the constructor's responsibility to handle the failure. For example, if an object requires two blocks of memory, and the second allocation fails, the constructor should deallocate the first memory block (and set the pointer to NULL for safety!). An alternative is examined a little further below, whereby the constructor simply initializes data members to NULL at the start of construction, and the destructor checks them before destroying them.

Also required for this status field method is a boolean "inspector" method to examine the status of an object. A typical definition would be a small inline function:

```
    public:
        int Bad() { return status == BAD; }
```

This method is used in at least two ways: (1) inside the class members to prevent operations on bad objects; and (2) outside the class for exception handling by users of the class.

First, Bad can be used by other class methods to ensure they don't operate on badly constructed objects. Other member functions should test the status to ensure the object is valid. If it is not valid, they can either perform a no-op or raise a more serious objection such as an error message or an abort call. The use of an error message (especially during the development phase) helps catch instances where a bad object has not been properly handled by the exception handling code surrounding *uses* of the objects. The destructor is a special case that probably should perform a no-op rather than report an error, because it is difficult to avoid calling the destructor on bad objects (e.g., bad local objects will have the destructor called when the corresponding scope is exited, and dynamic objects will have their destructor called when `delete` is called as part of the usual exception handling process). Thus a typical no-op destructor is:

```
Obj::~Obj()
{
    if (Bad()) return;  // no-operation
    // .. rest of the destructor
}
```

As an alternative to a no-op, the destructor could check the status of internal members before destroying them. For example, before applying `fclose` to a `FILE*` pointer (which is a data member), the destructor can check whether the pointer is `NULL`. Similarly, before applying `delete` to a pointer member it should be checked for a `NULL` value (actually deleting `NULL` is a valid no-op in ANSI C++, but it is still advisable to avoid it for portability to older C++ versions). Note that when this method is used, it becomes the responsibility of the constructor to ensure that these data members are correctly initialized to ensure that either they are `NULL` or point to a valid file pointer (for `fclose`) or a valid block of dynamic memory (for `delete`). The constructor initializations of these data members must occur before any constructor code that could possibly fail, so as to avoid uninitialized pointers. Thus a typical constructor and destructor pair may become:

```
Obj::Obj()
{
    status = BAD;
    file_ptr = NULL;   // initialize class data members
    data_ptr = NULL;   // avoids noninitialized pointers
    // ... rest of the constructor
    status = GOOD;
}
Obj::~Obj()
{
    if (file_ptr != NULL) fclose(file_ptr);
    if (data_ptr != NULL) delete data_ptr;
}
```

9.5.2 Testing for successful object construction

The second use of the `Bad` member function is to test for successful construction after the declaration of an object outside the class. Upon unsuccessful construction of an object, the constructor should have handled the failure as best it could, but there will usually be extra processing that the user code must attend to. Thus a typical automatic object declaration becomes:

```
Obj x;
if (x.Bad()) {
  // ... handle failure
}
```

and a typical dynamic allocation of an object becomes:

```
Obj *y = new Obj;
if (y->Bad()) {
    delete y;
    y = NULL;
    // ... handle failure
}
```

Note that one interesting possibility when using a status field is to make all member operations a no-op for badly constructed objects. This is the method used by `<iostream.h>` for its stream objects. It has the advantage of needing no user code in some instances, but can also make detection of failures more difficult as later code may fail as a result.

9.5.3 Using an initialization member instead of a constructor

It isn't possible to return a value from a constructor. This is unfortunate, as returning a status value is a very common method of handling exceptions. Furthermore, the alternative use of a status field is not space-efficient, wasting space in every object. Hence a brute-force alternative is to have the constructor perform very little processing, and delegate any parts that may fail to a separate initialization member function. This initialization function returns a status value to indicate failure. Thus, the method of constructing an automatic object becomes:

```
Obj x;
if (!x.Init()) {
    // ... handle "construction" failure
}
```

Dynamic allocation of an object can use a similar form:

```
Obj *y = new Obj;
if (!y->Init()) {
    delete y;
    y = NULL;
    // ... handle failure
}
```

Note that the destructor must be carefully defined when using this `Init` technique. It is difficult to avoid calling the destructor on a badly formed object (e.g., the `delete` operation above calls the destructor), and the destructor should ensure it never deallocates a bad address (or does some other form of mischief). Hence it is a good idea to have the constructor set all pointer data members to `NULL` rather than leaving them in a possibly uninitialized state. The destructor can then test for `NULL` before deallocation.

An alternative to calling `Init` for dynamically allocated objects is to provide a `static` member function to allocate dynamic instances of a class. This function merely passes any arguments along to the constructor in its internal call to the `new` operator. If there are multiple constructors, then overloaded versions of this `static` member function should exist, one for each constructor. An example of such a `static` member function without arguments is:

```
Obj* Obj::Alloc()    // NOTE: this is a static member function
{
    Obj* temp = new Obj;   // call constructor here
    if (temp != NULL && !temp->Init()) {
        // handle construction failure
        delete temp;
        temp = NULL;
    }
    return temp;
}
```

The main advantage of this method is that the user code need not deallocate the memory on construction failure. A test for failure becomes a test for a NULL pointer and construction failure handling can be combined with memory allocation failure handling (i.e., unless allocation failure is handled elsewhere by set_new_handler). Instead of calling the new operator, a dynamic object is allocated using the static member function Alloc:

```
Obj *z = Obj::Alloc();
if (z == NULL) {
    // ... handle failure
}
```

In summary, the technique of an explicit initialization method is cumbersome in that the automatic initialization of objects via constructors is circumvented, and the programmer must remember to initialize every object explicitly. However, it is more space-efficient than using a status field, and is no worse than the status field method in that it requires explicit tests of a member function's return value (i.e., the bad function for the status field idiom, and the Init function for this method).

9.6 Catching array bounds errors using classes

Since array indices out of bounds are not usually caught in C++ implementations, it can be useful to catch them explicitly. One method of doing so is to define a "safe array" class, which is used for array variables, instead of the usual method. Before diving into the details of this method, note that overall it's probably more worthwhile to find a compiler or debugging tool that finds these errors automatically.

9.6.1 Safe arrays using templates

Templates make it possible to allow all types and dimensions, permitting an almost exact mapping from ordinary arrays to safe arrays. The syntax for declaring an array has changed, but the same information is still required. An example of the usage method is:

```
SafeArray<int,10> data;   // int data[10];
int i = -1;
int x = data[i];          // run-time error!
```

The implementation of safe arrays using templates is as follows:

```
#include <iostream.h>
#include <stdlib.h>

void BOUNDS_ERROR(int,int);

template <class T, int size>
class SafeArray {
   private:
      T arr[size];
      void operator = (...);          // disallow assignment
      SafeArray(SafeArray<T,size> &);  // disallow copying
   public:
      SafeArray() { }    // nothing
      ~SafeArray() { }   // nothing
      inline T& operator [] (int index);
};

//----------------------------------------------------
// Overloaded [] operator with bounds checking
//----------------------------------------------------

template <class T, int size>
inline T& SafeArray<T,size>::operator [] (int index)
{
    if (index < 0 || index >= size)
        BOUNDS_ERROR(index, size);
    return arr[index];
}

//----------------------------------------------------
// Bounds error has occurred - report it.
//----------------------------------------------------

void BOUNDS_ERROR(int index, int size)
{
    if (index < 0) {
        cerr << "ERROR: SafeArray index less than zero ["
             << index << "]\n";
    }
    else if (index >= size) {
        cerr << "ERROR: SafeArray index out of bounds - "
             << index << " should be strictly < " << size << "\n";
    }
    exit(EXIT_FAILURE);
}
```

Naturally, the efficiency of safe arrays is less than than of ordinary arrays because of the extra checking. Note that the [] operator is a small inline function to avoid the inefficiency of a function call for each array access, except when an error is detected.

The [] operator calls a function to handle errors to avoid the wasted code space that would occur if the error reporting were performed inside the [] operator body. Note also that BOUNDS_ERROR is a global function rather than a static member function, to avoid the space wastage of having multiple copies of the function for each template type. Naturally, there are many alternatives to this use of a global function for handling the failure; for example, in ANSI C++ we would throw an exception.

The private declarations of the = operator and copy constructor should prevent assignments of arrays, which are now possible for safe arrays, because they are class objects. This is intended to provide compatibility between safe arrays and ordinary arrays. The declarations could be removed if these safe array copying operations were desirable!

One possibility for improving efficiency is a preprocessor macro for declaring arrays that uses safe arrays in the development phase and ordinary arrays in the production code:

```
#ifdef PRODUCTION
#define ARRAY(type,size,name)      type name[size]
#else
#define ARRAY(type,size,name)      SafeArray<type,size> name
#endif
```

For commonly used types, we can use `typedef` to require safe arrays or unsafe arrays. Again, we can use conditional compilation to choose the method:

```
#ifdef PRODUCTION
    typedef char *string[STR_LEN];
#else
    typedef SafeArray<char,STR_LEN> string;
#endif
```

Unfortunately, there are a few semantic differences between the two forms of array declarations that make this approach dangerous. For example, safe arrays are class objects passed by value, whereas ordinary arrays are passed by reference; another difference is that safe arrays have very reduced affinity with pointers. Nevertheless, if the operations on an array are restricted, this technique may be useful.

9.6.2 Safe multidimensional arrays

Extending this technique to multidimensional arrays is a more difficult problem, because there is no way to overload groups of [] operations as a single operator. The use of a 2-dimensional array such as `arr[i][j]` must be dealt with as two 1-dimensional array operations — `arr[i]` followed by `[j]` applied to the result. Therefore, the first [] operator must return a class object to allow overloading of the second [] operator.

One method of declaring 2-dimensional safe arrays is as follows. The first [] operation returns a "dummy" object, which is really a pointer to the relevant 1-dimensional subarray, and the second [] operation returns a reference to the correct array element. A simple implementation of a safe 2-dimensional array using this technique is provided in file "`chap9/safe_mul.cc`" on the source code disk. The extension of this technique to 3-dimensional arrays requires another level of dummy object definition, and is not discussed further here for obvious reasons.

9.6.3 Code size problems with templates

Unfortunately, the C++ template mechanism is not really very smart, and the use of a constant integer as a template parameter is not usually handled by the compiler in the manner we would wish. The problem is the generation of multiple member function definitions for each different array size. Array declarations of size 10 and 20 will create two different function definitions, even if they are the same type array. Naturally, we require different functions for different types, but it isn't hard to see that one function per size would suffice. Unfortunately, the compiler cannot see this and there is the danger of duplicated code space. The declaration of `inline` functions is helpful, but only a partial solution, as the compiler may arbitrarily decide not to inline certain functions. Hence, the code size should be monitored carefully when using safe array templates.

9.7 Catching bad pointers to classes

Uses of bad objects, which typically occur via uninitialized or wayward pointers, can be caught by adding some debugging code to each class. We will discuss one method of achieving this by clever use of the inheritance features of C++ classes. Note that our method has the important feature that it can be "compiled out" of production code simply by defining PRODUCTION as a macro name. The errors that can be caught by this technique include:

- uninitialized pointers to objects
- wayward/corrupted pointers to objects
- pointers to already deallocated/destroyed objects
- double destruction of objects (usually from double delete of object pointer)
- temporary objects used after destruction

The implementation of the debugging base class is given below. It consists of a single header file that defines a single class and a few macros to aid in using the class.

```
//--------------------------------------------------------------------
// BADCLASS.H:   Header file for class debugging
//    Errors found:   (1) Objects used after destruction
//                    (2) Bad pointers to objects (e.g., uninitialized)
//--------------------------------------------------------------------

#include <iostream.h>

#ifdef PRODUCTION
     // remove checking from production code
#define USE_DEBUG_CLASS   /* nothing */
#define DEBUG_CLASS_TEST(s)    /* nothing */
#else
#define USE_DEBUG_CLASS   : public DebugClass
#define DEBUG_CLASS_TEST(s)   DebugClass::TEST((s), __FILE__, __LINE__)
#endif

class DebugClass {
   enum { MAGIC_VALUE = -55 };
   private:
     int active;
     int magic;
   public:
     void TEST(char *method = "(Unknown)",
              char *file = "(Unknown)", int line = 0)
     {
         if (magic != MAGIC_VALUE) {
             cerr << "File '" << file << "', Line " << line
                 << ", Method '" << method
                 << "' used on bad object (bad magic value)\n";
         }
         else if (active != 1) {
             cerr << "File '" << file << "', Line " << line
                 << ", Method '" << method
                 << "' used on previously destroyed object\n";
         }
     }
     DebugClass() { magic = MAGIC_VALUE;   active = 1; }
     ~DebugClass() { TEST("Destructor",__FILE__, __LINE__); active=0;}
};
```

To catch bad objects, we will maintain a data member containing a "magic value" in the class, so that any uninitialized or bad object addresses will (most likely) have bad magic values. A status flag is also set by the constructor and cleared by the destructor, thus maintaining an indication of whether an object is currently active or has been destroyed. All methods applied to the object must first check the magic value and the status flag to determine whether the object is valid.

The only necessary changes to existing classes are (a) to #include the header file "badclass.h" at the top of the file; (b) to inherit from the debugging class using the USE_DEBUG_CLASS macro; and (c) to add a debugging test statement (using the DEBUG_CLASS_TEST macro) at the start of any class methods being debugged. A typical method of using the extra convenience macros is as follows:

```
class MyClass USE_DEBUG_CLASS {       // macro hides inheritance
   // ...
   public:
      void Print() {
         DEBUG_CLASS_TEST("MyClass::Print");   // use test macro
         // .. body of Print()
      }
   // ...
}
```

The header file will totally remove all the debugging features if the PRODUCTION macro is defined before including "badclass.h".

The implementation shown will print out the filename and line number details of the offending method, but not the details of where the call to the method occurred (which would be more useful). Note that the base class tests the destructor, so there is no need to add an explicit statement to a destructor in a user's class, and double destruction errors are caught without any need for any DEBUG_CLASS_TEST macro calls. However, it may be desirable to use an explicit DEBUG_CLASS_TEST call in the destructor if the debugging class in "badclass.h" is used for debugging multiple classes. The built-in destructor checking will always report the error as occurring in "badclass.h," which gives no indication what type of object caused the problem. To get an error with better details, a DEBUG_CLASS_TEST statement can be added to the start of the destructor in the same manner as for any other method. If this form of explicit calls in the destructor is preferred you may wish to remove the TEST call from the destructor ~DebugClass; otherwise two warnings will appear for a single double destruction error.

Naturally, this idea can be extended in many ways. For example, rather than use one debugging class for all other classes, you could add debugging code to the constructor and destructor of each class, put the testing function as a member of the class being tested, and thereby allow printing out of the object's data upon detected failure.

9.8 Catching NULL dereferences using smart pointers

The idea of "smart pointers" has largely arisen through examination of reference counting and garbage collection. However, the smart pointer idiom offers a simple method of catching both NULL pointer references and uses of uninitialized pointers.

A full implementation of a smart pointer idiom as a template is shown below. Only the pointer declarations need to be changed to use these smart pointers. The pointers are then used in exactly the same way as normal pointers and should not require any special treatment.

```cpp
#include <iostream.h>      // declare NULL
#include <stdlib.h>        // declare exit()

template <class T>
class SmartPtr {
    private:
        T * ptr;        // the real pointer
        void TEST() const
            { if (ptr == NULL) {
                cerr << "SmartPtr Error: NULL pointer dereference\n";
                exit(EXIT_FAILURE);
              }
            }
    public:
        SmartPtr() {  ptr = NULL; }    // default to NULL
        SmartPtr(const SmartPtr<T> &p2)    // copy constructor
            { ptr = p2.ptr; }
        SmartPtr(T *p) {  ptr = p; }  // initialized with address
        SmartPtr(const T *p)           // initialized with address
            {  ptr = (T*)p; }
        const SmartPtr<T>& operator=(const SmartPtr<T> &p)
            {  ptr = p.ptr; return *this; }
        T* operator=(T *p)             // assigned an address
            {  ptr = p; return ptr; }
        T* operator=(const T *p)       // assigned an address
            {  ptr = (T*)p; return ptr; }
        T& operator[](int i)                // array [] operator
            { TEST(); return ptr[i]; }
        const T& operator[](int i) const    // array [] operator
            { TEST(); return ptr[i]; }
        T& operator*()             // unary * (indirection)
            { TEST(); return *ptr; }
        const T& operator*() const    // unary * (indirection)
            { TEST(); return *ptr; }
        T* operator->()               // -> operator (indirection)
            { TEST(); return ptr; }
        const T* operator->() const   // -> operator (indirection)
            { TEST(); return ptr; }
        operator T*()              // conversion to T*
            { return ptr; }
        operator const T*() const    // conversion to T*
            { return ptr; }
        ~SmartPtr() { }              // destructor does nothing
};
```

Because of the inefficiency of the extra testing, it may be desirable to remove the use of smart pointers for the production version. A simple method is to use a `typedef` declaration based on conditional compilation for each pointer type required.

```
#ifdef PRODUCTION
   typedef int * IntPtr;              // ordinary int pointers
#else
   typedef SmartPtr<int> IntPtr;      // smart int pointers
#endif
```

Unfortunately, this requires a disciplined use of `typedef` names by programmers, and will be difficult to introduce into existing code. Nevertheless, the technique offers another means whereby in-code support for pointer error checking is possible. The extensions at the end of the chapter discuss some extra features that could be added to the `SmartPtr` class to increase the number of errors detected.

9.9 Extensions

1.   Modify the `handled_malloc` idea of Section 9.3 to support new features:

> • Only call the failure handler once; avoids infinite loop dangers.
> • Make the failure handler return an `int` for success in finding more memory.
> • Pass line and filename to `handled_malloc` and its handlers.
> • Intercept the `malloc`/`calloc` calls at link-time (difficult).

2.   Design a safe array class that avoids the code space wastage problems of the 2-parameter template method in Section 9.6.1, using a 1-parameter template that accepts the array size as a run-time variable in the constructor. That is, the array declaration becomes:

```
SafeArray<int> arr(10);
```

Unfortunately, this means that memory must be dynamically allocated, leading to slower array construction than the original method that uses stack-allocated memory. However, an advantage is that arrays are truly dynamic because the size need not be known at compile-time.

3.   Modify the `SmartPtr` error-checking class in Section 9.8 to use one bit per pointer to distinguish NULL dereferences from uninitialized pointer uses.

4.   Combine the `SmartPtr` error-checking class in Section 9.8 with a memory debugging library from Chapter 3 to catch extra errors such as:

> • array overruns of heap blocks (e.g., modify the `[]` operator)
> • dereferences of already deallocated memory blocks

5.   Design a safe `Int` class that detects overflow and underflow.

6.   [Hard] Design an entire mathematical library analogous to `<math.h>` with support for `Int`, `Float`, and `Double` classes. When an error is detected, the library should do something more useful than C's method of setting `errno`.

7.   Implement classes analogous to the `Handle_New` class for `set_new_handler` functions (see Section 9.2) to allow elegant hierarchical installation of the following handlers for exceptional conditions:

- `set_terminate` ANSI C++ exception handler functions
- `set_unexpected` ANSI C++ exception handler functions
- `signal` handler functions
- `malloc` failure (using the wrapper function idea)

Can one class be conveniently used for all handlers? Note that we won't want to install different handlers for every condition at every level — that is, we may wish to change only the `set_new_handler` at one level, or change all at another level.

8.   Make the pointer-to-object debugging class in Section 9.7 more space-efficient by combining the magic value and status variables into a single `char` variable. The status value needs only 1 bit, and the rest of the bits can contain the magic value.

9.   [Difficult] Improve the pointer-to-object debugging class in Section 9.7 so that it has different magic values for different classes. At present, the debugging class will not detect an error for methods of one class applied to the address of an object of a different class. Naturally, the technique must be hidden behind a macro for easy removal from production code.

   Note that I'm not sure how this can be done without using multiple debugging base classes. One attempt that partially fails is to pass the magic value to the base class constructor from all constructors of the class being debugged:

```
MyClass() : DebugClass(777) { ... }
```

Unfortunately, using this method, the debugging class does not know what magic value to check for and the `DEBUG_CLASS_TEST` macro must be changed to pass this magic value.

10.   Extend the methods of constructor failure handling in Section 9.5 to allow the cause of the failure to be stored in some manner. For example, the status field could contain more than two possible values.

11.   Provide a definition of the `Alloc` member function in Section 9.5.3 for allocation of arrays of objects.

Chapter 10

Reliable C coding

10.1 Handling malloc failure

One of the most common forms of exception that a program must handle correctly is running out of allocated heap memory. In the C library this is indicated by a NULL return value from malloc or calloc. For simplicity of exposition, this section will examine the options for handling failure of malloc; both calloc and realloc can be handled in an analogous manner.

The most common method of handling malloc failure is to always test the return value against NULL, such as:

```
p = malloc(100);
if (p == NULL) {
    /* .. handle the problem .. */
}
```

A slightly simpler method is to use a macro to perform the test and handle any detected failure, such as to call a handler function as shown in the following example:

```
#define malloc_test(ptr) ((ptr) == NULL ? malloc_handler() : 0)
    ...
p = malloc(100);
malloc_test(p);
```

However, either style of manually testing the return value is repetitive and therefore error-prone, and there are a variety of methods of automating the process, which we now discuss.

10.1.1 Avoiding tests of the malloc return value

If the required method of handling allocation failure is the same for the entire program, this simplifies the problem. For example, if program termination or a longjmp call is all that is required, then there are a number of alternatives for detecting malloc failure automatically. Once allocation failure is detected, a handler function can be called that then either terminates or calls longjmp.

One method of detecting allocation failure is to never call `malloc` or `calloc` directly, but instead to call them via a "wrapper" function. Such a wrapper for `malloc` is given below:

```
#include <stddef.h>    /* declare size_t */
#include <stdlib.h>    /* declare malloc */
#include <stdio.h>

void* my_malloc(size_t n)
{
    void *p = malloc(n);
    if (p == NULL) {
        fprintf(stderr,"Internal error: malloc failure\n");
        exit(EXIT_FAILURE);
    }
    return p;
}
```

This requires the programmer to habitually call `my_malloc` rather than `malloc`. Alternatively, such a change could be introduced into existing code that calls `malloc` by by placing a preprocessor macro in a global definitions header file:

```
#define malloc  my_malloc
```

A slightly better method would be to use a macro to indicate the line and file of the failed call. The macro definition of `malloc` becomes:

```
#define malloc(n)  my_malloc(n, __LINE__, __FILE__)
```

The definition of `my_malloc` is only slightly changed to accept two more arguments:

```
#include <stddef.h>    /* declare size_t */
#include <stdlib.h>    /* declare malloc */
#include <stdio.h>

void* my_malloc(size_t n, long int line, char *file)
{
    void *p = malloc(n);
    if (p == NULL) {
        fprintf(stderr, "Internal error: malloc failure: ");
        fprintf(stderr, "line %ld, file '%s'\n", line, file);
        exit(EXIT_FAILURE);
    }
    return p;
}
```

The above functions simply print a message to `stderr` and exit when a failure is detected. Naturally, there are other alternatives, such as a `longjmp` to a block of "recovery" code or logging the error in a log file.

The main disadvantage of such wrapper functions around `malloc` and `calloc` is that they handle all `malloc` failures in the same way, and do not allow each call to `malloc` to handle the failure in a separate way. Some calls to `malloc` are not crucial, and a block of code can test the return value of `malloc` to determine whether the block was allocated. For example, if an algorithm is trying to allocate a block of memory as temporary storage to use a fast algorithm, it might be able to detect `malloc` failure and use a less efficient algorithm instead:

```
char *block;
    ...
block = malloc(BYTES_NEEDED);
if (block != NULL) {
        /* fast algorithm using allocated block */
}
else {
        /* slower algorithm NOT using allocated block */
}
```

Therefore, there is a choice between calling wrapper functions for easy handling, and having the flexibility to handle `malloc` failure at each call. Consequently, it may not be desirable to `#define` the names `malloc` and `calloc`, but instead to directly call `my_malloc` and `my_calloc` when the "graceful termination" behavior is required.

10.1.2 Another preprocessing trick for malloc failure

Another preprocessor macro method to automatically check for a NULL return value from `malloc` (indicating failure to allocate memory) is given below. The action on failure in the macro given is to call a function that handles the exception, such as by printing a message and exiting, or restarting the program using `longjmp`. The header file for automatic `malloc` failure handling becomes:

```
static void *malloc_tmp;     /* temporary variable */
#undef malloc
#define malloc(n)   \
    ((malloc_tmp = malloc(n)) ? malloc_tmp : \
        (void*)malloc_error((long)__LINE__, __FILE__))
```

The importance of making the temporary variable `static` is that it allows the header file to be included in all files requiring automatic `malloc` testing, and avoids the need to define a global variable in a source library file. Thus all that is required is the header file, with no accompanying source code file or object library.

Defining `malloc` as a macro should work even if `malloc` has already been defined as a macro by the ANSI header files. ANSI always requires a function definition to be hidden behind a macro for a standard library function and thus if `malloc` is defined by `<stdlib.h>` as a macro, it must also hide a function prototype of the same name. The "real" function version of `malloc` is available by using `#undef`.

Note that in C or C++ compilers with a pre-ANSI preprocessor, the definition of the macro in terms of itself is not always possible, and may cause a compilation error. Also the `(void*)` type cast is necessary because the ternary conditional operator's return type depends on both the second and third operand. Moreover, the return value of `malloc_error` cannot be `void`; otherwise the type cast to `void*` would be illegal.

The definition of the `malloc_error` function should be provided in one source file, or in C++ it could be an `inline` function in the same header file.

```
void* malloc_error(long int line, char *file)
{
    fprintf(stderr, "Malloc failure: ");
    fprintf(stderr, "line %ld, in file '%s'\n", line, file);
    exit(EXIT_FAILURE);
}
```

10.2 Library function error return values

The simplest requirement of reliable code is that it should check the return values of library functions to determine whether an error occurred. The main area where this is important in the average program is in the use of file handling functions. Whereas a novice programmer would call `fopen` and assume that the file exists, a professional programmer will check the return value of `fopen` and perform some error handling if it is NULL; the simplest idea is to terminate with a message if the file fails to open:

```
fp = fopen(fname, "r");
if (fp == NULL) {
    fprintf(stderr,"File '%s' failed to open\n", fname);
    perror("The error was");
    exit(EXIT_FAILURE);
}
```

The return value of *all* file I/O functions should be checked; just because a file has opened satisfactorily doesn't mean that other operations will always succeed (e.g., a write may fail if the disk quota has been exceeded, or if the hardware environment has changed). Naturally, file input functions should be tested for failure; this is often done in any case to test for end of file. Some of the I/O functions whose return value should be tested are:

```
fprintf, fscanf,
fgets, fputs,
putc, getc, fputc, fgetc,
fread, fwrite.
```

The `fclose` function returns EOF on error, and a highly reliable program should test for its failure. Admittedly, there isn't much you can do when closing a file fails, except perhaps report the failure to the user.

Other less commonly used file functions that should be tested include:

```
fflush, freopen, vfprintf, vprintf,
ungetc, fseek, ftell, rewind.
```

There are a number of functions for which the return value is usually ignored when it should perhaps be examined in very highly reliable programs. For example, the `printf` function returns an integer value indicating how many characters were output, and −1 on error. One might wonder why `printf` would ever fail, but there are rare conditions under which it can fail when something has gone wrong with `stdout`; try the following code:

```
fclose(stdout);
ret = printf("hello\n");
fprintf(stderr, "ret = %d\n", ret);
```

Thus printf may fail if stdout has accidentally been closed, or if freopen has been used to redirect stdout to a file. Hence a highly reliable program should perhaps check the return value of the printf function. Similarly, functions such as puts and putchar may occasionally fail and should be checked. However, this level of care is unnecessary for most programs.

10.3   Reliable input: avoiding scanf and gets

One of the largest areas of reliability problems is input requests to the user. Human beings tend to stretch a program's ability to handle strange requests, when they intentionally or inadvertently fail to supply the input expected by the program. Some of the worst reliability problems can arise from the use of the scanf and gets library functions. The problem with both of these is that they do not limit the number of characters read into an internal string. Thus a general piece of advice for reliability is:

Don't use gets or scanf.

This can be qualified slightly, although not everyone will agree, to the more moderate statement:

Use fgets and/or sscanf instead of gets or scanf.

However, as I will discuss, my personal recommendation is to avoid using gets, fgets, and scanf by writing your own read_line function, and to use sscanf as rarely as possible.

One way to ensure that scanf and gets are never used in a project is to declare them as macros using compilation options. A typical pair of options would be:

```
-Dscanf=DONT_USE_SCANF   -Dgets=DONT_USE_GETS
```

Thus any use of these functions should be flagged by a linker diagnostic message complaining about undefined functions.

10.3.1 gets versus fgets

Let's examine the gets problem first. The following gets call is highly dangerous because of the absence of any character limit:

```
char s[100], *ret;

ret = gets(s);              /* DANGEROUS */
if (ret == NULL) { ... }
```

If the user types in more than 99 characters, this gets call will overwrite other memory with unpredictable results. The call is not robust, and can even represent a security problem: the use of gets in a common UNIX utility was a means used by hackers to circumvent UNIX security by typing in so many characters that gets overwrote the call stack.

The solution is to use a function that does have a limit on the number of characters written: fgets. The equivalent fgets call is:

```
ret = fgets(s, 100, stdin);
```

Unfortunately, there are differences between gets and fgets, notably that fgets retains the newline in the string read in. This newline can be removed as follows:

```
ret = fgets(s, 100, stdin);
if (ret != NULL) {
    len = strlen(s);
    if (len != 0 && s[len - 1] == '\n')    /* newline ? */
        s[len - 1] = '\0';  /* overwrite with null char */
}
```

The repetitive nature of the newline-removal technique make it a highly error-prone programming practice. Furthermore, when fgets finds a line that is too long, it will leave the unread portion of the line in the input for the next input request to read. This is rarely the desired behavior, and will typically lead to strange results later in the program when more input is requested.

Another problem is that the string is unchanged by fgets when end-of-file is received, and retains its old value. Although a good programmer should never use this string if fgets returns NULL, the potential for error is always there.

For these reasons it is recommended that you write your own read_line function, or its equivalent, to read in an entire line of text, and this is now discussed.

10.3.2 Writing your own read_line function

Presented here is the definition of a function read_line that is similar to fgets, except that it has the following extra reliability features:

• Always reads an entire line (discards unused characters).
• Always discards the end newline.
• String is empty when NULL is returned for end-of-file.

This implementation also has the convenience feature that read_line does not write the characters to the destination string if max is 0. This can be used to skip over a line of input. The source code for the function is:

```
/*----------------------------------------------------*/
/* READ_LINE: like fgets, but always read whole line */
/*----------------------------------------------------*/
char *read_line(char *s, int max, FILE *fp)
{
    int ch, i = 0;

    while ((ch = getc(fp)) != EOF && ch != '\n') {
        if (i < max - 1)
            s[i++] = ch;
    }
    if (max > 0) s[i] = '\0';   /* add terminating null */
    if (ch == EOF && i == 0)
        return NULL;  /* return NULL for end of file */
    return s;
}
```

10.3.3 scanf versus sscanf

The scanf function also has its own problems when reading in strings using the %s format. The following statement represents a reliability error:

```
char s[100];

scanf("%s", s);    /* DANGEROUS */
```

One slightly improved method of avoiding the problem with scanf is to restrict the number of characters to be read by scanf:

```
scanf("%99s", s);    /* BETTER, but error-prone */
```

The problems with this method include the need to hard-code the field limits as integers in the format string, and the fact that unread input remains in the buffer for the next input statement. Thus it is better to use fgets or preferably your own read_line function for string input.

The scanf function can also be considered for use with nonstring formats (i.e., other than the %s or %[..] formats) because other formats do not write an unlimited number of characters. For example, the %d format writes only a single int to the address provided, regardless of how many input characters are processed. However, there are many difficulties in covering all the cases (especially regarding whitespace skipping) and it is generally best to avoid the problem and use fgets combined with sscanf instead.

Naturally, using sscanf has its own set of difficulties. The return value must be tested to determine whether all conversions have been processed correctly, or whether there has been some error. Furthermore, if the format is so complicated that a single format string does not suffice, then it is difficult to keep track of the "current position" in the string — a second successive sscanf call does not automatically start where the previous call left off.

Because of these difficulties with the functions in the scanf family, it is often better to write your own input handling routine based on character-by-character input. sscanf could be called to handle conversion of a single integer or floating-point constant, but only after the input function has identified them as a token and read in all the relevant characters. However, even in this case you can probably use atoi, atol, or atof instead of sscanf.

10.4 Reliable strings: strcpy versus strncpy

A common issue in reliability is ensuring that character strings are null-terminated and limited to a fixed length. For example, how reliable is the following code fragment:

```
char s[20];

strcpy(s, s2);   /* how long is s2? */
```

If the length of s2 is greater than 19 the strcpy statement will cause an error. Of course, we can guarantee that the string isn't that long, right? Perhaps, but if we are relying on some other program component, it may be better to use "mutual suspicion" and not assume that the string is short enough. (During development, an assertion regarding the string length is probably in order, but this may not be satisfactory for the production version because termination via a failed assertion doesn't really exhibit the quality of "fault tolerance.")

For these reasons, it may be better to use `strncpy` to restrict the number of characters copied:

```
strncpy(s, s2, 20);
```

However, `strncpy` has a hidden danger in that it will leave s without a null-terminator if s2 contains more than 19 characters; in this case it copies exactly 20 characters and does not add a terminating null. Therefore, a safer method of using `strncpy` is to always explicitly add the terminating null after the call:

```
strncpy(s, s2, 20);
s[19] = '\0';
```

However, the need to place this assignment statement after each `strncpy` call is error-prone, and a macro may be better:

```
#define STRNCPY(s, s2, n) \
        ((void)(strncpy((s),(s2),(n)), s[(n)-1] = '\0'))
```

Note that the `(void)` cast prevents the programmer from erroneously using the return value of STRNCPY. If this return value is required, another possible macro definition is:

```
#define STRNCPY(s, s2, n) \
        (strncpy((s),(s2),(n)), s[(n)-1] = '\0', (s))
```

Alternatively, it may be better to write a "safe" version of the `strncpy` function that never leaves the string nonterminated. The version below has similar behavior to `strncpy` that should be satisfactory when using it for null-terminated strings (the reason for ANSI C's definition of `strncpy` is so that it can be used in advanced code for nonterminated strings). The function below copies at most n-1 nonnull characters and adds a terminating null; unlike `strncpy` it does not pad the rest of the destination string with null bytes if the string to be copied is too short, but this behavior isn't of much use for null-terminated strings.

```
void safe_strncpy(char *s, char *s2, int n)
{
    int i;

    for (i = 0; i < n - 1 && s2[i] != '\0'; i++) {
        s[i] = s2[i];
    }
    s[i] = '\0';   /* add terminating null */
}
```

Naturally, a far better solution is to always ensure that strings are shorter than the required length, making all the fuss over string length unnecessary.

10.5 <errno.h> and the errno global variable

Many of the standard library functions report an error by setting the errno variable to a nonzero value. The errno variable is declared as type int in <errno.h>, and can also be converted to a character string error message using the strerror or perror functions, also declared in <errno.h>.

The strerror function returns the address of a string constant referring to the error number. For example, to print out the current error message we can use:

```
printf("Current error message is '%s'\n", strerror(errno));
```

The perror standard library function is a more specialized error message output function. perror(mesg) is functionally equivalent to:

```
fprintf(stderr, "%s: %s\n", mesg, strerror(errno));
```

In some implementations (e.g., some UNIX variants) a few other non-ANSI features are available: sys_errlist is the array of string constants holding the error messages, and sys_nerr is an integer variable representing the number of string constants in the array.

10.5.1 Correct methods of testing errno

The value of errno should not usually be examined unless a library function has returned an error code. For example, the following method of testing for a file error is dangerous:

```
fp = fopen(fname, "r");
if (errno != 0) {            /* DANGEROUS */
    perror("File error"):
    exit(EXIT_FAILURE);
}
```

The problem is that library functions do not clear errno when they are successful. Therefore, errno may still contain a nonzero value from an earlier error.

The above method could be improved by setting errno to zero before the call to fopen, but there is still another problem. In some implementations errno may be set by a library function even when it is successful. A well-known portability problem is that on some early implementations the printf function would set errno because some (noncrucial) internal routine would fail. Although it is unlikely that fopen will accidentally set errno when successful, it is still not advisable to examine errno. The best method of using errno is to only examine it when an error code is returned by a standard library function:

```
fp = fopen(fname, "r");
if (fp == NULL) {
    perror("File error"):
    exit(EXIT_FAILURE);
}
```

There are some exceptions to this rule about the use of errno. In particular, when using errno to detect errors in the use of the <math.h> functions, it is not always possible to detect an error by examining the return value of the mathematical function. The detection of a "domain error" is such a situation. A domain error occurs when a function's parameters are outside the legal range (e.g., sqrt with a negative argument). The implementation sets errno to the macro EDOM (declared in <errno.h>) and returns an implementation-defined value. Therefore, there is no portable method of detecting domain errors from function return values and the only method is to examine errno after the function has returned:

```
errno = 0;      /* clear any previous value */
x = sqrt(y);    /* call <math.h> function */
if (errno == EDOM) {
    ...  /* domain error has occurred */
}
```

Naturally, for the sqrt function we could simply test whether y was negative, but for other functions it is not always simple to check their arguments for validity (i.e., it is easier to check errno afterwards).

There is a similar problem with detecting underflow errors in <math.h> functions. In this case the function returns zero, and may set errno to ERANGE. It is implementation-defined whether errno is set or left unchanged; on implementations where it is set we can detect underflow by examining errno after the operation.

10.6 Trapping and handling signals

A bug in a program will often cause the program to crash and on some platforms it is possible to intercept these failures by handling signals. Thus signal handling represents a last resort, as it indicates a very serious internal failure of the program. The signal handler should perform any required cleanup (e.g., saving important data) and then terminate with an appropriate message.

Signal handling is particularly useful under UNIX where the most common run-time errors — segmentation faults and bus errors, can be caught — because they generate the signals SIGSEGV and SIGBUS, respectively. Floating-point arithmetic exceptions can be caught using the signal SIGFPE, and integer exceptions can be caught using the signal SIGTRAP (although SIGTRAP also has other meanings). Note that arithmetic overflow does not usually cause an exception, and often cannot be detected.

DOS implementations typically offer far less in the way of support for signals. It is more likely that a program will "hang" than produce a signal (e.g., a NULL pointer assignment won't usually produce a signal, but may cause a hung program). Nevertheless, the technique can be useful for catching a few failures; refer to your compiler documentation for more details on supported signals.

Upon detection of of a fatal signal, the signal handler must choose some appropriate recovery action. Unfortunately, it isn't portable to use longjmp to jump to a safe location (e.g., in the main function) where the program can continue. Using longjmp in a signal handler is a dangerous practice (see Section 18.12.3). It is also dangerous to call main or some other function to continue execution (i.e., to continue or restart execution without rewinding the stack). The only portable solution is to report an error message and terminate gracefully using exit or abort.

A very advanced low-level trick under UNIX is that the handler can change the program counter to skip over the instruction causing the error. This is very advanced and the reader is referred to the UNIX manual entries for `signal` and `sigvec`.

A simple demonstration of signal handling is presented below. The signal handler simply reports the type of signal causing the failure, and then terminates using `exit`. The alternative termination method is `abort`, which may be desirable (especially during the development phase) as it produces a core dump for postmortem debugging:

```
#include <stdio.h>
#include <stdlib.h>
#include <signal.h>

void handler(int sig)
{
    fprintf(stderr, "UNRECOVERABLE INTERNAL ERROR: ");
    switch (sig) {
        case SIGFPE:
            fprintf(stderr, "Floating point exception\n");
            break;

        case SIGSEGV:
            fprintf(stderr, "Segmentation fault\n");
            break;

        case SIGTRAP:
            fprintf(stderr, "Overflow or divide by zero error\n");
            break;

        case SIGBUS:
            fprintf(stderr, "Bus error\n");
            break;
    }
    /* ... Perform any cleanup here */
    signal(sig, handler);    /* reinstall: needed on some systems */
    exit(EXIT_FAILURE);
}

main()
{
    signal(SIGSEGV, handler);    /* Segmentation fault */
    signal(SIGFPE, handler);     /* Floating point exception */
    signal(SIGBUS, handler);     /* Bus error */
    signal(SIGTRAP, handler);    /* Overflow or divide by zero */

    /* ... rest of the program ... */
}
```

Another dangerous alternative is to ignore the various signals. This can cause an infinite loop because ignoring a signal (or returning from a handler) can cause the same operation to be restarted, resulting in another signal immediately. Therefore, this method is inapplicable to signals like SIGSEGV and SIGBUS. However, ignoring signals may be useful for less dangerous signals. (Note that the infinite loop cannot occur on those systems where a signal gets set to its default state once handled.)

10.7 Arithmetic overflow

Detecting overflow in an arithmetic computation is a less frequently needed part of reliable programming. In most cases it is possible to program so as to ensure that overflow is never an issue. For example, the use of `long` variables makes integral overflow unlikely in most programs. Nevertheless, for complete reliability a program should ensure that overflow does not occur. Fortunately, some compilers have run-time options to automatically check for such errors, but the majority of current compilers do not, leaving the problem for the programmer to detect.

The most important aspect of checking for overflow is that is should be performed *before* the operation. Overflow can cause a run-time failure (e.g., a core dump under UNIX) in some environments; therefore, testing for overflow after the operation is not portable. This prevents the following technique of testing overflow from adding two positive integers from being useful:

```
/* Assertion: a and b both positive */
x = a + b;
if (x < 0)  WARN_OVERFLOW();
```

If `a` and `b` are nonnegative, then `x` will be negative only if an overflow has occurred. This technique is useful for machines where overflow doesn't cause a run-time failure, but is not useful in general.

Let us formalize the problem of detecting overflow by using a debugging function that tests for overflow. This function is called *before* an operation such as below:

```
check_add_overflow(a, b);
x = a + b;
```

How is the `check_add_overflow` function to be defined? The easiest method is to separate a number of cases on the basis of the signs of the arguments. If `a` and `b` have different signs there can be no overflow; if they are both negative or both nonnegative, then overflow checking uses computations involving INT_MIN or INT_MAX (declared in the ANSI C header file <`limits.h`>).

```
#include <stdio.h>
#include <limits.h>

void WARN_ADD_OVERFLOW(int a, int b)
{
    fprintf(stderr, "Arithmetic overflow of %d + %d\n", a, b);
}

void check_add_overflow(int a, int b)
{
    if (a >= 0 && b >= 0) {  /* both nonnegative */
        if (a > INT_MAX - b)
            WARN_ADD_OVERFLOW(a, b);
    }
    else if (a < 0 && b < 0) {   /* both negative */
        if (a < INT_MIN - b)
            WARN_ADD_OVERFLOW(a, b);
    }
    /* Note: can't overflow if different signs */
}
```

It is possible to write similar functions to check overflow for all operations that may overflow. The operators that can overflow are shown in Tables 10.1 and 10.2:

Table 10.1   Binary operators that can overflow

Operator	Usage	Problems
addition	x+y	overflow/underflow
subtraction	x-y	overflow/underflow
multiplication	x*y	overflow/underflow
left shift	x<<y	overflow
extended assignment	x+=y, x-=y	overflow/underflow

Table 10.2   Unary operators that can overflow

Operator	Usage	Problems
unary minus	-x	overflow (INT_MIN)
increment	x++	overflow
decrement	x--	underflow
type cast	(int)x	overflow

It may seem surprising that unary minus can overflow. This is caused by the 2's complement representation that is commonly used. In such a scheme, a 16-bit integer can represent values from −32,768 to 32,767. Since there is no way to represent +32,768, applying unary minus to the smallest negative (i.e., INT_MIN) will often lead to overflow. In fact, it is often true that overflow causes the following result:

```
-INT_MIN == INT_MIN
```

Therefore, when applying unary minus it is always important to ensure that the value is not the smallest negative. Note that this overflow is the reason that the abs and labs standard library functions will fail in many implementations when supplied the smallest negative value in the representable range of int and long respectively.

Although in practice it is undesirable to call overflow testing code before all arithmetic operations, it is important to be aware of the problems of overflow. For crucial operations it may be desirable to have overflow tests in the code, and later remove them from production code using #define.

10.7.1 unsigned types cannot overflow

The ANSI C standard guarantees that `unsigned` types cannot overflow or underflow, and this behavior is also expected to be ratified in the ANSI C++ standard. Perhaps it is better to say that `unsigned` types are allowed to overflow and underflow, but the results are always well defined and a run-time error can never result. Arithmetic on `unsigned` types is required to behave as modulo 2^n where n bits are used to represent the particular type. Therefore, incrementing the largest value will yield zero and decrementing zero will yield the largest value.

The fact that `unsigned` types cannot overflow can often be useful in avoiding the dangers of overflow. For example, consider the use of `unsigned int` in the following hash function computation:

```
#define SIZE 211   /* a prime */

int hash(char *key)
{
    int i;
    unsigned int sum;

    for (i = 0; key[i] != '\0'; i++)
        sum += key[i];

    return sum % SIZE;
}
```

The use of `unsigned` prevents problems if the sum happens to overflow. If the variable `sum` were "plain" `int`, an overflow could lead to a run-time failure (although most machines would ignore such integer overflow). If the machine did ignore overflow, then an overflow would cause the value of `sum` to become negative, and the `%` operator would be applied to a negative value, leading to unpredictable results. The result of `%` on a negative operand could well be a negative value, and the function would return a negative hash value, probably leading to a later crash if the negative value is used as an array index into the hash table.

The `unsigned` type is not a good solution to overflow in all situations. The overflow from a large value to zero is often just as bad as the plain `int` overflow to a negative value. However, `unsigned` types are a handy solution in cases where it is important that the value not be negative, and the magnitude of the value is not very important.

Chapter 11

Debugging and testing tools

There is a wide variety of software tools available for the C and C++ languages, and many of these can be used to improve the debugging and testing process. However, before launching into an examination of the various tools, let us raise an important point: *your compiler is a powerful debugging tool.* Using the full power of your compiler can aid the debugging process. There are two separate issues: compile-time checking and run-time checking. Enabling all the compile-time warnings is like running a static checker every time you compile, and enabling run-time checking can also save you time by pinpointing an error.

11.1 Summary of tools

Every UNIX implementation brings its own bag of tools and some are relevant to C and C++ programming. A summarized list of these tools is given in Table 11.1. Note that UNIX variants differ, and these tools may not all be available on your UNIX platform.

Table 11.1 Standard UNIX tools

Tool	Purpose
lint	Static checker for C errors and portability
ctrace	Debugging output program tracing tool
cflow	Call graph of function calls and external references
cxref	Cross-reference listing of C files
dbx	Symbolic debugger
xdbx	X windows front for dbx
nm	List global names in executable/object file
sdb	Symbolic debugger
adb	Debugger (rudimentary machine-level)

The Free Software Foundation (typically known as "Gnu") has produced an immense variety of free software. This chapter examines only those that are most relevant to debugging and testing as listed in Table 11.2. Note that a few of the tools in Table 11.2 are not actually produced by the FSF, but are additions to Gnu tools.

Table 11.2 Gnu-related free tools

Tool	Purpose
gdb	Symbolic debugger
xxgdb	X windows front for gdb
Duel	Enhanced commands for gdb
gcc/g++	C/C++ compiler
DejaGnu	Automated testing facility

All Gnu tools are freely available via FTP, and you can retrieve the tools discussed or examine other Gnu tools. The tools are available via FTP to one of the sites shown below in Table 11.3; the relevant directory is also shown in this table.

Table 11.3 Gnu FTP archive sites

Site	Directory	Country
archie.au	/gnu	Australia
ftp.uu.net	/packages/gnu	USA
gatekeeper.dec.com	/pub/GNU	USA
nic.funet.fi	/pub/gnu	Finland
prep.ai.mit.edu	/pub/gnu	USA (main site)
src.doc.ic.ac.uk	/gnu	United Kingdom
utsun.s.u-tokyo.ac.jp	/ftpsync/prep	Japan

There are also a lot of free tools available via anonymous FTP throughout the Internet. Unfortunately, these tools tend to be UNIX-based rather than multiplatform because of the predominance of UNIX for machines on the Internet. Some such tools are listed in Table 11.4.

Table 11.4 Free tools (non-Gnu)

Tool	Purpose
cparen	Parenthesize C expressions
cdecl	Convert or explain C/C++ expressions
ups	GUI-based symbolic debugger
idclib	Code checker and debugging library
com_err	Error reporting library
malloc_trace	malloc debugging library
gct	Testing coverage analysis
dbmalloc	Memory allocation debugging library
vmon/vmemcheck	Memory debugging library
dbug	Trace output library
sedcheck	Error checker using grep/sed

11.2 Source code analysis tools

The analysis of source code can provide many checks for common errors and is thus an important debugging technique. The UNIX `lint` utility is probably the best example of error detection by the examination of source code, but there are now a large number of tools that operate in this manner, effectively performing analysis at compile-time.

11.2.1 The lint checker (UNIX)

The `lint` checker is a UNIX debugging utility that examines the C source code for "obvious" mistakes. A number of slightly different versions are available on different UNIX variants, but the errors reported by these versions are comparable. Unfortunately, the author is not aware of a `lint` version for C++.

Some of the errors commonly identified by `lint` are shown in Table 11.5; the exact format of the error messages will depend on which version of `lint` you are running.

Table 11.5   Errors detected by lint

Error	*Example*
Function arguments have wrong types	`sqrt(2)`
Variable used before set	`char*s; strcpy(s,"ab");`
Null effect statement	`x<<1;`
Nonportable character comparison	`char c; if (c == EOF)`
Redefinition hides earlier definition	`{ int ; ... { int i; }}`
Function has `return(e);` and `return;`	
Evaluation order is undefined	`a[i]=i++;`
Variable defined but not used	
Possible pointer alignment problem	
Function returns value that is always ignored	
Function returns value that is sometimes ignored	
Long assignment may lose accuracy	`int x; x = 100000;`
Type cast of integer to pointer	`char *p = (char*)100`

Generally speaking, `lint` finds very few of the large number of possible mistakes that are listed in Part II of this book. Its major use in the past has been to find errors in type checking, particularly of function parameters and arguments. The introduction of ANSI C compilers with function prototyping has reduced the importance of `lint`, but `lint` can still find type errors when using multiple files and independent compilation, whereas compilers may fail to detect such errors (good environments using smart compilers and linkers can detect these type errors at link-time, but few currently do this).

The `lint` utility also finds such errors as variables not initialized before use, functions failing to return a value (i.e., falling through to the right brace), and functions used inconsistently. In addition to potential bugs, `lint` examines the source for wasteful code. For example, it finds statements not reached and variables declared but not used.

11.2.1.1 Problems with lint

Some implementations of lint are not particularly useful. This is not because the messages produced are incorrect, but because of the deluge of distracting messages that appear, concealing any important messages. It becomes necessary to search through every single message for relevant problems, or to painstakingly modify your code to resolve each message (e.g., delete unused variable declarations). A particular case in point is the "possible pointer alignment problem" warning message, which is often produced by lint when it sees any use of malloc. Many versions of lint are not aware of the generic pointers to void (i.e., malloc's return type in ANSI C is void*) and therefore warn about casting the value returned by malloc to some other type.

More recent implementations have largely solved this problem with too much error message output. A good implementation I have seen prints out only the important messages on a line-by-line basis, saving less dangerous warnings for a summary at the end (e.g., variables not used). The problem with malloc has also been alleviated, presumably by making lint aware of the type void*. This makes lint a very powerful tool without the annoyances. When a program doesn't run as expected, it is worthwhile to test it with lint before using other debugging methods.

11.2.1.2 lint options

There are a large number of command-line options for lint. A number of the options control whether a particular warning is enabled or disabled. Unfortunately, there is inconsistency between various implementations of lint because various options are on/off by default and the option toggles the options; on some systems it will enable the warning, and on other systems it will disable it. Such options are shown in Table 11.6 using both "enable" and "disable"; consult your local documentation to determine the effect on your system.

Table 11.6 Important lint options

Option	Meaning
-a	Enable/disable warnings about long assignments
-b	Enable/disable warnings about unreachable break statements
-c	Enable/disable warnings about type casts
-Dmacro	Define macro name (as for cc)
-h	Enable/disable heuristic error checks (e.g., null effect)
-Idir	Directory to search during #include (as for cc)
-n	Disable checking against standard lint library
-olib	Create lint library
-p	Enable checking against portable lint library
-Umacro	Undefine macro name (as for cc)
-u	Enable/disable warnings about unused functions and variables
-v	Enable/disable warnings about unused function parameters
-x	Enable/disable warnings about unused external variables

11.2.1.3 Conditional compilation using lint

lint defines a preprocessor identifier "lint". This can be used to hide dubious lines of code from lint (i.e., to stop it complaining):

```
#ifndef lint
    ...        /* not checked by lint */
#endif
```

For example, one use of this macro is to prevent lint from complaining about "constants in conditional context" when using fancy macro tricks. The "do-while(0)" trick for multistatement macros and the "if(1){}else" removal method are good examples. Consider the following macros:

```
#define SWAP(x,y)  do{ int tmp = x; x = y; y = tmp; }while(0)
#define DPRINTF  if(1){}else    /* remove debug statements */
```

Whenever SWAP or DPRINTF is used, lint will complain about the tests of the constants 0 and 1. A simple method of suppressing these annoying warnings is to use conditional compilation:

```
#ifdef lint
#    define ZERO  strcmp("a","a")
#    define ONE   (!strcmp("a","a"))
#else /* not lint */
#    define ZERO  0
#    define ONE   1
#endif
    ...
#define SWAP(x,y)  do{ int tmp = x; x = y; y = tmp; }while(ZERO)
#define DPRINTF  if(ONE){}else    /* remove debug statements */
```

This works because lint is not clever enough to identify the strcmp function calls as constants. Note that there is no loss in efficiency because the function calls are never compiled into object code. The compiler never sees them and only lint sees the strcmp calls.

11.2.1.4 lint comment directives

Directives can be given to lint from within the program. lint recognizes special comments, such as /*NOTREACHED*/ and /*NOSTRICT*/.

The /*NOTREACHED*/ comment specifies that the current position cannot be reached by flow of control. The most common necessity for this comment directive is that lint does not understand functions that do not return, such as exit or longjmp. For more information on these directives, refer to your manual entry for lint.

11.2.1.5 Incremental linting using make

When used with a large project, the command:

```
lint *.c
```

starts to become very slow. Not only does it take a long time for lint to produce the final results, but there is also the disadvantage that all files are checked, even if only one has changed. A better method is to use the -c option to lint and a makefile.

The -c option causes lint to produce its own version of an object file for each source file — this is not the same sort of object file as produced by the compiler, but the idea is similar. These object files contain information for the global analysis phase of lint; that is, the last messages from lint indicating things such as which functions have inconsistent argument types, or return values that are always ignored. The filename extension of lint object files is ".ln"; for example, the command:

```
lint -c file.c
```

will produce the object file "file.ln" with the ".ln" filename suffix. In the process it will also identify any "local" anomalies such as a "null effect" statement.

One method of using lint in a makefile is examined below:

```
.c.ln:
        lint -c $*.c

LINTOBJS=file1.ln file2.ln file3.ln    # lint object files

lint: $(LINTOBJS)
    lint $(LINTOBJS)
```

The method is fundamentally the same as used for incremental production of the executable version with the compiler. The command to use is:

```
make lint
```

The make utility will identify which lint object files are out of date with respect to the source files, and will apply "lint -c" to these files to produce the lint object files (and also find any local errors). Once all the lint object files have been updated, lint is applied to all of them to produce the global error listing. In this way only source files that have changed are "relinted," which saves time (since processing all the object files is much faster) and also avoids reexamining warning messages about unchanged files.

The above makefile can be slightly improved by using the UNIX touch utility. The problem is that even if all source files are unchanged, the global analysis phase will still occur. The solution is to use a dummy file called "lint" that indicates whether all the object files have been examined before. The modified makefile lines are:

```
lint: $(LINTOBJS)
    lint $(LINTOBJS)
    touch lint    # update dummy file
```

When this modification is made, the make utility will respond with "lint is up to date" when all source files are unchanged since the last "make lint" command.

11.2.1.6 Is lint redundant in ANSI C?

It is occasionally said that `lint` has no useful purpose in ANSI C. Although it is true that the importance of `lint` is slightly reduced, it is certainly wrong to say that `lint` has no use.

The main area where `lint`'s importance is reduced is in the area of function argument type checking. Pre-ANSI C compilers performed no type checking of argument types and parameter types, nor even of whether the correct number of arguments was passed. `lint` was very important in identifying such argument passing errors. The advent of ANSI C has meant that prototyped functions can be used, and these have the types and number of arguments checked by the compiler. However, there are still instances in ANSI C where the argument passing errors can arise:

(a) An ANSI C compiler is used with older code containing nonprototyped functions.
(b) A function is called in a file where it has not previously been declared (i.e., no previous definition nor prototype declaration has been supplied).

The `lint` utility also has importance in that it checks for a number of other common errors that can occur as often in ANSI C as in pre-ANSI C. Such errors include null effect statements, precedence errors, and type mismatch of global variable definitions with their `extern` declarations.

11.2.2 PC-Lint/Flexe-Lint from Gimpel Software

Gimpel Software has produced a highly advanced static analysis tool for C, and now also C++, based on the same principle as `lint` — detection of erroneous or nonportable code constructs. The author has reviewed PC-Lint 5.0, the DOS version, but the UNIX version called Flexe-Lint should be very similar (it is distributed as obfuscated source code).

PC-Lint 5.0 does not support C++, but Gimpel Software have just released version 6.0 of PC-Lint that supports both C and C++. Unfortunately, the author hasn't yet had a chance to review PC-Lint 6.0, but the advertised C++ support looks very promising with 130 new messages. Some of the common C++ errors detected are non-`virtual` destructors and missing copy constructor or assignment operator in a class where the constructor uses `new`. I would expect most of the comments below on version 5.0 also to apply to the new C++ version.

PC-Lint is much better than the UNIX Lint in numerous ways, including a much larger set of error checks and convenient suppression of individual warnings that the programmer considers unimportant. The level of error checking is very impressive with hundreds of distinct messages that you can receive from PC-Lint. The tradition of UNIX Lint continues in that a large number of the checks relate to types and their use across multiple files. The type checking is as strict as a good ANSI compiler by default, but can be made even stricter by using "strong types," which allows `typedef` types to be treated as separate types and mismatches to be caught (e.g., misusing your own `boolean` type). Naturally, type checking can also be made "looser" by setting the appropriate options.

In addition to type errors, there are a multitude of common errors that are detected. The long list includes evaluation order, `printf` formats, dubious indentation, returning an auto variable address, missing `break` in `switch` and suspicious semicolons.

The configuration options available are also impressive. Options can be passed at the command-line, in option files, and even within program comments (much more general than UNIX lint's `/*NOTREACHED*/` facilities, which incidentally are also supported by PC-Lint). Messages can be suppressed individually by number, by ranges of numbers, within system headers only, within individual files only, for specific identifiers, and the list goes on. In addition to message suppression, there are many more options, too numerous to mention fully; notable are the "size" options allowing specification of the byte size of integral types, and the many "flag" options that specify various aspects of PC-Lint behavior (e.g., whether char is signed or unsigned).

Overall, I am very impressed by PC-Lint — it is an excellent static checker and its regular usage should greatly reduce the time spent in debugging. The details of Gimpel Software are: 3207 Hogarth Lane, Collegeville, PA 19426, USA; telephone: +1(215)584-4261; fax: +1(215)584-4266.

11.2.3 CodeCheck from Abraxis Software

CodeCheck is a very powerful and versatile static analysis tool that applies to both C and C++. It is a commercial tool with a variety of supported platforms, including MS-DOS, Windows, VMS, and UNIX.

CodeCheck can be used as a static error checker for debugging and testing, but can also be used to enforce coding style guidelines and compute code metrics. The main difference between CodeCheck and other Lint-like checking tools is that every execution requires a "rule file" in addition to the source files being checked. This specialized design to support multiple rule files is what gives CodeCheck its high level of flexibility. There are a variety of example rule files shipped with CodeCheck, including files for error checking, portability checking, style checking, and computing code metrics (e.g., McCabe). There are even a few neat rule files such as "wrapper.cc" to detect header files that aren't "wrapped" using #ifdef, and "indent.cc" to check for correct indentation.

You can also write your own rule files. Rule files are set out in a similar manner to C code using if statements, variables, and function calls. The if statements test a variety of built-in variables that are set during the parsing performed by CodeCheck. The following excerpt from an example rule file checks for macro parameter misuse by testing the built-in variable pp_arg_paren:

```
if (pp_arg_paren)
    warn(102, "Enclose macro parameters in parentheses.");
```

The parser upon which this checking is built can be configured in many ways. For example, you can choose between K&R, ANSI C, and a variety of C++ dialects. There are also minor options, such as a flag to enable nested comments.

Overall, CodeCheck is a very professional static analysis tool that is so versatile that it has application in many areas of software development, including debugging, portability checking, and coding style enforcement. The details of Abraxis Software are: P.O. Box 19586, Portland, OR 97219, USA; telephone: +1(503)244-5253; fax: +1(503)244-8375; email: APPLELINK D2205.

11.2.4 gcc/g++: a free C/C++ compiler

The Free Software Foundation (FSF) has produced a free C/C++ compiler that has been ported to many platforms. Note that the FSF is typically referred to by the name "Gnu" and that gcc stands for "Gnu C compiler." The quality is very high (supporting ANSI C and C++ 3.0) and many programmers use gcc or g++ rather than the default compiler bundled with the operating system.

The manner of usage is very similar to that of other compilers, and we won't examine it in detail. However, one feature that stands out is the high quality of the warnings available, making gcc/g++ a good candidate for a de facto static checking tool, especially for C++ as there is no noncommercial UNIX lint for C++. Most warnings about common coding bugs are enabled using the -Wall option, but a few other warning options may be worth considering that are not implied by -Wall; the command line I use is:

```
gcc -Wall -Wpointer-arith -Wtraditional
```

The options -ansi and -pedantic can also be used to check strict conformance of programs to the ANSI C standard.

Gnu software can be copied via FTP from any of the Gnu sites discussed in Section 11.1. The relevant filenames should have a "gcc" prefix but are subject to change, so refer to the on-site documentation. Note that the gcc distribution includes g++.

11.2.5 Other limited lint-like C checkers

Ian Darwin reports on a number of other limited checkers for C in his book *Checking C Programs with lint*, published by O'Reilly & Associates. All the tools are aimed at fixing a particular limitation of lint and are not very general. The printfck tool is a front end to lint that enables it to detect printf argument type errors. The tools clash and shortc are used to detect portability problems due to identifier truncation to the first 7 characters. The cchk tool will catch assignments in if statements, dangling else errors and nested comments; the check tool detects a similar limited range of common errors. These tools are all available via FTP as part of the O'Reilly "nutshell" archive distribution; for example, from the site ftp.eu.net in the directory documents/nutshell/lint. printfck is also available in volume 4 of the comp.sources.unix archives.

The Omega checker for C is discussed by Wilson and Osterweil [1985] and is more of a research project than a practical tool; it detects data flow errors such as "use before initialization" and "dead assignments."

11.2.6 sedcheck: a new checker using grep and sed

This section examines a static checker written recently by the author that detects common C and C++ programming errors by specifying regular expressions for sed in a UNIX script file. The full implementation is given in the source code disk directory chap11/sedcheck. The number of errors that can be caught by searching for regular expressions is very large and even grep can be a powerful debugging tool if used well. The advantage of sed over grep is that it allows messages to be added to the erroneous program lines in the diagnostic output.

The data file containing the regular expressions (in a special form) along with their corresponding error messages is called "regexps." This data file of pseudo-regular expressions is converted into real regular expressions for sed using the "makesed" script file. The full source for the resulting tool produced by this process is the script file "sedcheck." It can be applied to C and C++ source files and will report the erroneous lines with an appropriate diagnostic message.

11.2.7 Further reading on static checkers

The lint utility is widely used and is discussed in most C books. Ian Darwin has written a neat book that gives fully detailed coverage of how to best use lint, and mentions a number of other "small" checker tools. The first publication about lint is the technical report written by the original author, S.C. Johnson. An interesting research paper showing a very advanced checker, but that detects only a limited range of errors is the paper by Wilson and Osterweil discussing the Omega checker. Lastly, there is my own research on a C checker, but unfortunately the code is not yet ready for public release.

DARWIN, Ian F., *Checking C Programs with lint*, O'Reilly & Associates, 1988.

JOHNSON, S.C., "Lint: a C Program Checker," Computer Science Technical Report No. 65, Bell Laboratories, 1978.

SPULER, David A., "Check: A Better Checker for C," Honours Thesis, Department of Computer Science, James Cook University, Townsville, Australia, 1991 (FTP to coral.cs.jcu.edu.au in the directory pub/techreports as the file spuler-hons.ps.Z).

SPULER, D. and SAJEEV, A.S.M., "Static Detection of Preprocessor Macro Errors in C," Technical Report 92/7, Department of Computer Science, James Cook University, Townsville, Australia, July 1992/7 (available via FTP to the site coral.cs.jcu.edu.au as file pub/techreports/92-7.ps.Z).

WILSON, C., and OSTERWEIL, L.J., "Omega — A Data Flow Analysis Tool for the C Programming Language," *IEEE Transactions on Software Engineering*, Vol. 11, No. 9, 1985, pp. 832–838.

11.3 Run-time error detection tools

There are now a variety of free and commercial debugging tools that detect errors at run-time. Some of these tools use techniques similar to the macro and linker interception of library functions in the libraries in Chapter 3.

The types of program errors detected by these tools are typically related to heap memory allocation and memory accesses, including array bounds violations, dangling pointer reads and writes, freeing unallocated memory, double deallocation, using already-freed memory, NULL dereferences, and many others. Although it might seem that the number of types of errors found by these tools is small in comparison with the total number of different types of errors that programmers can make (see Part II of this book!), this does not take into account the relative importance of detecting these types of errors. The majority of error types will lead to some fixed and tangible failure of the program and should therefore be found and corrected during normal testing. However, memory-access errors will often be intermittent and very hard to trace because the symptoms of memory corruption may bear no resemblance to the actual cause. In fact, many such errors are not detected at all, and remain hidden as potentially harmful problems. Therefore, immediate detection of memory corruption errors leads to a significant improvement in the debugging and testing process because these errors are actually detected, and the cause is identified rather than just the symptom.

Unfortunately, the implementation of run-time error checking has a few disadvantages. Space and time efficiency suffer somewhat because of the extra code required to perform the checking. Another problem is that programs performing low-level memory manipulations (e.g., redefining malloc and free, or use of sbrk) may require special effort to add the checking, although it depends on the particular tool. Nevertheless, these tools are still an important part of a professional programmer's toolkit.

11.3.1 dbmalloc: a free UNIX debugging library

dbmalloc is a high-quality UNIX debugging library built by Conor Cahill that supports the link-time interception of standard library calls related to dynamic memory allocation. The difficulty mentioned in Section 3.5 with link-time interception of malloc is overcome by implementing allocation primitives in terms of sbrk (which is similar to how the "real" version of malloc operates), thus allowing portability across many UNIX platforms. In addition to link-time interception, dbmalloc allows source files to include the header file "malloc.h" for reporting of the filename and line number of the statement causing the error.

As with most such libraries, the primary focus is on memory allocation debugging, including detection of errors such as block overwrites and bad free calls, and also memory leak reports. In addition to the interception of the standard memory allocation functions, a number of memory-related functions such as strcpy and memset are intercepted, as well as the X windows allocation functions. Unfortunately, although very good, dbmalloc is not quite a commercial-quality library because of disadvantages such as the requirement of in-code support for function call stack tracing, a lack of run-time configurability (e.g., dbmalloc cannot be left in production code), and its somewhat cryptic error messages.

`dbmalloc` was posted to `comp.sources.misc` in September 1992 and is available wherever `comp.sources.misc` is archived, as `dbmalloc`, Volume 32, Issues 6–15. There are various sites, including `ftp.uu.net` (USA) in the `usenet` directory, `archie.au` (Australia) in the `usenet` directory, or alternatively `gatekeeper.dec.com` (USA) in the `pub/usenet` directory; within these directories, go to subdirectory `comp.sources.misc/volume32/dbmalloc`.

11.3.2 SENTINEL from AIB Software Corporation

SENTINEL is a high-quality commercial debugging library for C and C++ aimed primarily at memory-related program errors, and is available for a wide variety of UNIX-based platforms. SENTINEL uses link-time interception of library function calls as described in Section 3.5. The main designer of SENTINEL is Conor Cahill, who also wrote `dbmalloc`, the success of which inspired him to build a commercial-quality version: SENTINEL.

The level of error checking is very high, including all the "usual" errors related to heap memory allocation (e.g., bad `free`, double `free`, etc.) and a variety of portability warnings (e.g., `free`'ing a NULL pointer, or `memcpy` arguments overlap). A number of other error checks are performed at every intercepted call, including checks for `malloc` chain corruption and stack corruption. A "magic value" technique is also used to detect reads of already-freed memory blocks or uses of uninitialized `malloc` blocks.

Memory leaks are another major form of error identified by SENTINEL. A variety of reports are available about "garbage" blocks, and these can be customized in many ways. Reports can be made to appear at the end of execution or can be achieved through calls to various API functions.

The main limitation of SENTINEL's error checking arises from its use of function call interception, which means that memory errors not arising directly from a function call (e.g., bad array index) are not caught immediately. Such errors can be caught only as early as the next call to an intercepted library function.

Error reporting is quite verbose, making the causes of errors simple to trace. Typically, the report includes a long human-readable description of the type of error, and stack traces of both the point at which the error is detected and the point when the allocation of the relevant memory block occurred.

SENTINEL is easy to use, with no changes to source code required. All that is needed is to invoke the "sentinel" command, which has a similar usage format to most compilers. This allows a `makefile` alteration to require only the addition of this single word in many cases.

The level of configurability is also very high, including aspects such as various forms of error report suppression and the ability to prevent certain expensive error checks if performance degradation is too high. Options are set by using configuration files and environment variables that are examined at program startup and can be reexamined via API calls.

An aspect of SENTINEL not related to its run-time error checking is its support for a run-time configurable debugging output library. There is a `printf`-like SEDBG macro that uses the double bracket removal method of Section 2.8.5, and another macro named SEDBG_CODE that is a "large" macro allowing an entire code block as its second argument. Both of the debugging output "areas" and "levels" idioms discussed in Section 2.10 are supported.

A notable feature of SENTINEL is its explicit support for using it to help in beta testing a product. The manual encourages SENTINEL to be left linked into the executable during beta testing, and error reports can be mailed electronically to the person supervising the beta test. Note that beta testers do not need a SENTINEL license to run the executable.

In summary, SENTINEL is an excellent C/C++ debugging tool for UNIX platforms, allowing convenient detection of the majority of memory-related errors. The details of AIB Software Corporation are: 46030 Manekin Plaza, Suite 160, Dulles, VA 20166, USA; telephone: 1-800-296-3000 (within USA only) and 1-703-430-9247; fax: 1-703-450-4560; email: info@aib.com.

11.3.3 Purify from Pure Software Inc.

Purify is a commercial run-time debugging tool for both C and C++ that detects many memory-related programming errors. Purify is currently available for Sun SPARC running either SunOS 4, or Solaris 2, and also for HP 9000 workstations running HP-UX.

Purify operates on a lower level than any other tool I have examined. Errors are detected by "object code insertion" during the linking phase and memory accesses are intercepted at object level. Hence *all* memory accesses are checked, even those in third-party libraries. Furthermore, any detected memory errors are reported immediately rather than only at the next call to an intercepted library function, which is the case for many similar tools.

Error checks include the usual heap memory related errors (e.g., bad free, double free, etc.), but the low level of memory access interception also makes it possible to find a slightly broader range of errors, including uses of uninitialized memory.

Memory leaks are another major form of error that is identified by Purify. A report of any memory leaks appears by default at the end of execution. The report provides a stack trace for every block, showing what sequence of functions caused the leak. More detailed memory leak reporting can be achieved by calling various API functions from within the program or from a debugger.

The error messages produced by Purify are detailed enough to trace the cause of an error. A stack trace is presented of function calls currently active when the error occurred, and also a stack trace of function calls that created the memory block involved in the error (if there is a related block). These error reports can be customized in a number of ways, including suppressing specific errors, saving error reports to a log file, and even mailing error reports to the main developer! Error suppression can be achieved via options in a ".purify" configuration file, and there are a variety of modes for suppressing a given error type, including all instances, all instances in a given function, all instances in functions called by a given function, and all instances in a given library. Purify allows C++ names to be used in full, and "unmangles" names in error reports.

Purify is very easy to use. All that is required is a relink of the object files using Purify's linker. Typically, all that is needed to build a Purify'd executable is an extra word, "purify," in the makefile.

Purify has a large number of other features to make it more useful in various contexts. For example, it has a large number of Purify-specific API functions to call from within a program or a symbolic debugger. These functions can be used to present various reports on memory usage and memory leaks, change the handling of errors, etc. Another feature is called "watchpoints" where the programmer can call a function at run-time to specify that accesses to a particular address or block of memory be reported by Purify. This can be used to detect changes to particular addresses; for example, Purify's manual suggests a watchpoint on `errno` to detect the next time `errno` is changed by a system call.

An impressive aspect of Purify's documentation was the discussion of how to overcome a limitation that is typical of this sort of tool — programs that do not use `malloc` and `free` in the usual way will need some modification. Purify's manual includes a number of sections discussing how programs can be modified so that Purify can still be used for situations such as fixed-size memory allocators, pool allocators, and use of `sbrk`.

In summary, Purify is an excellent tool for detecting a variety of otherwise difficult to detect memory errors, making it very valuable in the software development cycle. It is especially powerful because of the low-level interception of memory accesses and thus checks *all* memory accesses, rather than only those arising from library function calls. Pure Software Inc. can be reached at email address `info@pure.com` or telephone +1(408)720-1600 in the United States for current pricing and sales information.

11.3.4 vmon and vmemcheck (Brown University)

The Computer Science Department at Brown University offers a free package for memory debugging under UNIX. The package detects memory errors such as freeing bad memory or using uninitialized memory. The tool works at a low level by intercepting memory accesses and also calls to `malloc` and `free`. `vmon` produces trace output about memory accesses and `vmemcheck` can be used to analyze the traces either at run-time or postmortem.

The `vmon` and `vmemcheck` tools are available as part of AARD via FTP from `wilma.cs.brown.edu` as the file `pub/aard.tar.Z`. There is also a variety of other interesting software engineering projects at that site.

11.3.5 idClib: a free debugging library

The *idClib* library by Ian Cottam is a debugging library similar to those presented in Chapter 3. However, rather than using macro interception, it uses a compiler-like tool for precompilation of C files that converts standard C library function calls to `idC` library calls. The *idClib* functions perform argument checking and then call the corresponding standard functions. At present, version 1.4 does not perform any detailed checking of `malloc`/`free` blocks, but this would not be difficult to add.

One notable feature is that the precompilation tool also enforces a particular programming style, called *idC* for "Ian's disciplined C," and warns about infringements of this style. The style restrictions are discussed in Ian Cottam's interesting technical report:

COTTAM, Ian D., "idC: A Subset of Standard C for Initial Teaching," Tech Report UMCS-92-12-3, Dept. Computer Science, University of Manchester, England, 1992 (available via FTP from `ftp.cs.man.ac.uk` in directory `pub/TR` as file `UMCS-92-12-3.ps.Z`).

A distribution of the *idClib* library is currently available via anonymous FTP from `ftp.cs.man.ac.uk` in the `pub` directory as file `idclib_1.4.shar`.

11.3.6 malloc-trace: a Sun malloc debugging library

Yet another `malloc`/`free` debugging library is available for Sun called `malloc-trace`. It is a linkable library with implementations of `malloc` in terms of `sbrk`. Unfortunately, it is not highly portable, and the (limited) documentation refers only to the Sun platform. The `malloc-trace` library is available via FTP in volume 18 of the `comp.sources.unix` archive as found at many sites.

11.3.7 MemCheck from StratosWare Corporation

MemCheck is a commercial debugging tool available for detecting memory errors available from StratosWare Corporation. It works on similar principles to the debugging libraries examined in Chapter 3 using interception of library calls by preprocessor macros and also at link-time. This technique gives the product a high level of portability and MemCheck is available on many platforms, including DOS, Windows, and Macintosh. It is also available in source code form for any other platforms with ANSI or K&R compliant C compilers.

When adding MemCheck to a project, the main alteration is the addition of `#include <memcheck.h>` to each source file. This change can be performed manually, or automatically using a supplied tool. The environment variable MEMCHECK must also be set to enable checking.

MemCheck is a supported commercial product and the difference shines through, with many more features than the typical free `malloc` debugging package. The errors detected include heap-related memory errors, memory leaks, memory allocation failure, and bad arguments to various library functions. The performance is good with only 7-15K code overhead, and with good run-time efficiency because MemCheck uses a binary tree to track addresses. In fact, I was particularly impressed by the facility to track addresses either in memory or using a disk data structure in a temporary file should the space used by the in-memory binary tree become prohibitive.

MemCheck offers a high level of run-time configurability. MemCheck code never needs to be removed from a project's source code; it can be either (1) left in the production version, (2) "linked out" by linking with a particular library, or (3) "compiled out" by defining the macro name NOMEMCHECK. A variety of API functions are also available that I won't examine in detail.

A useful feature for DOS programmers is that MemCheck performs frequent tests for NULL pointer overwrites. This can be useful for narrowing down the cause of a "null pointer assignment" error message.

Debugging of C++ memory allocation with `new` and `delete` is supported in a few ways. The default method is link-time interception of the calls to `malloc` and `free` performed by the compiler's default `new` and `delete` operators. This means that all new and delete operations are checked, but any error messages about them are slightly misleading — referring to malloc rather than new, and without an accurate associated filename and line number. More accurate messages about new and delete can be achieved by adding definitions of the overloaded new and delete operators as a C++ source file in your project (usable sample definitions are provided with MemCheck), and defining the macro NEW_OVERLOADED to enable a macro definition of new.

The main limitations of MemCheck arise from its use of library function interception which means that memory errors arising in other ways (e.g., a bad index in an array access) are not necessarily detected immediately.

In summary, MemCheck represents a high-quality memory debugging library with numerous convenience features, which would make a useful impact on any programmer's debugging tasks. The relevant details about StratosWare Corporation are as follows: 1756 Plymouth Road, Suite 1500, Ann Arbor, MI 48105, USA; phone: +1(313)996-2944 or (within the United States only) 1-800-WE-DEBUG; fax: +1(313)996-2955 (preferred) or +1(313)747-8519; email: 70244.1372@compuserve.com.

11.3.8 TrackDeck from Dashboard Software

TrackDeck is a new type of graphical debugging and performance analysis tool for C and C++ under Windows. It allows the programmer to "look into" the program and examine data values during execution. This makes it sound like a symbolic debugger, but it isn't, and TrackDeck has two main advantages over symbolic debuggers: (1) a symbolic debugger must "step" through execution, but TrackDeck execution continues automatically; and (2) TrackDeck offers graphical viewing of data values.

This graphical viewing is the most important feature of TrackDeck. As their manual says, "a graph is worth a thousand print statements." Variables can be presented graphically as dials or history graphs. Naturally, the dials and graphs can be customized in various ways: size, color, etc. Data values can also be viewed as ordinary values (i.e., like a symbolic debugger watch window) and a message logging facility is also provided. There is also the flexibility to specify simple functions such as average, minimum, or maximum for a given value, or to supply a callback function for more complicated functions.

TrackDeck has two separate parts: a DLL that detects changes to monitored variables and a separate viewing program that extracts this information about variable values and presents it graphically to the user. Thus the debugging information is automatically updated as the program executes, but the performance degradation this causes is only a few percent.

Although it is definitely an interesting new tool, TrackDeck has some important limitations. A minor issue is that rather than grabbing variable names and their addresses from the executable or object files, using TrackDeck requires source code modification: one function call per address to be monitored. Presumably this limitation arises because TrackDeck supports multiple C/C++ compilers. Another minor problem is that the monitoring of variables on the stack suffers if the function returns, because the address becomes invalid. However, there are API functions provided to handle stack addresses. A more major issue is that only a few simple forms of expression can be monitored: single variables, and variables indirectly referred to by one or more pointers. TrackDeck does not present a graphical view into larger linked data structures, which is the logical extension of this idea.

In summary, TrackDeck is an interesting foray into the future world of graphical debugging tools, and is certainly a level above looking through reams of print statement output. The details of DashBoard Software are: 4 Louis Avenue, Monsey, New York, NY 10952, USA; phone/fax: +1(914)352-8071; email: `76620.750@compuserve.com`.

11.4 Symbolic debuggers

Almost all implementations of the C or C++ language come with at least one tool for debugging of programs: a symbolic debugger. Typically, this type of utility allows the programmer to set breakpoints in the program and examine values of variables during execution. Some of the more common debuggers under UNIX are `sdb`, `gdb`, and `dbx`. Note that the use of these debuggers requires that the `-g` option be used with the `cc` compiler. UNIX debuggers are reasonably good but tend not to be as useful as the multiwindow debugging often allowed on smaller machines. Some features can be very cumbersome, and my personal preference is to avoid the use of UNIX debuggers, except to trace segmentation faults.

UNIX debuggers are useful in tracking down a segmentation fault or arithmetic exception using postmortem debugging. When invoked after a crash, the debugger will examine the `"core"` file created by the crash, to pinpoint the cause of the crash.

11.4.1 dbx: a UNIX symbolic debugger

`dbx` is a symbolic debugger supported on many UNIX-based systems. A typical invocation is as follows:

```
dbx a.out
```

A summary of commands is given in Table 11.7. For full symbolic support it is necessary to compile the program using the `-g` option to the compiler. This causes the executable to contain symbolic information that is used by the debugger. If the program has not been compiled this way, `dbx` will still continue, but it will not recognize program names and most of its information will be in the form of hexadecimal addresses.

Table 11.7 dbx commands

Command	Meaning
`quit` (`q`)	Quit `dbx`
`run` (`r`)	Run the executable
`help` (`h`)	Help (online)
`where`	Stack trace
`print`	Print variable values

The `dbx` debugger can be used as a postmortem debugger to locate the cause of a program failure after a "core dump" (e.g., as caused by a segmentation fault or bus error). The command to achieve this is:

```
dbx a.out core
```

The where command can be applied at the dbx prompt to give a stack trace, which indicates the function, source file, and line number of the failure. All debugger features are invoked as if the program had just been executed by dbx up to the failure (e.g., the values of variables can be printed using the print command).

11.4.2 xdbx — X windows extension to dbx

An X windows front end for dbx called xdbx is available as part of the xxgdb distribution. Refer to Section 11.4.4 for acquisition details.

11.4.3 gdb: a free UNIX debugger

gdb is a free symbolic debugger produced by the Free Software Foundation. It is similar to other line-based UNIX debuggers such as dbx in terms of features and user interface. A typical invocation would be:

```
gdb a.out
```

When using gdb for postmortem debugging after a core dump, the command becomes:

```
gdb a.out core
```

Some of the most important commands are shown in Table 11.8. All commands can be abbreviated if the prefix is unique.

Table 11.8   gdb commands

Command	Meaning
quit (q)	Quit gdb
help (h)	Help (online)
where	Stack trace
bt (q)	Stack trace (same as where)
run (r)	Execute program from within gdb

For full symbolic support, the program must be compiled with debugging information included; typically this is achieved by the -g compiler option.

As with all Gnu software, it can be copied via FTP from the sites discussed in Section 11.1. The filenames usually have a "gdb" prefix but are subject to change.

11.4.4 xxgdb — X Windows extension to gdb

The xxgdb debugger is an X windows front end to gdb. xxgdb is available wherever comp.sources.x is archived and can be found in the volume11 directory, with patches also available in volumes 12, 13, 14, and 16. There are various archive sites, including ftp.uu.net (USA) in the usenet directory, archie.au (Australia) in the usenet directory, or gatekeeper.dec.com (USA) in the pub/usenet directory. Note that the distribution also includes the xdbx front end for dbx.

11.4.5 Duel: an extension to gdb

Duel is intended as an extension to existing debuggers, but currently only supports C debugging using gdb. All Duel commands are prefixed with the command dl, thus making the new features easy to add to existing debuggers. The many extensions offered by Duel include a large number of compact operators for more effective examination of data, and C-like if statements and loops. There are far too many extensions to examine in detail, but the power of Duel shows up clearly in the following use of the --> extended operator (two minus signs) to traverse an entire linked list and print the data field of each list node:

```
gdb> dl head-->next->data
```

Duel is free software available via FTP from ftp.cs.princeton.edu in the directory duel, which contains many files, including duel.tar.Z which is a complete distribution, and copies of a technical report as files usenix.paper.ps.Z and usenix.paper.dvi; the same report is also available separately in the file reports/1992/399.ps.Z from the top-level FTP directory.

11.4.6 ups: a free X windows debugger

ups is a free symbolic debugger for C that runs under X11 or SunView. The features of ups are too numerous to discuss in detail, but the basic concept is to have a GUI-based debugger rather than a text-based debugger. ups has been ported to a variety of UNIX architectures, including those running SunOS and Ultrix.

ups is available via FTP at numerous sites. It is part of the X11 distribution and appears in various directories at different sites: I found it at archie.au in the X11/contrib directory, but you are advised to perform an "archie" search to find a site close to you; another site is export.lcs.mit.edu in the contrib directory. All filenames have a "ups" prefix.

11.5 Automated testing tools

There are quite a few tools available for automating the testing process, especially the repetitive commands required for regression tests. This section presents a brief survey of a relatively small number of the tools in this area.

11.5.1 DejaGnu: free automated testing tool

DejaGnu is a free tool from Gnu for automated testing on many platforms, and is currently used to test other major tools produced by Gnu. DejaGnu tests are written in *expect*, which uses Tool Command Language (Tcl). Regression testing is an obvious application of DejaGnu's automated testing, but not the only one. DejaGnu is designed to allow consistent testing of a program across multiple platforms, with support for both batch and interactive programs (e.g., it has been used to test both gcc and gdb). Unfortunately, it does not currently support GUI-based testing, although this is an intended area of future work (and may be available by the time you read this!).

DejaGnu is available at any of the usual Gnu sites as discussed in Section 11.1. At the time of writing, the filename is dejagnu-1.0.1.tar.gz. The distribution also includes implementations of tcl and expect, and numerous test suites.

11.5.2 gct: a free test coverage analysis tool

Brian Marick has produced a free tool for automated test coverage analysis under UNIX, called gct for "Generic Coverage Tool". gct works by taking C files and adding source code to them. The process is transparent because gct automatically calls the system C compiler after augmenting the source code (alternatively, the modified source can be extracted). The resulting augmented executable produces a tracing log at program termination, which can be analyzed by a number of tools provided for this purpose. A variety of code coverage measures are provided, including branch coverage, multicondition coverage, loop coverage, relational operator coverage, routine coverage, and call coverage, just to mention a few.

gct is available via FTP from cs.uiuc.edu in the pub/testing directory. A brief overview is in the file GCT.README and the full distribution is in the gct.files directory (actually a link to another directory). The distribution includes plenty of good documentation and testing examples and is supported commercially by Brian Marick.

11.5.3 QA Partner from Segue Software

QA Partner is an advanced object-oriented tool for automated testing of GUI applications. It offers the same fundamental idea as capture/playback testing systems, but with a GUI twist. Some of its notable features include cross-platform testing (including Windows, NT, OS/2, Macintosh, OSF/Motif on most UNIX platforms), distributed testing, and performance testing.

The single most significant feature of *QA Partner* is its inherent support for GUI testing. Test scripts operate on a higher abstraction level than older testing tools. Objects in an application's GUI are treated as just that — *objects*. For example, input events are not tied to a particular screen location. Clicking on a window can be specified as an action on a window object and *QA Partner* will find the current location of that window at run-time. Similarly, the examination of test results goes beyond the old-style method of bitmap recording, which isn't really adequate for testing modern GUI applications.

The high abstraction level of test scripts offers an important advantage in cross-platform testing. The same scripts can be used to test an application on a variety of platforms, provided the *logical* organization of GUI objects is similar. Another interesting advantage is that testing international versions of the same product will not require major script changes.

All testing scripts are written in a 4GL language specifically designed for testing, called *4Test*. *4Test* offers low-level constructs such as variables and flow of control alongside the higher-level treatment of GUI objects. Notably, *4Test* is compiled rather than interpreted, so that scripts aren't a performance burden. Scripts are created using the *Script Development Environment*, which is a similar concept to a graphical environment for programming.

Overall, I am very impressed with *QA Partner* as an excellent tool for automated testing of GUI-based products. Segue Software can be reached at: 1320 Centre Street, Newton Centre, MA 02159, USA; telephone: +1(617)969-3771; fax: +1(617)969-4326; email: `info@segue.com`.

11.5.4 Cantata from IPL

Cantata is an automated testing tool for C and C++ programs that is commercially available from IPL. Cantata is available on a variety of platforms, including UNIX, VMS, PC-DOS, and OS/2.

Cantata offers three major features: dynamic testing, coverage analysis, and static analysis. Dynamic testing refers to the overall use of test scripts to execute tests; coverage analysis examines the extent to which the tests have exercised the program; and static analysis can be used to check code metrics and conformance to coding standards. Results from these three areas can be incorporated into a pass/fail scheme for test scripts.

The main test driver is the Cantata Test Harness (CTH), which is mainly a library of testing directives. A test script is actually a `main` function in C/C++ that uses a structured format. There are facilities for setting initial conditions, testing whether results are satisfactory, timing performance, and stubbing external modules, and all tests can be combined into a pass/fail scheme.

Coverage analysis can be incorporated into a dynamic test, and does not require postprocessing of result files. The supported coverage metrics are statement coverage, decision (or branch) coverage, condition coverage, and call coverage.

Static analysis can be incorporated into the testing phase, allowing both the enforcement of coding style standards and the computation of complexity metrics. There are two types of metrics available: "academic" metrics (e.g., McCabe's, Halstead's, Harrison's and others) and "common sense" metrics designed by IPL, such as statement counts. It is also possible to define your own metrics or coding standards.

Overall, Cantata is a flexible low-level testing system that should considerably ease the burden of manual testing during development. For more information refer to the documentation about Cantata on the source disk in the file `products/cantata.txt` or contact IPL at: Software Products Group, IPL, Eveleigh House, Grove Street, Bath BA1 5LR, UK; telephone: +44 225 444888; fax: +44 225 444400.

11.6 Miscellaneous tools

There are a few other free tools that don't fit into any of the categories above. Not all of them are particularly closely related to debugging and testing, but since they're free I decided they were worth discussing briefly.

11.6.1 The ctrace utility (UNIX)

An interesting debugging tool is the `ctrace` utility that is available in most versions of UNIX. The purpose of `ctrace` is to automatically produce debugging output without the programmer adding any debugging statements to the code. `ctrace` is a filter that accepts as input a C source file, and outputs a modified version of the C source file with output statements added. Thus the use of `ctrace` requires an extra stage during compilation.

Unfortunately, the `ctrace` utility has so many limitations that it isn't of great practical use for professional programmers. The version of `ctrace` that the author examined was so old that it would not accept ANSI C code, refusing to recognize function prototypes. The author is not aware of an ANSI C version of the `ctrace` utility. If such a version exists, `ctrace` could become quite a useful debugging tool.

11.6.2 dbug: a free debugging output library

The `dbug` library is a free package that provides a number of standard macros that the programmer can insert into the program. A typical example is the use of a `DBUG_ENTER` macro at the start of the function and replacing the `return` statement with a `DBUG_RETURN` macro. These macros will produce tracing output to the screen or a log file, which can be analyzed at run-time or postmortem. The overall configurability of the package is quite good, and the macros can be compiled-out easily. `dbug` is available via anonymous FTP and I found it at the site `ftp.germany.eu.net` in the `pub/programming/lib/dbug` directory, but it is a good idea to do an "archie" search to find a site close to you.

11.6.3 com_err: an error message library

`com_err` is a UNIX library aiming at a more uniform manner of handling library function errors. Note that it is not an exception handling library, but instead provides a simpler method of reporting error messages. `com_err` is available via FTP and it is a good idea to do an "archie" search to find a site close to you: the FTP site I used was `aeneas.mit.edu` in the directory `pub/tools`.

11.6.4 cparen: parenthesize expressions

cparen is a "small" tool that parenthesizes C expressions, and is useful for those who don't want to memorize the 15 precedence levels of C's operators. cparen accepts a single expression (not an entire C file) from stdin and produces the parenthesized version on stdout.

I had some difficulty in obtaining a copy of cparen via FTP; after a search using the "archie" tool, I finally found it at the site pluto.ulcc.ac.uk in the directory /convex_ug/us_archive_1992 as the file cparen.tar.Z. Note that cparen is primarily UNIX-based, mainly because of its use of lex and yacc in the building process.

11.6.5 cdecl: explain complicated declarations

cdecl is a UNIX-based free tool for converting C declarations into English text, and vice versa. Thus it can be used to explain complicated declarations and also to produce such declarations from an English explanation of a type.

cdecl is available via FTP as part of the comp.sources.unix archive. There are various archive sites, including ftp.uu.net (USA) in the usenet directory, archie.au (Australia) in the usenet directory, or gatekeeper.dec.com (USA) in the pub/usenet directory. Within these directories, the file appears in the subdirectory comp.sources.unix/volume14/cdecl2 as a shar archive in two parts. The distribution includes c++decl, which has support for C++ syntax.

Part II

Catalog

of

common

errors

Chapter 12

General forms of error

12.1 Special cases (boundary conditions)

Algorithms often fail on special cases. It is a good idea to ensure that your algorithms correctly handle all special cases. Test the program on all special cases. Special cases usually involve zero or one of some object, or the maximum number of such objects. Some examples of special cases (often called boundary conditions) are:

- empty lists
- single element lists
- empty arrays
- full arrays

Equality is often a special case. Always be careful when using the relational operators, greater-than and less-than. Does the algorithm make the correct choice on equality? Mistakes are commonly made with < instead of <=, and vice versa.

12.2 Off-by-one errors

Off-by-one errors refer to errors where the program does one too many or one too few actions. They are often referred to as "fencepost" errors.

A common example of off-by-one involves problems with array indices. Remember that array indices range from 0..n-1, and not 1..n. When counting elements in an array, there are n elements, but the highest index is n-1. If the size is confused with the highest index, the program is off-by-one.

Another example of off-by-one is whether to increment before or after an operation (i.e., prefix or postfix increment). Consider the for loop to copy a linked list into an array:

```
count = 0;
for (p = head; p != NULL; p = p->next)
    a[++count] = p->data;                    /* INCORRECT */
```

177

This is incorrect as the zeroth array element is missed. The problem is the use of the prefix ++ causing count to be incremented before its value is used for the array index. The correct statement uses postincrement:

```
a[count++] = p->data;              /* CORRECT */
```

Another example of an off-by-one error occurs in the use of arrays. Common style for setting or accessing all elements in an array is to use a for loop similar to:

```
for (i = 0; i < n; i++)
    a[i] = 0;
```

There are two ways this can go wrong — i can be wrongly initialized to 1, or the < operator can be mistakenly replaced with <=. In the first case, the zeroth array element is missed. In the second case, the array element a[n] is accessed, often causing a crash.

12.3 Infinite recursion

Recursion refers to a function that calls itself from within its own function body. Recursive functions offer highly elegant solutions to a number of different programming problems. However, they are quite tricky and there are many ways to go wrong. A recursive function requires a number of conditions to operate correctly:

- a base case when recursion stops
- recursive calls operate on "reduced" problems

The need for a base case is simply that if a program always calls itself it will never return. For example, consider the following erroneous factorial function:

```
int fact1(int n)
{
    return n * fact1(n - 1);    /* No base case */
}
```

This function will never return and the program will probably terminate abnormally after some delay, when the program stack is finally used up. Therefore, a simple rule about recursive functions is that they should contain a selection statement — an if statement, a conditional operator, or a switch statement. Otherwise, all flow paths will lead to a recursive call and infinite recursion cannot be prevented.

12.4 Unchanged arguments in recursive call

The idea of "reduced" problems for the recursive call usually refers to a change in the arguments to the recursive function. If the arguments do not change at all, this will cause infinite recursion as illustrated by the following function:

```
int fact2(int n)
{
    if(n == 0)        /* base case */
        return 1;
    else
        return n * fact2(n);   /* Unchanged argument */
}
```

Whenever this function is passed a nonzero argument such as 2, the `else` clause will be executed, but this will again try to compute the factorial of 2, leading to infinite recursion.

12.5 Recursive base case never reached

A totally unchanged argument is not the only problem related to the idea of "reduced" problems. The argument must change in a way that it will finally reach the base case. For example, even if we change the argument to `fact2` in the previous example to the correct expression `n-1`, the function still contains a dangerous reliability problem. It will work well for positive integers, but if a negative integer is accidentally passed, there will again be infinite recursion because the argument does not approach the base case — it is decremented further away from zero. Therefore, the program should explicitly check for a negative value of n, as follows:

```
int fact3(int n)
{
    if(n < 0)
        ERROR();
    else if(n == 0)   /* base case */
        return 1;
    else
        return n * fact3(n - 1);
}
```

12.6 Poor choice of recursive base case

Yet another common error made by novice programmers when first experimenting with recursion is to forget that the base case will always be reached. For example, examine the recursive function to print out a binary tree using an "inorder" tree traversal:

```
void print_tree(Node *root)
{
    if (root == NULL)
        printf("Empty tree\n");
    else {
        print_tree(root->left);    /* print left subtree */
        printf("%d\n", root->data);        /* visit node */
        print_tree(root->right);  /* print right subtree */
    }
}
```

The intention is to print the message "`Empty tree`" for a tree with a `NULL` root pointer, and it does indeed do this. However, it also prints the message for every `NULL` pointer in a nonempty tree. The base case is reached many times, and each time this messages is printed. The correct solution is to test for the empty tree *before* calling the recursive function, and making the base case of the recursive function do nothing. This can be achieved by making `print_tree` call another function that performs most of the work, as follows:

```
void print_tree_sub(Node *root)
{
    if (root != NULL) {
        print_tree_sub(root->left);
        printf("%d\n", root->data);
        print_tree_sub(root->right);
    }
}

void print_tree(Node *root)
{
    if (root == NULL)
        printf("Empty tree\n");
    else
        print_tree_sub(root);
}
```

12.7 Indirect recursion

Novice programmers will sometimes use incorrect methods to achieve the required flow of control. In the example below, the aim is to have a menu repeatedly shown and for the user to make a choice whereupon the program will do what the user requested and return to the menu. The following program achieves this but contains a hidden recursion problem:

```
void menu(void)
{
  char choice;

    while(1) {  /* infinite loop */
        printf("--- MAIN MENU ---\n");
        printf("1. Insert\n");
        printf("2. Delete\n");
        printf("3. Quit\n");
        printf("-----------------\n");
        printf("\nEnter your choice: \n");
        scanf("%c", &choice);
        switch(choice) {
            case '1':
                    insert_obj();
                    break;
            case '2':
                    delete_obj();
                    break;
            case '3':     /* quit */
                    exit(0);
            default:
                    printf("Unknown choice... try again\n\n");
        }
    } /* infinite loop */
}
```

```
void delete_obj(void)
{
  /* ... delete something */
  menu();  /* go back to menu */
}

void insert_obj(void)
{
  /* ... insert something */
  menu();  /* go back to menu */
}
```

There are no directly recursive functions in this example, but there is indirect recursion between the menu function and the insert and delete functions. The insert and delete functions will never return because they call the menu function as their last action. Therefore, the stack is never unwound and the program will gradually run out of stack space, thus causing a subsequent failure because of stack overflow. In the example above, the simple removal of the calls to menu will cause the program to run correctly.

The astute reader will also notice that the program contains a minor error involving scanf and the %c format; see Section 18.2.5.

A particular instance of indirect recursion is a call to the special function, main. Any explicit call to main indicates an error due to indirect recursion, and such a program will eventually fail because of stack overflow. Although calling main is legal in C, the C++ language definition prohibits explicit calls to main and compilation should fail with a diagnostic.

12.8 Aliasing problems

The term *aliasing* refers to a general idea of two names referring to the same object. If two names x and y are both aliases for the same object, then any modification to the object via x will also affect y. Two names can be aliases in a few different ways — they might be two pointers pointing to the same address, or two C++ reference parameters referring to the same variable or object. Although aliasing is a more common problem for compiler implementors because it prevents many winning code optimizations, there are also some errors that programmers must avoid.

12.9 Aliasing and pointer variables

In C the most common aliasing problem involves pointers because any number of pointer variables can point to the same object. This can lead to hidden dangers if code assumes that two pointers are pointing at different objects. For example, consider the situation when one string pointer is copied so that it contains the same characters as in the string pointed to by the other string pointer. The obvious code sequence will be:

```
free(s1);    /* deallocate old string */
s1 = malloc(strlen(s2) + 1);
strcpy(s1,s2);    /* copy the string */
```

This will work correctly in all situations but one. Consider what happens when s1 and s2 are aliases for the same string (i.e., s1==s2). The free operation deallocates the memory they point to and then the strlen and strcpy operations read the characters from a location that has just been deallocated (i.e., an illegal address). This may or may not cause some form of program failure. Worse still, after the code fragment, the pointer s2 is pointing at a deallocated location and its string value may change in an undefined way (e.g., if the memory is reallocated by a later call to `malloc`). Therefore, the problem of the alias of s1 and s2 can cause run-time program failure. The programmer should always be careful to consider whether two pointers could ever be equal, and if necessary, use special code for this case.

Pointer aliases can be a problem in less obvious ways. For example, the `strcpy` function has undefined behavior if the two strings overlap (i.e., if the two pointers are aliases for parts of the same string). A `strcpy` call of the following form may cause strange behavior:

```
strcpy(s + 1, s);
```

Similarly, incorrect behavior can occur when `sprintf` has aliases between its destination string and its arguments. For example, the following method of adding a prefix to a string is erroneous:

```
sprintf(s, "Prefix %s", s);
```

Interestingly, the main reason for the appearance of the `memmove` standard library function is as a safe replacement for `memcpy` when both pointers could be aliased to addresses within the same memory block.

12.10 Aliasing and reference parameters

In the C++ language aliasing is also possible when using reference variables, or more commonly when using reference parameters. A typical problem is illustrated by the code to compute the maximum of two values and return it in a third:

```
void max3(double &x, double &y, double &max)
{
    max = x;
    if (y > max) max = y;
}
```

This code will work well for all instances except a few involving aliasing. Consider the code sequence:

```
double a = 1.0, b = 2.0;

max3(a, b, b);
```

For this set of arguments, the reference parameters y and max are aliases that both refer to b. The first assignment to max also changes y. Therefore, the code is equivalent to:

```
b = a;
if (b > b) b = b;
```

The function will always return the value of a as the maximum of the two values, regardless of the value of b.

One solution to the problem is to avoid aliasing by making x and y value parameters (possibly losing some efficiency advantage). Alternatively, the function can be rewritten so that it works correctly even if aliasing exists:

```
void max3(double &x, double &y, double &max)
{
    if (x > y)
        max = x;
    else
        max = y;
}
```

A particular case of aliasing of reference parameters in C++ classes involves the overloaded = operator when an object is assigned to itself. This common error is discussed fully in Section 17.1.

12.11 Aliasing and macro parameters

Aliasing problems are not limited to pointer variables or reference parameters. Another situation is that the names of macro parameters can be aliases for the same object. Let us consider a well-known trick for swapping two integral variables without using a temporary variable. The trick uses properties of the bitwise exclusive-or operator, ^. The following code sequence will (usually) swap the values of x and y:

```
x ^= y;
y ^= x;
x ^= y;
```

The clever manner in which this code fragment swaps two values can be examined by following the effects of all three statements on the four different bit patterns that each bit of x and y could have (the ^ operator applies to each bit individually):

```
x   0  0  1  1
y   0  1  0  1
-------------
x   0  1  1  0      (x ^= y)
y   0  1  0  1      (Unchanged)
-------------
x   0  1  1  0      (Unchanged)
y   0  0  1  1      (y ^= x → original x value)
-------------
x   0  1  0  1      (x ^= y → original y value)
y   0  1  0  1      (Unchanged → original x value)
```

Therefore, it seems that it is possible to write a clever macro to swap two integers as follows:

```
#define swap_int(x,y)    (x ^= y, y ^= x, x ^= y)
```

However, there is a hidden aliasing error in using this method. What is the result when the macro parameters x and y are aliases for the same location, such as below?

```
swap_int(a, a);    /* DANGEROUS ALIASES */
```

The result is that all bits of a are set to zero. All of the three statements perform a^=a, which sets a to zero. Therefore, this method of swapping works only when x is not an alias for y. Note that the alias might be more obscure, as in the following call when i and j are equal:

```
swap_int(a[i], a[j]);
```

12.12 Dangers of common idioms

There are many dangerous programming practices that are commonly used by programmers. For example, the common method of receiving input using getchar is:

```
while ((ch = getchar()) != EOF)
    putchar(ch);
```

which has the inherent danger of a precedence error if the brackets around the assignment are omitted. The following code will output a whole stream of characters with ASCII value 1, since the != operator will return 1 (i.e., true) until EOF is found:

```
while (ch = getchar() != EOF)    /* ERROR */
    putchar(ch);
```

Another common idiom is the use of an integer loop variable in a for loop. A correct for loop header looks like:

```
for (i = 1; i <= 10; i++)
```

However, when programmers "cut-and-paste" program statements there are some errors that often arise. When asked to loop down from 10 to 1, a lazy programmer will copy and change the above for loop header — a highly error-prone practice. One such error is that ++ is not changed to -- as below:

```
for (i = 10; i >= 1; i++)    /* ERROR */
```

This will cause a loop that is (almost) infinite. It will terminate only when integer overflow causes i to become negative.

A similar use of cut-and-paste without due care has caused a similar error in the code below:

```
for (i = 1; i < n; i++)
    for (j = 0; j < n; i++)    /* ERROR */
        arr[i][j] = 0;
```

Another example of a common idiom is the addition of a "bool" type using either typedef or #define. The following declaration of a boolean-like type is an error:

```
typedef enum { TRUE, FALSE } bool;    /* WRONG */
```

The problem is that TRUE is given value 0, and FALSE is given value 1.

Chapter 13

Lexical errors

The first phase of compilation is the conversion of characters into tokens and is called "lexical analysis." There are a number of common errors that may arise when the programmer makes a typographical error or misunderstands a particular token.

13.1 Unclosed or nested comments

In ANSI C and C++, the presence of /* inside another C-style /* comment does not start a nested comment; instead, it is ignored. Leaving a comment unclosed accidentally can comment out part of your code, without a compilation warning on many implementations. The /* of the unclosed comment matches the */ of a second comment, leaving out any code between the two. In the example shown below, only the first printf statement is executed because the second is accidentally commented out:

```
printf("j = %d\n", j);    /* this is a comment - unclosed!
printf("i = %d\n", i);    /* this statement is commented out */
```

One likely culprit is an erroneous space between the * and / characters. The following code is identical in effect to that above:

```
printf("j = %d\n", j);    /* this is a comment - unclosed! * /
printf("i = %d\n", i);    /* this statement is commented out */
```

Another very strange instance of nested comment problems appears when the / and * operators are placed together, such as:

```
divisor = x /*ptr;
```

Instead of dividing x by what ptr points to, the /* sequence starts a comment. Like most instances of this error, the above code will usually cause a compilation error because divisor=x has no semicolon. However, there are pathological examples where no error is generated, and the / operation simply disappears!

Another common pitfall is attempting to comment out a statement that already contains comments. However, this is less of a problem than the pitfalls above in that the */ sequence of the enclosing comment is no longer actually in a comment, and is parsed as if it were part of a statement. Thus the error typically provokes a compilation diagnostic. The solution is to use #if 0 and #endif rather than comments.

There is not usually any problem with C++-style // comments. The appearance of another // sequence before the newline is simply ignored. Using a /* comment to surround multiple lines containing // comments is also no problem. A minor danger may occur if the programmer accidentally uses // to comment out the beginning of a multiline C-style /* comment, such as below:

```
//  ...      /* this is a
             multiline comment */
```

Fortunately, this situation will almost always cause a compilation error either from the contents of the comment or from the closing */ sequence. It is possible to generate pathological examples where the code will compile cleanly and fail at run-time, but such instances are so rare that I can't think of a likely one. Can you?

A very rare problem involving the C++-style // comment is that of accidentally commenting out a statement. One potential danger appears in the common practice of converting C-style /*..*/ comments into // comments by changing /* to // and deleting */. Consider what could happen to the code below during conversion:

```
for (i = 1; i <= 10; i++)
    /* do nothing */ ;
assert(i == 11);
```

The code becomes:

```
for (i = 1; i <= 10; i++)
    // do nothing   ;
assert(i == 11);
```

The null statement (the semicolon) is commented out, and the assert macro call becomes the body of the loop.

13.2 Multibyte characters

Because C and C++ compilers accept more than one character in a char constant, there are some common errors made by novices. The compiler does not complain about a space in a char constant, as below:

```
if (ch == ' A')                  /* WRONG */
```

but interprets the code as testing whether ch is equal to some integer derived from the codes for A and a space. The result is not defined by ANSI and is machine-dependent and nonportable. Assuming an ASCII character set where A has value 65 and a space has value 32, the value of the character constant ' A' is often 65*256+32, or 32*256+65, or even just 32.

Similarly, it is wrong to confuse string constants with char constants, as in the code below. Unfortunately, many older C compilers will not complain about this statement, but will convert this strange character constant to an address (i.e., conversion to type char*) and this address is passed to printf, thereby causing unpredictable behavior:

```
printf('Hello World\n');        /* WRONG */
```

13.3 Trigraphs in string constants

Trigraphs are a new feature of ANSI C and C++ that are intended to support machines with limited keyboards or character sets. For example, instead of typing #, the programmer can type the 3-character sequence ??=, and the compiler will automatically convert this trigraph into #. The full list of trigraphs is shown in Table 13.1.

Table 13.1 Trigraph sequences

Trigraph	Meaning
??=	#
??/	\
??'	^
??(	[
??)	]
??!	|
??<	{
??>	}
??-	~

For the most part a programmer can ignore the existence of trigraphs. The only danger is that of accidentally placing a trigraph in a string literal, such as:

```
printf("What??!");    /* DANGEROUS */
```

On a strictly ANSI-conforming C compiler (or a modern C++ compiler) this will become:

```
printf("What|");
```

The solution is to use the \? escape to ensure that no trigraph sequence is seen by the compiler:

```
printf("What\?\?!");    /* CORRECT */
```

This method has a slight portability problem in that pre-ANSI C and early C++ compilers may not support the escape \? — they may produce a compilation warning, but fortunately they should convert it to an ordinary ? character.

13.4 Line splicing string constants

The placement of a backslash as the last character on a line is called line splicing, as it causes the lines to be joined as if there had been no backslash or newline. This feature is convenient for writing long string constants on multiple lines, such as:

```
char *prompt = "Hello \
world";
```

There is one danger involving whitespace characters. The programmer must be careful about the number of spaces or tabs before the backslash, and also on the beginning of the next line, because these spaces will become part of the string constant. The following code fragment illustrates both mistakes:

```
char *prompt = "Hello       \
        world";
```

The resulting string literal has many spaces between the two words. One solution to the problem is to use the facility of adjacent string literal concatenation wherever it is necessary to extend string literals over more than one source code line. Unfortunately, string literal concatenation is not available for pre-ANSI C compilers and early versions of C++.

Note that this danger involving whitespace does not exist for the other common use of line splicing in creating multiple-line macros, because these spaces will not be "inside" a token.

13.5 Octal integer constants

Any integer constant beginning with 0 is treated as an octal constant. This creates no problem with 0 itself since its value is the same in both octal and decimal, but there are dangers in using prefix zeros on integer constants. For example, the following use of prefix zeros to line up columns of integer initializers is erroneous:

```
int powers_of_10[] = {
    0001,    /* Octal 1 == decimal 1 */
    0010,    /* Octal 10 == decimal 8 */
    0100,    /* Octal 100 == decimal 64 */
    1000,    /* Decimal 1000 */
};
```

The correct solution is simply to use spaces instead of prefix zeros. Nevertheless, the temptation to use initial zeros can arise occasionally. For example, consider representing 4-digit phone extension numbers as integers:

```
struct {  char *name;  int ext_number; } arr[] = {
    { "Mary",    7234   },
    { "John",    3467   },
    { "Elaine",   0135  }    /* ERROR! */
};
```

13.6 Lowercase l suffix on integer constants

A problem can arise with programmers who use lowercase *l* as the suffix to indicate long constants. In some printed fonts, and to some extent on the screen, an *l* letter looks almost identical to 1 (one). Therefore, the use of lowercase *l* as a suffix is highly error-prone because it can be easily mistaken for a 1. For example, consider the constant 10l; is it 10 of type long or 101 of type int? Unfortunately, the chance of the compiler noticing that the constant is of the wrong type is very slim, and this error can be very hard to detect. The simple solution is: *use the uppercase suffix L.*

13.7 Character escapes

Novice C programmers occasionally confuse / with \ when used in `printf` format strings. The error is usually quite harmless, as it will appear as erroneous output. A typical example is:

```
printf("Hello world/n");
```

A rare error can occur when using hexadecimal or octal escapes in string literals. If the programmer uses too many digits for the escape, the succeeding digits will be included as characters in the string. For example, the string literal `"\xffff"` contains 3 characters: `'\xff'`, `'f'` and `'f'`. Hexadecimal escapes with \x use at most 2 hexadecimal digits and octal escapes use at most 3 octal digits.

These rules also create a portability problem for old pre-ANSI C code (and early C++) where there were different rules. In pre-ANSI C the escape \000002 would be a single character in a string literal; in ANSI C it is 4 characters.

13.8 Tabs in output statements

Using tab characters to align columns of output is an error-prone practice. For example, try placing a tab character in a C++ output statement such as:

```
0123456701234567012345670123456
cout << "ABC    DEF";  /* Single tab between headings */
```

The alignment of columns to tab stops will be different in the source code from how it appears in the output, because the source code is already indented a number of characters by whitespace and by the characters that make up the program statement (i.e., `"cout <<"` in the example). As a result, the output will have a different number of spaces for the tab character; in this case it is one extra space:

```
0123456701234567012345670123456
ABC    DEF
```

Assuming tab stops every 8 characters, the tab character in the source code above starts at position 4 and the tab finishes at position 7; in the output the start of the tab is position 3, and its finish is still position 7.

13.9 Backslash in DOS filenames

A common error for UNIX programmers converting to DOS occurs when a DOS filename is encoded with its full path name. The apparently simple change of the slash character in UNIX filenames to the backslash in DOS filenames has a major danger — the backslash starts an escape. Hence the filename below is wrong:

```
fp = fopen("c:\file.c", "r");      /* WRONG */
```

The backslash character starts the escape \f. The correct statement uses two backslash characters to form the escape representing a single backslash:

```
fp = fopen("c:\\file.c", "r");      /* CORRECT */
```

13.10 Misspelled default label

A very rare but bizarre error can occur if the programmer mistypes the "default" label.
For example, consider the following code:

```
switch (x) {
   case 1:  printf("case 1"); break;
   case 2:  printf("case 2"); break;
   defalut: printf("default"); break;    /* TYPO! */
}
```

The default label is spelled incorrectly and becomes a goto label by accident. When
none of the cases match during program execution, the default code is simply skipped
because there is no default label and the program continues with the statements
following the switch statement. Fortunately, this error is usually detected by a warning
about an unused label "defalut" or unreachable code (the printf call).

13.11 Mistyping :: in C++

Another error related to goto labels occurs when the programmer accidentally misses
one of the colon characters in the :: token. Consider the following example:

```
void Derived::fn()
{
    Base:fn();    // call Base method?
}
```

The intention is to forward a derived method to the base class version of the same
method, but what actually occurs is infinite recursion! The error is a missing colon
character from the :: token. The sequence "Base:" becomes an unused goto label,
and thus the call "fn();" is a recursive call.

13.12 Confusing NULL, 0, '0', and '\0'

There are so many versions of zero that it isn't surprising that they are misused. Novice
programmers may write '0' when they mean the null byte that terminates a string. The
correct method is to use 0 or preferably '\0' which is equivalent and considered better
style by many because it makes it clear that we are using character zero rather than
integer zero.

It is a common mistake for programmers to use NULL when they really mean the
string terminating byte. Some reasons for the confusion are that the ASCII name for
character zero is NUL, and many C/C++ programming texts refer to it as the null byte.
Consider the following example:

```
char s[10];
    ...
if (s[0] == NULL)    /* if empty string */
```

Fortunately, on many compilers the macro NULL expands out to 0 and the program does
not fail. On other platforms, NULL may expand out as (void*)0, but even here there is
unlikely to be a run-time failure as all the implicit type conversions preserve the intended
meaning of the test. Therefore, the error is mainly one of style.

13.13 Single letter variables

Novice programmers learning their first language may not immediately appreciate the significance of the single quotes around character constants. An occasional source of errors are tests such as:

```
if (A <= ch && ch <= Z)
```

where the novice has actually declared the variables A and Z, because the compiler complained that they were not declared! The correct expression is:

```
if ('A' <= ch && ch <= 'Z')
```

Programmers using such expressions should be encouraged to use the library functions in <ctype.h> instead. The expression isupper(ch) would be more portable, more readable, and more efficient than the test above.

13.14 Anachronistic tokens and ancient C compilers

In a very early definition of the C language the extended assignment operators such as -= had the characters reversed (i.e., =- was an operator in ancient C). Fortunately, this usage quickly died out, and neither ANSI C nor C++ supports these tokens. However, for very old C compilers there is some ambiguity in statements such as:

```
x=-1;
```

Some very old compilers could conceivably treat =- as the extended subtraction operator and subtract 1 from x. However, in the author's experience the worst that occurs is an annoying warning about using an "anachronism." The problem can be removed by adding a space to separate the - and = characters:

```
x = -1;
```

Chapter 14

Expression errors

Expressions in C and C++ programs can become very complicated and are prone to error. The sheer number of different operators can cause confusion, and errors occur when operators are used improperly or are applied in an order different from that intended by the programmer because of confusion about precedence and associativity.

14.1 Assignment and equality (= and ==)

The most common error for beginning C and C++ programmers is to use the assignment operator (=) instead of the relational equality operator (==). The assignment operator is legal in `if` statements. It evaluates to the value of its right operand. In the example below, the value 3 is assigned to x, and the result returned is 3, which is always true. If instead there had been "if(x=0)" it would always be false, because the value of the expression "x=0" is 0, which is false. The problem is illustrated below:

```
if (x = 3)      /* INCORRECT */
if (x == 3)     /* CORRECT */
```

Fortunately, many modern compilers warn about such expressions, although most old compilers do not consider assignment in logical conditions to be an error and do not generate any warning. The best solution is practice — get used to typing ==.

14.2 Logical and bitwise operators (& and &&)

Another common mistake that novice programmers make with double character operators is using & or | (which are bitwise operators) instead of && or || (which are logical operators). This bug is not shown by the compiler, as it is not a syntax error. The erroneous use of bitwise operators can cause intermittent bugs. The difference between & and && does not always cause an error. The bitwise-and operator, &, causes a bit operation on each bit of its two operands, and returns the result, which can be any integer. The logical operator, &&, returns only two possible values — zero or one. It returns 1 (true) if both operands are nonzero, otherwise it returns zero.

If both operands are either zero or one, there is no difference between the result of & and &&. This is often the case in conditions such as (x==y)&&(z>3), because the relational operators return only zero or one. However, problems occur when using a

nonzero value to indicate the truth of a condition. Incorrect results can occur below if &
accidentally replaces &&:

```
if (flag && x > y)                    /* if flag != 0  and  x > y */
```

If & replaces && here, the test is effectively a bit mask on the lower bit of flag. The test
"(x>y)" returns 0 or 1, which is then used as a mask for the & operator. If, for example,
flag is 2 (nonzero means true) the condition will return false anyway, because the lower
bit is zero.

There are also differences between & and && in terms of their order of evaluation.
The logical operator && uses short-circuiting and does not evaluate its second operand if
the first operand is false. In the code below the incorrect use of & will cause an error if p
is NULL:

```
if (p == NULL & p->next != NULL) ...
```

The best solution to this problem is to be aware of it, and get used to typing characters
twice. The preprocessor could be used to help (e.g., #define and &&), but this is not
recommended, mainly because it is not common practice. It is also good to use explicit
comparisons with zero (i.e., flag!=0) since this reduces dangers of error, increases
readability, and should not reduce efficiency on any reasonable compiler.

14.3 Boolean expressions: De Morgan's laws

A common mistake for novice programmers is to incorrectly interpret complicated
boolean expressions. Unless you are very familiar with the rules of boolean algebra,
check them carefully. A good idea is to hand-evaluate a few cases to check that the
condition gives the correct result.

One problem area involves the combination of the ! operator with either of && or ||.
De Morgan's laws of boolean algebra are counterintuitive to the average programmer.
For example, do not be fooled into thinking that the expression *not (A or B)* is the same as
not A or not B. De Morgan's laws state:

```
!(x || y)   ≡    (!x) && (!y)
!(x && y)   ≡    (!x) || (!y)
```

For example, when testing whether x is in the range 1..10, the expression is simply:

```
if (1 <= x && x <= 10)
```

Problems may arise when this if statement is inverted to test whether x is not in this
range. An obvious (and correct) method is to use the ! operator:

```
if (!(1 <= x && x <= 10))
```

However, many programmers are tempted to simplify this code for efficiency (although in
practice a good compiler will perform these changes automatically during code
generation). The trap here is to change just the <= operators without changing the &&
operator to ||:

```
if (1 > x && x > 10))    /* WRONG */
```

The above test is testing whether x is less than 1 *and* greater than 10 — obviously an impossible condition. The correct solution is to change both the relational operators (<=) and the logical operator (&&):

```
if (1 > x || x > 10))    /* CORRECT */
```

14.4 Real number equality

Real numbers behave strangely on computers. The problems are due to the internal representation of real numbers. Computers can store real numbers only to a limited precision (i.e., a limited number of significant figures). Inevitably, roundoff errors occur in calculations. The most common mistake made with real numbers is comparing them for equality. For example, the for loop below checks for inequality (i.e., not equal):

```
double x, inc;
   ....
for (x = 0.0; x != 10.0 * inc; x += inc)    // DANGEROUS
```

This could cause an infinite loop, because when x nears 10*inc, it might not be exactly equal. The test for inequality would still succeed, and the loop would continue infinitely, incrementing x further away from 10*inc at each iteration.

Instead of comparing two real numbers for exact equality, programs should examine their difference. When the absolute value of this difference is smaller than some defined tolerance, consider them equal. A greater difference than the tolerance means not equal. The tolerance value should be very small (e.g., 0.00001). The for loop becomes:

```
for (x = 0.0; fabs(x - 10.0 * inc) > TOLERANCE; x += inc)
```

Tests for real number equality might be better hidden behind a macro or inline function:

```
#define REAL_EQ(x,y)    (fabs((x) - (y)) <= TOLERANCE)
#define REAL_NEQ(x,y)    (fabs((x) - (y)) > TOLERANCE)
int REAL_EQ(double x,double y) {return fabs(x-y) <= TOLERANCE;}
int REAL_NEQ(double x,double y) {return fabs(x-y) > TOLERANCE;}
```

Note that changing the original loop to use < instead of != would also probably fail, although not as drastically. The loop:

```
for (x = 0.0; x < 10.0 * inc; x += inc)
```

might not iterate exactly 10 times. It might perform one extra iteration because at the end of the 10th, the value of x might be very close to 10.0*inc, but not exactly equal, causing the < operator to still return true (it is still less than, albeit only very slightly).

14.5 Array index out of bounds

During execution, a C/C++ program does not check array references to determine if indices are too large for the array. A very common error is an array index passing the end of the array. This can cause other variables to be overwritten, crashing sooner or later. Most commonly, the mistake is that an array extends only from `0..n-1`. Declaring an array of size n does not allow the nth array element to be accessed or modified. A common form of this error is:

```
int arr[MAX];
    ...
for (i = 1; i <= MAX; i++)
    printf("%d\n", arr[i];
```

This code demonstrates the misconception that arrays start at 1 and extend to the declared size. The correct `for` loop starts at 0 and use < instead of <=, as below:

```
for (i = 0; i < MAX; i++)
```

You might have read that ANSI C allows pointers to hold values one past the end of an array (i.e., hold the address `&arr[n]`). However, do not be confused into thinking that it is then legal to dereference these pointers to access or modify the value they point to. Pointers are allowed to hold such values only for the purposes of pointer comparisons.

14.6 Operator precedence errors

The precedence of some operators is not as you might expect it to be and nasty bugs can creep in. The only real solution is to become more familiar with the precedence of various operators, but placing extra brackets causes no harm and does eliminate the problem. The precedence of the various operators is shown in Table 14.1.

Note that C++ overloaded operators still retain their usual precedence, and it is therefore not possible to fix any "inaccuracies" in the precedence table (and also not possible to introduce further precedence errors).

When masking bits and then comparing them with a value, brackets are needed to ensure the correct ordering:

```
if (x & MASK != 0)          /* INCORRECT */
if ((x & MASK) != 0)        /* CORRECT */
```

Similarly, when testing a function return value by assigning it to a variable, brackets are necessary:

```
if (c = getchar() != EOF)        /* INCORRECT */
if ((c = getchar()) != EOF)      /* CORRECT */
```

When using the shift operators to replace multiplication or division, the low precedence of the shift operators causes problems. For example, consider the conversion of `a+b*2` to use shifting:

```
x = a + b >> 1;          /* INCORRECT */
x = a + (b >> 1);        /* CORRECT */
```

Table 14.1 Operator precedence

Operator	Precedence
() [] -> .	highest precedence
! - + ++ -- ~ * & (type) sizeof	
* / %	
+ -	
<< >>	
< <= > >=	
== !=	
&	
^	
|	
&&	
||	
?:	
= += -= *= /= %= &= |= <<= >>=	
,	lowest precedence

The use of the shift operators with C++ output streams declared by `<iostream.h>` can occasionally be the cause of a precedence error. There is no problem for any operators with higher precedence than << in Table 14.1, and this includes the most used operators. However, the relational operators, bitwise operators, logical operators, and the conditional operator can all cause precedence errors because of their low precedence. The code fragment below illustrates these dangers:

```
cout << x & y;       // Compilation error
cout << x > y;       // Compilation error
cout << x && y;      // Warning?
cout << x ? x : y;   // Warning?
```

The use of the bitwise or relational operators will cause a compilation error because there is an attempt to apply an operator such as & or > to a stream object. However, the incorrect use of the && operator will receive only a warning about the value of the && expression not being used, and not all compilers will have warnings this sophisticated. Similarly, the use of the conditional operator may not even receive a warning. The solution is simply to bracket the subexpressions being printed:

```
cout << (x & y);
cout << (x > y);
cout << (x && y);
cout << (x ? x : y);
```

The use of increment or decrement operators with either of the pointer dereference operators is quite error-prone. There are always two interpretations, depending on whether brackets are used:

```
++p->len;      /* Increment p->len */
(++p)->len;    /* Increment p, then access p->len */
*p++;          /* Increment p, then access what p pointed to */
(*p)++;        /* Increment what p points to */
```

The last two statements illustrate a common error: the use of *p++ is incorrect when trying to increment what p is pointing to.

The high precedence of the type cast operator means that care is necessary when using it in expressions. For example, when trying to convert the result of x/y to int, the code below is incorrect:

```
z = (int)x / y;        /* INCORRECT */
```

The correct method is to use brackets:

```
z = (int)(x / y);      /* CORRECT */
```

14.7 Null effect operations

This error refers to use of operators where the returned result is ignored. It can occur because of a major misconception by the programmer about some operators, or because of operator precedence problems. For example, the statements below have no effect:

```
x << 1;        /* INCORRECT */
~x;            /* INCORRECT */
```

The first statement is an attempt to double x using bit shifting, and the second is an attempt to complement x using the one's complement operator. Unfortunately, the << operator in the statement "x<<1;" does not affect x at all. Instead, the statement merely evaluates the value of x doubled and then "throws away" this value because it is not used. Compilers usually do not complain about throwing away values because this effect is commonly used by function calls (e.g., the printf function always returns a value, but this value is rarely used). The statements above are executed normally despite the fact that they actually do nothing at all. The correct statements are:

```
x <<= 1;
x = ~x;
```

Another common example occurs when Pascal programmers call a function with no arguments and omit the empty pair of brackets, as below:

```
fn_name;       /* INCORRECT */
```

This is interpreted as a null effect statement that simply evaluates to the address of the function, rather than calling the function.

Another example of the problem, related to operator associativity, occurs in the statement:

```
*ptr++;        /* INCORRECT */
```

The intention is to increment what `ptr` is pointing to, but right-to-left operator associativity causes ++ to be evaluated first, followed by the dereference operator. Hence `ptr` is incremented, and the * dereference operation has no effect — the value of what `ptr` points to is calculated and then thrown away. Brackets are needed to enforce the desired associativity.

14.8 Missing brackets on function calls

The most common example of missing brackets on a function call is illustrated below. The statement below is a null effect statement (see Section 14.7) that simply evaluates to the address of `fn_name` (and then throws it away), rather than calling the function:

```
fn_name;     /* INCORRECT */
```

The situation is also dangerous in C++ where omitting the brackets from a call to a member function with no arguments can cause wrong behavior. This is a common pitfall for C programmers moving to C++ since the presence of brackets on a construct like C's structure members is new to C programmers. An example is:

```
stack.pop;   // INCORRECT - should be stack.pop();
```

Even worse is the fact that most compilers will not detect missing brackets on function calls in conditional expressions. For example, the C++ expression with missing brackets:

```
if (stack.is_empty) {  // MISSING BRACKETS
   ....
}
```

may not provoke a warning on many compilers. It is interpreted as testing whether the pointer-to-function constant `stack.is_empty` is not equal to NULL; therefore the condition will evaluate to true. An equivalent problem exists in ANSI C where tests such as `if(fn_name)` test whether `fn_name` is non-NULL.

14.9 Side effects and short-circuiting

Expressions that use the binary logical operators (`||` or `&&`) or the ternary conditional operator (`?:`) can have problems if the subexpressions contain *side effects*. Side effects are operations that affect a variable, consume input, or produce output. Thus, the increment and decrement operators and the assignment operators all cause side effects because they change a variable. A function call can be a side effect if it consumes input, produces output, changes one of its arguments, or alters a *global* variable.

The problem is that C and C++ use *short-circuiting* in the evaluation of the binary logical operators and the ternary conditional operator. Not all of a boolean expression involving these operators is always evaluated. In fact, only as much of the expression as is necessary to determine the result is actually evaluated. Parts of the expression having no effect on the result are ignored.

If the first operand of an `&&` is false, or the first operand of an `||` is true, then the second operand is not evaluated at all. If either of these cases occurs, the result is completely determined by the first operand. There is no need to evaluate the second operand to determine the result. The identities below show the justification for short-circuiting:

> False AND anything ≡ False
> True OR anything ≡ True

This short-circuiting process is guaranteed by the ANSI C standard and also occurs in C++. Short-circuiting improves the efficiency of evaluating a boolean expression by doing as little work as necessary. However, it can also cause strange errors.

Short-circuiting means that not all subexpressions in an expression are always executed. If a subexpression containing side effects is not executed, the (usually important) effect of these side effects is lost. For example, in the expression:

```
if (x < y && (ch = getchar()) != EOF)
```

if the first term (x<y) is false, the call to the `getchar` function is not executed and no input is consumed.

The only real solution is to avoid the use of side effects in boolean expressions. This is quite reasonable since such expressions are bad style anyway. The problem of short-circuiting and side effects is also covered in Section 14.10.1.

14.10 Order of evaluation of operators

In C and C++ the order of the evaluation of *operands* for most binary operators is not specified. This makes it possible for compilers to apply very good optimizing algorithms to the code. Unfortunately, it also leads to some problems that the programmer must be aware of.

Order of evaluation of *operands* is a different concept from order of evaluation of *operators*. The evaluation of operators is completely specified by brackets, operator precedence, and associativity, but evaluation of operands is not. To see the effect of order of evaluation of operands, consider the expression:

```
(a + b) * (c + d)
```

Which is to be evaluated first: (a+b) or (c+d)? Neither bracketing, precedence nor associativity decides this order. Bracketing specifies that both additions must be evaluated before the multiplication, not which addition is evaluated first. Associativity does not apply, because the two + operators are not near one another (they are separated by a * operator). Precedence does not apply because the brackets override it.

The order of evaluation depends only upon how the compiler chooses to evaluate the operands of the * operator. Intuitively, we would assume that the evaluation would take place left-to-right. However, the order of evaluation of the operands to the multiplication operator, and most other binary operators, is not specified in C or C++. Different compilers may choose different orderings.

Usually the order does not matter. In the example above, it does not matter which addition is done first. The two additions are independent, and can be executed in any order. However, if an expression involves side effects, the result is sometimes undefined. The result may be as intended, or it may be incorrect. Sometimes it will be correct when compiled without optimization, but incorrect after optimization. Results may differ on different machines and the code is not portable.

A *side effect* is an operation that affects a variable being used in the expression or affects some external variable used indirectly in the expression. The most common example of a side effect is the increment or decrement operator. Any assignment operation deep inside an expression is also a side effect to the variable it changes. A function call can also be a side effect if it modifies a variable used in the expression (as a parameter or globally), modifies some other external variable on which another subexpression depends (i.e., a global or local `static` variable), or if it produces output or accepts input. The full list of side effects is given in Table 14.2.

Table 14.2   Side effects

Operation	Meaning
++	Decrement
--	Increment
=, +=, etc.	Assignment operators
fn()	Function call (some kinds)

To see the effect of side effects, consider the increment operator in the expression below. It is a dangerous side effect.

```
y = (x++) + (x * 2);
```

Because the order of evaluation of the addition operator is not specified, there are two orders in which the expression could actually be executed. The programmer's intended order is:

```
temp = x++;
y = (temp) + (x * 2);
```

and the incorrect order is:

```
temp = x * 2;
y = (x++) + (temp);
```

In the first case, the increment occurs before x*2 is evaluated. In the second, the increment occurs after x*2 has been evaluated. Obviously, the two interpretations give different results.

If there are two function calls in the one expression, the order of the function calls can be important. For example, in the code below:

```
f() + g()
```

if both functions produce output or both modify the same global variable, the result of the expression may depend on the order of evaluation of the + operator (which is undefined).

Most binary operators have unspecified order of evaluation — even the assignment operators. A simple assignment statement can be the cause of an error. Consider the example:

```
a[i] = i++;
```

This has two interpretations. Is the array subscript the old or new value of i? It isn't clear whether a[i] or a[i+1] will be assigned the value. The intended order is:

```
temp = i;                    /* Programmer intended meaning */
a[temp] = i++;               /* Index is OLD value of i */
```

and the incorrect alternative order that the compiler can also legally implement is:

```
temp = i++;                  /* Incorrect order */
a[i] = temp;                 /* Index is NEW value of i */
```

14.10.1 Safe and unsafe operators

The following discussion applies to C operators and also to nonoverloaded C++ operators. The use of overloaded C++ operators is similar to a function call, and the evaluation order of the operator then has no importance; instead the order of evaluation of function arguments applies.

There is no order of evaluation problem with *unary operators* as they have only one operand to evaluate. The *structure operators* also give no problem as only one of the operands can be evaluated (the first). The second operand is a field name that needs no evaluation — it is not an expression. The *comma operator* is also a completely safe operator. Its specified order for evaluation of operands is left-to-right. Furthermore, it always evaluates both its operands.

The *logical operators*, && and ||, are almost safe. Their specified order of evaluation is left-to-right. However, it is possible to *not evaluate* some operands. Depending on the value of the first expression, any side effect in the second expression can occur once or not occur at all. This occurs owing to the *short-circuiting* of logical operators.

Short-circuiting refers to the fact that when evaluating expressions involving the logical operators (&& and ||), the expression is evaluated only up to what is necessary to determine the result of the expression (i.e., true or false). If the first operand of the && is false or the first operand of the || is true, the second operand is not evaluated. Consider the example:

```
if (x == 0 && y == z++)
    ...
```

If x equals zero, the second expression is evaluated and z is incremented. However, if x is nonzero, short-circuiting prevents the evaluation of the second operand and z is not incremented. Note that there is no problem if only the first expression contains side effects, as all the side effects will be executed exactly once, and will be executed before the second expression is evaluated.

The *ternary conditional operator* (?:) has its order of evaluation fully specified: evaluate the first operand; if true then evaluate the second, else evaluate the third. Hence the order of evaluation is fixed, but, as with the binary logical operators, whether each operand is actually evaluated is not fixed. There is a problem when the second or third expression involves side effects. Depending on the value of the first expression, the side effect can occur once or not occur at all. As with the logical operators, side effects in the first expression pose no problem.

The *ordinary binary operators* are completely unsafe. This includes the arithmetic, relational, bitwise, shift, assignment, and extended assignment operators. The order of evaluation of their operands is not specified at all.

14.10.2 Sequence points

UNIX programmers have a partial solution to order of evaluation problems: `lint`. The `lint` utility will find many simple order of evaluation ambiguities: it will find those involving increment, but will not find those involving function calls.

No amount of brackets can be a solution. Brackets do not affect the order of evaluation of operands. They affect only the order of evaluation of operators (i.e., they change only the precedence and associativity).

An extreme solution follows this motto: if there are no side effects, there is no problem. With that aim, the code is written so that increment and decrement operations are done in separate statements (i.e., different lines). Never increment a variable inside a complicated expression or in a function argument. Assignments are not placed in the middle of expressions. Function calls that may cause dangerous side effects are also separated out to separate lines. For example, the expression:

```
a[i] = i++;
```

can be rewritten as:

```
a[i] = i;
i++;
```

A less extreme solution is to separate any *dangerous* side effects. Some side effects are no problem. For example, if a variable with a side effect appears only once in an expression, it is not a problem. Only dangerous side effects need be separated out, and side effects that are not dangerous are left alone. To separate side effects, temporary variables may be necessary to hold values of subexpressions.

The concept of *sequence points* is useful in determining how to break up an expression into subexpressions. Sequence points are points in the program where it is guaranteed that all side effects in the code so far have taken place. The sequence points are summarized in Table 14.3.

Table 14.3 Sequence points

Token	Meaning
;	End of a statement
||	Logical-or operator
&&	Logical-and operator
,	Comma operator
?:	Ternary operator

The main example of a sequence point is the semicolon terminating a statement. Once the whole expression has been evaluated, all side effects will have occurred. Other examples of sequence points are after the first operand of the comma operator, ternary conditional operator, or a binary logical operator, and also at the (only) operand of a unary plus operator.

When writing code, try to satisfy the following condition: between successive sequence points, any variable with a side effect is referenced only once. Simply put, if a variable has a side effect in a statement, ensure that the variable occurs only once in that statement. If such a variable occurs twice, the subexpression causing the side effect should be separated out. If a variable has no side effect in a statement, it may occur any number of times in the statement.

14.11 Order of evaluation of function arguments

Another form of the order of evaluation problem occurs because the order of the evaluation of arguments to a function is not specified in C or C++. It is not necessarily left-to-right, as the programmer expects it to be. For example, consider the function call:

```
fn(a++, a);
```

Which argument is evaluated first? Is the second argument the new or old value of a? The compiler can legally implement this statement as if it were equivalent to either of:

```
fn(a, a),   a++;
fn(a, a+1),   a++;
```

Another example occurs where the side effect is a global variable. In the following example, the global variable is the file stream:

```
void process_2_chars(int first_char, int second_char);
  ...
process_2_chars(getchar(), getchar());   /* ERROR */
```

It is undefined whether the function will receive the 2 characters in the intended order, or in reverse order.

14.12 Evaluation order of C++ overloaded operators

When a class has overloaded operators declared to operate on itself and other values, there are order of evaluation errors that can creep in. Consider the output statement:

```
cout << i++ << " " << i++;
```

This use of the overloaded << operator suffers the same order of evaluation problems as any other function call. Overloaded operators are just like any other functions in terms of evaluation of their arguments. The above statement is equivalent to:

```
cout.operator<<(i++).operator<<(" ").operator<<(i++);
```

which is similar to a function call such as:

```
fn(fn(fn(cout,i++)," "), i++);
```

There is no specified ordering of the two i++ side effects. It could be equivalent to any of the following statements:

```
(cout << i << " " << i), i++, i++;
(cout << i+1 << " " << i), i++, i++;
(cout << i << " " << i+1), i++, i++;
```

14.13 Side effects to sizeof

The sizeof operator can be applied to an expression, and yields the size of the type of the resulting expression. Any side effects in this expression are not evaluated at run-time.

Unfortunately, some compilers do not implement this correctly. Although most programmers won't willingly place useful side effects in a sizeof expression, it is reasonably common practice to call malloc as below:

```
ptr = malloc(sizeof(*ptr));
```

and this is quite valid in ANSI C. However, on deficient compilers that implement sizeof incorrectly this can cause a dereference of ptr, which is possibly NULL or a wayward pointer (e.g., uninitialized). Nevertheless, a compiler bug is not necessarily a good reason to avoid this style.

14.14 sizeof operator applied to array parameter

There is one situation when the sizeof operator computes surprising results — when applied to a function parameter of array type. The error is illustrated by the following function:

```
void test_sizeof(int arr[3])
{
    printf("Size is %d\n", (int) sizeof(arr));
}
```

The computed size is expected to be 3*sizeof(int) — usually either 6 or 12. However, the actual result will usually be 2 or 4. This is because the sizeof operator is actually being applied to a pointer type. An array parameter is converted to the corresponding pointer type and it is this type that sizeof applied to. Therefore, the output result is exactly sizeof(int*), which is commonly 2 or 4.

14.14.1 sizeof and string literals

Another bizarre situation related to sizeof in ANSI C is that the computed size for a string literal is not the same as a pointer size. For example, sizeof("hello") is not 2 or 4 (i.e., a pointer size), but is actually 6, because "hello" has array type char[6], with 5 bytes for the letters and one byte for the null. Presumably most pre-ANSI and some modern "ANSI" C compilers will get this wrong.

14.15 Overflow of 16-bit ints

Perhaps the single most common portability problem for code written on UNIX (or other 32-bit systems) when ported to DOS is the 16-bit int problem. Many major compilers for DOS use 16-bit integers for the type int. However, this is not merely a portability problem, since any programmers working with 16-bit compilers must always consider carefully whether any values they declare as "int" will ever overflow.

The range of a 16-bit int is −32,768...32,767 which is quite small. Numbers like 50,000 and 100,000 are commonly used in programs and the programmer must make a careful choice between int and long. If a value stored in an int becomes too large (or too small) it will overflow and change sign, leading to strange errors. By contrast, a 32-bit int will have a huge range of values (−2,147,483,648...2,147,483,647) and is much less likely to overflow in common usage.

14.15.1 Loop iterations and 16-bit int

Even the use of an int variable as a for loop counter is not immune from error. For example, consider the simple for loop below:

```
#define ITERATIONS   1000
 ....
int i;
 ...
for (i = 0; i <= ITERATIONS; i++)
   ... /* do something */
```

If i is an int variable, we must be careful how high we set the ITERATIONS constant. If it is set higher than 32,767, the loop will be an infinite loop with i going up to 32,767 and then overflowing to become −32,768. The loop is infinite because i can never get a value higher than 32,767 and the loop condition is always true. Fortunately, some compilers will warn that the comparison can never fail.

14.15.2 fseek and 16-bit int

Let us examine a dangerous error that has bitten the author quite badly in the past. However, it is unlikely to occur again as it occurred because of a compiler's lack of conformance with the ANSI C standard, and the problem has now been corrected.

A program that was using a binary file of records worked well for a small number of records, but suddenly failed when a large number of records were stored. The strangest symptom was that the binary file was exactly 65,536 bytes in length (i.e., 64K bytes).

The error was finally traced to the fact that the compiler (an early non-ANSI version of a popular DOS compiler) had declared fseek to have an offset argument of type size_t, and ftell to return size_t. Since size_t was declared as unsigned int the number of bytes accessible via fseek was exactly the range of a 16-bit unsigned integer: 0..65,535. Therefore, any offset values larger than 65,535 produced an unsigned overflow (i.e., they wrapped around to smaller values within the limited range). Storing a record that should have been a long way into the file was actually overwriting some of the earlier records with disastrous results.

Fortunately, the said compiler has since come round to ANSI standard conformance with the `fseek` argument and `ftell` return type corrected to become `long int` — a 32-bit integer.

14.15.3 Integer calculations and 16-bit int

When performing mathematical computations involving integers, the choice between `int` and `long` should be made carefully. For example, consider the `factorial` function to compute the product 1*2*3...*n. The use of `int` as the return type is shown below:

```
int factorial(int n)
{
    int i, result = 1;

    for (i = 1; i <= n; i++)
        result *= i;
    return result;
}
```

However, this will perform poorly on a 16-bit machine since it will overflow the return type for $n \geq 8$. The corrected function becomes:

```
long int factorial(int n)
{
    int i;
    long int result = 1L;

    for (i = 1; i <= n; i++)
        result *= i;
    return result;
}
```

However, in this case the improvement from using 32-bit calculations is not particularly great because of the explosive nature of the factorial function. The result of the function overflows the 32-bit upper bound of 2,147,483,647 for $n \geq 14$.

14.15.4 The rand function and 16-bit int

An example of a nonportable practice on 32-bit implementations is the extraction of high-order bits from the return value of `rand`. On some implementations the low-order bits of the random number exhibit nonrandom patterns (e.g., `rand()&01` may produce the pattern 0,1,0,1...), and programmers solve this problem by extracting bits from the higher 16 bits. A common method of producing random binary values is:

```
bit = rand() & (1 << 16);    /* extract 17th bit */
```

This will usually return zero on a 16-bit machine because `1<<16` is an overflow. Some compilers will warn about a shift count larger than the operand size.

14.16 Right shift is not division

The shift operators << and >> are often used to replace multiplication by a power of 2 for a low-level optimization. However, it is dangerous to use >> on negative numbers. Right shift is not equivalent to division for negative values. Note that the problem does not arise for unsigned data types that are never negative, and for which shifting is always a division.

There are two separate issues involved in shifting signed types with negative values: firstly, that the compiler may choose two distinct methods of implementing >>, and secondly, that neither of these approaches is equivalent to division (although one approach is often equivalent).

It is unspecified by the ANSI standard whether >> on negative values will:

(a) sign extend, or
(b) shift in zero bits.

Different compilers must choose one of these methods, document it, and use it for all applications of the >> operator. The use of shifting in zero bits is never equal to division for a negative number, since it shifts a zero bit into the sign bit, causing the result to be a nonnegative integer. Shifting in zero bits is always used for unsigned types, which explains why right shifting on unsigned types is a division.

The second method of implementing right shift on negative values is sign extension. This is similar to division, but is not always equivalent. However, note that integral division of negative values is also not well defined by ANSI C (i.e., rounding down or rounding up), and so it may happen that / and >> produce the same results. Try the following statement to examine whether >> and division are the same:

```
printf("-17 / 2 =  %d, -17 >> 1 =  %d\n", -17 / 2, -17 >> 1);
```

14.17 Integer wrap around

Integer overflow can lead to an interesting problem. Consider the following code to print out the 256 characters in a particular implementation's character set:

```
char ch;

for (ch = 0; ch <= 255; ch++)
    printf("%d  %c\n", ch, ch);
```

There are a few problems with this loop. It is implementation-specific whether the type char behaves as signed or unsigned on any system. If char is signed by default it cannot hold the values 128..255 and the loop test cannot fail. However, even if char is unsigned by default, there is another error causing the loop never to terminate. As soon as ch reaches 255, it is incremented, but instead of becoming 256 it "wraps around" to become 0. The for loop condition never fails.

Similar problems can occur with short, int, and long, as these have only a finite range of values and will wrap around to zero (for unsigned types) or negative (for signed types).

14.18 Divide and remainder on negatives

Extreme care is needed when the division and remainder operators / and % are applied to negative values. Problems arise if a program assumes, for example, that $-7/2$ equals -3 (rather than -4) or that $-1\%3$ equals 2 (rather than -1). The direction of truncation of / is undefined if either operand is negative; therefore the following are undefined:

```
-7 / 2
 7 / -2
-7 / -2
```

It is likely that the last case, $-7/-2$, is implemented equivalently to $7/2$ with rounding down to the result 3. However, the ANSI standard does not specify that dividing two negatives is well defined, and thus it is safer to assume that it is not.

Similarly, the % remainder operator is undefined on negative operands. However, if n>0 and p<0 it is guaranteed that n%p is in the range:

```
p < n % p < -p
```

Therefore, x%-5 is between -4 and 4, inclusive. Note that this restriction can also be formed as:

```
abs(n % p) < abs(p)
```

Although the above discussion seems to indicate that the results of / and % on negative operands are very unpredictable, there is a relationship between / and % that restricts the implementation. An implementation must ensure that the following identity remains true for x and y (except y==0):

```
(x/y)*y + x%y == x
```

The / and % operators also have undefined behavior when their second operand, the divisor, is zero. On some machines this will raise an arithmetic exception that can be trapped by signal; on other machines it is ignored, but the result is undefined.

14.19 Incorrect use of relational operators

A common error made by novice programmers is to assume that programming language operators are like mathematical notation. For example, although $x \le y \le z$ is valid mathematical notation, the expression x<=y<=z is erroneous. Even worse is the confusion that the 3-way assignment x=y=z is legal, but the 3-way equality test x==y==z is incorrect. Unfortunately, such uses rarely cause compilation errors because of the flexibility to mix operators freely. Such expressions will compile and run, but won't produce the expected results. For example, the test:

```
if (x <= y <= z)
```

will actually compare the value of z with the 0 or 1 (i.e., false or true) result of the x<=y relational operation. The left associativity of <= ensures this evaluation order.

14.20 Equality tests on string constants and arrays

Applying either `==` or `!=` to string constants is usually an indication of a novice's misunderstanding about strings. The expression:

```
if (str == "YES")
```

does not test whether the string equals YES. Instead, it tests whether the address of `str` equals the address of where the string constant is stored, and will usually evaluate to false. The correct method for comparing strings is to call the `strcmp` function.

Applying the `==` or `!=` operators to array variables is often an indication of an error. In particular, if the array is an array of `char`, this is probably the indication of a misunderstanding about how to test equality of strings. The correct method of testing strings is to call `strcmp`. For equality tests on other arrays, the `memcmp` function may be useful.

14.21 Character set portability issues

One pervasive area of portability problems is those programs that rely on the underlying ASCII representation of the character set. Although the most common, ASCII is not the only representation; another major representation is the EBCDIC character set.

There are many ways that a program can have a dependency on the ASCII representation. The most blatant is the use of integers instead of character constants. For example, the following code testing for capital A works in ASCII:

```
if (ch == 65)    /* Nonportable */
```

This works only because capital letter A is 65 in ASCII; this test will probably fail in a non-ASCII environment. Naturally, the completely portable method is to use character constants, since the compiler will always supply the correct integer for the given implementation's character set:

```
if (ch == 'A')    /* Portable */
```

Another dangerous programming style is the use of order tests involving character constants. For example, consider the test whether ch is a lowercase letter:

```
if ('a' <= ch && ch <= 'z')   /* Nonportable */
```

This test relies on the fact that the letters `'a'...'z'` are consecutive integers in ASCII. This is not guaranteed in a non-ASCII environment. As an example, in EBCDIC there are more than 26 values in the range of `'a'...'z'` and this test will incorrectly accept a number of nonletter characters. The required test for EBCDIC, because of the two "holes" in the sequence, is as follows:

```
if ('a' <= ch && ch <= 'i') ||
   ('j' <= ch && ch <= 'r') ||
   ('s' <= ch && ch <= 'z'))
```

Fortunately, there is a portable alternative using the ANSI C standard library functions in <ctype.h>, which will always be correct for each implementation:

```
if (islower(ch))  /* Portable */
```

The use of islower is also likely to be more efficient than either of the above tests, because most implementations use fast macros accessing precalculated tables for <ctype.h> functions. Hence making good use of <ctype.h> will solve most character set portability problems. However, occasional errors are still made:

```
char c;

do {  /* do while invalid */
  printf("Enter choice A..E\n");
  scanf(" %c", &c);
} while(c < 'A' || c > 'E');  /* Nonportable */
```

Although this will work with both ASCII and EBCDIC, it is conceivable (although unlikely) that the < and > tests on characters will cause wrong behavior on some obscure character set. Furthermore, if the character range was A..J (or some other range covering a "hole" in EBCDIC), the use of < and > would be incorrect.

14.21.1 Portable conversion between characters and integers

There are also a few common mistakes made by programmers involving conversions between characters and integers. For example, how does one convert the integers 0..25 into the letters 'A'...'Z'? Most programmers would use:

```
ch = i + 'A';   /* Nonportable */
```

This will fail in the EBCDIC character set for any letters after I since the EBCDIC character set has 3 contiguous sequences of letters: 'A'..'I', 'J'..'R', and 'S'..'Z'. The obvious portable method is to use a switch statement with 26 case labels, but one neater portable method is:

```
ch = "ABCDEFGHIJKLMNOPQRSTUVWXYZ"[i];   /* Portable */
```

This uses the character string as an array of characters and chooses the *i*th character. A similar idea can be used to portably convert a number 0..15 into a hexadecimal digit:

```
hex_dig = "0123456789ABCDEF"[i];   /* Portable */
```

A similar nonportable practice is to iterate through characters in a particular range using an increment or decrement. Consider the following code to iterate through all the letters of the alphabet:

```
for (ch = 'A'; ch <= 'Z'; ch++)  /* Nonportable */
  ....
```

A portable method is:

```
char * letters = "ABCDEFGHIJKLMNOPQRSTUVWXYZ";

for (i = 0; i <= 25; i++) {
  ch = letters[i];   /* Portably choose ith letter */
  ....
}
```

Conversions from characters to integers are a little more difficult to perform neatly. For example, conversion of a letter in the range $'A'..'Z'$ into an integer 0..25 can be performed simply but nonportably in ASCII using:

```
i = ch - 'A';   /* Nonportable */
```

The simplest portable method is to use a `switch` statement similar to the following:

```
switch(ch) {         /* Portable */
  case 'A':  i = 0; break;
  case 'B':  i = 1; break;
  /* etc... all 26 cases */
}
```

One reasonably neat method is to use the `strchr` function, although this may be less efficient than a `switch` statement because of the function call overhead. The code below uses `strchr` to search the letters for the given character, and then uses pointer arithmetic to return the integral position of that character. Note that `strchr` will not return NULL, provided that `ch` is an uppercase letter.

```
char *letters = "ABCDEFGHIJKLMNOPQRSTUVWXYZ";

i = strchr(letters, ch) - letters;
printf("%c -- > %d \n", ch, i);
```

Another instance where character set dependencies arise is in data structures that use string representations, notably tries and hash tables. Although a reasonable hash function will work for any character set (although it will generate different numbers, this doesn't matter since it does so consistently for a given implementation), any hash function or trie indexing access that uses, say, the 26 letters to refer to an array of 26 "buckets" is error-prone. Care must be taken to portably convert the 26 letters into the 26 integer values. Unfortunately, efficiency is lost by writing portable code in this situation.

Chapter 15

Flow of control errors

There are a number of common errors in the use of the flow of control statements — that is, the selection, iteration, and jump statements. Some of these errors are particularly hard to track down because control can pass through a function along many different paths and the error may occur only on one particular path.

15.1 Function return inconsistencies

There are a number of problems with the use of a `return` statement. A simple example of such an error is a non-`void` function with no `return` statement at all — obviously the function will return an undefined value. The same problem can occur in less obvious ways when a `return` statement is not found on some execution paths. The function exits at the closing right brace and returns an undefined value. For example, the function below returns a value only if the condition in the `if` statement is true:

```
int positive(int x)
{
    if (x > 0)
        return TRUE;
    /* MISSING RETURN STATEMENT */
}
```

Another situation where a function may return wrong values is when an `int` function uses the `return` statement:

```
return;          /* return NO value */
```

An older C compiler might not produce a warning message because pre-ANSI C programs often used `int` return type instead of `void` (usually by declaring the function with no explicit return type, thereby defaulting to `int`).

15.2 main must return a value

A particular example of problems with function return values concerns the `main` function. The following simple C program contains a subtle error — the return value of `main` is undefined:

```
#include <stdio.h>

main()
{
  printf("Hello world\n");
}
```

Although the program is rarely directly concerned with the value returned by `main`, the operating system may examine this value. It is important for a program always to return a value, as some operating systems may fail if a strange value is returned. Although the above program will work in most environments, there are a few for which it may fail.

The most common method of returning a value in ANSI C is to use the `exit` library function (declared in `<stdlib.h>`). The ANSI standard macros `EXIT_SUCCESS` and `EXIT_FAILURE` are also declared in `<stdlib.h>` to represent program success and failure; typically they have values 0 and 1. Hence a minimally correct "hello world" program in ANSI C should look like:

```
#include <stdio.h>
#include <stdlib.h>

main()
{
  printf("Hello world\n");
  exit(EXIT_SUCCESS);
}
```

15.2.1 main must have int type

Another related error is the declaration of the `main` function as a `void` function:

```
void main()     /* WRONG */
{
}
```

This is incorrect because some environments rely upon `main` having an `int` return value. The correct declaration of `main` is having `int` return value, using either explicit or implicit typing:

```
int main()  /* CORRECT */
main()       /* CORRECT (FOR NOW) */
```

Note that the use of `main()` with an implicit `int` return type is correct now, but may not survive an update to the ANSI C standard in coming years.

The declaration of `main` as an `int` function has the annoying side effect of provoking warnings from some compilers to the effect that `main` "does not return a value" or similar. This is because although `main` calls `exit`, it contains no return value. One cumbersome method of suppressing the error is to add an unreachable `return` statement after the `exit` call:

```
int main()
{
    exit(EXIT_SUCCESS);
    return EXIT_SUCCESS;
}
```

15.3 Accidental empty loop

A common error with loops is to place a semicolon just after the header of a `for` or `while` loop. Syntactically, this is correct, so the compiler gives no error message. However, it changes the meaning of the loop. For example:

```
for (i = 1; i <= 10; i++);        /* Extra semicolon */
    ...            /* body of loop */
```

is interpreted as:

```
for (i = 1; i <= 10; i++)
    ;  /* empty loop */
    ...    /* body of loop - executed only once */
```

The effect of this is that the body of the loop is assumed to be an empty loop by the compiler. The block after the loop header (the real loop body) is executed after the loop has finished, and is executed only once. Worse still, the accidental empty loop may cause an infinite loop if the condition is not being changed in the header.

15.4 Missing break in a switch statement

Leaving out a `break` statement in a `case` clause causes execution to fall through to the next `case`. The statements for more than one `case` are then executed. If a program appears to be doing two things when it should be doing only one, this could be the problem. For example, consider the following `switch` statement to convert an error code to an error message:

```
switch (err) {
    case E_TOO_LONG:
        fprintf(stderr, "String too long\n");
    case E_UPPER_CASE:
        fprintf(stderr, "String should be lower case\n");
    default:
        fprintf(stderr, "Unrecognized error\n");
}
```

All of the cases should have `break` statements after the `fprintf` statement. As above, when `err` equals `E_TOO_LONG` the statement will fall through all the cases and also the `default` case; that is, it prints all three error messages. The corrected `switch` statement is shown below. Even the `default` code has a `break` statement. Although it doesn't need one, this is a safety net in case another `case` clause is later added to the bottom of the `switch` statement.

```
switch (err) {
    case E_TOO_LONG:
        fprintf(stderr, "String too long\n");
        break;
    case E_UPPER_CASE:
        fprintf(stderr, "String should be lower case\n");
        break;
    default:
        fprintf(stderr, "Unrecognized error\n");
        break;
}
```

Another problem that can appear in a switch statement is failure to cover all cases, such as a forgotten case or a missing default clause. For this reason it is good practice to ensure that every switch statement has a default code block. Even if it seems "obvious" that the control value will always match one of the values, it is good defensive programming practice to have a default block that reports an error if this "impossible" situation occurs.

15.5 Noninitialized local variables

This problem occurs when an automatic variable is used before it has been assigned a value, either by explicit initialization or by an assignment statement. For example, the function below is incorrect because the local variable sum is not set with an initial value of zero:

```
int sum(int n)
{
    int i, sum;

    for (i = 1; i <= n; i++)
        sum += i;
    return sum;
}
```

ANSI C does not require the compiler to initialize local automatic variables to zero, although some compilers and debuggers do. If not explicitly initialized, the values are undefined at the start of the function.

Another common example of this form of error is uninitialized pointers. A pointer without an initializer will contain an undefined address and dereferencing the pointer can cause a run-time failure. A common mistake with novices is to use a string pointer without first allocating some memory:

```
char *s;

strcpy(s, "abc");  /* ERROR */
```

15.6 Mismatched else clauses

The rule that an `else` always matches the closest `if` is usually satisfactory. However, there are occasions where errors can arise in nested `if` statements such as:

```
if (y < 0)
    if (x < 0)
        x = 0;
else                /* DANGER */
    y = 0;
```

Here the `else` clause is presumably intended to match the first `if`, as suggested by the indentation. However, the compiler matches the `else` with the second (closest) `if`, and compiles the code as if it were written as:

```
if (y < 0) {
    if (x < 0)
        x = 0;
    else
        y = 0;
}
```

The method of avoiding this error is to always use braces around the inner `if` statement when using nested `if` statements.

```
if (y < 0) {        /* CORRECT */
    if (x < 0)
        x = 0;
}
else
    y = 0;
```

15.7 Unreachable statements

It is possible to have code in a program that cannot be reached under any circumstances. This type of code occasionally indicates the presence of a bug, but more commonly indicates that unnecessary code has not been removed. Good compilers should produce a warning message — the `lint` utility finds many instances of this error. One dangerous example of an unreachable statement is a missing `case` label at the start of a `switch`:

```
switch(x) {
    putchar('0');   /* Unreachable - missing case */
    ....
}
```

15.8 Dead assignments

An assignment statement that has no effect because a later assignment always overwrites the value is sometimes called a "dead assignment" or "dead definition." In many cases a dead assignment is merely indicative of old obsolete code statements that have not been removed. However, occasionally it can arise because of a programming error. An example of this situation is:

```
if (*s == '\0')
    empty = TRUE;
    empty = FALSE;
```

The assignment of TRUE to empty is "dead" because it will always be overwritten by the second assignment, setting it to FALSE. In this case the error is that the source code line containing "else" has been accidentally lost.

Although dead assignments are rarely caught by the compiler, the author has seen one example where the optimization phase of compilation warned that it was removing an assignment because it had no effect.

15.9 switch bypasses local variable initializations

A common error in C (but not C++) involving the switch statement is to initialize local variables in the block containing the cases. The following code shows the error:

```
switch (x) {
    int y = 2;    /* ERROR */

    case 1: ...
    case 2: ...
    default: ...
}
```

C programmers get into the habit of declaring new variables at the start of a new block, and declare a variable at the top of a switch. However, this declaration is always bypassed by the switch statement jumping to a case or default label, and so the initialization may never occur.

Fortunately, C++ prohibits code that bypasses initializations and a compilation error is produced. Furthermore, C++ programmers are not as restricted in the placement of variable declarations and are less prone to declaring variables at a left brace.

15.10 goto bypasses local variable initializations

A rare error (in C but not C++) involving the goto statement occurs because it is legal for a goto to jump anywhere within a function. Therefore, it can jump into the middle of a compound statement. This jump will bypass any initializations of variables at the start of the block:

```
    goto middle;

    if (.. ) {  int j = 1;     /* initialization skipped */
        middle:   ...
    }
```

The C++ language prohibits programs that use goto in this manner, by requiring a compilation error to be emitted when an initialization is bypassed. However, the error can arise in C since the ANSI C standard permits this code.

Chapter 16

Types and declarations

Although C and C++ compilers type-check most uses of variables, there are still some areas where the compiler ignores types. For example, when nonprototyped function declarations are used in C the compiler does not check the types of arguments passed to functions (to permit compatibility with old C code). Similarly, arguments to variable-length argument list functions such as `printf` and `scanf` are not checked in either C or C++ (because the compiler cannot check them).

16.1 Nonprototyping problems

Prototyping refers to the placing of types of parameters inside the parameter list. With nonprototyping, the types are specified in a list after the end of the parameter list. Note that nonprototyping is considered obsolete in ANSI C (although it must still be supported by compilers) and it is not allowed in C++ (although some compilers permit it for upward compatibility of old C code).

In older C compilers that do not support prototyping (or if you choose not to use prototyping for some reason), there is no checking of the types of arguments passed to functions. If the types are not consistent, or if the wrong number of arguments is passed to a function, this usually causes some form of run-time error. The most common error this causes on UNIX systems is the notorious "segmentation fault."

If the program crashes for some reason, one of the first things to check is the types and number of function arguments. Be careful to check for &'s on arguments that need them, as this form of type mismatch error is a common problem. To summarize, check for the following errors:

- wrong types of arguments
- wrong number of arguments
- missing &'s on arguments

Note that nonprototyping problems also occur if a function is used before it has been declared. For this reason it is good practice always to have forward declarations (i.e., prototypes) for all functions at the top of the file (or preferably in a header file). This problem is common when using independent compilation of multiple file programs. It also arises when <math.h> is not included by a file using mathematical functions.

16.2 Mixing prototyping and nonprototyping

The ANSI C standard introduced a new form of function declaration: the prototype. ANSI also specified certain conditions under which the mixture of prototyped and nonprototyped functions was legal. Note that C++ compilers need not support nonprototyped declarations at all, but many do for upward compatibility from C to C++.

There are two main restrictions on the mixing of prototyping and nonprototyping. The first is that it is not allowed if function parameters have type `char`, `short`, or `float` because these are the types affected by the default argument promotions. For example, the following code is not legal:

```
void fn(char c);    /* Prototype should use int */

void fn(c)          /* Illegal Redeclaration */
char c;
{
 ...
}
```

This situation is not too dangerous since the compiler should detect it and complain about a "redefinition" of `fn`. However, if a function is *defined* using a prototype, but is called in a separate file without a previous declaration, this causes the compiler to believe it is nonprototyped. Hence the argument will be promoted to `int`, whereas the prototyped definition in the first file expects a `char`.

The second instance where mixing prototyping and nonprototyping is not legal is for variable-argument functions. ANSI requires that all variable-argument functions be *defined* using the "`...`" ellipsis token. Therefore, such functions must be defined using the `<stdarg.h>` header file and any programs defining variable-argument functions using the pre-ANSI header file `<varargs.h>` are illegal.

Furthermore, even if a variable-argument function is correctly defined using `<stdarg.h>`, it must always be called with a prototype currently in scope, with that prototype containing an ellipsis (i.e., it must be currently *declared* with a prototype using an ellipsis). One danger this creates is that programs that use the variable-argument functions `printf` or `scanf` without including `<stdio.h>` may fail in ANSI C, whereas they were previously correct. More generally, any variable-argument function needs a prototype declaration containing the ellipsis in any file that uses it.

The requirement of an ellipsis for all variable-argument functions means that the compiler can use aggressive optimizations of function calls. Some of the common tricks in pre-ANSI C will now fail in ANSI C; for example, when a function is passed fewer arguments than expected, as in the following "debugging output" function:

```
dprintf(format, x, y, z, any, number)
char *format;
int x, y, z, any, number;
{
    fprintf(stderr, format, x, y, z, any, number);
}
....
dprintf("x = %d", x);               /* ERROR */
dprintf("x = %d, y = %d", x, y);    /* ERROR */
```

Passing too few arguments can cause a program failure in ANSI C. The correct solution is to properly define `dprintf` as a variable-argument function using `<stdarg.h>`.

16.3 Problems with independent compilation

Independent compilation refers to using multiple files for one program. This can lead to the problems with nonprototyped functions in C (and also functions *defined* using the prototyping syntax but not *declared* using prototypes in files where they are used). There is usually little problem with functions in C++ because prototypes are required. However, both C and C++ programs can exhibit errors related to mismatched declarations and definitions of global variables.

The use of separate files for different functions can lead to a number of problems with types. The basic problem is that C compilers assume the types of function names not already declared. When an undefined identifier is found used as a function name, the C compiler assumes that this function returns `int`. If the function (as defined in another file) does not return `int`, there can be problems. For example, consider a function returning a `short`, but not declared in the current file. If the returned value is assigned to a variable of type `short`, the compiler thinks that an `int` function is being assigned to a `short` variable. It may generate some code to perform the type conversion from `int` to `short`. This type conversion code is the problem. When the program runs, the function actually returns a `short`. This `short` is treated as an `int`, and the type cast is applied, leading to incorrect results.

A similar problem can occur if a function is used before its declaration in the same file. This is not as dangerous because a compilation warning is usually generated about a "redeclaration" of a function when the definition is found by the compiler.

Another problem is that when a function name is not defined in the current file, the compiler assumes nonprototyping for the function's parameters. With nonprototyping it then performs no type checks on arguments passed to the function. This can lead to the problems of arguments not matching the types of parameters (or the wrong number of arguments passed), as discussed above.

Further problems occur in both C and C++ if an `extern` variable is declared incorrectly (i.e., with the wrong type) in any file. The compiler cannot detect the incorrect use of types, as it deals with each file separately. There is not usually an error from the linker as there is only one definition of the variable. In theory, a good programming environment could provide a smarter linker that detects this, but no environment known to the author does this.

A similar (but less dangerous) problem is that of accidentally declaring two global variables, or two functions with identical names, in different files. The compiler cannot usually detect the multiple declaration, but its linker often can. Unfortunately, linkers differ between different machines and some linkers will detect multiple declarations as an error, but other linkers will join the two declarations into a single location (i.e., the two variables refer to the same memory address). This can obviously cause incorrect results.

One partial solution to the problems of independent compilation (for UNIX users) is to use the `lint` checker, which checks for type problems over multiple files and is able to detect the errors discussed above. A better solution to these problems is to declare every variable or function used. The best way to do this is with a header file containing extern declarations of every global variable and prototype declarations of every function. The header files are included in every C or C++ source file — even the files containing the actual function definitions. Including an extern declaration or function prototype declaration in the file containing the proper definition ensures that the header file and the definition are consistent. In this way, any difference in declarations is immediately detected as a compilation error.

16.4 Passing structs by value, arrays by reference

Parameter passing can be very confusing in C and C++. All struct variables, C++ class objects, and simple variables are passed by value, which means that when a function is called, the arguments are copied and these copies are used inside the function. The original arguments cannot be changed within the function, and thus the values of variables passed as arguments to a function cannot be changed by the function.

Arrays are the exception. When arrays are passed as arguments, the elements of an array can be changed inside the function. The reason for this exception is that arrays are considered to be pointers to the first element of the array. This distinction can cause errors when a function does modify its parameters (e.g., to use as working variables). One solution is never to modify pass-by-value function parameters; another is judicious use of const to receive compilation warnings about modifying parameters.

16.5 Implicit type conversions

The large number of type conversions performed implicitly by the compiler leaves room for error. Be careful when mixing real and integral types because conversion from a real to an integer truncates to the nearest integer. When mixing these types it is important to use the correct form of constant. For example, the code below may not have the effect intended by the programmer:

```
int x = 7;
float f;
...
f = x / 2;        /* Set f = 3.5 ? */
```

This code will perform integral division on x, thereby truncating it to the nearest whole integer, and then convert this integer to float, yielding the value 3.0 and not 3.5. The problem is that both x and 2 have type int and therefore the / operator performs integral division. The correct code uses the constant 2.0, which has type double:

```
f = x / 2.0;
```

Even better would be to also use an explicit cast to indicate a conversion of int to float:

```
f = (float)x / 2.0;
```

Conversion from double to float, or from one integral type to a smaller integral type, may lose information. Some good compilers will issue a warning for instances of such conversions, but many compilers do not. Generally speaking, such conversions should be avoided wherever possible through the use of consistent variable types. For example, always use int to represent an integer even if it will be small enough to be stored in a char or a short. Don't use a char or a short to represent an integer value unless you really need a performance improvement (either space or time) and you have measured the code to determine that this will yield an improvement. Use type int for most integral values; use type char only for characters; use type long when a value may exceed 32,767 (for portability to 16-bit machines); and use type short very rarely.

Similar comments apply to the choice between float and double. The type double is slightly preferred because it is the default type of floating-point constants.

16.6 Type defaults to int

It is a dangerous feature of C and C++ that if no type is supplied, the type defaults to int. One example of the dangers is the constant declaration:

```
const half = 0.5;    // ERROR
```

The constant half is accidentally declared as type int, and given the (truncated) value of 0. A good compiler will warn about converting double to int. The correct declaration is simply:

```
const double half = 0.5;
```

16.7 signed and unsigned char

The type qualifiers signed and unsigned can also lead to implicit type conversion problems. In particular, char variables are implicitly signed char on some platforms, and conversion of a character in the range 128..255 to an integer would yield a negative number. Fortunately, in ASCII all common alphanumeric characters fall into the range 0..127 and present no problem. However, when accessing bytes from a binary file (i.e., characters in the range 0..255) or using a character set other than ASCII, the type "unsigned char" should be used.

For similar reasons, it is often bad practice to use the type char to represent small integral values because the possibility of overflow is so high. The type char cannot portably represent values outside 0..127. Using explicitly signed or unsigned char can increase the portable range to −128..127 and 0..255, respectively.

Another related problem is comparing a char variable with EOF. Because EOF is represented as integer value −1, it should not be directly compared with a char type. Although it will usually work if characters happen to be signed for a particular implementation, if characters are unsigned, the comparison of a char type with EOF is not correct since −1 is promoted to unsigned int, yielding a huge value not representable by a char. A common instance of this error occurs in the usage of getchar or getc as described in Section 18.4.

16.8 Implicit conversion of negatives to unsigned

The unsigned qualifier can be a problem when dealing with negative values. For example, consider the code below:

```
unsigned int x = 0;
int y = -1;

if (x > y)
    printf("x > y \n");
```

The operands of > are converted to the "larger" type — in this case, unsigned int. Hence −1 is converted to an unsigned quantity, yielding a very large positive value.

A similar problem with unsigned types can be hidden by the ANSI type size_t. Since many of the library functions return or use this type it is not uncommon style for programmers to declare variables of type size_t. However, in my opinion, this is a dangerous and unnecessary practice since the type int will usually adequately handle the same task. One danger is illustrated by the following function to print a string in reverse:

```
#include <stdio.h>
#include <string.h>
#include <stddef.h>   /* declare size_t */

void print_reverse(char *s)
{
    size_t len = strlen(s);

    for ( ; len >= 0; len--) {
        putchar(s[len]);
    }
}
```

The programmer has declared len having type size_t because strlen has this return type. This function will have an infinite loop if size_t is an unsigned type, because the comparison with 0 will never fail. If the particular implementation defined size_t as a signed type, the code will work but hides a potential portability problem. Fortunately, some compilers will produce a warning about a comparison of an unsigned type with zero.

16.9 Order of initialization errors

The order of evaluation of initializers is not defined. Therefore, the following declaration may cause strange program results on some compilers:

```
int i = 1, j = i;     /* DANGEROUS */
```

There is no problem if evaluation is from left to right, but if it occurs right to left then j will be assigned the value of i before i has been initialized — that is, j will contain garbage rather than 1.

Fortunately, the use of the address of a variable is no problem since the address does not depend on whether the variable has been initialized with a pointer. Therefore, the initialization below is not dangerous:

```
int i = 1, *ptr = &i;    /* SAFE */
```

A problem related to order of evaluation of initializers occurs with the order of initialization of constructors in C++ classes. The following constructor typifies the problem:

```
Object::Object(int x) : i(x), j(i)      // ERROR
{
    // ...
}
```

The order of initialization, although well defined, is not necessarily left-to-right as the above code requires. Determining the order of initialization is quite a complicated process, depending on the ordering of the declarations of the data members being initialized, rather than the order in which they appear in the initializer list. Hence, depending on what i and j refer to, and in what order their declarations were placed, j may be initialized using i before i has itself been initialized by x.

16.10 Pascal-like arrays and case labels

A common error made by Pascal programmers moving to C is to use Pascal syntax for declaring multidimensional arrays and also for case labels in switch statements. Pascal uses commas for both these declarations, leading to the following erroneous declarations:

```
int arr[10, 20];
case 5, 7:
```

Although many compilers will warn about such uses (e.g., they are usually a syntax error on the traditional UNIX C compiler), there will be no warning on some compilers. The problem is that the comma is treated as an operator in both these contexts, since the syntax requires a constant expression for both the array size and a case label. Therefore, the above declarations will be treated by the compiler as:

```
int arr[20];
case 7:
```

The behavior of a program misusing these declarations may appear strange. The switch statement will execute the default code for the value 5, leading to erroneous results. Any use of arr will probably be erroneous; for example, the statement:

```
x = arr[i, j];
```

might be treated as a one-dimensional array with the expression "i,j" as the index, which is equivalent to:

```
x = arr[j];
```

Therefore, on some poor compilers that do not warn about commas in constant expressions this error can lead to very strange run-time behavior.

16.11 Scopes and inner redeclaration

Variables can be declared in inner scopes with the same names as variables in outer scopes, without even a compilation warning. This is often called "inner redeclaration" or "shadowing." It is a very convenient feature but can occasionally lead to confusion.

16.12 Redeclaration of global variables

An example of inner redeclaration is a local variable having the same name as a global variable:

```
int x;      /*  Global variable */

main()
{
    int x;   /* Local variable */
    ...
}
```

Although problems are quite rare, it is possible that a programmer will use the name x intending the global variable to be accessed, but instead the local variable is accessed.

If the above declarations are used in C there is no way to access the global variable x since it is hidden by the local variable. In C++ the : : operator can be used to access global variables:

```
::x = 3;    // Access global x
```

It is good C++ style to use : : for all accesses to global variables since it avoids the potential pitfalls described here.

16.13 Redeclaration of local variables

Redeclaration of a variable is also possible in different blocks in a program. Every pair of braces introduces a new scope in both C and C++, and new declarations are permitted after every left brace (of course, C++ is even more flexible than this, as we will discuss a little later). Such variables are local to the innermost enclosing block and are often called "block-local" declarations. The following code is legal in both C and C++:

```
main()
{
    int i;

    for (i = 0; i <= 10; i++) {
        int i;    /* declare block-local variable */

        printf("%d\n", i);   /* Uses block-local variable */
    }
}
```

In this code the "outer" loop variable i is hidden by the declaration of the "inner" block-local variable. Although the above code is obviously erroneous, there are valid uses for hiding a name by declaring a variable in a new scope, such as to introduce a temporary variable. In C++ there may be a performance improvement from declaring an object at its first point of use, rather than at the top of a function.

Although hidden global variables can be accessed in C++ using the :: operator, this is not possible for hidden local variables. Hidden local variables cannot be accessed at all while another declaration hides the name.

16.14 Redeclaration of local variables: C++ problems

C++ provides the programmer with increased flexibility in the placement of variable declarations. Whereas C programmers were restricted to placing all declarations at the beginning of a block (after the left brace), C++ programmers can place declarations in almost all locations where a statement is allowed. The scope of a variable so declared extends to the closing right brace of the innermost block in which it is declared.

One common C++ idiom using this new freedom is the declaration of a for loop variable in the first expression of the for loop header:

```
for (int i = 1; i < N; i++)   // declares i
```

This is a very useful idiom but has the nonintuitive feature that the scope of the variable is not restricted to the loop body, but instead extends to the end of the enclosing block. (There have been some proposals to change this, but so far the draft ANSI C++ language standard agrees with the previous sentence.) If i is already declared in that block a compilation error will occur. This can be annoying because it prevents uses such as two loops one after the other:

```
for (int i = 1; i < N; i++)
    do_something(i);

for (int i = 1; i < N; i++)  // Error: i multiply defined
    do_something_else(i);
```

A far worse problem is that if i is declared in an outer block, the new declaration of i will hide the outer declaration, and the program may access the wrong variable. This is the case below since the if statement introduces an extra scope level between the two declarations of i:

```
int main(void)
{
    int i = 0;

    if (some_test()) {
        for (int i = 1; i < 10; i++) {
            do_something(i);
        }
        cout << "i = " << i << "\n";  // .. using i is ambiguous
    }
    cout << "i = " << i << "\n";     // .. using i is safe
}
```

The first output statement will output 10, since it is referring to the i declared in the for loop. However, once the enclosing scope (from the if statement) closes, the i declared in the for loop is no longer accessible and using i will refer to the outer local variable.

Another possible error is that nesting two of these for loops can cause an error, as shown in the (somewhat contrived) example below:

```
#include <iostream.h>

main()
{
    const int N = 10;
    int matrix[N][N];

    for (int i = 0; i < N; i++) {
        int sum = 0;
        int *p = &matrix[i][0];    // address of the row

        for (int i = 0; i < N; i++) {
            sum += p[i];
        }
        cout << "Row = " << i << ", row sum = " << sum << "\n";
    }
}
```

Although the row sums are computed correctly, the value of i that is output will always be 10 because the output statement is inside the enclosing block containing the inner declaration of i.

16.15 Shadowing parameter names in pre-ANSI C

Errors due to redeclaration of variables with the same name are not very common in C because programmers usually don't use common names for global variables and also tend to avoid "block-local" declarations. However, one very common error in pre-ANSI C was the accidental redeclaration of a parameter name by a local variable:

```
int fn(x, y)
int x, y;
{
   int x;    /* ERROR: hides parameter name */

   /* .... */
}
```

In the example above the parameter x is no longer available in the function, and the local variable is used instead. Many old C compilers would compile this code without error because the parameter declarations were considered in a scope "outside" the block containing the local variables. However, ANSI C requires that a compiler complain about the above code, by specifying that parameters have the same scope as the topmost block in the function body. Therefore, an ANSI C compiler will complain that x is multiply defined.

16.16 Plain int bit-fields

Bit-fields should be explicitly declared as either signed or unsigned int. If a bit-field is left to have type int, it is implementation-defined whether it will receive signed or unsigned type. For example, the following declaration relies on the compiler using unsigned representations by default:

```
struct { ...
    int flag : 1;    /* WRONG */
};
```

This will fail if the compiler uses `signed int` because a `signed` type requires at least one bit to represent the sign bit. The correct declaration of the bit-field is:

```
unsigned int flag : 1;    /* CORRECT */
```

16.17 Missing initializers

There is a very neat syntax for the initialization of arrays and structures, using a comma-separated list of expressions inside a pair of braces. Unfortunately, the compiler will rarely warn about having too few initializers, and it is a common error to accidentally omit an expression. The code below is an example of this situation:

```
struct { int x,y,z; } a = { 10, 20 };    /* z is missing */
```

The uninitialized fields are set to zero (for both global and automatic objects in ANSI C), but this is not adequate if another value was intended to be stored.

16.18 Initialization squeezing out the null byte

The initialization of character arrays with string constants in ANSI C has an unfortunate feature (although this is disallowed in C++). If the number of letters in the string is exactly equal to the specified size of the array, as in:

```
char s[3] = "YES";    /* ERROR */
```

the null byte is not stored at the end of the string, and the string is unterminated. This allows experienced programmers to use nonnull terminated strings, but makes it easy for novices to make mistakes by forgetting to leave room for the null byte. Few C compilers will emit a warning for this situation, but C++ compilers should produce a compilation error. A better style is to let the compiler count the characters:

```
char s[] = "YES";    /* GOOD */
```

16.19 Accidental string literal concatenation

String concatenation is a relatively new feature of ANSI C and C++ that allows consecutive string literals to be merged into a single string literal. Concatenation of string literals takes place after the usual preprocessing tasks (i.e., after macro expansion), but before parsing. It is most useful for writing long string literals on multiple lines, and avoids the pitfalls that line splicing has involving whitespace (see Section 13.4). An example of its usage is that the following code:

```
char *prompt = "Hello "
        "world";
```

will be equivalent to:

```
char *prompt = "Hello world";
```

Unfortunately, the fact that the compiler (or preprocessor) performs this concatenation automatically without any warning can lead to strange errors. Consider the following definition of an array of strings:

```
char *arr[] = { "a", "b"  "c" };   /* MISSING COMMA */
```

The absence of the second comma causes `"b"` and `"c"` to be concatenated to produce `"bc"` and `arr` is defined to hold 2 strings instead of 3. Even if the array size were explicitly declared as 3 (i.e., `char*arr[3]`) many compilers would still not produce a warning, since having too few initializers is not an error in C or C++.

16.20 Problems with size_t, ptrdiff_t, clock_t, time_t

ANSI C attempts to enhance portability by declaring various types as special names in header files. For example, `size_t` and `ptrdiff_t` are defined in `<stddef.h>`, and `time_t` and `clock_t` are defined in `<time.h>`. In most situations there is no problem with the use of these types, but in the situations where the compiler does not check types there can be problems. The main danger is when passing these types as arguments to a nonprototyped function. A common error is:

```
printf("size of int = %d\n", sizeof(int));
```

The `sizeof` operator returns type `size_t`, which may or may not be an `int`. The code above will fail if `size_t` is a `long`. The solution is simply to use a cast:

```
printf("size of int = %d\n", (int) sizeof(int));
```

An even worse problem arises with the use of `scanf` because type casts cannot solve the problem. Consider what happens if the user intentionally uses the type name `size_t` as the type of a variable:

```
size_t n;

scanf("%d", &n);   /* DANGER */
```

This program will fail if `size_t` is not the same size as an `int`. Hence, the use of `size_t` as the type of variables is inherently dangerous.

Obviously, similar problems can arise with the use of any of the standard `typedef` names. An example involving `clock_t` is:

```
printf("%d seconds used\n",
    clock() / CLOCKS_PER_SEC);   /* needs cast */
```

The corrected code using a type cast is:

```
printf("%d seconds used\n",
    (int)clock() / CLOCKS_PER_SEC);   /* needs cast */
```

An example involving `ptrdiff_t` occurs in a common idiom for calling the `bsearch` library function to search a sorted array:

```
int *result, arr[HOW_MANY], key, n = HOW_MANY;
...
result = bsearch(&key, arr, n, sizeof(int), cmp);
printf("Found at index %d\n", result - arr);  /* needs cast */
```

The correct code is:

```
printf("Found at index %d\n", (int)(result - arr));
```

16.21 Automatic arrays

When a function makes use of a large array variable, or even a huge structure (perhaps containing a large array), the variable should probably be declared as `static`, even if it need not retain its value between calls. If the variable is too large, it can easily cause a stack overflow, particularly on DOS systems where the stack has at most 64K available.

A large automatic variable in a recursive function is particularly dangerous (because multiple copies may be stored on the stack) and should be avoided wherever possible. Unfortunately, in this case, converting the variable to `static` may introduce errors if each invocation of the recursive function needs a distinct copy of the variable.

There are also various problems with automatic array initialization. In pre-ANSI C the following declaration is valid only if the array is declared globally or as a local `static`; otherwise it is illegal:

```
int arr[2] = { 1, 2 };
```

This form of initialization of automatic arrays is legal in ANSI C (and C++). Unfortunately, this means that programmers occasionally make mistakes about initialized array declarations; consider the following code:

```
char *convert(int day)
{
  char *days[] = { "Monday", "Tuesday", "Wednesday",
        "Thursday", "Friday", "Saturday", "Sunday" };

  return days[day];
}
```

The initialize array `days` illustrates a minor problem — inefficiency. The initialization of `days` occurs every time the `convert` function is entered. It would be much more efficient to declare `days` as a `static` variable. Although this is not a bug, but only an inefficiency, it shows that care must be taken with array initializations.

16.22 Identifier truncation clashes

This discussion applies to C only and not usually to C++; a C++ implementation usually allows a much larger significance in its identifiers. To write fully portable C code, all identifiers representing functions or external variables should have unique prefixes in the first 6 characters, with uppercase and lowercase letters considered identical. Although there is no problem for many modern programming environments, some linkers will map external names to 6 characters and one case. There may be problems for code such as where two function names use the same prefix:

```
void error_message1() { ... }
void error_message2() { ... }
```

On environments with linker name truncation, both of these functions will map to error_me. Hence as far as the linker is concerned there are two functions with the same name, and the result is undefined — usually either a linker error will occur, or one of the functions will be arbitrarily chosen, leading to obscure run-time errors.

Another instance of the problem is identifiers that use different case letters. For example, it is bad practice to define an identifier such as Strcmp to represent your own version of strcmp that checks only for string equality:

```
int Strcmp(char *s1, char *s2)
{
    return strcmp(s1, s2) == 0;
}
```

The linker may map both functions to the same identifier, and may or may not produce a diagnostic warning message. If the linker allows the program to compile and run, the program may exhibit strange behavior. For example, all calls to Strcmp might call the ordinary strcmp, leading to exactly the opposite test to that desired; or all calls to strcmp might change to Strcmp, leading to infinite recursion within Strcmp.

Exactly the same problem can arise with names of global variables. Two different variables may have their names truncated to 6 characters and mapped to one case. Either an error will occur because of multiply defined variables or strange run-time behavior will result.

There is rarely any problem with "internal" names such as type names, static function names, local variable names, and structure tag names. The ANSI standard requires that internal names be unique in the first 31 characters, but few identifiers are ever this long.

One hack solution to identifier clashes is to use #define to map long names to unique short names. This works because the preprocessor typically permits longer names than may be supported by the linker.

```
#define error_message1    errmsg1
#define error_message2    errmsg2
```

Obviously, a better solution is to avoid identifiers with nonunique prefixes. However, the use of #define can help in porting existing code to problematic environments.

Chapter 17

C++ class errors

The class facility available in C++ gives the programmer increased freedom of expression, and therefore more opportunities to err. There are a number of common mistakes made by programmers as they attempt to create complicated class objects.

17.1 Aliasing in the overloaded assignment operator

The definition of an `operator=` for a class should always check for an assignment to itself (i.e., of the form x=x). Consider the following simple `String` class:

```
class String {
    private:
        char *str;
    public:
        String() { str = new char[1];  str[0] = '\0'; }
        String(char*s)
            { str = new char[strlen(s)+1];  strcpy(str,s); }
        void operator =(const String&s);
        ~String() { delete [] str;}
};

void String::operator = (const String&s)
{
    delete [] str;                      // delete old string
    str = new char[strlen(s.str)+1];    // allocate memory
    strcpy(str, s.str);                 // copy new string
}
```

This contains a hidden error that appears only if a string is assigned to itself. Consider the effect of the code:

```
String s("abc");

s = s;      // assignment to itself
```

When the assignment operator is called, the argument s is the same as the object to which the member function is applied. Therefore, the addresses `str` and `s.str` are the same, and the `delete` operator deallocates an address that is immediately used in the subsequent `strlen` and `strcpy` function calls. Thus, these operations apply to an illegal address and the behavior is undefined.

233

This error is an example of a general problem of *aliasing* in the use of overloaded operators, especially the = operator. The object to which the operator is applied is an alias for the object passed as the argument. Any modifications to the data members also affect the data in the argument object. This type of error is very difficult to track down because it occurs only for one particular special case, and this case may not occur very often. This error is not restricted to operator=, although this is its most common appearance. Similar aliasing errors may also occur in other operators such as +=, or in nonoperator member functions that accept objects of the same type.

The correct idiom to avoid this problem of aliasing is to compare the implicit pointer, this, with the address of the argument object (which must be passed as a *reference* type). If these addresses are the same, the two objects are identical and appropriate action can be taken for this special case. For example, in the String class the correct action when assigning a string to itself is to make no changes, and the operator= function becomes:

```
void String::operator = (const String&s)
{
    if (this != &s) {
        delete [] str;                      // delete old string
        str = new char[strlen(s.str)+1];    // allocate memory
        strcpy(str, s.str);                 // copy new string
    }
}
```

17.2 Missing copy constructor or assignment operator

There is a well-known idiom in the design of good classes that requires four major member functions to be defined as shown in Table 17.1.

Table 17.1   Four function C++ class idiom

Function	*Declaration*
1. Ordinary constructor(s)	Object(), Object(int), etc.
2. Copy constructor	Object(const Object &)
3. Destructor	~Object()
4. Assignment operator	operator=(const Object &)

This idiom is good style for all classes, but is very important for particular types of classes. The most common error is a failure to supply either a copy constructor or assignment operator in a class that makes use of dynamically allocated memory. This error causes the delete operation in the destructor to be applied to memory that has already been deleted by the destructor of another object. The following naive String class illustrates the error:

```
#include <string.h>
class String {
    private:
        char *str;
    public:
        String() { str = new char[1];   str[0] = '\0'; }
        String(char*s)
            { str = new char[strlen(s)+1];   strcpy(str,s); }
        ~String() { delete [] str;}
};

main()
{
  String s1("abc"), s2("xyz");
  s1 = s2;      // Dangerous bitwise copy
}
```

The problem is that the assignment of one string to another defaults to a bitwise copy of
the str field. (Note that you may hear that C++ 2.0 and higher versions implement
"memberwise" copying instead of bitwise copying, but this occurs only for data members
that are themselves classes and does not apply to primitive types — str is a pointer
which is a primitive type and therefore the str member is bitwise copied.) This means
that the above assignment overwrites s1.str with s2.str, and causes both str fields
to point to the same address. When s1 and s2 are destroyed, the delete operator in
the destructor is given the same address twice, usually leading to a run-time error. The
solution is to declare an overloaded assignment operator for the class, as follows:

```
#include <string.h>

class String {
    private:
        char *str;
    public:
        String() { str = new char[1];   str[0] = '\0'; }
        String(char*s)
            { str = new char[strlen(s)+1];   strcpy(str,s); }
        ~String() { delete [] str;}
        void operator =(const String&s);   // Assignment operator
};

void String::operator = (const String&s)
{
    if (this != &s) {    // Avoid aliasing problem
        delete [] str;                       // delete old string
        str = new char[strlen(s.str)+1];   // allocate memory
        strcpy(str, s.str);                  // copy new string
    }
}
```

This means that any use of the assignment operator is no longer dangerous. However,
this class declaration still contains a similar problem because of the absence of a *copy
constructor*. A String variable that is initialized using another String variable is still
dangerous. Some examples of declarations that call the copy constructor are below:

```
String s3(s1);
String s4 = s2;      // equivalent to String s4(s2);
```

Note that the = sign in a declaration is not the assignment operator, but is instead a form of initialization. The copy constructor is also called when objects are passed by value (i.e., not as a reference type) as arguments to a function, and also at a `return` statement where the return type is an object type.

The same problem with the `delete` operator in the destructor deallocating the same address twice occurs because the C++ compiler generates a default copy constructor that performs *bitwise* assignment of the `str` field (because it is a primitive type). After the above declarations the `str` field of s3 is the same address as that for s1, and this is also true for s4 and s2. The solution is to declare an explicit copy constructor for the `String` class that allocates new memory for the `str` field of the newly constructed `String` (rather than just copying the `str` fields). The `String` class finally becomes:

```
#include <string.h>

class String {
    private:
        char *str;
    public:
        String() { str = new char[1];   str[0] = '\0'; }
        String(char*s)
            { str = new char[strlen(s)+1];   strcpy(str,s); }
        ~String() { delete [] str;}
        void operator =(const String&s);   // Assignment operator
        String(const String &s);           // Copy constructor
};

void String::operator = (const String&s)     // SAME AS ABOVE
{
    if (this != &s) {    // Avoid aliasing problem
        delete [] str;                        // delete old string
        str = new char[strlen(s.str)+1];   // allocate memory
        strcpy(str, s.str);                   // copy new string
    }
}

String::String(const String&s)      // Copy constructor
{
    str = new char[strlen(s.str)+1];   // allocate memory
    strcpy(str, s.str);                   // copy string
}
```

The `String` class is by far the most common class for which this error from the omission of the assignment operator and copy constructor arises, but it is not the only such class. In general, this error can occur in a number of situations, including:

1. A class uses dynamic memory, pointed to by a data member of the class object, and there is a `delete` operation in the destructor.
2. A class contains a file descriptor, such as a `FILE*` pointer from the standard C library, `<stdio.h>`, and the file is closed in the destructor.

The error due to dynamic allocation can be solved by copying the dynamic memory inside both the copy constructor and assignment operator (as done above for the `String` class). The similar error, where a file descriptor is "closed" twice, is more difficult to avoid, as copying file descriptors is more difficult. One solution may be to declare the file descriptor as a `static` data member, and also add another `static` boolean data member that indicates whether the file is currently open or closed.

17.3 Return type of the assignment operator

The return type of the overloaded assignment operator should usually be a reference type or `void`. A common mistake is to make it return a class object. Consider the following class declaration:

```
class Integer {
   private:  int val;
   public:
      Integer operator = (const Integer &x);
      // ...
};

Integer Integer::operator = (const Integer &x)
{
    val = x.val;    // copy data
    return *this;   // return left operand
}
```

This declaration of the assignment operator to return an object permits expressions using the result of assignment, such as:

```
Integer x,y,z;

x = x + (y = z);   // embedded assignment
x = y = z;         // C-style multiple assignment
```

However, it needlessly calls the constructor and destructor for a temporary object, leading to inefficiency, and occasionally to error. The correct declaration of the assignment operator is to return a `const` reference to `Integer`. This simply requires an `&` in the return type declaration, as follows:

```
const Integer& Integer::operator = (const Integer &x)
{
    // ... same as above
}
```

Note that the use of a non-`const` reference is slightly undesirable because it allows the very strange (and probably incorrect) multiple assignment:

```
(x = y) = z;
```

Although the failure to declare the return type as a reference is quite harmless for this class, it can be more dangerous. For a string class with dynamic allocation, using a return type of `String` instead of `String&` will cause a temporary object to be created at the `return` statement, using the copy constructor with "`*this`" as the argument. If the copy constructor is defined correctly, this is often just an instance of inefficiency, but it may also lead to fatal errors related to temporary objects as discussed in Section 17.13. If the copy constructor isn't defined correctly, the programmer has the error in the previous section with an increased level of complexity caused by temporary objects.

Note that it may be far better simply to declare the return type of the assignment operator as `void`. Although this prohibits embedded assignments in expressions and also multiple assignments, these are poor style anyway and should probably be discouraged. Using return type `void` is also slightly more efficient because no value need be returned. However, not all C++ programmers agree that the assignment operators should return `void`. For example, Scott Meyers and Moses Lejter argue that a `void` return type is incorrect and only a `const` reference return type is correct (see the citation at the end of this chapter).

17.4 Derived class copy constructor

Since the default constructor for a derived class will automatically call the default constructor for the base class (even if both are user-supplied) we would naturally expect the same effect to occur for the derived copy constructor. Unfortunately, it does not, and this expectation leads to a common C++ pitfall.

The example below illustrates the problem. When the derived copy constructor is called (e.g., to pass an object by value or to return an object), the base data members are not copied because the base class copy constructor is never called by the derived copy constructor. Instead, the *default* constructor for the base class is implicitly called. So the situation is not as bad as it could be since at least we have initialized data members in the base class, but the effect is not what we usually require.

```
class Base {
    int base_data;
  public:
    Base() {                // Base default constructor
          base_data = 0;
        }
    Base(const Base &b) {  // Base copy constructor
          base_data = b.base_data;
        }
};
class Derived : public Base {
    int derived_data;
  public:
    Derived() {
          derived_data = 0;
        }
    Derived(const Derived &d) {
          derived_data = d.derived_data;
        }
};
```

The solution is the use of the base class initialization syntax in the function header of the derived copy constructor. The following use of `":Base(d)"` causes the base class copy constructor to be called correctly:

```
Derived(const Derived &d) : Base(d) {
      derived_data = d.derived_data;
    }
```

17.5 Derived class assignment operator

The above error with derived class copy constructors has an almost identical companion error with the assignment operator. As with the copy constructor, we would hope that the derived class assignment operator would call the base class assignment operator to assign the base class data members. However, this does not occur, and in fact, the base class data members are unaffected by a derived class assignment operator. Consider the following class:

```
class Base {
    int base_data;
  public:
    void operator=(const Base &b) {   // Base assignment
          base_data = b.base_data;
      }
};

class Derived : public Base {
    int derived_data;
  public:
    void operator=(const Derived &d) {   // Derived assignment
          derived_data = d.derived_data;
      }
};
```

In this class, the derived assignment operator does not call the base assignment operator. The solution is the placement of an explicit call to the base class assignment operator inside the derived class assignment operator. Unlike in the copy constructor case, there is no neat initialization syntax to use. Instead, there are various ways of explicitly calling the base assignment operator; one example is shown below:

```
void operator=(const Derived &d) {
        (Base&)(*this) = (Base&) d;   // Call base assignment
        derived_data = d.derived_data;
    }
```

This expression needs some decoding: firstly *this is used to get the derived object that we are currently operating upon. This is then cast to a reference to a base object, and this causes the = operator to apply to a base object, and thus the base assignment operator is called. The right-hand-side of the base assignment is the derived object, but truncated to a reference to a base object — hence it is an assignment between both base subobjects of the derived objects.

The above statement is not the only way of calling the base assignment operator. Other possibilities include the use of an explicit call to the "operator=" member function:

```
((Base&)(*this)).operator= ( (Base&) d);
(*this).Base::operator= ( (Base&) d);
```

Note that in all cases, the type cast of d to Base& is unnecessary because conversion of a derived reference to a base reference will occur automatically. However, it makes what is occurring a little clearer.

17.6 Calling exit from a destructor

The exit library function should never be called from within a destructor. Doing so may cause an infinite loop when a static or global object of that class is destroyed. The exit function invokes the destructors of all static or global objects. If one of these destructors calls exit, the destructors may be called again. This may cause a nonfatal infinite loop or may exhibit a fatal error when the same destructor is called again (e.g., if heap memory is deallocated twice).

It isn't difficult for the implementor to code exit so that it does not invoke destructors the second time it is called, but this is only a partial solution. How should the exit function react when called the second time? Should it invoke the destructor of the objects it hasn't yet destroyed, or abandon destruction of all objects? The result of calling exit twice is undefined. For example, the g++ compiler under UNIX when executed on the following program:

```
#include <iostream.h>
#include <stdlib.h>

class Obj {
 private:
    char *name;
 public:
    Obj(char *s) { name = s;
                cout << "constructor: " << name << "\n";   }
    ~Obj() { cout << "destructor: " << name << "\n";
             cout.flush();
             exit(0);    // DANGEROUS
           }
};

Obj a("xyz");            // global objects
Obj a2("abc");

main()
{
   exit(0);
}
```

produced the following output:

```
constructor: xyz
constructor: abc
destructor: abc
```

It appears that g++ abandons all destructors on reentry to exit. This explains why only one of the objects has its destructor called.

17.7 Order of initialization of static objects in C++

A special order of evaluation error exists because the order of initialization of static or global objects is not defined across files. Within a single file the ordering is the same as the textual appearance of the definitions. For example, the Chicken object is always initialized before the Egg object in the following code:

```
Chicken chicken;    // Chicken comes first
Egg egg;
```

However, as for any declarations there is no specified left-to-right ordering for initialization of objects within a single declaration. Therefore, it is undefined which of c1 or c2 is initialized first in the code below:

```
Chicken c1, c2;
```

If the declarations of the global objects chicken and egg appear in different files that are linked together using independent compilation, it is undefined which will be constructed first. Try compiling and linking the following two files. The file "egg.c" is as follows:

```
#include <iostream.h>

class Egg {
    public:
        Egg() { cout << "Egg initialized\n"; }
};

Egg egg;          // global object
```

The file "chicken.c," which also contains the main function, is:

```
#include <iostream.h>

class Chicken {
    public:
        Chicken() { cout << "Chicken initialized\n"; }
};

Chicken chicken;      // global object

main()
{
  // do nothing;  only constructors executed
}
```

Different compilers will have different orders of appearance of the two output messages at run-time, and in fact, the order may well change for a particular compiler, depending on the order in which the object files are passed to the linker:

```
cc chicken.o egg.o      # may have different results
cc egg.o chicken.o
```

Fortunately, the above problem is not serious, but imagine if chicken required egg to be constructed. Such a dependency could well produce a run-time error. Therefore, a good general rule is that programs should avoid dependencies between global objects in constructors, particularly if objects are defined in separate files. If a global object is accessed in the constructor for another global object, the access may occur before the global object has been initialized.

The order of *destruction* of class objects is also undefined across files, so there is a similar error if destructors have dependencies between objects in different files. Unless care is taken the destructor for one global object might use another global object that has already been destroyed.

17.8 Order of initialization of static variables in C++

Note that the problems with order of initialization across files are not limited to class objects; the order of evaluation of any global or `static` variables is undefined across files. Although there is not usually any problem for variables initialized with constant expressions (which is why this error did not arise in C), there is still potential danger in any initializations that involve nonconstant expressions that must be evaluated at run-time (i.e., immediately before `main` is called). For example, consider the problem if a program uses a global pointer variable initialized to point to dynamic memory:

```
char *buffer = new char[BUFFER_SIZE];
```

This is legal C++ code, but it is quite dangerous. If `buffer` is used in a different source file by initialization code that is executed before `main` is called (e.g., a global object's constructor), then any such uses may use the value of `buffer` before it has been initialized properly (i.e., the value NULL). The moral of the story is to think carefully before using global variables with nonconstant expressions.

17.9 Overloading the new and delete operators

The operators `new` and `delete` can be overloaded on a class-by-class basis. This allows the programmer to take over the memory allocation for a class, which is occasionally desirable. A simple example of this form of overloading is shown below, where the operators merely call the global `new` and `delete` operators to allocate the right number of bytes:

```
#include <stdlib.h>
#include <stddef.h>    // declare size_t
#include <iostream.h>

class Obj {
        int x;
    public:
        void *operator new(size_t n);
        void operator delete(void *p);
};

void *Obj::operator new(size_t n)
{
    return ::new char [n];
}

void Obj::operator delete(void *p)
{
    ::delete [] p;
}
```

This illustrates some of the pedantic syntactical restrictions, which although not causing a run-time error, make it difficult to get the code to compile. These include:

- `operator new` must have return type `void*`.
- `operator delete` must have return type `void`.
- The parameter to `operator new` must have type `size_t`.
- The parameter to `operator delete` must have type `void*`.

There are also a number of run-time errors that must be avoided. Naturally, the two operators must work in complementary ways and there are any number of ways to define these operators incorrectly and foul up the memory allocation scheme. However, some of the causes of common pitfalls are:

- There are inconsistencies between `new` and `delete`.
- The operators are called for derived class objects.
- The operators are *not* called for arrays of class objects.
- The operators are allocators, not constructors and destructors.

The next few sections examine the variety of errors that can arise when overloading `new` and `delete`.

17.9.1 Inconsistencies between new and delete

When overloading `new` and `delete`, it is important to ensure symmetry between both operators. Naturally, there are any number of ways that programmers can make these two operators do the wrong things, but some of the more common problems are:

- not defining an overloaded `delete`
- using `::new char[]` but not `::delete[]`

The first error is a blatant failure to observe an important rule: always overload `delete` when you overload `new`. For example, in the example given in Section 17.9, if the `delete` operator is missing, this is not particularly dangerous, except that the pointer is allocated using `::new[]` and deallocated with the global `delete` operator, probably without the `delete[]` syntax. Typically the failures will be worse, since the usual purpose of overloading `new` is to replace the usual memory allocation with some special form, and this will not usually be compatible with the usual deallocator.

A second problem with overloading `new` and `delete` is that care must be taken to ensure consistency between the calls to global `new` and `delete` (i.e., `::new` and `::delete`). The example given in Section 17.9 is correct in this respect, but there would be a dangerous error if the overloaded `delete` operator did not call `::delete[]`.

17.9.2 Allocation problems with derived classes

If a class is derived from the `Obj` class it will still call these overloaded `new` and `delete` operators (which are inherited from `Obj`) for memory allocation. Therefore, the `size_t` parameter to `operator new` can have different values that must be considered. For example, if the new operator had been defined using the statement:

```
return ::new Obj;
```

this would cause a failure when a derived class object was allocated. The use of the `size_t` parameter is better than assuming a particular object size. However, consider the problem of derived classes if the purpose of overloading the new and `delete` operators is to perform some memory management for one particular size of object. For example, an efficiency improvement may be possible by packing small objects into large memory blocks. In this case the allocation will work only if the correct size is received, and will fail for a derived object. Therefore, the code should check whether the size is correct, and call the global new operator if not (i.e., for a derived object):

```
void *Obj::operator new(size_t n)
{
    if (n != sizeof(Obj)) {     // handle derived objects
        return ::new char[n];   // call global new operator
    }
    ... // advanced allocation for the Obj class
}
```

A similar test of the size is required in `operator delete`, although to do so requires the use of a second argument for `delete`, which is the size of the object being deallocated. The `delete` operator is defined as follows:

```
void Obj::operator delete(void *p, size_t n)
{
    if (n != sizeof(Obj)) {  // handle derived objects
        ::delete [] p;       // call global delete operator
        return;
    }
    ... // advanced deallocation for the Obj class
}
```

Unfortunately, the overloading of `new` and `delete` is an area where compiler differences are common and some compilers may not allow the two-argument form of `operator delete`. In this case the only method of avoiding dangers with derived objects is the redefinition of the `new` and `delete` operators in the derived class so that they simply call the global new and `delete` operators (as shown in the first example in this section). Always remember that overloaded `new` and `delete` operators are inherited!

17.9.3 Overloading array allocation is impossible

The second major pitfall when overloading these operators is that they are not called for allocation or deallocation of arrays of objects. Statements such as those below will not invoke the overloaded operators, but will instead call the global operators:

```
Obj *p = new Obj[10];   // allocate array
delete [] p;            // deallocate array
```

Therefore, when using a fancy user-defined memory allocation scheme for a class it is important not to allocate dynamic arrays of objects; otherwise all sorts of problems can arise, since arrays of objects are allocated by the global allocator, and single objects are allocated by the overloaded versions. Perhaps this will not create errors (assuming your program uses the correct choice between "`delete ptr`" for deallocating single objects and "`delete[] ptr`" for arrays of object), but it is unlikely to be what was intended.

17.9.4 new is an allocator, not a constructor

An error that can arise when overloading the `new` and `delete` operators is one of understanding the purpose of `new` and `delete`. `new` and `delete` are an allocator and deallocator — not a constructor and destructor. When a dynamic object is allocated using `new`, the overloaded `new` is called, and then the constructor is called with the address returned by `new` (i.e., returned by the allocator). The basic idea is this: `new` allocates some "raw memory" and the constructor turns that memory into an object. Similarly, when an object is deleted, the reverse procedure occurs: first the destructor turns the object into raw memory, then the overloaded `delete` operator is called to deallocate that raw memory. The process can be understood using the following class with output statements to show what is happening:

```
#include <stdlib.h>
#include <stddef.h>    // declare size_t
#include <iostream.h>

class Obj {
        int x;
    public:
        Obj() { cout << "Constructor called\n"; }
        ~Obj() { cout << "Destructor called\n"; }
        void *operator new(size_t n);
        void operator delete(void *p);
};

void *Obj::operator new(size_t n)
{
    cout << "Operator new called\n";
    return :: new char [n];
}

void Obj::operator delete(void *p)
{
    cout << "Operator delete called\n";
    ::delete p;
}

int main(void)
{
  Obj *a = new Obj;
  delete a;
  exit(0);
}
```

The output of this program is:

```
Operator new called
Constructor called
Destructor called
Operator delete called
```

This shows that the overloaded new is called before the constructor and the overloaded delete is called after the destructor. Therefore, the overloaded new and delete operators *do not apply to an object, only to raw memory.*

Some of the possible erroneous actions in new and delete include setting or using a non-static data member, calling a non-static member function, and explicitly calling the destructor. Any attempt to use (non-static) data members in delete is erroneous, since they will have been "destroyed" by the destructor. Any attempt to set (non-static) data members in new is erroneous, although perhaps not always dangerous, because the data members will be reset when the constructor is called on the given object. Naturally, any calls to (non-static) member functions are dangerous since there is never a "real" object, only raw memory with undefined contents.

17.10 Postfix ++ and --

There is a potential error when only the prefix version of the overloaded operators ++ or -- are declared. The same overloaded operator is called for both prefix and postfix usages. This creates problems because users of a class with these operators defined may expect different behavior. For example, in the declaration of a "smart" pointer class, the user of a class may assume the following C idiom to work correctly:

```
SmartPtr p1, p2;

while(*p1 != 0)
    *p1++ = *p2++;       // postfix ++ works?
```

However, the postfix ++ operator may be actually calling the overloaded prefix ++ operator. The return value of the prefix version is (probably) the new value of the object after increment (to be consistent with prefix usage), rather than the old value before increment (which is the expected behavior because this is the behavior of the built-in postfix ++ operator on primitive types).

The solution is to always declare a postfix version of each operator with appropriate behavior (or at least one that reports an error so as to warn the programmer if it is accidentally called; it can be declared as private so as to cause a compilation error when used). Unfortunately, in C++ versions 2.0 and earlier it is not possible to distinguish between prefix and postfix increment and decrement for class objects. Indeed there are some reported compiler bugs where the prefix version is always called, even if a postfix version is supplied.

17.11 Nonvirtual destructor

When a class is used as a base class in an inheritance hierarchy there are some errors that can occur if the destructor is not `virtual`. If a class declaration contains even a single `virtual` function, the destructor should probably also be declared as `virtual`. Doing so will not impose any extra space overhead since the existence of even a single `virtual` function already imposes this overhead on the class and its objects. Even if a class contains no `virtual` functions it may be advisable to declare the destructor as `virtual` if the class is to be used as a base class for other classes (note that this comment applies to other member functions too).

The main problem with having a non-`virtual` destructor involves the problems when `delete` is applied to a base class pointer. If the base class pointer actually holds the address of a derived class object the base class destructor will still be invoked unless the destructor is `virtual`. Any useful work in the derived class destructor is lost: deallocating memory, closing files, etc. The following code illustrates the problem:

```
#include <iostream.h>

class Base {
        int x;   // ... member data fields
    public:
        ~Base() { cout << "Base destructor\n"; }
};

class Derived : public Base {
    public:
        ~Derived() { cout << "Derived destructor\n"; }
};

main()
{
    Derived *d = new Derived;
    Base *b = d;      // conversion to base pointer
    delete b;         // Which destructor is called?
}
```

The base class destructor is called because the destructor is not `virtual` and the pointer variable b is assumed to be pointing at a "real" base class object. Declaring the base class destructor as `virtual` will cause the true type of the object pointed to by b to be inspected, and the correct destructor called (i.e., the derived class destructor is called, which then also calls the base class destructor automatically).

Because of the problems associated with having a non-`virtual` destructor, it is often advisable when declaring a library to declare the destructor (and other member functions) as `virtual` because users of the library are likely to derive further classes from the class in the library. However, the decision should not be taken lightly since adding a `virtual` function to a class with no other `virtual` functions imposes a space overhead on every object and may cause reduced run-time efficiency in the use of references or pointers to these objects.

17.12 Templates and primitive types

Template classes and template functions are a means whereby the programmer can write one generic block of source code that should work for many different data types. For example, the programmer can design a `Stack` class so that it can hold any type of data, and the user of the class can later specify which data type is to be stored. Templates are therefore a very powerful tool, but there are some dangers because of the fact that they are, in a certain sense, just "clever" macros.

The most common problem is that operations on the primitive data types (i.e., integers, characters, floating-point values, and pointers) are not fully "orthogonal." The same operation does not necessarily have the same meaning for all types. For example, the > operation is valid and has the same meaning for integers, characters, and floating-point values but has erroneous meaning for strings declared as `char*` — it compares the pointer values rather than lexically comparing the two strings. Therefore, the use of this operator in a template may have problems if the template is later instantiated with type `char*`. Consider the template for a generic `max` function that returns the maximum of its two arguments, as below:

```
template <class Type> Type max(Type x, Type y)
{
    if (x > y)
        return x;
    else
        return y;
}
```

This performs correctly for basic types, but when used to test the lexical ordering of two strings it can produce incorrect results. The following code illustrates its usage:

```
cout << max(1,2) << "\n";             // Integers ok
cout << max('b','a') << "\n";         // Characters ok
cout << max("abcd","defgh") << "\n";  // DANGEROUS!
```

Because of these problems with templates, the programmer is allowed to explicitly define particular instances of the generic function, so as to handle special cases. A special version of the max function can be declared for type `char*` as follows:

```
#include <string.h>      // declare strcmp

char* max(char* x, char* y)     // specialized char* version
{
    if (strcmp(x,y) > 0)
        return x;
    else
        return y;
}
```

17.13 Temporary objects and destruction

Temporary objects are created automatically by the compiler in a number of situations. This is a similar idea to that of a C compiler generating temporary values for intermediate results of a computation. However, in C++ a temporary with class type will have its constructor and destructor activated. For example, try the following class to demonstrate how a temporary object is defined for intermediate expression results, particularly that returned by the + operator:

```cpp
#include <iostream.h>

class Integer {
private: int val;
public:
        Integer() { val = 0; cout << "Constructor\n";  }
        ~Integer() { cout << "Destructor\n"; }
        Integer(const Integer &x)
            { val = x.val;
              cout << "Copy Constructor\n";
            }
        void operator=(int x) { val = x; }
        void operator=(const Integer &x) { val = x.val; }

        friend Integer operator+(Integer &x, Integer &y);
};

Integer operator+(Integer &x, Integer &y)
{
        Integer temp;    // user-defined temporary

        temp.val = x.val + y.val;
        return temp;     // creates compiler temporary
}

main()
{
        Integer i, j, k;

        k = i + j;
}
```

There are 4 calls to the ordinary constructor corresponding to i, j, k, and temp; there is a single call to the copy constructor that occurs when the return statement creates a temporary object for the object returned from operator +. This temporary object is the result of i+j and is then assigned to k.

In this case there are no errors related to temporary objects and in most cases, temporary objects are transparent to the programmer for a correctly defined class (i.e., having both assignment operator and copy constructor). However, if the programmer unwittingly stores a reference or pointer to members of a temporary object, there may be errors in a later use of the reference or pointer. The problem is that temporary objects can be destroyed by the compiler as soon as they have been used in the computation, and so the reference or pointer is no longer valid. However, since the timing of the destruction of temporaries is undefined, some compilers will not exhibit an error for such code because they leave the destruction of temporaries till late; it depends on how aggressively a particular compiler performs its internal code optimization.

The classic example of this error is concatenation using an overloaded + operator in a string class with dynamically allocated memory and a `char*` type conversion member operator. A fully coded example of such a string class is given below:

```cpp
#include <stream.h>
#include <string.h>

class String {
    private:
        char *str;
    public:
        String() { str = new char[1];   str[0] = '\0'; }
        String(char *s);
        String(char *s, char *s2);
        ~String();
        void operator =(const String &s);
        String(const String &s);
        operator char*();          // TYPE CONVERSION OPERATOR
        friend String operator+(String &s1, String &s2);
};

String::String(char*s)          // Constructor
{
    str = new char[strlen(s)+1];
    strcpy(str,s);
}

String::String(char*s, char*s2)    // Constructor
{                                  // concatenates 2 strings
    str = new char[strlen(s) + strlen(s2) + 1];
    strcpy(str,s);
    strcat(str,s2);
}

String::~String()            // Destructor
{
    cout << "Destructor for " << str << "\n";
    delete [] str;
}

void String::operator = (const String&s)
{
    if (this != &s) {
        delete [] str;
        str = new char[strlen(s.str)+1];
        strcpy(str, s.str);
    }
}

String::String(const String&s)      // Copy constructor
{
    str = new char[strlen(s.str)+1];
    strcpy(str, s.str);
}

String::operator char*()         // Type conversion operator
{
    return str;      // Return pointer to 'str' data member
}                    // DANGER!

String operator + (String &s1, String &s2)     // Concatenate
{
    return String(s1.str,s2.str);         // returns temporary
}
```

This string class looks wholly correct, but there is the hidden danger of using temporary objects after their destruction. The following `main` function using this class illustrates the problem:

```
main()
{
    String s1("abc"), s2("xyz");

    cout << s1 + s2 << "\n";          // ERROR
}
```

On some C++ implementations the above code will produce the following output:

```
Destructor for abcxyz
abcxyz
Destructor for xyz
Destructor for abc
```

This indicates that the destructor has been called before the concatenated string has been output. Destruction has occurred after computation of s1+s2 but before output using the << operator. The output statement was taking characters from a deallocated address.

The problem is that the + operator returns a class object, which creates a temporary object when the function is called. Therefore, s1+s2 is evaluated into a temporary object. There seems to be no problem since it is immediately used, but this is not so. In fact, the type conversion operator for conversion to char* is called, and this returns a pointer to the str field of the temporary object. Once this conversion has been performed, there is no further need for the temporary object and the compiler can destroy it. This destruction can occur before the char* address is passed to << for output, in which case the address becomes a dangling reference pointing to memory that has been deallocated by the delete operator in the temporary object's destructor.

17.14 delete versus delete [ ]

There are two distinct styles for the allocation and deallocation of memory — one for arrays and one for nonarrays. The two styles are distinguished by different syntax, particularly the presence or absence of square brackets. The styles for the new operator are:

```
Obj *p = new Obj;        // one object (nonarray)
Obj *p = new Obj[2];     // two objects (array)
```

and the corresponding styles for the delete operator are:

```
delete p;        // delete nonarray
delete [] p;     // delete array
```

Mixing the two styles is a common C++ programming error. The programmer is often lazy in the use of the delete operator and forgets the [] specification for the deallocation of an array. In fact, the implementation is often quite forgiving if the array objects are not class objects, or they are class objects for which the destructor does nothing important. Therefore, the programmer is rarely reminded of the necessity of using the correct syntax, and the error is much more difficult to track when it does finally catch the unwary programmer. The problem causes a run-time failure when an array of objects is deallocated without the [ ] syntax *and* the destructor for these objects does important work (e.g., deallocating memory allocated to class members). The error is illustrated by the following example program:

```
#include <iostream.h>

class Obj {
    public:
        Obj() { cout << "Constructor\n"; }
        ~Obj() { cout << "Destructor\n"; }
};

main()
{
    Obj *p = new Obj[2];
    delete p;        /* WRONG */
}
```

The correct method of allocation using the `new` operator causes the constructor to be called for both objects. However, the incorrect `delete` syntax means that only the destructor for the first object in the array is executed. The compiler sees only a pointer to the class object, p, and does not detect that it is actually pointing to an array of objects.

Note that although the wrong `delete` syntax is rarely fatal for the deallocation of arrays of primitive types, this need not always be true. The current C++ language definition defines the situation when the ordinary `delete` syntax is used to delete an array as "undefined," and there is no reason to expect that the ANSI C++ standard will change this. For example, the following code sequence is harmless on most (all?) current C++ implementations, although the compiler need not always be this forgiving.

```
char *p = new char[2];
delete p;      /* DANGEROUS? */
```

17.15 Function overrides inherited virtual method

A common error in the use of `virtual` functions for derived classes is to accidentally change the *signature* of the member function — that is, to declare the parameter types in a derived class member function differently from the base class member function. Although the compiler will detect and complain about a `virtual` member function given a different return type (and the same parameter types), it will allow a program using functions with changed parameter types to compile and run. The following code illustrates the strange behavior that can arise:

```
#include <iostream.h>

class Base {
    public:
        virtual void print(int x)
        { cout << "Base::print entered\n"; }
};
```

```
class Derived : public Base {
    public:
        void print(long x)      // WRONG! Parameter changed
        {  cout << "Derived::print entered\n"; }
};

main()
{
    Base * b;
    Derived * d = new Derived;

    b = d;
    b->print(0);    // Calls Base::print
}
```

If Derived::print were declared with an int parameter type, we would expect it to be called rather than Base::print. However, the problem is that the Derived class has no print(int) function and therefore the call using the Base pointer uses the base class function rather than the derived function.

Note that whether or not the Derived::print function declaration is qualified with virtual has no effect on the problem. If the virtual keyword is used this will only affect the member function print(long) in classes derived from the Derived class; it has no effect on any print(int) member functions in any of the classes.

17.16 Name of default constructor misspelled

The fact that the C++ compiler creates a default constructor for any class without one can lead to problems. The author came across this error when changing an implementation of a stack to use the uppercase letter S. A substitution of Stack for stack was performed but one important substitution was accidentally missed, leading to the following class declaration:

```
class Stack {
    private:
        int arr[SIZE];      // array holding stack
        int sp;             // stack pointer
    public:
        stack() { sp = 0; }   // CONSTRUCTOR (or is it?)
        ....
};
```

The compiler treats Stack::stack as a member function and creates a default constructor for the class Stack. The stack pointer, sp, remains an uninitialized data member. Fortunately, this error was discovered by a warning that the non-void function Stack::stack does not return a value.

17.17 throw inside a destructor

It is bad practice to use the `throw` statement to raise an exception from within a destructor. The problem is that destructors are invoked during the stack unwinding caused by handling a thrown exception. Consider the following code:

```
class Error {};   // exception class

class X {
    public:
        ~X() { throw Error(); }    // DANGEROUS!
};

void fn(void)
{
    X obj;

    if (something)
        throw Error();
}
```

When the function throws the exception, the destructor for `obj` will be called. If that destructor throws another exception, it seems to be an infinitely looping process because throwing that exception will again lead the destructor to be called. However, Bjarne Stroustrup, the designer of C++, has taken care to avoid this form of infinite looping in the use of exceptions. The requirements for exception handling state that when an exception is thrown from within a destructor that has been called as a result of stack unwinding from an earlier exception, this results in a call to the `terminate` function (instead of again unwinding the stack leading to an infinite loop). Therefore, a `throw` statement inside a destructor will often cause the program to terminate rather than returning to earlier exception handling code.

17.18 Portability to early C++ versions

The large number of different versions of C++ leads to a number of portability problems when attempting to write C++ code that is compatible with older C++ compilers. Although many of the changes relate to language syntax and will cause compilation errors, there are a few "quiet" changes, where the program will compile, link, and run on different C++ versions, but will produce unexpected results. The next two sections are examples of such problems.

17.19 Constructor with default parameter values

Early versions of C++ have an unfortunate feature (or bug) relating to constructors with default values for parameters. In versions 2.0 and earlier, a constructor where all parameters had default values was not recognized as the default zero-argument constructor, and the compiler created one automatically (as it does for any class with no zero-argument constructor). For example, try executing the following program:

```
#include <iostream.h>

class Obj {
    public:
        Obj(int x = 0) {  cout << "constructor called\n"; }
};

int main()
{
    Obj X;
    Obj Y(1);
}
```

If the constructor is called for both X and Y, then the compiler is correct. However, if the constructor is called only for Y, then the compiler does not support C++ version 2.1 or later versions. In this case the compiler has created its own default constructor and this will be called for all objects declared without arguments.

This anomaly in the language definition was fixed in C++ version 2.1 but may remain in some older compilers. Therefore, for improved portability it is recommended to declare a default constructor with zero arguments as a separate function, ensuring that all other constructors have at least one parameter with no default value.

17.20 Type of character constants — int or char

In versions of C++ prior to version 2.0 the type of a character constant such as 'a' was int. The reason for this is simply that this was (and still is) the situation in C because the difference between char and int is not particularly important in C, with the large number of implicit conversions between the two types. However, in C++ having a character constant with type int leads to strange anomalies in function and operator overloading. The most well known problem was the method of outputting a single character using:

```
cout << 'A';
```

In early versions of C++ this didn't output the character A, but instead produced the number representing it (e.g., 65 in ASCII). On the other hand, a sequence such as:

```
char ch = 'A';
cout << ch;
```

correctly produced the single character. The problem is caused by character constants having type int, so the first usage called the overloaded << operator with the int parameter.

The problem with cout is only one particular problem. Whenever a character constant was applied to an overloaded function or operator there was some risk of the programmer being surprised. An error would occur if the overloaded function or operator had versions with both char and int parameters.

This anomaly was corrected in C++ version 2.0 and character constants now have type char. Nevertheless, it is still a portability problem for older C++ versions and character constants should be handled carefully if compatibility is required for older C++ compilers. For example, some portable methods of outputting a single character are:

```
cout << (char) 'A';    // explicit cast
cout << "A";           // output string (inefficient)
```

There is also the minor issue that `sizeof('A')` will be 1 in C++, but `sizeof(int)` in C, because character constants have type `char` in ANSI C.

17.21 Further reading

One book I have no hesitation in recommending to any aspiring C++ programmer is *Effective C++* by Scott Meyers, which I found to be an excellent book. It contains 50 sections on specific methods of improving C++ programming, and not surprisingly a number of these sections relate to avoiding common pitfalls. Hence, there are a large number of sections (at least 20 out of the 50, according to my calculations) that are relevant to the C++ errors covered in this chapter (and elsewhere in this book). In addition, Items 35–44 in Meyers' book cover a variety of issues in avoiding design pitfalls when using C++ for object-oriented programming, which are not covered in this book.

An interesting paper on C++ errors and algorithms for their automatic detection by the compiler is that by Meyers and Lejter. The errors examined include mismatched `new` and `delete`, non-`virtual` destructor, missing copy constructor or assignment operator, return type of the assignment operator, and no check for self-assignment in the overloaded assignment operator.

Another interesting paper on C++ is "Programming in C++: Rules and Recommendations" by Mats Henricson and Erik Nyquist. Although the main aim of the paper is the establishment of C++ programming style guidelines, there are a number of sections relevant to common C++ errors (i.e., styles to avoid them!).

HENRICSON, Mats, and NYQUIST, Erik, "Programming in C++: Rules and Recommendations," Technical Report, Ellemtel Telecommunication Systems Laboratories, Sweden, 1990–1992 (see Bibliography for acquisition details).

MEYERS, Scott, *Effective C++: 50 Specific Ways to Improve Your Programs and Designs*, Addison-Wesley, 1992.

MEYERS, Scott, and LEJTER, Moses, "Automatic Detection of C++ Programming Errors: Initial Thoughts on a lint++," Technical Report CS-91-51, Department of Computer Science, Brown University, Providence, Rhode Island, 1991 (see Bibliography for acquisition details).

Chapter 18

ANSI C library errors

The ANSI C standard specifies a number of library functions that can be portably used by C programs. Most of these functions can also be used by C++ programs, and will presumably be part of the ANSI C++ standard when it is released. Therefore, most of the errors discussed in this chapter apply to both C and C++ programs.

18.1 Errors with printf

The compiler cannot type-check arguments to functions with a variable number of arguments, such as `printf` and `scanf`. Even worse, functions with variable arguments cannot themselves check for correct types. If the wrong types are passed to `printf` or `scanf`, a number of different run-time errors can occur. The most harmless problem is that a meaningless number will be printed (i.e., garbage characters as output). The worst that can occur is a segmentation fault or some other abnormal termination.

There are a number of common errors in calling `printf`. The simplest error is to simply forget the argument:

```
printf("%d\n");    /* MISSING ARGUMENT */
```

This causes an integer to be extracted from the stack even though one was not passed as an argument. The usual result is output of a weird integer value.

The other similar error is to pass too many arguments to `printf`, as below. Fortunately, this causes no harmful effects since the extra argument is ignored.

```
printf("%d\n", i, j);    /* EXTRA ARGUMENT */
```

Even if the correct number of arguments is passed, their types must also be correct for the corresponding format. For example, accidentally passing an `int` argument for a `%s` format will cause the integer to be treated as an address, causing abnormal termination or at least the output of unexpected string data:

```
printf("%s", 10);    /* ERROR */
```

Fortunately, the default argument promotions that are applied to variable arguments reduce the frequency of type mismatches. Arguments of type `char` or `short` are promoted to `int`, and `float` is promoted to `double`. This explains why the `printf`

formats %e, %f and %g are valid for both float and double, and also why there is no
special format for short values. Therefore, accidentally passing a char or short
instead of an int, or a float instead of a double, will not cause an error; in fact,
these situations are quite common.

```
char ch;
short sh;
float fl;

printf("%d %d %f\n", ch, sh, fl);    /* OK */
```

Nevertheless, there are a few situations where a mismatch is possible. The major types
and their formats that cannot be mixed are int (%d), long (%ld), double (%f), and
char* (%s). The error in passing an integer to %s has been discussed above. Passing an
integer for a %f format or a float for a %d format will also cause an error. There is no
implicit conversion between integral and floating-point types when they are passed as
arguments to a variable-argument function, although there are conversions when they are
passed to a fixed-argument prototyped function. An example of an erroneous call passing
an integer to %f is:

```
#define COST  10
....
printf("Cost is %4.2f dollars\n", COST);
```

One source of trouble with portability is the type of large integer constants on 16-bit
implementations. Consider the following printf statement:

```
#define SALARY  50000
..
printf("The manager has salary %d dollars\n", SALARY);
```

On a 16-bit machine the value 50000 is too large for int and becomes a long constant,
causing a type mismatch between %d and long. One portable method is to use the %ld
format with a type cast to long (or a suffix L on the constant):

```
printf("The manager has salary %ld dollars\n", (long)SALARY);
```

18.1.1 Unnecessary type casting to float

Another minor mistake made by novice programmers is to unnecessarily type-cast
arguments to %f to float even when they are already double. The following
statement is an example:

```
printf("x*2.0 = %f\n", (float)(x*2.0));
```

The type cast is not necessary because %f applies to both float and double. This is
not a dangerous error, since the value is simply converted to float by the type cast and
then promoted back up to double with argument promotions. However, it is bad style,
and indicates a dangerous misunderstanding that may lead to a later error. For example,
this programmer might believe that %f applies to float and %lf applies to double
(as is the case for scanf), whereas %lf actually applies to long double in printf.

18.1.2 Missing FILE* argument to fprintf

Another type-related error that is prevalent in pre-ANSI C code is a missing FILE* argument in a fprintf call. Typically, this occurs when the programmer forgets to use stderr. The following statement illustrates the error:

```
fprintf("Error...file %s didn't open!\n", filename);
```

Unfortunately, many compilers (particularly pre-ANSI C compilers) will not detect this coding error because (a) argument types are not tested if fprintf is declared using nonprototyping; and (b) even if there is a prototype for fprintf, the type of the format string, char*, is a pointer type that many implementations will allow to be converted to the type FILE*. Even high-quality modern ANSI compilers commonly only produce a *warning* for this statement, allowing the program to be executed even though it contains this error. Naturally, the corrected code is:

```
fprintf(stderr, "Error...file %s didn't open!\n", filename);
```

18.1.3 Printing a string with printf

One dangerous practice that introduces a subtle error is a common method of printing a string using printf. The following statement contains a hidden error:

```
printf(str);      /* DANGEROUS */
```

This will print the string correctly unless it happens to contain a % character, in which case printf will expect extra arguments. No arguments are present, and a fatal error may result. The correct method is:

```
printf("%s", str);      /* CORRECT */
```

18.2 Errors with scanf

The scanf function exhibits similar type-related errors to printf because it is also a variable-argument function, and the compiler cannot type-check its arguments. This problem is compounded by the common misconception that the format string for scanf can be the same as that used for printf, which causes the programmer to use the wrong type arguments.

18.2.1 Missing & on scanf argument

A very common instance of passing wrong argument types to scanf is forgetting the & in front of the arguments. Instead of a pointer to the variable being passed, the variable's value is passed as if it were a pointer value. This is usually an illegal address and a dereference of this address inside the scanf function will cause undefined run-time behavior. The error is seen in the following code:

```
int x;
....
scanf("%d", x);      /* ERROR */
```

The correct `scanf` statement is:

```
scanf("%d", &x);    /* CORRECT */
```

An `&` is needed for input of all basic types, including integers, characters, and floating point values. However, it is not needed for string arguments corresponding to the `%s` format. Accidentally using an `&` for a `char[]` argument is often harmless (perhaps causing a compilation warning about `&` being "ignored"), but using `&` on a `char*` argument to `%s` can cause a fatal error similar to that from omitting `&` on basic types:

```
char s1[10];
char *s2;
   ....
scanf("%s", &s1);    /* HARMLESS */
scanf("%s", &s2);    /* ERROR */
```

18.2.2 Wrong argument types to scanf

Even if `&` is used correctly, the `scanf` function is still more prone to argument type errors than `printf` simply because the default argument promotions offer little safety for scanf. Whereas `printf` allowed both `float` and `double` for the `%f` format, scanf has `%f` for `float` and `%lf` for `double`. Similarly, scanf has a special format `%hd` for `short int`, whereas `printf` simply used `%d` for both `short` and `int` values. The difference occurs because the default argument promotions do not apply to addresses, and all arguments to scanf are addresses. Consider the following erroneous code:

```
double f;

scanf("%f", &f);      /* ERROR */
```

This will attempt to store a `float` value at an address that actually contains a `double`. Although this should not cause a run-time error, the value of `f` is likely to be incorrect (unless the implementation has `float` and `double` the same size).

A similar, more dangerous example is the confusion between `%d` and `%hd`, as follows:

```
short x;

scanf("%d", &x);      /* ERROR */
```

This statement attempts to store an `int` at an address that points to a `short`. If a `short` is 2 bytes and `int` is 4 bytes the program is unwittingly modifying some unknown extra 2 bytes. Note that such errors can lie dormant in a program as portability problems if `short` and `int` are the same size for a particular implementation.

18.2.3 scanf and printf format strings differ

A common error that even reasonably experienced programmers may make is the assumption that the format strings for `printf` and `scanf` are the same. There is some overlap in the common formats such as `%d` and `%s`, but there are many differences and programmers should study `printf` and `scanf` separately, rather than assuming a one-to-one mapping of facilities.

One common mistake with scanf involves the input of floating-point numbers. Since printf uses %f for double types it is quite common for a programmer to mistakenly use %f for a double variable in a scanf call:

```
double x;
...
scanf("%f", &x);
```

This is incorrect since %f is the format for float, and %lf is the correct scanf format for double. There is further confusion in that the %lf format is not correct for printf (it specifies long double); instead simply %f should be used for both float and double.

This form of error can lie dormant in a program since many implementations use the same representation for float, double, and long double. It becomes a portability problem for other implementations where the representations differ.

18.2.3.1 scanf has no precision specifier

Another common error with using the same format string for printf and scanf is using a field width and precision. Suppose you have generated a data file using:

```
fprintf(dat, "%6.4f\n", val);
```

The following statement is erroneous, even if val has float type (if it has double type then we have the error discussed in the previous section):

```
fscanf(dat, "%6.4f", &val);   /* WRONG */
```

The error is that scanf formats do not allow two integers. Whereas printf has both a field width and a precision, scanf only allows a single integer indicating field width. The above statement is interpreted by scanf as if the format specification were "%6.", where the '.' character is an undefined format specifier. Therefore, the format string is erroneous, and scanf will return zero, and will not alter val, and will not even read any characters in the file.

18.2.4 Whitespace in scanf format strings

Programmers get into the habit of adding \n at the end of a printf call, and because of the similarity between printf and scanf format strings, they can accidentally do so for a scanf call. A newline in the scanf format string causes characters up to the next non-whitespace character to be read. For example, if the following program is executed, the user will have to enter a number and then another character other than space, tab, or newline:

```
#include <stdio.h>

int main()
{
  int x;
  printf("Enter an integer: ");
  scanf("%d\n", &x);
}
```

In fact, any whitespace in a scanf format string is usually misplaced, although it is often harmless. A common indication that something is wrong is when two or more adjacent whitespace characters appear in a scanf format string. Two whitespace characters have the same effect as one, so the usage is probably erroneous.

Even a single space character is often not necessary. The scanf format string "%d %d" needs no space before the second %d specification because scanf skips whitespace when looking for a number. Hence, whitespace is skipped twice and the space is redundant. The only specifications that may require a preceding space character are the %c and %[specifications, since these do not skip whitespace by default. The programmer should consider carefully whether to put a space before a %c specification; using a space will read the first non-whitespace character, and omitting the space will be similar to getchar:

```
scanf("%c", &c);    /* act like getchar */
scanf(" %c", &c);   /* read first non-whitespace */
```

18.2.5 Whitespace and the %c scanf format

Not using a space before a %c format is a reasonably common error in scanf usage. An example of such an error is given in Section 12.7. The crucial function is:

```
void menu(void)
{
  char choice;

    while(1) {  /* infinite loop */
        printf("--- MAIN MENU ---\n");
        printf("1. Insert\n");
        printf("2. Delete\n");
        printf("3. Quit\n");
        printf("----------------\n");
        printf("\nEnter your choice: \n");
        scanf("%c", &choice);             /* ERROR! */
        switch(choice) {
            case '1': insert_obj(); break;
            case '2': delete_obj(); break;
            case '3': exit(0);    /* Quit */
            default:
                printf("Unknown choice... try again\n\n");
        }
    } /* infinite loop */
}
```

Using %c without a preceding space for the input will cause strange behavior. When the user chooses 1 or 2 the program will perform the insertion or deletion operation (which we assume to consume no input), and will then read the newline (or any other whitespace typed by the user) as the next user choice. Hence choosing 1 or 2 and hitting return will cause a complaint about an "Unknown choice" (because the newline character is processed as a choice) and an extra appearance of the menu. The solution is to add a space to the format string in the scanf statement:

```
scanf(" %c", &choice);    /* CORRECT */
```

18.3 Misusing feof

A common erroneous practice is to use `feof` to control whether or not to read input from a file. The error arises because of a misunderstanding of how `feof` operates. The `feof` function returns true if a previous read operation tried to read past the end of the file. Therefore, unlike the similar `eof` function in Pascal, `feof` can return false (i.e., not end of file) even if there are no more characters to read (i.e., the previous read operation read the last character, but did not try to read past the end of the file). Therefore, it is important to always check the return value of input functions even if `feof` has returned false. The error is illustrated in the code below to copy a file to `stdout`:

```
#include <stdio.h>

main()
{
    FILE *fp;
    char *fname = "dummy";
    char s[100];
                            /* Copy file to stdout */
    fp = fopen(fname, "r");
    while(!feof(fp)) {
        fgets(s, 100, fp);
        printf("%s", s);
    }
}
```

The main error that occurs is that the last line is printed twice. The return value of `fgets` has not been examined to check for a NULL return indicating end of file. The `feof` test will not indicate end of file after reading the last line because it has just read the last newline in the file and hasn't yet tried to read past the end of the file. When `fgets` returns NULL on end of file its string argument is unchanged, and in this case it contains the previous line. A slightly better method is to test the return value of `fgets`:

```
while(!feof(fp)) {
    char *ret = fgets(s, 100, fp);
    if (ret = NULL) break;
    .....   /* process the line */
}
```

However, it is rather pointless to use `feof` to control the loop iteration, since the loop will never actually exit from the `feof` test. The following idiom for reading from a file is much better:

```
while(fgets(s, 100, fp) != NULL) {
    .....   /* process the line */
}
```

This idiom where an input statement is involved in the loop condition is very common in C. For example, it is commonly used with `getchar`, `getch` and `fread`:

```
while((ch = getchar()) != EOF) { .... }
while((ch = getc(fp)) != EOF) { .... }
while(fread(buf, sizeof(int), 1, fp) != 0) { .... }
```

Another fairly common error involving `fgets` is the method of removing the newline from the string that `fgets` reads (recall that `gets` removes newlines, but `fgets` leaves the newline in the string). Therefore, code such as the following is often seen after an `fgets` call:

```
len = strlen(s);
s[len - 1] = '\0';    /* overwrite the newline */
```

This is erroneous if there is not a newline at the end of the string, which can occur from reading in a long line (in which case the `fgets` call may not have read the newline), and also since it is not always guaranteed that there will be a newline on the end of the last line of a file. The correct method is:

```
len = strlen(s);
if (len > 0 && s[len - 1] == '\n')
    s[len - 1] = '\0';    /* overwrite the newline */
```

18.4 getchar and getc return int not char

It is all too common for programs to assign the character returned from `getchar` or `getc` to a variable of type `char`. However, this is an incorrect practice because these functions return EOF upon end of file, and EOF is an `int`, not a `char`. Consider the common method of copying input to output:

```
char c;   /* WRONG */

while( (c = getchar()) != EOF)
    putchar(c);
```

In practice, EOF is always equal to −1, which is a value that cannot always be represented by the type `char`. The result of the above code depends on whether the compiler treats plain `char` as `signed` or `unsigned char`, which is unspecified by the ANSI C standard.

If characters are `unsigned`, the above expression causes −1 to be promoted to `unsigned int` for comparison with the returned character. However, the variable c can never hold a value equivalent to `(unsigned)-1`, and the `while` loop becomes an infinite loop that continues to read characters even after end of file.

If characters are `signed`, the code above will mostly perform as expected because −1 can be represented as a `signed char`. However, there is a rare error that if the input contains the character with ASCII value 255, then it too will be represented as −1 and the loop will terminate prematurely.

The solution is simply to declare c as an `int`. An int type should always hold the returned value of `getchar` or `getc` as long as the value could be EOF. As soon as the presence of EOF has been tested, the value could be assigned to a `char` variable (such as for efficiency). The idea is illustrated below:

```
int c;   /* CORRECT */

while( (c = getchar()) != EOF) {
    char c2 = c;     /* no longer need be int */
    /* ... do something with c2 */
}
```

18.5 setbuf buffer is local array

The buffer used in a call to `setbuf` or `setvbuf` must be a `static` or global array variable, or an allocated heap block. If it is an automatic local array variable, a run-time failure may occur because when the function containing the local array returns, the space on the stack for that array is no longer used for that array (and may in fact be used by different variables).

It is not even safe to declare the buffer for `setbuf` or `setbuf` as an automatic array in `main` since the flushing of buffers by the `exit` function may occur after `main` has returned. The following code contains the error:

```
#include <stdio.h>
#include <stdlib.h>

main()
{
    char buf[BUFSIZ];  /* should be static */

    setbuf(stdout, buf);
    /* ... do work */
    exit(EXIT_SUCCESS);
}
```

18.6 Direct access on text files

There is no difference between text files and binary files on UNIX systems. The return value of `ftell` is an integer indicating the number of characters along the file. However, this is not necessarily so for other operating systems and it is common to abuse direct access on a text file. The `long` value returned from `ftell` is not necessarily a count of how many characters have been read.

Some implementations of text files will use two characters to represent each newline. Instead of a single newline character, the file will contain a newline \n character and a line-feed character (\r). Although the I/O libraries on such implementations will usually hide this fact from the user (by ignoring \r on input and automatically adding \r when outputting a \n), this can create problems when using direct access on text files where these conversions are not performed. Text files should not be opened using binary mode unless you really need low-level processing; otherwise there is a high probability that the \r-\n problem will not be handled correctly.

18.7 fflush on an input file

The fflush function is used to flush the buffer associated with a file pointer. Unfortunately, it can only be used to flush an output buffer, causing output to appear on screen (or be flushed to a file). Applying fflush on an input file leads to undefined results; it will succeed on some systems, but cause failure on others. The problem is typified by the following statement that often appears in code:

```
fflush(stdin);
```

The intention is to flush all input characters currently awaiting processing (i.e., stored in the buffer), so that the next call to getchar (or another input function) will only read characters entered by the user after the fflush call. This functionality would be very useful, but is unfortunately not possible in general, as the effect of fflush is undefined on input streams. There is no portable way to flush any "type ahead" input keystrokes; fflush(stdin) may work on some systems, but on others it is necessary to call some non-ANSI library functions.

18.8 fread and fwrite without intervening fseek

When a binary file is opened for update using a mode such as "rb+", the programmer must be careful when using fread and fwrite. It is an error to mix fread and fwrite operations without an intervening call to a repositioning function such as fseek or rewind. For example, do not assume, after sequentially reading all records in a file using fread, that a call to fwrite will write data to the end of the file; use an fseek call to explicitly reach the end of the file. The best method of avoiding this error is to call fseek immediately before every fread or fwrite call.

18.9 Buffering problems with <stdio.h>

Consider the following method of prompting for and accepting input with printf and scanf:

```
#include <stdio.h>

main()
{
    int n;

    printf("Enter a number: ");
    scanf("%d", &n);
    printf("The number is %d\n", n);
}
```

This simple program contains an error that is far from obvious. Since stdout is line-buffered, and the call to printf does not contain a newline character, the initial prompt need not appear until the second printf statement (which contains a newline). The program could well wait for input from the scanf statement before the prompt has appeared. Fortunately, most implementations of the <stdio.h> library seem to silently flush stdout whenever an input function such as scanf or getchar is called. However, such behavior is not required by ANSI C, and there are implementations that do not do this. Therefore, this simple program contains a dangerous portability problem.

There are a number of solutions to this problem. One method is to always place a newline at the end of a `printf` statement, thereby forcing the characters in the internal buffer to appear. Another method is to call `fflush(stdout)` before any input statement.

There is no similar problem in C++ between `cout` and `cin` statements. The relationship between these streams is explicitly documented, and in fact there is a member function `tie` that allows a programmer to "tie" an input and output stream so that requesting input will flush the corresponding output stream.

18.10 Mixing <stdio.h> and <iostream.h>

It is poor C++ style to intermingle usages of functions from the C `<stdio.h>` library and the C++ `<iostream.h>` library (or the older `<stream.h>` library). Although mixing the two is often harmless, there are some errors that may occur. One problem is that they use different buffers and different buffering methods. Try executing the following program:

```
#include <stdio.h>
#include <iostream.h>

main()
{
    printf("Hello ");
    cout << "World\n";
}
```

This program may well produce the erroneous output:

```
World
Hello
```

The problem is that `printf` is line-buffered and will not output characters until it outputs a newline. `cout` uses a different buffering scheme and its output appears immediately. The characters in the `printf` buffer do not appear until the program terminates, causing the buffers to be flushed. Although it is far better to avoid mixing operations, one "quick-and-dirty" fix for this problem is the use of `fflush(stdout)` after `<stdio.h>` output statements, particularly `printf` statements when the format string does not end with a newline.

Buffering problems can also appear related to input. Consider the following sequence of statements when given the input 35a, with no space between the number and the character:

```
int x;
char c;

scanf("%d", &x);
cin >> c;
```

The second input statement using `cin` will not see the 'a' character because it has been read into the `<stdio.h>` internal buffer. To read an integer, `scanf` must keep reading characters until it finds a nondigit character. Thus it always reads one extra character, and pushes that character back onto the input buffer to be read next time. Unfortunately, scanf and cin don't read from the same buffer, so cin cannot read the character; any later call to scanf or getchar will receive the character.

The same problem with input buffering means that the explicit use of pushback using ungetc from <stdio.h> or pushback from <iostream.h> will not permit the pushed back character to be read by input functions from the opposite library.

Sometimes it is necessary to mix both C and C++ input libraries, such as when linking C++ code with existing C code. In such cases the basic rule to follow is to mix operations between the different libraries only on a line-by-line basis.

18.11 <stdarg.h> errors

There are a number of common errors when declaring variable-argument functions using the <stdarg.h> macros: va_start, va_arg, and va_end. Some of these errors are:

- va_end not called at the end of the function
- va_start uses a register parameter
- va_start uses an array parameter
- va_start uses a char, short, or float parameter
- va_start doesn't use a parameter (e.g., uses a variable)
- va_start doesn't use the last named parameter
- va_start uses a C++ reference parameter
- va_arg uses a complicated type declarator
- va_list type passed to printf
- va_arg uses the type char, short, or float
- relying on call-by-value when passing the va_list variable
- va_end not called in the same function as va_start
- mismatched multiple calls to va_start and va_end

The simplest error is to forget to call va_end at the end of the function. The va_end macro performs any necessary cleanup, possibly deallocating memory allocated by va_start. This error is not dangerous in many cases because va_end is a "do nothing" macro in many implementations, but it is still a dormant portability problem.

The restrictions on the parameter used by va_start are caused by the fact that, in most implementations, it applies the address-of operator (&) and the sizeof operator to the parameter. If the parameter is declared as register, then applying the address-of operator is illegal and should provoke a compilation error.

If the parameter used by va_start is an array type, the sizeof operator computes the size of the corresponding pointer type instead of the size of the array and all its elements (this behavior of sizeof is also covered in Section 14.14). Therefore, the process of extracting arguments with va_arg is corrupted because an incorrect size is computed and the bytes in the array parameter might be returned by later calls to va_arg.

Similarly, if the parameter used by va_start is of type char, short, or float it can corrupt the argument extraction. Although the author is unsure of the reason for this restriction, one conjecture is that a small type would corrupt alignment of the argument list. Note that the use of `char`, `short`, or `float` with `va_arg` is a different error, and is discussed in the next section.

Naturally, `va_start` must use a function parameter; using a variable can cause any manner of failure. Another error is applying `va_start` to the wrong parameter. If the parameter supplied to `va_start` is not the *last* named parameter, subsequent calls to `va_arg` may return values of the named parameters.

Another form of rare error when using `va_start` in C++ occurs when the last named parameter is a reference parameter, as in:

```
void fn(int &x, ...)     // pass x by reference
{
    ....
    va_start(ap, x);     // ERROR
    ....
}
```

The problem is that most `va_start` implementations are simply macros that will involve computing `&x`. Unfortunately, the address of a reference cannot be computed, and `&x` evaluates to the address of the value referenced by x — that is, the address of the argument passed to x. All manner of failure is possible, since later `va_arg` calls will extract values from near where the *argument* is stored, rather than near where the *parameter* is stored. Perhaps the ANSI C++ standard, when it is finalized, will modify `va_start` to work correctly in this situation, but for the time being this area represents a limitation of `<stdarg.h>` in C++.

18.11.1 va_arg with pointer-to-function type

The `va_arg` macro is often implemented in a way that simply appends a `*` to the type argument to create a new type. For example, with `va_arg(ap,int)` it will make some internal use of the type `int *`. However, there are some types for which appending a star will not create a legal type, and such uses will cause a syntax error at the `va_arg` call. Typically, the problematical types are those containing brackets. For example, trying to extract a pointer-to-function argument using:

```
ptr_to_fn = va_arg(ap, void(*)(int));
```

is likely to cause a syntax error because appending a star will not work. The solution is to use a `typedef` name:

```
typedef void (*pfn)(int);
    ....
ptr_to_fn = va_arg(ap, pfn);
```

18.11.2 va_list type passed to printf

A common error made by inexperienced programmers when coding up their first function using <stdarg.h> is to misunderstand how the pointer to the list of arguments (i.e., the va_list variable) should be used. A typical error is to assume that printf will understand variable argument lists:

```
#include <stdarg.h>
#include <stdio.h>
#include <stdlib.h>

void debug_print(char *format, ...)
{
    va_list ap;

    va_start(ap, format);
    printf(format, ap);   /* should be vprintf */
    va_end(ap);
}

main()
{
    debug_print("x = %d\n", 3);
    exit(0);
}
```

The result will usually be incorrect output, although some more drastic failure could also occur. The problem is that the value of ap is used as data (i.e., the address of the start of the argument block) rather than what ap points to being used. Hence, printf has only one argument, a 4-byte pointer value, which is used as the data for the %d format. Unfortunately, the compiler does not produce a warning about this incorrect use of va_list because printf's arguments cannot be type-checked. The correct solution is to call one of the functions that are specially designed to accept a va_list argument: vprintf, vfprintf, or vsprintf.

18.11.3 va_arg uses char, short, or float

A common error where the use of char, short, or float types is dangerous is the use of va_arg. The va_arg macro is used to extract unnamed arguments to the variable-argument function, and these arguments will have had the default promotions applied: char and short promote to int; float promotes to double. Consider the effect of the following erroneous use of type char:

```
char c;
 ....
c = va_arg(p, char);     /* WRONG */
```

The va_arg macro usually applies the sizeof operator to the second type parameter. The use of char will compute the size as 1, whereas the correct number of bytes is sizeof(int) — usually 2 or 4 bytes. Therefore, the extraction of a 1 byte value is incorrect and va_arg may return an incorrect character value. The remaining extra bytes will cause erroneous behavior of subsequent calls to va_arg. The correct method of extracting a character argument is:

```
c = va_arg(p, int);    /* CORRECT */
```

The variable c can be left declared as type char. Using type int may be preferable style, but leaving the variable with the intended type will not cause a failure since the returned value of va_arg will be truncated to the required type.

The use of short or float as types for va_arg will cause a failure analogous to the one described above regarding char. On some implementations they may cause no failure — using short is not dangerous if sizeof(short) is the same as sizeof(int), and similarly, using float is not dangerous if sizeof(float) equals sizeof(double).

Some implementations use very clever macros to handle erroneous types to va_arg correctly. For example, the va_arg macro might include a constant conditional expression that compares the size to ensure that it is at least as large as an int. Alternatively, the implementor could use a hidden built-in operator, which is similar to sizeof except that it returns the size of the type after the default promotions. Even on implementations where such usage is harmless, it represents a dangerous portability pitfall and should be avoided.

Naturally, the restriction on va_arg also applies to the types signed char, unsigned char, signed short, and unsigned short. However, pointers to these types are allowed because no promotions are applied to pointer types. Therefore, uses such as va_arg(p, char*) are legal.

18.11.4 Passing va_list function arguments

The pointer of type va_list initialized by va_start can safely be passed to another function, and it is satisfactory to define a function with a va_list parameter. The standard library functions vprintf, vfprintf, and vsprintf have this property, and we can also define new functions. The va_arg macro can be called in a different function from that in which the corresponding va_start macro was invoked. However, there are a few pitfalls to avoid when passing va_list arguments around.

Firstly, after processing all the arguments, the va_end macro must be invoked in the same function that called va_start. This means that a variable-argument function can pass its argument list to another function, but the second function cannot call va_end.

The second problem relates to the type of va_list. The majority of implementations declare va_list as a pointer type, typically char*. This means that passing a va_list parameter to a function will not change the parameter in the top-level function because of call-by-value parameter passing of pointer types. However, other implementations could declare va_list as an array type that would display pass-by-reference semantics, and would be changed in the top-level function. Hence any code that passes va_list types to other functions should take care that it works for any type of va_list. For example, the following code relies on call-by-value passing of the va_list variable:

```
#include <stdarg.h>
#include <stdio.h>

void addlog(char *format, va_list ap)
{
    extern FILE *logfile;
    vfprintf(logfile, format, ap);
}

void debug_print(char *format, ...)
{
    va_list ap;

    va_start(ap, format);
    addlog(format, ap);    /* to log file */
    vprintf(format, ap);   /* to screen */
    va_end(ap);
}
```

The problem is that the addlog function could modify ap (i.e., if vfprintf modifies ap) if va_list is an array type. Hence this code exhibits a portability problem for some implementations.

One solution is to use a temporary variable of type va_list, either in the top-level function (as in the example below) or in the lower-level function. The copying of the temporary must be performed using memcpy rather than the assignment "temp=ap;" because the latter will fail with a compilation error when va_list is an array type.

```
void debug_print(char *format, ...)
{
    va_list ap;
    va_list temp;

    va_start(ap, format);
        /* use temporary va_list variable */
    memcpy(&temp, &ap, sizeof(va_list));
    addlog(format, temp);
        /* No need to use temporary for last usage */
    vprintf(format, ap);
    va_end(ap);
}
```

Alternatively, the top-level function could use va_start to restart the processing of arguments at the beginning of the argument list. And here there is another pitfall: va_end must be called to finish off the current processing before calling va_start to restart another pass over the arguments.

```
void debug_print(char *format, ...)
{
    va_list ap;

    va_start(ap, format);
    addlog(format, ap);    /* to file */
    va_end(ap);            /* Finish ....*/
    va_start(ap, format);  /* .. and restart */
    vprintf(format, ap);   /* to screen */
    va_end(ap);
}
```

Naturally, the reverse of this error can arise, where the programmer assumes call-by-reference either because va_list is an array type for that implementation, or more likely, just a mistaken assumption about va_list. The following dummy example shows the incorrect way to extract multiple arguments by passing the va_list pointer to a function:

```
#include <stdarg.h>
#include <stdio.h>
#include <stdlib.h>

void extract_and_print(va_list ap)
{
    printf("%d\n", va_arg(ap,int));
}

void unusual_print(int how_many, ...)
{
    va_list ap;
    int i;

    va_start(ap, how_many);
    for (i = 1; i <= how_many; i++)
        extract_and_print(ap);
    va_end(ap);
}

main()
{
    unusual_print(5, 1,2,3,4,5);
    exit(0);
}
```

On most implementations, va_list will be passed by value and the program will print out five 1's, because the same argument is repeatedly extracted. The program is correct only if va_list is an array type for the chosen implementation.

If it is necessary to pass a va_list type in such a way that changes must be propagated to the top-level function, then the solution is to use the type pointer-to-va_list to give the effect of pass-by-reference. This is the same as passing any other scalar type by reference using pointers: use the type va_list* for the function parameter, pass the address of ap as the argument corresponding to that parameter, and deference that pointer type inside the function. The corrected implementation of the above example becomes:

```
#include <stdarg.h>
#include <stdio.h>
#include <stdlib.h>

void extract_and_print(va_list *ap)   /* pointer type */
{
    printf("%d\n", va_arg(*ap,int));    /* dereference ap */
}

void unusual_print(int how_many, ...)
{
    va_list ap;
    int i;

    va_start(ap, how_many);
    for (i = 1; i <= how_many; i++)
        extract_and_print(&ap);    /* pass the address */
    va_end(ap);
}
```

18.12 Errors with setjmp and longjmp

The ANSI C standard is very picky about legal methods of calling setjmp. This allows implementors freedom in not supporting the most general usage, which may be difficult to achieve. Some of the most common legal usages are:

```
if(setjmp(...))
if(setjmp(...) == ...)
switch(setjmp(...))
if(!setjmp(...))
```

A common but strictly non-ANSI method is the assignment of its return value to a temporary variable, as below. Therefore, the following usage of setjmp may fail on some implementations:

```
temp = setjmp(...);    /* NON-ANSI */
```

This restriction appears because some implementations have difficulty in implementing setjmp so that it can keep enough "context" so as to continue the evaluation of an expression after a return via longjmp. Therefore, ANSI specifies a minimal number of call methods that the compiler must support.

18.12.1 Use of local variables after setjmp call

The setjmp function, when it returns with a nonzero value from a longjmp call, causes the values of non-volatile automatic local variables to be indeterminate in a particular situation. If a local variable is modified between the setjmp call, and the later longjmp call its value is indeterminate. (Note that a variable that has *not* been modified in this period will have the expected value.) The local variable may contain the value it had when setjmp was originally executed, or it may contain the updated value (strictly speaking, it might have any value because the ANSI standard merely says it is "indeterminate," but one of these two values is the usual behavior). The following code illustrates the problem:

```
#include <stdio.h>
#include <stdlib.h>
#include <setjmp.h>

jmp_buf env;

main()
{
  int i;    /* Local automatic variable */

  i = 1;
  if (setjmp(env) != 0) {
        /* longjmp has occurred */
        printf("i = %d\n", i);    /* Value of i is 1 or 2 ? */
        exit(1);
  }
  i = 2;    /* change i after setjmp */
  longjmp(env,1);
}
```

Does the variable i contain the value 1 or 2 after the return from the longjmp call? If longjmp restores the values of automatic local variables it will have value 1; otherwise, it will have value 2.

If variables must be accessed after the return from a longjmp call they should be declared volatile or static. The program above will report i as having value 2 if it is declared as either volatile or static. Note that the values of automatic local variables are not affected in the original call to setjmp, when it returns 0 (i.e., it is just like any other function call in the initial call).

18.12.2 setjmp returns before longjmp

The setjmp function should be called in a function that will not finish before the longjmp call is executed. If the function calling setjmp has terminated when longjmp is executed, the behavior is undefined and the result is probably a fatal error. For example, it is erroneous to write a neat function to set up the exception handling facilities, such as the init_handler function in the test program below:

```
#include <stdio.h>
#include <stdlib.h>
#include <setjmp.h>

jmp_buf env;

void init_handler(void)          /* WRONG!! */
{
  if (setjmp(env) != 0) {
        /* longjmp has occurred - exception handler here */
        fprintf(stderr, "\nFatal error\n");
        exit(1);
  }
}

main()
{
  init_handler();
  longjmp(env,1);
}
```

This method of handling exceptions is totally flawed. In fact, the execution of this short program on one system produced the fatal error message "longjmp botch" and did not execute the fprintf statement. The usual method of avoiding this problem is to call setjmp in a function that never returns, typically the main function.

18.12.3 longjmp inside a signal handler

It is bad programming practice to call longjmp from within a signal handler that may have been invoked owing to an asynchronous hardware signal. For example, if the user presses *ctrl-c* to provoke the SIGINT signal, this can occur at any time. The program may have been executing any code, and prematurely leaving that code block may have left a data structure corrupted. Therefore, attempting to continue after a signal by using longjmp is dangerous. The only portable method of handling a signal is to report an error and then terminate.

18.13 Errors with <math.h>

The first obstacle that novice programmers working under UNIX must overcome is how
to get a program using mathematical functions to link. For example, in a simple program
using sqrt, the linker may complain that _sqrt is undefined. The problem is probably
that the math library is not linked. UNIX compilers have the annoying feature that they
do not try to link in math functions unless this is requested by the -lm option:

```
cc file.c -lm
```

Note that -lm must be at the end of the statement. A common mistake in the use of -lm
is to put it first, in which case the linker error messages persist:

```
cc -lm file.c    # WRONG
```

Once this obstacle has been overcome and the program is finally running, the
programmer is free to discover other forms of run-time errors involving the <math.h>
library functions.

18.13.1 <math.h> not included

The most common error in the use of <math.h> is to forget to include it using
#include. Consider the following simple program:

```
#include <stdio.h>

main()
{
    int i;

    for (i = 0; i <= 10; i++)
        printf("i = %d, sqrt(i) = %f\n", i, sqrt(i));
}
```

The absence of a prototype for sqrt (which is in <math.h>) causes two problems:
(1) the compiler assumes that sqrt returns int, and (2) the compiler assumes its
parameter type is int. The first problem causes the compiler to generate code as it
would for any other function returning int. Since sqrt actually returns double this
leads to a run-time error (e.g., always outputting the result of sqrt as zero). The second
problem and the absence of a type cast on i cause the compiler to pass i as an int to
sqrt, which expects a double parameter. This is a parameter passing error with
undefined effect of the type that was more common in pre-ANSI C code with
nonprototyped functions.

   If you are using a good-quality compiler there should be a warning about sqrt being
used without being previously declared. This indicates that <math.h> has not been
included; you should always include the appropriate header file rather than declaring your
own prototype for a library function.

18.13.2 Trigonometric functions use radians

The trigonometric functions `sin`, `cos`, and `tan` declared in `<math.h>` require their arguments in radians, not degrees. Usages such as below are likely to be erroneous:

```
double cos_60 = cos(60.0);    /* PROBABLE ERROR */
```

The natural assumption is that `cos_60` will be `0.5`, but in fact the call to `cos` computes the cosine of 60 radians, which is approximately 3437 degrees. The correct code should convert the degree value to radians using the relationship that π radians equals 180 degrees. Therefore, the following is one method of converting degrees to radians:

```
#include <math.h>    /* declare non-ANSI constant M_PI */
#define CONVERT(degrees)  (((double)(degrees) * M_PI) / 180.0)

double cos_60 = cos(CONVERT(60));
```

Note that the use of computations of this nature may involve roundoff errors, and the value need not be exactly equal to `0.5`. In fact, when printed out using the `printf` format `%.20f` to show 20 decimal places, the calculated result of `cos_60` on my implementation was actually:

```
0.50000000000000011000
```

18.14 Side effects to assert macro

It is incorrect to place any side effects in a call to the `assert` macro. Although the side effects will be evaluated when assertions are turned on, the program will fail as soon as assertions are disabled by setting NDEBUG. Side effects include assignment, increment, decrement, accessing a `volatile` variable, and calling certain types of function. An example of an incorrect use of `assert` is the tricky code:

```
assert(++count < MAX);    /* WRONG */
```

The increment to `count` may be an important side effect. Removing assertions by defining the macro NDEBUG will cause the increment to disappear. The correct code is simply:

```
++count;
assert(count < MAX);
```

Although an experienced programmer is unlikely to intentionally place side effects in an `assert` macro, it can occur by accident:

```
assert(x = 3);        /* WRONG */
```

This assertion exhibits the =/== error and accidentally assigns 3 to x.

18.15 Errors with <string.h>

Strings are a quite complicated area of C and C++ because they cross into the areas of memory allocation, especially when programmers use char* to represent a string. Hence, there are many pitfalls for the unwary programmer.

18.15.1 strncpy leaves string nonterminated

A rather dangerous feature of the strncpy function is that it can leave a string nonterminated. It is reasonably common practice to use strncpy as a more reliable method of copying strings than strcpy, because it prevents too many characters from being copied. An example of such a usage is:

```
char s[MAX];
    ...
strncpy(s, s2, MAX);
```

This will prevent s from being overwritten by too many characters, regardless of the length of s2. However, if strlen(s2) is greater than or equal to MAX, then s will not be left null-terminated. Exactly MAX nonzero characters will be copied to s and no terminating zero character is appended by strncpy. A more reliable method of using strncpy that avoids this danger is given below:

```
strncpy(s, s2, MAX - 1);
s[MAX - 1] = '\0';
```

Unlike the strncpy function, the strncat library function does not have this dangerous feature and always leaves a string null-terminated.

18.15.2 sscanf twice on the same string

Programmers are sometimes confused about the behavior of sscanf, and assume that two successive calls to sscanf will read along a string in the same way as two successive scanf calls would read input. However, sscanf does not save its position and the second call to sscanf will simply restart from the beginning of the string. Consider the code:

```
char s[] = "10 20";

sscanf(s,"%d", &i);
sscanf(s,"%d", &j);    /* INCORRECT */
```

The value of i and j will always be the same after this code sequence — both will equal 10.

18.15.3 Misusing strcat

A common mistake in the use of `strcat` is to assume that it concatenates its two arguments, and returns the resulting string. This leads to uses such as:

```
char *str2;
    ...
str2 = strcat("The cat sat on the ", str);   /* WRONG */
```

The actual behavior of `strcat` is to concatenate the second argument onto the end of the first, and return the address of the first string. Hence this return value is quite useless in most circumstances, and is mostly ignored by programmers. However, the fact that it does return a value means that the above code will compile and run, but its behavior is undefined in ANSI C. In fact, the statement will correctly concatenate the two strings, and `str2` will point to the new string. However, the code is appending `str` on the end of the string constant. Hence the statement overwrites the memory where string constants are stored, and could lead to quite bizarre behavior. In fact, the instance of this error that inspired this section had the above statement inside a loop, similar to the following:

```
for (;;) {
    char *str2 = strcat("The cat sat on the ", str);
    puts(str2);
}
```

This produces the following very strange output, caused by repeatedly concatenating `str` onto the end of the string constant:

```
The cat sat on the mat
The cat sat on the matmat
The cat sat on the matmatmat
The cat sat on the matmatmatmat
The cat sat on the matmatmatmatmat
    .........
```

There are many methods of achieving the desired results of the above `strcat` statement. One correct method is:

```
char str2[MAX_LEN];
    ...
strcpy(str2, "The cat sat on the ");
strcat(str2, str);
```

18.15.4 Confusing strcpy and strcmp

This is an error often made by the author when tiredness causes the typing of the wrong function name. These are probably the two most common string functions and their occasional transposition is not surprising. Consider the following statements:

```
strcmp(s1, s2);
if (strcpy(s1,s2) == 0) ....
```

The use of `strcmp` is a null effect statement, and the test of `strcpy` copies rather than comparing. Neither usage will receive a compilation warning. The similar expression `strcpy(s1,s2)>0` may receive a warning about a suspicious pointer comparison.

18.15.5 strcmp compared with –1 or 1

Although it would probably be quite sensible, the strcmp function is not restricted to returning only 1, 0 and –1. It can return any negative or positive number instead of –1 or 1, respectively. Thus, only comparisons of the return value with zero are safe. The following comparison is incorrectly determining if s1 is lexically after s2:

```
if (strcmp(s1, s2) == 1)    /* WRONG */
```

The correct version is:

```
if (strcmp(s1, s2) > 0)    /* CORRECT */
```

18.15.6 qsort/bsearch using the strcmp function

The strcmp function is not an appropriate comparison function for passing to qsort for sorting arrays of strings, as in:

```
qsort(arr, n, sizeof(arr[0]), strcmp);    /* WRONG */
```

This is true regardless of whether the array of strings is declared as char*[] or char[][]. The solution is to write a comparison function that contains a call to strcmp, such as the following code:

```
#include <stdio.h>
#include <stdlib.h>   /* declare qsort */

int cmp(const void *p, const void *p2)
{
    return strcmp(*(char**)p,*(char**)p2);
}

main()
{
    int n = 3, i;
    char *arr[] = { "abc", "def", "abcd" };

    qsort(arr, n, sizeof(arr[0]), cmp);
    for (i = 0; i < n; i++)
        printf("'%s'\n", arr[i]);
}
```

The main point to note is that the void* pointer received by the cmp function is actually of type char**, and not type char*, which strcmp requires. Using strcmp would cause it to operate on strings starting at &arr[0], which is actually a pointer value (i.e., it treats the bytes of the pointer as a string).

18.16 clock wrap around

The clock function returns the number of clock ticks since the program began execution (or since the first clock call in non-ANSI implementations). If the system clock is incremented every microsecond, or more frequently, the number of clock ticks rapidly increases. The declaration of clock_t is usually a long, but even this has only a finite maximum value. After a certain amount of time, the number of ticks will be larger than that which can be represented by `clock_t`, and will wrap around (either to a large-magnitude negative value if `clock_t` is a `signed` type, or to zero if `clock_t` is an `unsigned` type).

One UNIX-based system takes approximately 36 minutes to wrap around, and timing a program that takes longer than this fails. Consider the timing of an operation:

```
clock_t before, after;

before = clock();
 ....  /* Do something */
after = clock();
printf("Time taken is %5.2f seconds\n",
        (after - before) /(double) CLOCKS_PER_SEC):
```

One possible solution that was appropriate for my problem (timing the search times of nearly optimal binary trees) was to detect wrap around and redo the operation if it had occurred. This involves testing the two clock tick values for wrap around, as below:

```
do {
    before = clock();
    ....  /* Do something */
    after = clock();
} while (after < before);       /* Until no wrap around */
printf("Time taken is %5.2f seconds\n",
        (after - before) /(double) CLOCKS_PER_SEC):
```

However, this solution is not valid if the operation being timed takes longer than the wrap around period. In this situation, it may be necessary to use the `time` function, which does not have the fine resolution of `clock`, but does not have the wrap around problem.

18.16.1 clock called only once

Although the ANSI C standard states that `clock` should return the time elapsed since the program started, some implementations return the time since the first call to `clock`. Therefore, the first call to the `clock` function will always return zero. Thus, it is dangerous (nonportable) to measure execution time by a single call to clock at the end of the `main` function. The portable method is to use a "before" and "after" count:

```
#include <stdio.h>
#include <time.h>    /* declare clock and clock_t */

main()
{
    clock_t before = clock();
    /* ..... do something */
    printf("Time taken is %5.2f seconds\n",
        (clock() - before) / (double) CLOCKS_PER_SEC);
}
```

This method will not time the startup sequence of the program (i.e., the time used before main was called). However, using a single call to `clock` might also not return an accurate count of startup time, depending upon when during the startup sequence the clock's counter was initialized.

18.17 Boolean library function compared with TRUE

A similar problem to that involving `strcmp` is that a number of library functions return a "boolean" value. For example, the character test functions in <ctype.h> such as `isdigit` do not only return 0 and 1 for false and true. These functions usually return a nonzero integer for true (it is usually positive, but some obscure implementations might return a negative). Hence the following test is incorrect:

```
if (isdigit(ch) == TRUE)      /* WRONG */
```

and the correct version is simply:

```
if (isdigit(ch))             /* CORRECT */
```

The comparison of the return result with zero is correct, but indicates a dangerous habit:

```
if (isdigit(ch) == FALSE)     /* DANGEROUS */
```

and the correct style is:

```
if (!isdigit(ch))            /* CORRECT */
```

Other boolean functions for which this pitfall exists include the `feof` and `ferror` library functions:

```
if (feof(fp) == TRUE)        /* WRONG */
if (ferror(fp) == TRUE)      /* WRONG */
```

18.18 The lower bits of rand

There are some very poor existing implementations of the `rand` standard library function. On some implementations the low-order bits of the return value are not random at all. A common failing is using the least-significant bit to produce a random binary value. The expression:

```
bit = rand() & 01;
```

may produce the nonrandom pattern 0,1,0,1... One solution is to extract bits from the higher 16 bits of the random number as below, since they are less likely to repeat:

```
bit = rand() & (1 << 16);   /* extract 17th bit */
```

However, this has a portability problem for 16-bit implementations. A better solution may be to use the % operator with a prime number:

```
do {
   ret = rand() % 17;
} while(ret == 0);   /* Until nonzero */
bit = (ret <= (17/2));
```

The utility of the loop is to avoid biasing the sequence since there are 9 values in 0..8, but only 8 in the range 9..16.

18.19 Redefining ANSI library functions

The names of the ANSI standard library functions are reserved in the sense that the programmer should not use such names for external variables or for other functions. It is a common error to accidentally redefine one of the existing functions, such as the ANSI C "remove" function. Redefining an existing library function may cause some strange failures because some library functions may call each other. For example, some functions may call malloc and these functions may fail if malloc has been redefined by the program. On the other hand, redefining a function might also be harmless on a particular implementation, and a dangerous portability problem will remain undetected.

18.20 Confusing identical library function parameters

There are a number of library functions that have two parameters of the same type. For example, many functions accept two parameters of type char*, and therefore novice errors such as the following will compile without warning:

```
fp = fopen("r", filename);   /* WRONG */
strcpy("hello", dest);       /* WRONG */
```

There are also a number of functions with two integer parameters indicating number and size of the objects concerned. These functions include fread, fwrite, calloc, bsearch, and qsort. Unfortunately, the ordering of these parameters differs across these functions. For example, the prototypes of fread and calloc illustrate the different orderings of the "size" and "number" parameters:

```
size_t fread(void *p, size_t size, size_t number, FILE *fp);
void* calloc(size_t number, size_t size);
```

Therefore, the roles of the two parameters may be occasionally confused. Because both parameters have the same types the compiler will not warn about erroneous calls such as the following:

```
p = calloc(sizeof(int), 100);
fread(buf, 100, sizeof(struct rec), fp);
qsort(arr, sizeof(int), 100, cmp_fn);
```

Fortunately, such errors may be harmless for calloc (and also for fread and fwrite if their return value is ignored) since the effect of the call depends mainly on the product of the two arguments. However, passing the wrong arguments to qsort or bsearch can lead to disastrous results.

18.21 Miscellaneous ANSI library errors

There are many other areas of ANSI standard library usage that are undefined by the ANSI C standard. Some of these areas are listed below:

- wrong `fopen` mode (e.g., applying `fseek` to file opened as `"r"`)
- `ungetc` cannot push back 2 or more characters for one file (undefined behavior)
- `ungetc` causes the file position pointer to become indeterminate (on a *text* file)
- `ungetc` won't work with the C++ `<iostream.h>` library
- `remove` applied to a file that is currently open (undefined behavior)
- `rename` when the new file already exists (undefined behavior)
- `printf` producing more than 509 characters (undefined behavior)
- arguments overlap for `strcpy`, `strncpy`, `strcat`, `strncat`, `memcpy`
- destination and arguments overlap (e.g., for `%s`): `sprintf`, `vsprintf`, `sscanf`
- `memcmp` cannot be portably used to compare `struct`s because of padding "holes"
- `abs` may fail (overflow) for the "largest" negative, i.e., `abs(INT_MIN)`
- `labs` may fail (overflow) for the "largest" negative, i.e., `labs(LONG_MIN)`
- `time_t` is not necessarily a count of seconds elapsed
- bad format string to `strftime`

Note that there are many additional portability problems with some pre-ANSI C implementations. Some of these problems are:

- `ungetc(EOF)` is illegal in pre-ANSI C, but has no effect in ANSI C.
- `free(NULL)` is illegal in pre-ANSI C, but has no effect in ANSI C.
- `tolower` (`toupper`) required an upper (lower) case letter in some pre-ANSI C implementations; ANSI C allows any letters, leaving inappropriate arguments unchanged.
- Spaces in `scanf` format strings were ignored in some pre-ANSI implementations rather than causing whitespace skipping. The main problem with this appears with spaces preceding the `%c` format specification.

Chapter 19

Pointers and memory allocation

The use of pointers in C and C++ can be fraught with danger. There are some common pitfalls to watch out for and even experienced programmers have not always managed to avoid them.

19.1 Dereferencing a NULL pointer

A common error is to dereference a pointer that is NULL. This causes an immediate crash. It is one of the most common causes of a "segmentation fault" error on UNIX machines. Dereferencing a NULL pointer can occur with either of the two indirection operators (i.e., *ptr and ptr->field) and also via array indexing of a pointer variable (i.e., ptr[i]), which is equivalent to using the * operator. Dereferencing NULL is most common when using dynamic data structures, but can occur any time you forget to set a pointer. An example is given below:

```
if (ptr->next != NULL && ptr != NULL)        /* WRONG ORDER */
```

When ptr is NULL, the first condition ptr->next is calculated first, causing a NULL pointer to be dereferenced. Simply reversing the order of the operands solves the problem:

```
if (ptr != NULL && ptr->next != NULL)        /* CORRECT */
```

If ptr is NULL, the first condition evaluates as false and the short-circuiting of the && operator causes the second condition to be skipped, avoiding the dereference of the NULL pointer.

19.2 Dangling references

Dangling references occur when a pointer points to the wrong place or, more precisely, when it points to memory that is not at present controlled by the program. This is a common problem in algorithms involving linked data structures, where pointers point to blocks that have already been freed. The most well known example is the method of deallocating all blocks on a linked list. The incorrect code is:

285

```
for (ptr = head; ptr != NULL; ptr = ptr->next)
    free(ptr);
```

This code applies the -> operator to a dangling reference, since ptr has already been deallocated before the -> operation. In this particular case, many implementations are forgiving since the recently freed block is unlikely to have been changed. The correct code uses a temporary variable:

```
for (ptr = head; ptr != NULL; ptr = next_node) {
    next_node = ptr->next; /* compute ptr->next before free() */
    free(ptr);
}
```

Another common occurrence of dangling references is saving structures containing character pointers to a binary file. If strings have been allocated using malloc or the C++ new operator, when saving the structs only the pointers are being saved and not the actual character strings themselves. When the structs are loaded back in, the pointers are dangling references and the strings have been lost.

19.3 Garbage and memory leakage

Garbage refers to memory allocated by malloc (or new) that no longer has any pointer pointing to it. It is unused by the program, and unusable by the program because neither malloc nor the new operator can find it. This problem in a program is often called a "memory leak."

In a sense, garbage is the opposite problem to dangling references — dangling references are pointers without allocated memory, while garbage is memory without a pointer to it. The problem is not a major one unless memory is short. If memory is limited, then gradually accumulating garbage can lead to a program eventually running out of memory (and crashing if out-of-memory is not tested for). One method of detecting memory leaks in C is the memory allocation debugging library in Section 3.1.

19.4 Deallocating a nonallocated memory block

Programmers occasionally make the mistaken assumption that *any* memory can be deallocated by the free library function or the C++ delete operator. However, it is a bad error to use free or delete on a pointer to memory that has not been allocated by malloc, calloc, or realloc. The effect of this is not defined, but usually causes a program failure. A variable, such as a global array, cannot be freed to the heap:

```
int arr[10];
 ...
free(arr);    /* ERROR */
delete arr;   // ERROR (2 errors actually! See later)
```

The problem is that the array variable was not dynamically allocated by the corresponding allocation library (i.e., malloc or calloc for free, and new for delete). Therefore, the block has the wrong format and the deallocation can cause a strange run-time error. Memory allocated by malloc, calloc, or new has a special format — in many implementations it has a few information bytes before it.

The author recently discovered this form of error in a piece of software written some time ago, namely an ANSI C preprocessor. The program used structures that contained a token and a string pointer:

```
struct node {
    int token;
    char *text;   /* text corresponding to token */
    struct node*next;   /* linked list pointer */
};
```

At a number of points in the program it was convenient to change a node from an identifier to whitespace (easier than removing the node from the linked list). The code used to achieve this was:

```
ptr->token = WHITESPACE;
ptr->text = " ";
```

The problem with this method was that when these nodes were no longer needed, they were deallocated using `free`. Deallocating the linked list nodes was not a problem in itself, but the `text` fields were also deallocated (having been allocated much earlier in the tokenizer). However, any `text` fields that had been assigned a string constant as above were no longer pointing to an allocated block. Once the error was identified (using the memory allocation debugging package in Section 3.1), the solution chosen was to modify the characters in the existing allocated string:

```
ptr->token = WHITESPACE;
strcpy(ptr->text, " ");
```

19.5 Mixing C and C++ allocation

An important point to remember is that the `malloc`-based allocation scheme may be different from the C++ `new` and `delete` operators. It is an error to use `delete` to deallocate a block allocated using `malloc` or `calloc`. Similarly, applying `free` to a block allocated using `new` is also incorrect:

```
p = malloc(20);
delete p;   // ERROR
p = new char[20];
free(p);   // ERROR
```

19.6 Double deallocation

Another common memory allocation error is deallocating the same address twice. The first time is no problem, but the second time is an error — the memory is no longer allocated. In most environments this will result in a run-time error, possibly immediate abnormal termination.

Applying the C++ `delete` operator to the same address twice is a similar error. In C++ the error of deleting an address twice is often the result of having a missing copy constructor or assignment operator in a class that allocates dynamic memory for one of its data members (e.g., a dynamic string class); see Section 17.2 for a full discussion.

19.7 Not allocating enough memory for strings

Problems occur if not enough memory is allocated for an object. Storing an object at this address may overwrite other variables, or cause a crash. The most common example of this is forgetting that a string has an extra zero character at the end. If memory is not allocated for this extra character, there is the potential for a program failure. For example, the use of strlen below is wrong. The strcpy function copies the terminating zero, but strlen does not count it.

```
new_str = malloc(strlen(str));
strcpy(new_str, str);
```

The correct call to malloc is:

```
new_str = malloc(strlen(str) + 1);
```

It is also possible to have the same problem using C++ allocation. When allocating memory for strings the correct size must be supplied to the new operator. An example of the error in C++ is:

```
new_str = new char[strlen(str)];    // INCORRECT
strcpy(new_str, str);
```

Again the correct method is to add 1 to the length:

```
new_str = new char[strlen(str) + 1];
```

Another common error with this string allocation idiom is to accidentally place the "+1" inside the strlen argument list:

```
new_str = malloc(strlen(str+1));    /* WRONG */
new_str = new char[strlen(str+1)];  // WRONG
```

The compiler will not produce an error because it is legal to add 1 to a pointer type. This code will usually allocate 2 bytes fewer than are required, because not only is the "+1" not adding to the count of bytes, but also strlen calculates the length of the string starting at &str[1] rather than character &str[0].

19.8 realloc can move the block

When the realloc function is called to increase the size of a dynamically allocated block, there is a danger that this can create dangling references. If realloc cannot increase the size of the existing block it allocates a new larger block, copies the data from the old block to the new larger block, and then deallocates the old block. The following use of realloc illustrates the erroneous belief that realloc simply resizes the current block:

```
realloc(ptr, NEW_SIZE);     /* WRONG */
```

If realloc moves the block, then ptr becomes a dangling reference pointing to a block that has already been deallocated. The correct call is simply:

```
ptr = realloc(ptr, NEW_SIZE);    /* CORRECT */
```

However, even if the correct calling method is used it is important that there be no other pointers to the old block that would become dangling references. For example, this may occur if the block is part of a dynamic linked data structure such as a list or binary tree.

19.9 malloc does not initialize data

The malloc function does not necessarily initialize any allocated bytes of memory to zero, although this is a common feature of many implementations. However, dependence on this form of initialization will lead to portability problems for implementations without this extension. An example of an error that leaves part of a structure uninitialized is:

```
typedef struct node {
    int data;
    struct node *left, *right;
} * Ptr;

Ptr new_node(int data)
{
    Ptr temp;

    temp = malloc(sizeof(*temp));
    temp->data = data;
    return temp;
}
```

The new_node function assumes that malloc initializes its memory to zero, thereby setting the left and right pointers to NULL. However, if malloc does not initialize memory, these pointer fields are dangerous dangling references that could cause any form of program failure when the allocated node is later used.

A common solution is to use calloc instead of malloc, because the calloc function *does* initialize its allocated memory:

```
temp = calloc(sizeof(*temp), 1);
```

However, as we will see in Section 19.11, this is not necessarily a fully portable solution, although few implementations will actually cause a problem.

19.10 new operator does not initialize memory

As was the case for malloc, the C++ new memory allocation operator also usually leaves its memory uninitialized when used to allocate a primitive type. There is no problem when allocating a class type, since the constructor is automatically called (and this should initialize all data members). However, when allocating memory for types without constructors, namely, all primitive types, the memory is not initialized:

```
Obj  *p = new Obj(1);      // No problem
char *s = new char[100];   // s is not initialized
```

19.11 calloc initialization is nonportable

The calloc function initializes all its allocated bytes to zero; all implementations have this feature and it is specified by ANSI C. However, making use of this initialization feature is nonportable to machines where either floating-point zero (i.e., 0.0) or NULL are not all-bytes-zero. The initialization of calloc is portable only when allocating arrays of characters. The problem is that the floating-point zero, 0.0, is not always represented by a sequence of zero bytes (or equivalently zero bits). Consider the following loop to print out a double variable as a sequence of bytes:

```
double x;

x = 0.0;   /* floating point zero */
for (i = 0; i < sizeof(double); i++)
    printf("Byte %d is %d\n", i, ((unsigned char*)&x)[i]);
```

On most machines this will produce the information that all bytes are 0 bytes. However, this is not guaranteed and there are a few machines in existence where this is not true. On such machines it is incorrect to rely on the initialization feature of calloc when allocating objects containing double or float values, since these will be initialized to some value other than 0.0 (because 0.0 differs from all-bytes-zero).

Analogous portability problems exist for machines where the null pointer is not all-bytes-zero. Although ANSI C considers integer 0 and NULL to be almost identical within C source code, there is no guarantee that the value actually stored to represent the null pointer will be equivalent to integer 0. Try the following code to examine your machine's representation:

```
int * p;

p = NULL;
for (i = 0; i < sizeof(int*); i++)
    printf("Byte %d is %d\n", i, ((unsigned char*)&p)[i]);
```

On machines where the null pointer is not 0, the compiler is required to add conversion code when 0 (or NULL) is used in a pointer context. This shields the programmer from the actual representation of NULL in most situations. For example, the initialization of global pointer variables to NULL is performed correctly by the compiler, since it recognizes that a pointer type is being initialized. However, the initialization by calloc is one situation where the compiler cannot know that pointer data is being initialized. calloc blindly sets all bytes to zero and sets the pointer data to address 0, which does not correspond to NULL for the implementation.

The same portability problems with floating-point zero and NULL arise in the use of the memset function; in fact, calloc is similar to a malloc followed by a memset call. The only fully portable solution to initializing allocated memory is to explicitly initialize the data in your own program.

It is common style to avoid the use of calloc since its initialization feature is usually nonportable, and therefore the memory must be explicitly initialized in any case. Hence it is more efficient to call malloc, which does not waste time performing the initialization. It is unfortunate that neither calloc nor memset can be used since they are usually much faster than explicit initialization.

19.12 Pointer and object confused

It is common to confuse a pointer with what it is pointing to. Assigning one pointer to another is not the same as assigning the items they point to. For example, if the statement "p=q" is used instead of "*p=*q", when *q is modified, *p is also modified (i.e., the value p points to is also modified). One common example of this occurs when copying character strings:

```
s1 = s2;              /* INCORRECT */
strcpy(s1, s2);       /* CORRECT */
```

19.13 Returning the address of a local variable

If a function returns the address of a local variable, this is a major error. Because the local variable is stored on the stack, when the function terminates that value is no longer defined. Any pointer that holds the address has become a dangling reference.

This error is reasonably common when writing a function to return a string. Consider a function, label, to allocate a new string label ten characters long. The implementation shown below generates a unique label and stores it in a local string variable, returning the address of the string:

```
char *label(void)
{
    static int count = 0;
    char s[10];

    sprintf(s, "XXX%d", count++);
    return s;    /* ERROR - returning address */
}
```

The behavior of this function is undefined. It may work correctly if, by coincidence, the string value stored on the stack is not corrupted. However, it is more likely to fail in some way, resulting in the production of a very strange label.

19.14 Returning the address of a static local variable

The obvious method of resolving the problem from the previous section is to declare the string array as static. However, this creates a different problem. The second time the function is called, the same pointer value will be returned, and the first label will be overwritten. All pointers will point to the same label. Changing one label will change them all.

One "hack" solution to this problem is to use a small fixed number of different addresses. In this way there can be a small number of labels returned from the function active at the same time without affecting each other. This method isn't a general or reliable solution and is likely to introduce obscure bugs if more than the maximum number of labels is used, but it has occasional uses.

```
#define MAX_LABELS   5   /* how many distinct labels */
#define STR_LEN      10   /* length of string label */
char *label(void)
{
  static int count = 0;
  static int sp = 0;
  static char names[MAX_LABELS][STR_LEN];

  sp = (sp + 1) % MAX_LABELS;
  sprintf(&names[sp][0], "XXX%d", count++);
  return &names[sp][0];
}
```

One apparent solution to this problem is to use malloc to allocate some dynamic memory each time. However, this imposes the problem of how to deallocate the memory once it is no longer needed. The label function cannot do this, so the rest of the program must remember to deallocate the labels when they are no longer needed.

Note that many library functions use this method of returning the address of internal static storage, and this is satisfactory because the program using these library functions can make explicit copies of the values, rather than accessing them through the address returned. Therefore, returning the address of a static variable may be the best solution to the particular problem.

19.15 Address arithmetic and incrementing pointers

When accessing bytes of data, it is common to use pointers to step through. It is important to remember that ++ and -- increment a pointer by a number of bytes (one or more), depending on the type of the pointer. Incrementing a char* pointer will move along one char (i.e., byte); incrementing an int* pointer will move along one int. In general, the expression:

```
p++;
```

is equivalent to:

```
p = (char*)p + sizeof(*p);
```

Similarly, adding an integer to a pointer does not necessarily add that number of bytes — the change is implicitly multiplied by the size of the object the pointer points to (i.e., the type of the pointer).

If access to memory at a byte level is needed, use pointers of type char* because the size of char is one byte. Alternatively, it may be useful to use type casts to char* in expressions that perform fancy address calculations.

19.16 Inconsistent types for malloc

Errors can creep in when programmers cut and paste statements. One dangerous problem that the compiler will not detect is calling `malloc` with the `sizeof` operator computing the wrong size. An example of this problem is:

```
struct A *p;

p = malloc(sizeof(struct B));    /* should be struct A */
```

One way to avoid this problem is to use the following method:

```
p = malloc(sizeof(*p));
```

but unfortunately this will fail on some deficient compilers, which (erroneously) evaluate the expression to `sizeof` at run-time. However, a rare compiler bug such as this is poor justification for avoiding a technique.

This technique also has the danger that the `*` will be accidentally left out, and too few bytes will be allocated:

```
p = malloc(sizeof(p));   /* ERROR */
```

19.17 Errors with the new operator

There are fewer opportunities for typographical errors involving the `new` operator than for `malloc`, because `new` is type-safe. However, the author has observed one dangerous problem. Consider the following code:

```
char* my_strdup(char *s)
{
    int len = ::strlen(s) + 1;
    char *temp = new char(len);
    ::strcpy(temp, s);
    return temp;
}
```

Can you see the error? Perhaps you can, but the C++ compiler can't, and in fact, the program will often run correctly despite a memory allocation problem. The problem is the expression involving the `new` operator — it should be "`new char[size]`" with square brackets instead of round brackets. The compiler views "`char(size)`" as a pointer-to-function type, and will therefore allocate enough bytes to hold a function pointer, typically 4 bytes. Therefore, for any reasonably long string, the `new` operator returns too few bytes and the `strcpy` call is overwriting bad memory.

19.18 Operations on far pointers

Many DOS compilers support a non-ANSI extension that allows the declaration of pointers as near, far, or huge. This can improve efficiency by allowing the programmer to take advantage of the particular memory model, but can also lead to errors.

Pointer variables declared as far pointers, when compiled in the huge model, should not be compared to each other. They are not normalized, and the comparisons are meaningless. Not even equality tests have meaning. The pointers should be declared as huge if these comparisons are required.

The increment operation on far pointers increments the pointer only within its particular segment. This means that a far pointer can only be moved through a 64K segment with the increment operator. When the pointer is at the end of the segment, the increment operation will set it to point to the beginning of the segment. Hence, far pointers cannot be used to iterate through objects larger than 64K. Again, huge pointers are needed for this purpose.

19.19 Calculation of an address outside an array

It is common on many implementations for an access or dereference of an out-of-bounds address to cause a run-time program failure (e.g., an array index being out of bounds). However, on some implementations even the calculation of such an address without a dereference can cause a failure. Even if the address is an intermediate address that is never used this can cause a failure. Because of such implementations, the ANSI C standard defines the situation when an illegal address is computed as "undefined."

A common situation where this can be important is the use of a common trick to achieve arrays addressable via indices 1..n instead of 0..n-1. The trick is to use a second pointer variable to act like an array:

```
int a[10];        /* a[0..n-1] */
int *b = a - 1;   /* b[1..n] */
```

Unfortunately, the computation of a - 1 is an illegal address and computing it may cause a run-time failure before b is even used. It is a shame that such a useful technique for changing array indexing is subverted by this portability problem.

19.20 Pointer alignment

Some implementations have restrictions on the addresses that particular data types can be stored in. A typical situation is that an integer must be stored on a word boundary (i.e., an even-valued address); on such a machine the following code would probably cause a run-time error such as a "bus error" or "fixed up unaligned data access":

```
int x;
char *p = (char*) &x;

*(int*)(p+1) = 10;  /* ERROR */
```

The problem is that since &x is word-aligned, the expression p+1 will not be word-aligned. The attempt to store an integer through a nonaligned address will cause some form of error (on some machines).

Although the above example is obviously contrived, there are situations in practice where alignment must be considered. Fortunately, the most common uses of addresses are safe:

- addresses returned by malloc, calloc, or realloc
- pointers to characters (i.e., strings)

Any address returned by malloc is guaranteed to be compatible with the most restrictive alignment requirement for all data types for the given implementation. Therefore, it is safe to store any data type, whatever its alignment, at an address returned by malloc or calloc. Furthermore, the char* type (and its qualified variants) will have the least restrictive alignment requirements; typically there is no restriction on the addresses that are legal.

It is unclear what alignment may be assumed from an allocation using the new operator; presumably the ANSI C++ standard will ensure that the alignment is such as to satisfy the type of memory being allocated. Note that there is a major difference here between C's malloc and C++'s new operator in that malloc cannot determine what type of object is being allocated, whereas the C++ compiler can determine at compile-time the type of object being allocated by new and perform the allocation accordingly. malloc must have the most general alignment, but new need not.

Some implementations of lint attempt to diagnose instances where alignment error may arise, but are notoriously bad at it. The most common problem is that lint does not know about malloc or calloc, or about the type void*, and will complain about every call to malloc or calloc.

19.21 void* cannot store function pointers

A portability problem that can arise on some machines is that code addresses differ in size from data addresses. This creates problems if a program ever uses the same type to represent pointers to data and pointers to functions. The most common such mistake is the erroneous belief that the generic pointer type "void*" can hold pointers to functions. For example, it is incorrect to use a void* type to represent a function pointer of unknown type, such as when two types of function pointers are being passed to a function:

```
typedef char (*char_fn)(void);
typedef char (*int_fn)(void);
typedef void * generic_fn_ptr;     /* WRONG! */

void output(int type, generic_fn_ptr fn)
{
    if (type == CHAR)
        printf("%c", (*(char_fn)fn)());
    else
        printf("%d", (*(int_fn)fn)());
}
```

The above function will usually fail whenever data pointers are smaller than function pointers, which may occur on some large machines and also on personal computers when compiled in the medium model.

The correct type of a generic function pointer is void(*)(), which can be used to represent any type of pointer to function (but not any type of pointer to *data*). The correct declaration is:

```
typedef void (*generic_fn_ptr)();
```

To examine the different representations of data pointers and code pointers, try executing the following program in your environment. Possibly the values will be the same, or they may differ. On a personal computer, try executing the program when compiled using different memory models:

```
#include <stdio.h>

main()
{
    printf("data ptrs = %d, function ptrs = %d\n",
         (int) sizeof(void*), (int) sizeof(void(*)()) );
}
```

19.22 Modification of string literals

String literals should not be modified in ANSI C or C++ because they could potentially be stored in read-only memory. They should be thought of as having type const char*. Therefore, using char* string types without caution can lead to errors, such as applying strcpy to a pointer that currently points to a string literal, as below:

```
char *result = "yes";

if (...)
    strcpy(result, "no");    /* WRONG */
```

The effect of this code is to try to modify the memory containing the string literal "yes". If this is stored in read-only memory the strcpy function has no effect (or possibly a run-time failure). Even if string literals happen to be modifiable for the particular implementation this form of modification can lead to strange errors. Overwriting "yes" with "no" means that the initialization of result will never again set result to "yes". The code can be thought of as equivalent to the following code:

```
char yes_addr[4] = { 'y', 'e', 's', '\0' };
char *result = yes_addr;

if (...)
    strcpy(result, "no");    /* WRONG */
```

Hence the strcpy call changes yes_addr and the initialization will always set result to whatever yes_addr currently contains.

Worse still is the problem that many compilers merge identical string literals so as to save space. Hence, the above strcpy call will change *all* uses of the constant "yes" to be "no" throughout the program (all appearances of that constant use the same address, yes_addr). Therefore, one change to a string constant will affect all other instances of the same string constant — a very severe form of *aliasing*.

Avoiding the modification of string literals is not all that difficult, requiring only a better understanding of strings. One solution to the above problem is to use an array of characters instead of a pointer:

```
char result[] = "yes";

if (...)
    strcpy(result, "no");    /* RIGHT */
```

In this case the compiler allocates 4 bytes for result, rather than making it point at the 4 bytes for the string literal (which was the same address that all uses were given).

19.23 No memory allocated for string

A particularly common example of an error involving strings is to use a char* string type without allocating any memory for the string. The underlying problem is usually a misunderstanding of strings. This error is shown in the code:

```
char *s;
strcpy(s, "Hello world\n");    /* WRONG */
```

Here s is an uninitialized pointer variable and the strcpy function will store the copied string at whatever value this pointer holds, leading to undefined behavior (usually a run-time failure). Fortunately, many compilers will warn that s is used before being initialized in this example. However, the misunderstanding about strings will lead to many more complicated examples of such errors that the compiler will not detect.

Chapter 20

Preprocessor macro errors

Preprocessor macros can cause two types of problems: compilation errors and logical errors. Compiler diagnostics due to incorrect macro definitions can sometimes be difficult to understand. This is because the compiler receives input after the preprocessor has done its substitutions. Comments have been deleted, and any macros or symbolic constants have been replaced by their corresponding text. Hence, the diagnostic lines printed up by the compiler (supposedly program lines) may bear no resemblance to your program.

The second problem with macros is a logical error. This occurs when the macro expansion is syntactically correct, but is not what was intended by the programmer. This kind of bug can be very difficult to track down. Many of the mistakes mentioned below do not cause a compilation warning and this makes them very dangerous.

20.1 Semicolons on the end of macro definitions

In a macro definition there should not be a semicolon on the end. The preprocessor replaces text exactly as it is asked to, and putting a semicolon on the end usually leads to there being an extra semicolon in the wrong place. For example, the code:

```
#define MAX   10;
x = MAX * 2;
```

leads to the incorrect statement:

```
x = 10; * 2;
```

In this example the extra semicolon terminates the assignment to x and causes "*2;" to be seen as a pointer dereference of the constant 2. As is the case with most instances of this error, this example causes a compilation error because the constant 2 is not a legal pointer type.

If the operator in this example had been the + operator, there would be at most a warning about the statement "+2;" since unary + is legal in ANSI C and C++. A good compiler would warn about a "null effect" statement.

20.2 Assignment operator in macro declaration

A less common misconception about declaring symbolic constants using #define is that they require syntax similar to that for initializations. The macro definition below shows this error:

```
#define MAX = 10
```

Fortunately, most instances of this error will cause a syntax error during compilation wherever the symbolic constant is used.

20.3 Spaces between macro name and left bracket

In a macro definition there cannot be any whitespace (spaces or tabs) between the macro name and the left bracket. Spaces indicate to the preprocessor where the replacement text begins. If there is space, the preprocessor assumes that the definition is for a parameter-less symbolic constant and that the left bracket is part of the replacement text. For example, in the definition:

```
#define  abs (x) (x > 0) ? (x) : (-(x))
```

the identifier abs is replaced by:

```
(x) (x > 0) ? (x) : (-(x))
```

For example, the macro call:

```
a = abs(b);
```

is expanded into the syntactically incorrect code:

```
a = (x) (x > 0) ? (x) : (-(x)) (b);
```

As in most occurrences of this error, the above example will cause a compilation error alerting the programmer to the problem.

20.4 Operator precedence: bracketing of parameters

When using macros with parameters, where the parameters form an expression in the definition, always place brackets around the parameter. Without brackets, problems occur because of operator precedence. To see this, consider the following example of an incorrect macro definition:

```
#define  cube(x)   x * x * x      /* INCORRECT */
```

The macro call:

```
y = cube(z + 1);
```

expands out as:

```
y = z + 1 * z + 1 * z + 1;
```

which is equivalent to the incorrect expression:

```
y = z + (1 * z) + (1 * z) + 1;
```

To solve this problem, place brackets around each macro parameter in the replacement text in the macro definition:

```
#define  cube(x)   (x) * (x) * (x)     /* BETTER */
```

Then the macro call expands out correctly as:

```
y = (z + 1) * (z + 1) * (z + 1);
```

However, the above "better" macro definition is not completely safe. It is still prone to precedence errors involving the entire expression, as discussed in the next section.

20.5 Operator precedence: bracketing of expression

Although placing brackets around macro parameters solves most operator precedence problems, there is still one further safety measure needed. Consider the macros:

```
#define twice(x)      (x) << 1       /* INCORRECT */
#define inc(x)        (x) + 1        /* INCORRECT */
```

When called by:

```
z = 1 + twice(y);
p = 3 * inc(q);
```

these expand out to be:

```
z = 1 + (y) << 1;
p = 3 * (q) + 1;
```

which are equivalent to the incorrect expressions:

```
z = (1 + (y)) << 1;    /* Precedence of + higher than << */
p = (3 * (q)) + 1;     /* Precedence of * higher than + */
```

The solution to this problem is to place brackets around the entire expression in the macro definition. The examples become:

```
#define twice(x)      ((x) << 1)    /* CORRECT */
#define inc(x)        ((x) + 1)     /* CORRECT */
```

The calls become what was intended:

```
z = 1 + ((y) << 1);
p = 3 * ((q) + 1);
```

20.6 Side effects in macro arguments

Macros are not function calls. If there is a side effect (e.g., an increment operator) in an argument passed to a macro call, it is possible that the side effect will occur more than once, or not at all. For example, consider the cube macro definition:

```
#define cube(x)        ((x) * (x) * (x))
```

When called with:

```
c = cube(a++);
```

the macro expands to:

```
c = ((a++) * (a++) * (a++));
```

and the side effect a++ is executed three times.

A real-world example of this problem is the XtSetArg macro, which is part of the toolkit for X Windows programming. The first parameter of XtSetArg appears twice in the macro replacement text, and thus the following is a common pitfall for novice X Windows programmers:

```
XtSetArg(args[n++], XmNwidth, 500);   /* ERROR */
```

Instead, a typical usage style for XtSetArg that avoids the error is:

```
XtSetArg(args[n], XmNwidth, 500); n++;
```

The problem is even less obvious in macros such as min and max, where the number of times a side effect occurs depends on the values of the arguments. For example, with the following definition of min:

```
#define min(x, y)       (((x) < (y)) ? (x) : (y))
```

the macro call:

```
c = min(a++, b);
```

expands out to give:

```
(((a++) < (b)) ? (a++) : (b))
```

where the a++ side effect is executed twice if a<b, otherwise once.

In macros where each parameter appears only once, there is usually no problem. For example:

```
#define twice(x)        ((x) << 1)
```

has no problems, as any side effects are executed exactly once. However, some macros where parameters appear only once can still give trouble — if some parameters are not evaluated. Some side effects may not be executed at all. For example:

```
#define choose(x, y, z)     ((x) > 0 ? (y) : (z))
```

Depending on x, any side effect of y or z may or may not be executed.

The simplest solution for C++ programmers is to use `inline` functions instead of macros; they have the same efficiency but are far safer. Unfortunately, there is no easy solution in C. One solution is to use (inefficient) functions instead of macros when a parameter must appear twice in a macro, or when sometimes not all parameters are evaluated. Another incomplete solution is just to be aware of the problem, and to avoid side effects in macro calls.

20.7 Flow errors with multiple statement macros

If a macro contains more than one statement, it should have braces around it. Consider the `swap` macro below:

```
#define swap(x, y)    temp = x; x = y; y = temp    /* INCORRECT */
```

When called by:

```
if (a > b)
    swap(a, b);
```

the result is:

```
if (a > b)
    temp = a; a = b; b = temp;
```

which is (accidentally) equivalent to:

```
if (a > b) {
    temp = a;
}
a = b;
b = temp;
```

because only the first statement is considered to be the statement for the `if`.

There are a number of possible solutions. Placing braces around any sequences of statements prevents the problem:

```
#define swap(x, y) {temp = x; x = y; y = temp;}    /* IMPROVED */
```

This is satisfactory, but gives minor problems with the `else` statement, where the code below will cause a compilation error because of a semicolon after a right brace and before an `else` statement:

```
if (...)
    swap(a, b);    /* semicolon causes error */
else
    ...
```

This expands out to give:

```
if (a > b)
    { temp = x; x = y; y = temp; };         /* extra semicolon */
else
    ...      /* etc. */
```

The semicolon before the `else` and after the right brace causes a compilation error. If `swap` was a single statement with no braces (e.g., a function call), the semicolon before the `else` would be syntactically correct. However, the `swap` macro has expanded out to be a block (with braces), and a semicolon after a right brace and before an `else` is a syntax error.

Another solution is to use the comma operator. The comma operator joins two expressions together to make a single expression. In this way, the sequence is considered as a single statement, and both problems are resolved — the original problem with the `if` statement and also the syntax error with the semicolon before the `else`.

```
#define swap(x, y)    temp = x, x = y, y = temp    /* CORRECT */
```

The comma operator cannot be used if some of the statements are flow of control statements such as `if` statements, loops, or `return`. These statements are not allowed as operands of the comma operator. In such cases, a special form of `do` loop can be used:

```
#define swap(x, y)    do { temp = x; x = y; y = temp; } while(0)
```

This macro avoids syntax error problems with a semicolon before an `else` statement because the semicolon terminates the `do` loop statement. Note that the block of statements inside the loop is only executed once because `while(0)` is always false.

A similar solution is to use an `if` statement with a condition that is always true:

```
#define swap(x, y)    if (1) { temp = x; x = y; y = temp; } else
```

This also works correctly because the semicolon ends the `if` statement. However, this method is slightly worse than the `do` loop because accidentally omitting the semicolon after the macro call may silently introduce a major bug. The statement following the macro call will become part of the `else` clause and, for all practical purposes, disappears from the code at run-time. The `do-while(0)` method is preferred because a compilation error occurs when a semicolon is omitted. One minor problem with both these solutions is that `lint` will warn about a "constant in conditional context."

A slightly different solution is to use a different style for all `if` statements and loops — use blocks instead of single statements. This is generally sound practice, and can be combined with any of the other solutions, just to be safe. Admittedly, this solution leads to longer programs (extra lines), and sometimes less clear programs.

20.8 Macros containing if: dangling else problem

Consider the (very simplified) `assert` macro:

```
#define assert(x)   if (!(x)) error()   /* INCORRECT */
```

When called by:

```
if (i == 1)
    assert(a > b);
else
    ...   /* etc. */
```

it expands out as:

```
if (i == 1)
    if (!(a > b)) error();
else
    ...   /* etc. */
```

This is equivalent to the code below, because an `else` matches the closest `if`. The dangling `else` is resolved by choosing the inner `if`. This is not what was intended by the programmer.

```
if (i == 1) {
    if (!(a > b))
        error();
    else
        ...       /* etc. */
}
```

There are many possible solutions. The most obvious solution is to place braces around the replacement text. This solution is effective, but gives the minor problem with the syntax error before the `else` (discussed earlier).

```
#define assert(x) {if (!(x)) error();}   /* IMPROVED */
```

Another solution is to use an empty `else` clause, to make sure that the macro has an `else` to match the `if`. Note the added semicolon after the `error`, before the `else`, and also the lack of semicolon after the `else`.

```
#define assert(x) if(!(x)) error(); else   /* CORRECT */
```

When an assertion is expanded out, the semicolon after the macro call's right bracket is immediately after the `else` keyword, creating an empty `else` clause. However, this solution has a danger that if the programmer accidentally forgets the semicolon following the `assert` macro call, the statement immediately following is made part of the `else` clause and introduces an error into the program's flow of control. The problem is analogous to the problems with the `if(1)` method of implementing the `swap` macro in the previous section, but is worsened by the fact that a saving warning about unreachable code is unlikely because the `if` statement condition is probably not constant.

Another similar solution is to reverse the sense of the conditional test to make sure that the macro has an `else` to match the `if`. The `if` part then does nothing, and the `else` does the work. Note the semicolon before the `else` and no semicolon after the `error`.

```
#define assert(x)  if (x) ; else  error()     /* CORRECT */
```

Another solution involves converting the `if` statement into an expression using the ternary conditional operator. Note that the second case, after the colon, is a dummy expression (i.e., the constant 1). If the `else` clause is used by the macro, this second case will be executed (and have no effect). If the macro passes back some other type (i.e., not `void`), replace "`void`" with that type.

```
#define assert(x)    ((void)(!(x) ? error() : 1))    /* CORRECT */
```

Note that the above macro must be changed in ANSI C if error returns void. ANSI C requires that the second and third operands of the conditional operator have the same type; therefore a type cast to void of the constant 1 is necessary if error is a void function:

```
#define assert(x) ((void)(!(x)? error():(void)1))    /* CORRECT */
```

An obscure method of implementing the assert macro is to convert the if statement into an equivalent expression, using the short-circuiting of the logical operators to get the effect of the control flow of an if statement:

```
#define assert(x)    ((void)((x) || error()))    /* CORRECT */
```

If x is true, the short-circuiting comes into effect and the error is not executed. The use of the ternary conditional operator is just as effective, and the extra complexity of this method is hard to justify.

Another partial solution is to change your programming style instead of changing the macro definition — don't use single statements in if statements or loops.

20.9 Lost type checks in macros

Because the replacement of macro parameters is by simple text replacement, there is no type checking of these parameters. However, wherever the parameter is used, type checking of its usage inside the replacement text may cause compilation errors. This is no guarantee, and types of arguments to macros should be checked carefully by hand. An example of an error caused by the use of macros is:

```
#define PRINT_FLOAT(x)   (printf("%f", (x)))
   ...
PRINT_FLOAT(3.14);    /* OK */
PRINT_FLOAT(3);       /* ERROR */
```

The problem with this macro is that the implicit conversion of integral types to double is not performed by macro replacement of parameters, whereas it would be performed if PRINT_FLOAT were a function accepting x as a double parameter. Passing the integer constant 3 fails because it has type int instead of double and therefore corrupts the list of arguments. This macro can be improved by adding an explicit type cast to remove the problem:

```
#define PRINT_FLOAT(x)   (printf("%f", (double)(x)))
```

The loss of type checking within macros is yet another reason to avoid using preprocessor macros in C++. The use of inline functions can achieve the same efficiency gains without the dangers.

20.10 Name clashes involving macro local variables

There are some very obscure errors that the use of parameterized macros can cause. One problem is a clash between the names of local variables and variables in a macro argument. Consider the following macro to swap two integers:

```
#define swap_int(x,y)                    \
    { int temp;                          \
        temp = x; x = y; y = temp;       \
    }
```

This macro will work correctly for almost all arguments. However, there is one dangerous situation when an obscure error may occur. Consider what happens when one of the macro arguments is "temp," as may occur if the programmer uses the name "temp" frequently. The macro call:

```
swap_int(temp,temp2);
```

will expand to become:

```
{ int temp;
    temp = temp; temp = temp2; temp2 = temp;
}
```

Instead of using the temp in the argument, the macro uses only the local variable, and the results are erroneous. Although a good compiler will warn that temp is "used before set," many compilers will compile this code without warning.

The best solution is to always take care in naming local variables created by macro definitions. The name could be capitalized, given a unique prefix, or changed by any other method to any name, making it unlikely that the rest of the program will use such an identifier. One common solution is to use _temp. Although ANSI C prohibits programs from using prefix underscores on external names, it is quite valid for a program to do so for local variables.

This error would not arise were swap_int declared as a function with parameters x and y — another reason for C++ programs to use inline functions rather than macros.

20.11 Accidental macro expansion

Macro expansion occurs before any other phase of compilation. Consider what happens to the function definition below if "min" is already defined as a macro:

```
int min(int x, int y)
{
    ... /* etc. */
}
```

The macro expansion occurs, leading to absurd syntax. This causes the compiler to output nonsensical error messages and garbled diagnostic lines. The solution is to undefine the macro name *before* the function definition using:

```
#undef min
```

The #undef line is also needed in any other file that *calls* the function.

A more dangerous problem is that if the macro is defined where the function is called, the macro will be invoked without problem, and the function will never be called! This is a far worse problem because it will not cause a compilation error. An example of this problem would be trying to define your own version of the `getchar` function. The problem is that `getchar` is actually a macro and will expand out before compilation — the new `getchar` function is never called.

20.12 Conditional compilation error: name misspelled

The preprocessor does not check whether macro names used in `#if`, `#ifdef`, or `#ifndef` directives are actually the correct names. An error that is very difficult to trace can occur if such a macro name is misspelled. Consider a program using the macro name `TEST_DRIVER` to control bottom-up testing of a single source file. If this macro is defined (by a `-D` compiler option) then this indicates that testing is currently in progress and the function performs many self-tests. If the macro is not defined this indicates creation of the production version and the function runs more quickly without performing any tests. Some of the code might look like:

```
void do_something(void)
{
   int i;
#ifdef TEST_DRIVER
   int count = 0;
#endif

   for (i = 0;  test(i); i++) {
#ifdef TESTDRIVER          /* TYPO HERE! */
   count++;
#endif
   }

#ifdef TEST_DRIVER
   assert(count > 0);     /* loop entered at least once */
   assert(count <= 10);   /* but not more than 10 times */
#endif
}
```

The self-testing code surrounded by conditional compilation tests involving the `TEST_DRIVER` macro name is intended to check that the loop is actually entered at least once, and not more than 10 times. However, the unfortunate programmer who tests this module will find that the first `assert` macro will always fail — apparently the loop is never entered. But there is no error in the program flow; the error is a typographical mistake in the `#ifdef` directive. The underscore in `TEST_DRIVER` has been accidentally omitted, and the `#ifdef` always fails — the `count++` instruction is never executed regardless of whether the code is compiled in self-testing or production mode.

This form of error is not found by any compilers known to the author, although future compilers might one day be smart enough to watch out for "suspiciously similar" macro names. The error can arise in the use of any of the `#ifdef`, `#ifndef`, `#if`, or `#elif` directives and the author is not aware of any particular programming style that can avoid this hazard.

20.13 Using #define instead of typedef

A common macro error is to use #define to declare a type name. There are no problems for basic types or structure types, and the following declarations are quite safe:

```
#define   INTEGER   int
#define   PIECE     enum piece
#define   NODE      struct node
```

However, there is a subtle error when #define is used to declare a pointer type. The problem is typified by the declaration of a string type as:

```
#define string char *     /* ERROR */
```

This declaration is dangerous because of the strange binding rules of the * token in declarators. There is no problem for declaring single variables, but an error arises when two variables are declared in a single declaration:

```
string s;        /* OK */
string s1, s2;   /* ERROR */
```

The problem is that the second declaration expands out to become:

```
char *s1, s2;
```

Because of the binding rules of * the second variable s2 is not declared as a pointer type. The above declaration is equivalent to:

```
char *s1;
char s2;
```

Fortunately, this mistake using #define for a pointer type usually causes a compilation error alerting the programmer to the problem (although what the problem is may be difficult to see!). The solution to this problem is simply to use a typedef declaration for all type declarations (good style dictates this even for nonpointer types). A typedef name has different binding rules for * and the following sequence works correctly:

```
typedef char * string;
string s1, s2;          /* OK */
```

20.14 C++ comments in macros

A common error made by programmers with older C++ compilers is the use of // comments in macro lines. The problem is that many older C++ compilers used the existing C preprocessor rather than a proper C++ preprocessor. The traditional C preprocessor does not handle // comments well, and will leave them for the next phase of compilation. Consider the effect of the following code:

```
#define   MAX   10   // C++-style comment

y = MAX;
```

The preprocessor will treat the // and any text following it as ordinary C tokens. Hence the // comment becomes part of the replacement text for MAX and the statement expands out to become:

```
y =   10  // C++-style comment ;
```

This statement is then passed to the C++ compiler, which removes the C++ comment, including the semicolon on the end. Hence, when used with an old preprocessor, this code will (usually) cause a compilation diagnostic message because the semicolon will be accidentally "commented out" by the // comment. Therefore, it may be desirable to avoid using // comments on preprocessor lines since they may lead to obscure errors. Fortunately, most instances of this problem will cause a compilation diagnostic.

An example of a coding practice that explicitly relies on the use of older preprocessors is the method of removing debugging statements using // comments. Consider the following erroneous method of removing DPRINTF debugging output statements:

```
#define DPRINTF  //
   ...
DPRINTF("x = %d", x);
```

On an old preprocessor, the DPRINTF statement expands out to become a do-nothing comment:

```
//   ("x = %d", x);
```

However, this method will fail on any standard C++ compiler. Any code that relies on this interaction between C preprocessor and C++ compiler is incorrect. A proper C++ compiler will have its own preprocessor that correctly handles // comments.

20.15 Pre-ANSI preprocessing

The ANSI C preprocessor works on a token basis, whereas earlier preprocessors often worked differently. Although in many situations there is little difference, there are a few common pitfalls, as described below.

20.15.1 Expansion inside string constants

Consider the following pre-ANSI method of "stringizing" a macro argument:

```
#define str(x)   "x"
s = str(A);
```

A pre-ANSI compiler would probably have considered x to be the macro parameter; the result would be:

```
s = "A";
```

However, an ANSI C preprocessor would see "x" as an entire token, rather than examining characters inside the string. The token "x" is very different from the macro parameter x and the result is:

```
s = "x";
```

To get the required "stringize" behavior in ANSI C, the program should use the # preprocessor unary operator:

```
#define str(x)  #x
```

A similar situation arises in the expansion of identifiers inside single quotes. An ANSI preprocessor will never expand the x inside the character constant in the macro below; many pre-ANSI C preprocessors will do so.

```
#define chr(x)  'x'
```

It is difficult to write a "char-ize" macro in ANSI C. One possibility is:

```
#define chr(x)  ( * #x )
```

The expression:

```
chr(A)
```

will expand out to become:

```
( * "A" )
```

This method uses the stringize # preprocessor operator to build the string, and then applies the * operator to get the first character. Unfortunately, it is likely that the compiler will execute the * operation at run-time rather than compile-time.

20.15.2 Whitespace and token pasting

Pre-ANSI preprocessors had no explicit syntax for pasting together two tokens. The most common method was to make use of the fact that comments were removed by the preprocessor. This gave rise to the following macro:

```
#define PASTE(x,y)  x/**/y
```

The comment would be removed and the replacement text would be effectively xy, although both x and y would be expanded independently as macro parameters. When called with PASTE(a,10) the preprocessor would produce the single token a10, which was read by the tokenizing phase of compilation.

However, an ANSI C preprocessor is required to replace a comment with a single space character (or at least to act as if it did). Hence the call to PASTE would appear as two tokens: a and 10. The correct method of token pasting in ANSI C and C++ is the ## preprocessor operator:

```
#define PASTE(x,y)  x##y
```

20.15.3 Token streams

The output of the preprocessor must be a token stream, not a stream of characters. Consider the following code:

```
#define PLUS +

x PLUS= 3;     /* x += 3 ? */
```

The intention is to have the two tokens PLUS= expand into the single token +=. However, although this will work on many pre-ANSI compilers, it should receive a compilation error from an ANSI C compiler. The ANSI preprocessor should produce the token stream:

```
x PLUS = 3 ;
```

Then all macros are expanded; in this case this means expanding the PLUS macro. The token stream becomes:

```
x + = 3 ;
```

Therefore, an ANSI C compiler should treat this statement as if it had a space between PLUS and =, making it equivalent to:

```
x + = 3;
```

where the + and = characters are two separate tokens; therefore the code should receive a compilation error. Note that one correct method is to ensure that the macro text has whole tokens, such as:

```
#define PLUS  +=

x PLUS 3;    /* OK */
```

20.15.4 Quotes in commented out code

A common mistake is to assume that code ignored by the preprocessor, such as by using #if 0, can contain any text. Unfortunately, for an ANSI C preprocessor, such text must contain valid preprocessor tokens. The following code illustrates the problem, since the apostrophe in the text should start a character constant token:

```
#if 0
 this code shouldn't compile cleanly in ANSI C
#endif
```

The solution is to place this text inside comment delimiters, in which case the apostrophe is harmless:

```
#if 0   /* the comment below is incorrect! */
 /* this code shouldn't compile cleanly in ANSI C */
#endif
```

Chapter 21

UNIX programming errors

Most UNIX-based environments support a number of extra library functions that are not part of the ANSI standard. These library functions can be portably used across UNIX platforms, but are not usually available elsewhere. There are a number of well-known errors in using these functions, and also some errors related to using ANSI standard library functions (e.g., `system`) in a UNIX environment.

21.1 The fork UNIX system call and buffering

A problem can occur when forking a subprocess to perform some related work. Since the `fork` function copies the entire contents of memory, it also copies input/output buffers. If there are any characters left in buffers they will be in the buffers of both the parent and the child process. The most common problem is that `stdout` is line-buffered, so any output characters remain in the buffer until a newline character is output. A simple dummy example of the problem is:

```
#include <stdio.h>

main()
{
    printf("Hello world");   /* NO NEWLINE */
    fork();
    printf("\n");
}
```

Because there is no newline in the first `printf` statement the characters "Hello world" remain in the internal buffers, and only appear when the newline is printed. However, after the `fork` call, both parent and child process execute the second `printf` statement, and therefore the characters are output twice.

The solution is to apply `fflush` to `stdout` before calling the `fork` function. However, note that the error does not occur when `execve` or one of its relatives is called immediately following the call to `fork`. In this case the buffers are discarded; they are overlaid with the memory of the newly started executable.

21.2 Metacharacters in filenames

Consider writing a software tool under UNIX that must read a resource file ".toolrc" from the home directory. The obvious method will be:

```
FILE * fp;
    ...
fp = fopen("~/.toolrc", "r");    /* WRONG */
```

This is an example of a common misunderstanding by programmers new to UNIX. The tilde character (~) is a metacharacter that is expanded by many UNIX shells to represent the home directory. However, the fopen function does not run a shell to expand the filename and therefore looks for a file starting with a tilde. There will be no such file, and so fopen will return NULL and set errno appropriately.

The correct method of accessing a file in a user's home directory is to use getenv("HOME") to return the full name of the home directory and then catenate "/.toolrc" onto the end of that name.

An error similar to the use of the tilde occurs if the programmer assumes that fopen will expand regular expressions in its filename argument. Naturally, these errors can occur using any method of opening files that does not invoke the shell, such as the declaration of streams in C++ using <iostream.h>.

21.3 File permissions use octal constant

The file permissions for files on UNIX use the lowest 9 bits of the integer value of the permissions. This means that the file permission constants for the functions using these permissions must use octal constants rather than decimal constants. Therefore, the following use of creat is erroneous:

```
fd = creat("myfile", 755);    /* WRONG */
```

A prefix zero is needed on the permissions to make it into an octal constant:

```
fd = creat("myfile", 0755);    /* CORRECT */
```

The UNIX (non-ANSI) functions that use file permission arguments include open (when using the O_CREAT flag), creat, umask, and chmod. Information about file permissions extracted by functions such as stat must be treated carefully — that is, when the file permissions are extracted, they must be compared with octal constants.

21.4 Unclosed file descriptors with pipe and fork

The pipe function is used with fork to generate a communications channel between a parent process and a child process spawned using fork. These processes can use the file descriptors returned by pipe (i.e., p[0] and p[1]) to communicate down the inter-process pipeline. The following example sets up a simple pipeline between parent and child processes:

```
#include <stdio.h>
#include <stdlib.h>
#include <unistd.h>    /* declare fork(), pipe() etc */

#define WRITE_STRING(fd, s)    write(fd, s, strlen(s))

int main()
{
    int temp, pid;
    int p[2];       /* pipe descriptors */
    char buf[2];    /* buffer used by read/write */

    temp = pipe(p);      /* Set up the pipe */
    if (temp == -1) {    /* Check for errors */
        perror("Pipe failure");
        exit(EXIT_FAILURE);
    }
    pid = fork();    /* Fork a child to read the pipe */
    if (pid == 0) {    /* Child */
        close(p[1]);    /* Close unused descriptor: OFTEN FORGOTTEN! */

        while ( read(p[0], buf, 1) > 0)    /* read 1 char from pipe */
            write(1, buf, 1);               /* write 1 char to stdout */
        printf("Child exiting\n");
        exit(EXIT_SUCCESS);    /* child exits */
    }
    /* Parent process here */
    close(p[0]);    /* Close unused pipe input descriptor */

            /* Send output down the pipe to child */
    WRITE_STRING(p[1], "This is a test of parent writing down pipe\n");

    close(p[1]);    /* close parent process's descriptor down pipe */
                    /* parent can no longer communicate with child */
    (void) wait(NULL);    /* wait for child process to finish */
    exit(EXIT_SUCCESS);    /* parent exits */
}
```

Although the above code is error-free, it illustrates one of the most common errors with using pipe followed by fork. The statement close(p[1]) in the child process is often forgotten, thereby introducing a bug. The fork statement duplicates all process data, and this includes file descriptors; hence in the child process p[1] is still a live file descriptor and can be used to send output down the pipeline. The problem with leaving this descriptor live in the child process is that EOF is never transmitted down a pipeline unless no file descriptors apply to that pipeline (refer to the manuals for pipe and read). Hence if the child does not close p[1], there is still an active file descriptor applying to the pipeline and its read statement in the while loop will never receive end-of-file; the while loop will never terminate until the child process is killed.

The example above illustrates the problem in two ways. If the child does not have the close(p[1]) statement, then the "Child exiting" message is never printed by the child process. The while loop can only finish if the child is killed, such as by the parent exiting when the user hits <ctrl-c> (i.e., the child process can only terminate abnormally). Hence the wait function call will never return and both parent and child processes hang indefinitely. The child process has its read statement waiting for input, and the parent process is waiting for the child to finish.

Note that the parent process also closes its copy of the pipe-input file descriptor p[0], which it does not use. Omitting this statement is perhaps not as dangerous, although it wastes one file descriptor and the parent process could gradually run out of available file descriptors if the code is repeatedly executed.

The above example explicitly used p[0] and p[1] file descriptors. Another common method is to redirect stdin and stdout so that normal output goes down the pipe and the other process reads input from the pipe. Now consider a more complicated example. The program below will fork off two children, creating a pipe between them. It is equivalent to the shell command:

```
ls -l | cat -n
```

where ls -l provides a long listing of the directory and cat -n prefixes each line with a line number.

```
/*-------------------------------------------------------------*/
/* Pipe Test:    equivalent to command:  ls -l | cat -n        */
/*-------------------------------------------------------------*/

#include <stdio.h>
#include <stdlib.h>
#include <unistd.h>
#include <sys/wait.h>

main()
{
    int pid1, pid2;   /* Process id's */
    int p[2];         /* Pipe descriptor */
    int ret;

    ret = pipe(p);
    if (ret < 0) {
        perror("Pipe failed");
        exit(EXIT_FAILURE);
    }
                    /* Parent forks first child */
    pid1 = fork();
    if (pid1 == 0) {    /* Child */
        dup2(p[1], 1);          /* Redirect stdout down pipe */
        close(p[1]);            /* Close pipe file descriptors */
        close(p[0]);

        execl("/bin/ls", "ls", "-l", NULL);     /* ls -l */
        perror("Execl failed");
        exit(EXIT_FAILURE);
    }
                    /* Parent forks another child */
    pid2 = fork();
    if (pid2 == 0) {    /* 2nd Child */
        dup2(p[0], 0);          /* Redirect stdin from pipe */
        close(p[0]);            /* Close pipe file descriptors */
        close(p[1]);

        execl("/bin/cat", "cat", "-n", NULL);   /* cat -n */
        perror("Execl failed");
        exit(EXIT_FAILURE);
    }
                    /* Parent */
    close(p[0]);                /* Close pipe file descriptors */
    close(p[1]);
    while (wait(NULL) > 0)      /* Wait for all children to die */
        { }        /* empty loop */
    exit(EXIT_SUCCESS);
}
```

Handwritten annotation: dup2 (old, new); = close (new) + copy old → new

There are a few important points to note. First, the program uses dup2 to redirect input-output instead of a close-dup sequence. This is equivalent, but may not be supported by all implementations.

Second, note that the pipe descriptors are closed in a number of different places. There are two reasons for closing them. The first reason is that it is simply good practice to close file descriptors that are no longer needed, as otherwise a process may run out of file descriptors, causing failure of any subsequent request to open a file. The second, more compelling reason is that the program will hang if more than one file descriptor writing down the pipe is left alive. Removing either of the close(p[1]) statements in the second child or the parent process would cause the program to hang since the second child would never receive EOF from the piped input. Note that fork has created the copy in the parent process, and dup2 has created the copy in the second child. The removal of the close(p[1]) statement in the first child is not as dangerous since the ls process closes all descriptors when it terminates. Of course, the close(p[1]) in the first child process and the close(p[0]) in the second child process are part of the correct usage of dup2. Closing p[0] in many places is not as crucial to the success of the program but is desirable in order to avoid a "file descriptor leak."

Third, note the method for waiting for all children to terminate. The program simply waits until an error is returned, and assumes that error to be indicating that there are no more children. This is effective under normal circumstances, but a slightly better method would be to check if errno is ECHILD, or check the pid returned by wait each time to compare with pid1 and pid2.

21.5 The system function invokes Bourne shell

It is often forgotten by UNIX programmers who habitually use shells such as csh, ksh, or tcsh that the system library function calls the Bourne shell, sh. This creates problems when a syntax is used that sh does not support (e.g., the ~ metacharacter or the >& redirection), or when built-in commands specific to other shells are used. For example, the following call is erroneous:

```
system("make >& log.out");    /* WRONG */
```

21.6 The system function creates a new shell

Under UNIX, the system library function always invokes a new shell every time it is called. Any change to shell variables, change of directory, or use of the history mechanism will not work across multiple calls. For example, the following method of listing the parent directory will fail:

```
system("cd ..");        /* WRONG */
system("ls");           /* current directory listed */
```

The correct version is to ensure that the same shell invokes both commands:

```
system("cd ..;  ls");    /* CORRECT */
```

21.7 getenv does not access all shell variables

Under UNIX, the `getenv` function will only find those shell variables that have been exported. The `export` command must be used in `sh`, and the `setenv` command must be used in `csh`. As an example, the following call will fail:

```
char *p = getenv("path");    /* WRONG */
```

because `path` is a `csh` variable and is not exported. Either the `setenv` command must be used, or the `PATH` variable can be examined (since `csh` always exports `PATH` with a value the same as `path`). Hence, a correct version is:

```
char *p = getenv("PATH");    /* CORRECT */
```

21.8 mktemp modifying string constants

A common example of code that modifies string literals (see Section 19.22) involves the `mktemp` UNIX library function. This function requires a string with 6 trailing X characters that it modifies to create a unique filename. The most common usage is:

```
filename = mktemp("abcXXXXXX");
```

This will overwrite the string literal passed as its argument. Therefore, the program will fail if string literals are stored in read-only memory. Furthermore, since the string literal is changed, the second time this code is executed the argument will not contain 6 trailing X's, and so will return the same filename — the code cannot be used to create two temporary filenames. Furthermore, any other occurrence of the string literal `"abcXXXXXX"` may be changed (if the compiler merges identical string literals) and therefore using the same argument to `mktemp` might return the name unchanged, even if the call to `mktemp` occurs in a totally different function.

One partial solution is to use an array instead of a string constant as below:

```
char template[] = "abcXXXXXX";    /* BETTER */
...
filename = mktemp(template);
```

This avoids modifying a string literal because `template` is an array of `char` stored in writable memory. (Note that declaring `template` as a `char*` pointer would be erroneous, again leading to string literal modification.) Unfortunately, the use of a `template` character array does not avoid problems when executing the same statement twice since the first call has changed `template`. Executing `strcpy` before the `mktemp` call to reset `template` resolves this problem as below:

```
#define TEMPLATE   "abcXXXXXX"
char template[] = TEMPLATE;
...
strcpy(template, TEMPLATE);
filename = mktemp(template);
```

Note the use of the initialization to determine the correct size for the `template` array; equivalent but less elegant would be:

```
char template[10];
```

Although this solves most of the problems with `mktemp`, there is still a danger if the `filename` is left as the value returned from `mktemp`, rather than copied using `strcpy`. If the return value of `mktemp` is used in more than one location, then all these pointers will point to the same string (i.e., pointing to `&template[0]`).

The best solution is to avoid using `mktemp`, which is considered obsolete, and use the ANSI function `tmpnam`, which has similar functionality. `mktemp` is not an ANSI C library function and its use is not portable.

Appendix A
Symptom-based error diagnosis

It is very beneficial to the debugging process to be able to identify the cause of an error from its symptoms. Unfortunately, this is a very difficult process — otherwise debugging would be easy! Nevertheless, there are some common run-time errors with well-known causes, and this section attempts to provide a brief catalog of common error causes. In a sense, this section is a reverse index into Part II, mapping observable failure symptoms into the common errors.

A.1 UNIX core dumps: segmentation fault, bus error

There are a number of run-time error messages that occur mainly on large UNIX machines, but not usually on personal computers. Some of the common run-time error messages are:

- segmentation fault
- bus error
- illegal instruction
- trace/BPT trap

The message "core dumped" will often accompany the error message if it causes program termination, and this indicates that a file named "core" has been saved in the current directory. The "core" file can be used for postmortem debugging (see Section 2.5) to locate the failure with a symbolic debugger.

Note that the dump of the core file can be prevented by providing an empty file named "core" that is set to protection mode 000 using chmod. This may be useful if disk space is limited and the core dumps are huge.

A *segmentation fault* occurs when the hardware detects a memory access by the program that attempts to reference memory it is not allowed to use. For example, the address NULL cannot be referenced, and in fact, the single most common cause of a segmentation fault (at least for the experienced programmer) is a NULL dereference, but there are many other causes.

A *bus error* occurs when an attempt is made to load an incorrect address into an address bus. Although this leads us to suspect bad pointers, this error can also arise via stack corruption (because this can cause bad pointer addresses), and so there are a variety of potential causes.

Segmentation faults and bus errors may be reported as the program receiving signal SIGSEGV or SIGBUS in some situations. The most common causes of a segmentation fault or bus error are listed below. Different architectures will have different results for these errors, but will usually produce either a segmentation fault or bus error.

- NULL pointer dereference
- wayward pointer dereference (memory allocation problem)
- noninitialized pointer dereference
- array index out of bounds
- wrong number or type of arguments to nonprototyped function
- bad arguments to scanf or printf
- forgetting the & on arguments to scanf
- deallocating nonallocated location using free or delete
- deallocating same address twice using free or delete
- executable file removed/modified while being executed (dynamic loading)
- stack overflow

Another common abnormal termination condition for UNIX machines is the message "illegal instruction," which usually causes a core dump. The most common causes of this method of termination are:

- assert macro has failed (causes abort call)
- abort library function called
- data has been executed somehow (uninitialized pointer-to-function?)
- stack corruption (e.g., write past end of local array)
- stack overflow
- ANSI C++ exception problem causing abort call
  — unhandled exception was thrown
  — unexpected exception from function with interface specification
  — exception thrown in destructor during exception-related stack unwinding

Another run-time error message for UNIX machines is the message "fixed up nonaligned data access," although this does not necessarily lead to program termination. This indicates that hardware has detected an attempt to access a value through an address with incorrect alignment requirements. Typically it refers to attempting to read or write an integer or pointer at an odd-valued address (i.e., an address that is not word-aligned). Note that on machines without this automatic "fix-up" the same code will probably cause a bus error.

A.2 Program hangs infinitely

When one is faced with debugging a program that seems to get stuck, it is important to determine what type of "hang" has occurred. If the program is simply stuck in an infinite loop, you will still have control of the program and can interrupt it. One method of finding out where the program is stuck is to run the program from a debugger, or (under UNIX) to use the keyboard interrupt `<ctrl-\>` to cause a core dump, which can then be examined by a debugger. Some causes of this form of infinite looping are:

- NP-complete algorithm (!)
- infinite loop
- accidental semicolon on end of `while`/`for` loop header
- `exit` called within a destructor of global object (C++ only)
- handled/ignored signal is recurring (e.g., `SIGSEGV`, `SIGBUS`)
- waiting for input: `getc`/`getch` assigned to `char`
- linked data structure corrupted (contains pointer cycles)

If the program hangs for a period of time and then crashes, a likely candidate is a runaway recursive function. This will loop (almost) infinitely, consuming stack space all the time, until it runs out of stack space and (a) terminates abnormally (e.g., under UNIX or DOS with stack checking enabled), or (b) the stack overwrites some important memory and the second, more severe form of "hang" occurs (e.g., under DOS without stack checking).

The most severe form of a "hung" program is one that will not respond. This rarely occurs under UNIX or other large systems because of memory protection, but it is common for personal computers. You know it's a bad bug when the reset button is the only thing that works. When this occurs, I recommend the use of any compiler run-time checks, especially stack overflow checking and array bounds checking (if available). An additional method is to recompile using a memory allocation debugging package such as that in Section 3.1. Some possible causes of a nonresponsive program crash are:

- infinite recursion
- stack overflow (e.g., `_stklen` not set in Turbo C/C++ program)
- array index out of bounds
- modification via wayward pointer
- modification via noninitialized pointer
- modification via `NULL` pointer
- freeing a nonallocated block
- freeing a string constant
- nonterminated string was copied
- inconsistent compiler/linker options (e.g., object files with different memory models)

Note how many of these errors will cause a hung program on "smaller" computers but will receive segmentation fault or bus errors on UNIX systems.

A.3 Failure after long period of successful execution

A very annoying error is that of a program that runs perfectly for a long period of time and then suddenly fails for no apparent reason. This usually indicates a "memory leak" causing the system to use up all available memory and `malloc` to return `NULL`. However, there are other causes and a more complete list is:

- untested rare sequence of events is causing the error (try to repeat it)
- heap memory leak causing allocation failure (allocated memory not deallocated)
- running out of `FILE*` handles (files opened but not closed)
- some form of memory corruption (symptom of bug doesn't appear immediately)
- integer overflow (e.g., of some 16-bit counter)
- disk filling up
- peripheral error (e.g., printer out of paper)

A.4 Failure only when optimizer used

A program that runs correctly with normal compilation but fails when the optimizer is invoked is a well-known problem. The immediate reaction is to blame a bug in the optimizer. However, although such bugs are not so rare as one would wish, there are a number of other potential causes. It is usually an indication that some erroneous or nonportable code has been working correctly more by luck than good programming, and the more aggressive optimizations have shown up the error. Some possible causes are:

- order of evaluation errors (optimizer rearranges expressions)
- special location not declared `volatile`
- use of an uninitialized variable
- wrong number/type of arguments to nonprototyped function
- wrong arguments to prototyped function not declared before use
- memory access problems (optimizer has rearranged some memory)

In this situation it may be useful to examine what compiler options are available to choose which optimizations are chosen. For example, there may be an option to choose between traditional stack-based argument passing and pass by register. If so, recompilation with and without that option can help to test for argument passing errors. Argument passing errors can also be found more quickly by `lint` under UNIX.

A.5 Failure disappears when debugger used

A really annoying situation is a program that crashes when run normally, but does not fail when run via a symbolic debugger or interpreter. One fairly well known cause is the use of an uninitialized automatic variable. The error may disappear when run via the debugger, because some debuggers set these local variables to zero or `NULL` initially. Thus some possible causes are:

- using uninitialized variable (especially a pointer)
- memory access problems (debugger has rearranged memory somehow)
  — array index out of bounds
  — modification via wayward pointer
  — modification via noninitialized pointer
  — NULL pointer dereference
  — modification via NULL pointer
  — freeing a nonallocated block
  — freeing a string constant

The list of errors possibly causing a memory-related problem is comparable with the list of errors causing a nonrecoverable hung program.

A.6 Failure when memory model changed

When changing the memory model used by a program in the DOS environment, there are a few things that can go wrong. Typically, you will be "upgrading" to a larger model as your program increases size. Some possible causes of the problem are:

- not all object files recompiled with new memory model (usually hangs program)
- NULL assignment (warning in small/medium models, but crashes in other models)
- comparing `far` pointers
- pointer/memory problem
  — pointers change size; no longer same size as integers
    e.g., `char**arr=malloc(10*sizeof(int))` should be `sizeof(int*)`

A.7 Program crashes at startup

When a C++ program crashes on program startup, without even executing the first statement in `main`, we must suspect constructors of global objects. Use a run-time debugger to determine if `main` has been entered; but note that some debuggers allow debugging of constructors before `main` and others do not. Alternatively, place an output statement as the very first statement in `main` (even before the first declaration!) to ensure that the problem really is arising before `main`, rather than from instructions in `main`.

Once a constructor problem has been identified, finding the root cause of the problem is a debugging matter. There are no forms of error particular to constructors, so refer to the other sections herein that discuss the most appropriate symptoms.

A.8 Program crashes at end of successful execution

The program can fail in a few obscure ways at the end of execution. Careful consideration of what actions are taking place at the end of execution is important (e.g., destructors are invoked in C++; any functions registered with `atexit` will be called). In the author's experience this failure is most common during the learning phase of C++ programming, when destructor errors are common.

- `delete` operation in object destructor is trashing memory
- destructor in global object calls `exit`
- `main` accidentally declared returning non-`int`
  e.g., missing semicolon on `class` or `struct` declaration above `main`
- `setbuf` buffer is a non-`static` local variable of `main`
- no call to `exit`, and no `return` statement in `main` (a few platforms only)

A.9 Function apparently not invoked

Consider the situation where you are debugging a program, and discover that a particular function seems to be having no effect. You put an output statement at its first statement and no output appears. Why isn't the function being invoked? Some possible causes are:

- no call to the function (!)
- missing brackets on function call
- function is a macro at call location
- function is a reserved library function name
- nested comments deleting call to function

A.10 Garbage output

When a program runs and produces strange output there are a number of possibilities (mostly related to misusing string variables). Note that it is important to distinguish whether the output of a statement is entirely garbage or whether it has a correct prefix (which may indicate a nonterminated string). Some causes are:

- missing argument to `printf` `%s` format
- wrong type argument to `printf` `%s` format
- returning address of automatic local string array
- stack corruption
- `strncpy` leaves string nonterminated
- pointer variable not initialized

A.11 Failure on new platform — portability errors

When a program appears to be running successfully on one machine, it is by no means guaranteed that porting the source code and recompiling on a new machine will not lead to new errors. When a new error is discovered, the first thing that must be tested is whether the same error exists for the same test data on the original machine. The bug might not be a portability problem — it might be an untested case.

However, if the bug appears on one machine but not on another there are a few common causes. The most frequent portability problem is a memory corruption error since these will often lurk undetected on one machine, and appear in the new memory layout of a different environment.

Another common class of portability problems that typically arise when porting software from UNIX to DOS is that many DOS compilers have 16-bit int, whereas UNIX compilers use 32-bit int. For these errors it is worthwhile to examine all compiler warnings, since the compiler will often identify errors such as an integer constant that is too large to be stored in an int, or an attempt to compare an int with a value outside the range stored in 16-bits.

Other possible causes are different compilation results that may arise when a new compiler uses more aggressive optimization. Hence code that relies on an undocumented compiler feature (e.g., left to right function argument evaluation) may suddenly fail. Note that this implies that portability errors can arise after a compiler upgrade on the same machine, as well as when moving code to a new machine. Some common causes of portability errors are:

- memory corruption errors
    - array index out of bounds
    - modification via wayward pointer
    - modification via noninitialized pointer
    - NULL pointer dereference
    - modification via NULL pointer
    - freeing a nonallocated block
    - freeing a string constant

- 16-bit int problem
    - arithmetic overflow
    - bit-shifting: 1<<16 should probably be 1L<<16
    - assuming rand returns 32 bits
    - scanf/printf using %d (%ld) on a long (int)

- stack overflow (64K stack limit for IBM PCs)
- function has no return statement
- order of evaluation error
    - operators: a[i]=i++;
    - function arguments: fn(i,i++);
    - global object construction in separate files
- special location not declared volatile
- use of an uninitialized variable
- bit-field is plain int
- plain char is signed/unsigned
    - getc/getchar return value assigned to char

Most of these causes are fairly self-explanatory. However, the appearance of "function has no return statement" in the list may appear surprising — surely this will cause a bug on all implementations? However, it has been observed surprisingly frequently that a function that terminates without a return statement might accidentally return the correct value. Typically, this surprising outcome occurs if, by coincidence, a local scalar variable that is intended to be returned happens to be in the hardware register that is used to hold the function return value. Since that register is not loaded when no `return` statement is found, the correct result is accidentally returned, and there is no failure until a different compiler or environment is used.

Some compilers have compilation options to change various compiler-dependent features. For example, there may be options to change the default type of plain `char` and/or plain `int` bit-fields to `signed` or `unsigned`. If it is suspected that this may be the cause of the error, the code can be recompiled with different option settings to confirm this. Any run-time error checking options such as stack overflow checking should also be enabled.

A.12 Null pointer assignment

A number of common compilers for IBM PCs can produce an error message such as "Null pointer assignment" after the program terminates. These compilers examine the value stored at `NULL` before program execution, and then reexamine it after execution and complain if the value has changed. In this way any assignment to `NULL` is detected, albeit a long time after the actual error has occurred. Typically a number of bytes are examined close to address zero, so that assignments such as:

```
p->key = 10;
```

where p is `NULL` will provoke the error. This statement will not change the value at address zero, but at the offset of the `key` field.

Unfortunately, this error can only be detected in the `small` and `medium` models; in other models an assignment via `NULL` will probably change the interrupt vectors at address 0000:0000, thereby provoking a fatal crash. Only the `small` and `medium` models have `NULL` addresses that lie safely within a (single) writable segment.

It is also unfortunate that these compilers do not provide run-time testing of every pointer dereference. It would not be difficult to implement such a run-time check in a manner similar to the run-time stack overflow checking that is common. However, this "Null pointer assignment" message is the best available on these compilers, and we must examine the difficult task of tracing the cause of the error. There are a number of possible debugging methods:

- Set a "watch" on address zero using a debugger (small/medium models only)
  — for Turbo Debugger, watch `"*(char*)0,4m"` and `"(char*)4"`.
- Use postmortem debugging under Windows (see Section 2.5.2).
- Port the code to UNIX and use postmortem debugging to trace segmentation faults.
- Find a compiler or debugger supporting run-time `NULL` checking.
- Use roving `exit` calls.
- Use calls to a routine to check for `NULL` assignments.

Only the last two methods require elaboration. A brute-force method is to put `exit` calls at different places in the program to determine how early in program execution the `NULL` assignment takes place. However, this is a very laborious method because it requires repeated compilation and the same input case must be supplied.

A more effective method is to sprinkle calls to a function that detects the error throughout the program. Microsoft C/C++ supports the non-ANSI function _nullcheck. However, it is not difficult to write your own testing function if using other compilers; let's call ours nullchk. In addition to detecting the error, the preprocessor can be used to allow diagnosis of the line and filename of the nullchk call that first detects the error. This call will be the one "closest" in terms of execution time to the cause of the error.

The following version of nullchk has been tested using Turbo C/C++, but should work for all compilers (except possibly that the #if-#error-#endif test might need to be changed or deleted).

```c
/*------------------------------------------------*/
/* NULLCHK.C: Detect NULL pointer assignments     */
/*------------------------------------------------*/

#include <stdio.h>
#include <stdlib.h>

#define FALSE 0
#define TRUE  1
typedef int bool;

#define BYTES_TESTED 20 /* how close to NULL? */

#if ! __SMALL__ && ! __MEDIUM__
# error   nullchk() will only work for small/medium models
#endif

long int nullchk_line = -1;
char *nullchk_file = "???";

void nullchk(void)
{
    static unsigned char bytes[BYTES_TESTED];
    static bool first = TRUE;
    bool ok;
    int i;
    unsigned char *p;

    if (first) {     /* if first nullchk call */
        first = FALSE;
                        /* store the bytes */
        for (p = NULL, i = 0; i < BYTES_TESTED; i++, p++) {
            bytes[i] = *p;
        }
    }
    else {   /* Not the first call; check for changes */
        ok = TRUE;
        for (p = NULL, i = 0; i < BYTES_TESTED; i++, p++) {
            if (bytes[i] != *p) {
                if (ok)  /* first change only */
                    fprintf(stderr,"Line %ld, File '%s': nullchk fails\n",
                            nullchk_line, nullchk_file);
                fprintf(stderr, "Byte %d changed from %d to %d\n",
                                i, bytes[i], *p);
                ok = FALSE;
            }
        }
        if (!ok) exit(EXIT_FAILURE);   /* terminate */
    }
    nullchk_line = -1;        /* Reset to dummy values ... */
    nullchk_file = "???";     /* .. in case next time doesn't use macro */
}
```

If it is desirable to continue execution after an error has been identified, this can be achieved by deleting the line that calls `exit`.

The header file `"nullchk.h"` is shown below. This allows `nullchk` to report the line and filename where the error was detected, in a similar manner to the reporting of the `assert` macro.

```
/*-----------------------------------------------*/
/*  NULLCHK.H:   Detect NULL pointer assignments  */
/*-----------------------------------------------*/

void nullchk(void);
extern long int nullchk_line;
extern char *nullchk_file;

#define nullchk()   nullchk_line = __LINE__,  \
                    nullchk_file = __FILE__,  \
                    nullchk()
```

The line and filename are passed via global variables rather than as function arguments so that `nullchk` can be used both with and without the inclusion of the header file.

A.13 Floating-point run-time error messages

There are a few common run-time error messages produced by popular compilers for IBM PCs. Borland compilers such as Turbo C/C++ and Borland C/C++ may produce the error message:

```
Floating point format not linked
```

Typically, this error arises when a `printf` statement attempts to output a `float` or `double` value in a small program that doesn't use `float` or `double` for any other purpose. This error message is caused by what amounts to a bug in the compiler. The compiler attempts to deduce when the code to perform conversions of floating-point values to characters (e.g., for `%f`), but occasionally gets it wrong, and leaves out the code. When the `printf` statement is reached, the absence of this code is detected and the error occurs. One suggested workaround to force the linking of this code is to place the following function in one file (but don't call it!):

```
static void forcefloat(float *p)
{
    float f = *p;
    forcefloat(&f);
}
```

Microsoft C/C++ compilers have been known to produce the run-time error message:

```
Floating point not loaded
```

This indicates that the compiler has assumed the presence of a coprocessor, and has not loaded instructions to emulate the operations. Execution terminates when it detects the absence of the coprocessor. The solution is to relink with the correct library; consult your manual for details.

Bibliography

The following is a list of books, papers, and documents that were of use to me while writing this book. A number of documents have FTP availability details. To use this facility your organization will require Internet access. If you aren't sure whether you have it, or if you do have access but aren't familiar with how to copy files using FTP, please read the tutorial "`ftpinfo.txt`" on the source code disk.

AMSTERDAM, Jonathan, "Some Assembly Required: Taking Exception to C," *Byte*, August 1991, pp. 259–264.

ANDERSON, Paul, and ANDERSON, Gail, *Advanced C: Tips and Techniques*, Hayden Books, 1988.

BAKER, Emanuel R., and FISHER, Matthew, J., "Software Quality Program Organization," in *Handbook of Software Quality Assurance* (2nd edn), Schulmeyer & McManus, eds, 1992, pp. 49–74, esp. pp. 63, 67, 69–72.

BALDWIN, John T., "An Abbreviated C++ Code Inspection Checklist," Testing Foundations, 1992 (available via FTP to the site `cs.uiuc.edu` in directory `pub/testing` as filename `baldwin-inspect.ps`).

BATES, Rodney M., "Debugging with Assertions," *The C Users Journal*, Vol. 10, No. 10, October 1992.

BENGTSSON, Johan, "C++, Without Exceptions," Telia Research, Lulea, Sweden (available via FTP to the site `euagate.eua.ericsson.se` in directory `pub/eua/c++` with filename `Exceptions_920511.ps.Z`).

BINDER, Robert, *Application Debugging*, Prentice Hall, 1985.

BROWN, A.R., and SAMPSON, W.A., *Program Debugging*, Elsevier Publishing Company, 1973.

Brown University, "vmon and vmemcheck tools," Department of Computer Science, Brown University, Providence, Rhode Island, (anonymous FTP from the site `wilma.cs.brown.edu`; as filename: `pub/aard.tar.Z`).

CAHILL, Conor P., "The 'Art' of Debugging C Programs," *X Journal*, March/April 1993.

CASSELL, Don, *The Structured Alternative: Program Design, Style and Debugging*, Reston Publishing Company Inc., 1983.

CHANDRASEKARAN, B., and RADICCHI, S. (eds), *Computer Program Testing*, North Holland Publishing Company, 1981.

comp.software-eng, "comp.software-eng archives," Available via FTP to `ftp.qucis.queensu.ca` in the directory `pub/software-eng` as various filenames, including `inspect`, `fault`, `verification`, `testTools`, `regress`, `static`, `horror`.

COPLIEN, James O., *Advanced C++ Programming Styles and Idioms*, Addison-Wesley, 1992.

COTTAM, Ian D., "idC: A Subset of Standard C for Initial Teaching," Tech Report UMCS-92-12-3, Department of Computer Science, University of Manchester, England, 1992 (available via FTP from `ftp.cs.man.ac.uk` in directory `pub/TR` as file `UMCS-92-12-3.ps.Z`).

COTTAM, Ian, "idC Toolkit," anonymous FTP to `ftp.cs.man.ac.uk`; filename: `pub/idclib_1.4.shar`.

DARWIN, Ian F., *Checking C Programs with lint*, O'Reilly & Associates, 1988.

DAVIS, Stephen R., *C++ Programmer's Companion: Designing, Testing and Debugging*, Addison-Wesley, 1993.

DUNHAM, Alan, "Crash Tracebacks in UNIX," *Dr Dobbs Journal*, September 1992 (code via FTP to `ftp.mv.com` in `pub/ddj/1992.09` as file `trace.arc`).

ELLIS, Margaret A., and STROUSTRUP, Bjarne, *The Annotated C++ Reference Manual*, Addison-Wesley, 1990.

ERDELSKY, Philip J., "A Safer setjmp in C++," *C Users Journal*, Vol. 11, No. 1, January 1993, pp. 41–44.

FRAKES, William B., FOX, Christopher J., and NEJMEH, Brian A., *Software Engineering in the UNIX/C Environment*, Prentice Hall, 1991.

HENRICSON, Mats, and NYQUIST, Erik, "Programming in C++: Rules and Recommendations," Technical Report, Ellemtel Telecommunication Systems Laboratories, Sweden, 1990–1992; available via anonymous FTP to the site `euagate.eua.ericsson.se` in directory `pub/eua/c++` as numerous files including `rules.ascii.Z`.

HORSTMANN, Cay, "Memory management and smart pointers," *C++ Report*, Vol. 5, No. 3, March/April 1993, pp. 28–34.

ISO 9000 News, "ISO-9000 Quality Standards in 24 Questions," available via FTP to `ftp.uni-erlangen.de` in the directory `pub/doc/ISO/english` as file `ISO-9000-summary`.

JOHNSON, S.C., "Lint: a C Program Checker," Computer Science Technical Report No. 65, Bell Laboratories, 1978.

JURAN, J.M., and GRYNA, Frank M., *Quality Planning and Analysis* (3rd edn), McGraw-Hill, 1993 (especially Chapter 23).

KERNIGHAN, Brian W., and PLAUGER, P. J., *The Elements of Programming Style*, McGraw-Hill, 1974.

KOCHAN, Stephen G., and WOOD, Patrick H., *Topics in C Programming* (rev. edn), John Wiley and Sons, 1991.

KOENIG, Andrew, *C Traps and Pitfalls*, Addison-Wesley, 1989.

KUHN, Markus, "Standards FAQ," Frequently Asked Question (FAQ) list for the Internet news group `comp.std.misc` (also available via anonymous FTP to the site `rtfm.mit.edu` in the directory `pub/usenet/comp.std.misc` as filename `Standards_FAQ`).

LADD, Scott Robert, "Debugging Dynamic Memory in C++," *PC Techniques*, Vol. 3, No. 5, December/January 1993, pp. 38–43.

LEARY, Sean, and D'SOUZA, Desmond, "Catch the Error: C++ Exception Handling," *Computer Language*, October 1992, pp. 63–77.

LEE, P.A., "Exception Handling in C Programs," *Software — Practice & Experience*, Vol. 13, 1983, pp. 389–405.

MARICK, Brian, "A Question Catalog for Code Inspections," Testing Foundations, 1992 (available via FTP to `cs.uiuc.edu` in directory `pub/testing` as filenames `inspect.n` and `inspect.ps`).

MASTERS, David, *Introduction to C with Advanced Applications*, Prentice Hall, 1991.

MEYERS, Scott, *Effective C++: 50 Specific Ways to Improve Your Programs and Designs*, Addison-Wesley, 1992.

MEYERS, Scott, and LEJTER, Moses, "Automatic Detection of C++ Programming Errors: Initial Thoughts on a lint++," Technical Report CS-91-51, Department of Computer Science, Brown University, Providence, Rhode Island, August 1991 (also published USENIX C++ Conference Proceedings, April 1991, p29–40); available via FTP to `wilma.cs.brown.edu`; directory: `techreports/91`, file: `cs91-51.ps.Z`.

MILLER, Edward, and HOWDEN, William E (eds), *Tutorial: Software Testing & Validation Techniques*, IEEE Computer Society Press, 1981.

MILLER, W.M., "Error Handling in C++," *Computer Language*, May 1988, pp. 43–52.

MILLER, W.M., "Exception Handling without Language Support," *USENIX C++ Conference Proceedings*, Denver, Colorado, USENIX Press, 1988.

MYERS, Glenford J., *Software Reliability: Principles and Practices*, John Wiley and Sons, 1976.

MYERS, Glenford J., *The Art of Software Testing*, John Wiley and Sons, 1979.

OULD, Martyn A., and UNWIN, Charles (eds), *Testing in Software Development*, Cambridge University Press, 1986.

PIETREK, Matt, "Postmortem Debugging," *Dr Dobbs Journal*, September 1992, pp. 18–31.

PUGH, Ken, *All on C*, Scott, Foresman/Little, Brown Higher Education, 1990.

SCHILDT, Herbert, *C: The Complete Reference*, Osborne-McGraw-Hill, 1987.

SCHULMEYER, G. Gordon and McMANUS, James, I. (eds), *Handbook of Software Quality Assurance* (2nd edn), Van Nostrand Reinhold, 1992.

SHOOMAN, Martin, *Software Engineering — Design, Reliability and Management*, McGraw-Hill, 1983.

SMITH, William M., "Debugging with Macro Wrappers," *The C Users Journal*, Vol. 10, No. 10, October 1992.

SPULER, David A., *C++ and C Efficiency: How to Improve Program Speed and Memory Usage*, Prentice Hall, 1992.

SPULER, David A., *Comprehensive C*, Prentice Hall, 1992.

SPULER, David A., "Check: A Better Checker for C," Honours Thesis, Department of Computer Science, James Cook University, Townsville, Australia, 1991 (FTP to `coral.cs.jcu.edu.au` in the directory `pub/techreports` as the file `spuler-hons.ps.Z`).

SPULER, D. and SAJEEV, A.S.M., "Static Detection of Preprocessor Macro Errors in C," Technical Report 92/7, Department of Computer Science, James Cook University, Townsville, Australia, July 1992/7 (available via FTP to the site `coral.cs.jcu.edu.au` as file `pub/techreports/92-7.ps.Z`).

STRAKER, David, *C Style: Standards and Guidelines*, Prentice Hall, 1992.

STROUSTRUP, Bjarne, *The C++ Programming Language* (2nd edn), Addison-Wesley, 1991.

VIDAL, Carlos, "Exception Handling," *C Users Journal*, Vol. 10, No. 9, September 1992, pp. 19–28.

WEINBERG, G.M., *The Psychology of Computer Programming*, Van Nostrand Reinhold, 1971.

WILLIAMS, Ross N., "A C Exceptions Package Written Using the FunnelWeb Literate Programming Tool," available via FTP to `ftp.adelaide.edu.au` in the directory `pub/funnelweb/examples`.

WILSON, C., and OSTERWEIL, L.J., "Omega — A Data Flow Analysis Tool for the C Programming Language," *IEEE Transactions on Software Engineering*, Vol. 11, No. 9, 1985, pp. 832–838.

WINROTH, Harald, "Exception Handling in ANSI C," Computational Vision and Active Perception Laboratory (CVAP), Royal Institute of Technology (KTH), Stockholm, Sweden (available via FTP to `ftp.bion.kth.se` in directory `cvap/2.0` as file `exception-1.2.tar.Z`).

Index

F

falling through in `switch` 214
`farmalloc` Borland C/C++ function 53, 59
fault tolerance 145
`feof` library function 263–264
`fflush` library function 24, 266
`fgets` library function 263
`fgets`, instead of `gets` 142
file errors, detecting 55
file handle leak 55, 322
`__FILE__` preprocessor special name 23, 26, 36
files (text) and debug output 32
fixed up nonaligned data access 320
fixed-argument DPRINTF 16
fleshed out stubs 66
Flexe-Lint (Gimpel Software) 82, 158–159
floating-point errors 328
floating-point format not linked 328
floating-point not loaded 328
flushing buffers 24
`fopen` library function 141, 189, 283, 284, 313
`fork` UNIX function 312, 313
`form <iostream.h>` facility 22
formalized common sense 71
`fread` library function 266, 283
`free` library function 46, 125, 284, 286, 320
Free Software Foundation 152
`freopen` library function 142
`fseek` library function 266
FTP archives for Gnu 153
`__FUNCTION__` Gnu extension 23
`fwrite` library function 266

G

garbage memory 46, 58, 104, 120, 135, 286
`gcc/g++` free Gnu C/C++ compiler 160
`gct` free test coverage tool 171
`gdb` Gnu debugger 169
generic pointers 295
`getchar` library function 184, 264–265
`getenv` library function 317
`getpid` UNIX function 11
`gets`, don't use 142
Gimpel Software (PC-Lint/Flexe-Lint) 158–159
global error flag 86
global `new` and `delete` 48
global variables 226
Gnu (Free Software Foundation) 152
`goto` statement 86, 190, 217
GP (general protection) fault 11
graceful termination 37, 86, 119
`graceful_assert` macro 37
guidelines, testing 61

H

hack nonprototyped DPRINTF 21
handle exception macros (Hood's) 108
`Handle_New` debugging class 121
`harmless_assert` macro 38
hashing (hash table) 151, 211
header files versus compiler options 14
heterogeneous exception handling 88
hidden variable macro trick (Winroth's) 112
hierarchical exception handling 87
hierarchies of exception, ANSI C++ 96
hierarchies of exceptions via `structs` 110
high-level reliability 85–90
Hood's exception library 108
horror stories 82
Horsmeier's exception library 105–107
hung program 147, 321

I

`idClib` debugging library 165
`if(0)` removal, errors from 18
`if(1){}else` removal method 17
`#ifdef` versus `#if` 13
`#ifdef-#endif` pair 13
illegal instruction 319, 320
in-code support for debug output 30
incremental count, self-tests 40
incremental linting 157
independent compilation 221
independent tester 61
infinite loop 321
`inline` do-nothing function 22
`inline` functions and debuggers 12
inspections, code 63–65
interactive programs, regression testing 69
interception, library function 45
interface specifications (ANSI C++ exceptions) 98
internal failure reporting 77
interrupts (keyboard) and debug output 30, 42–43
INT_MIN ANSI C constant in `<limits.h>` 150
`ioctl` UNIX function 68
`<iostream.h>` C++ header file 267
IPL (Cantata testing tool) 172
`isdigit` library function 282
ISO quality standards 72

K

`kbhit` Turbo C/C++ function 68
keyboard interrupts 30, 42–43
`kill` UNIX library function 11

DATE DUE